U.S. ARMY WEAPONS SYSTEMS 2016–2017

All inquiries should be addressed to Skyhorse Publishing, 307 West 36th Street, 11th Floor, New York, NY 10018.

Skyhorse Publishing books may be purchased in bulk at special discounts for sales promotion, corporate gifts, fund-raising, or educational purposes. Special editions can also be created to specifications. For details, contact the Special Sales Department, Skyhorse Publishing, 307 West 36th Street, 11th Floor, New York, NY 10018 or info@skyhorsepublishing.com.

Skyhorse® and Skyhorse Publishing® are registered trademarks of Skyhorse Publishing, Inc.®, a Delaware corporation.

Visit our website at www.skyhorsepublishing.com.

10 9 8 7 6 5 4 3 2 1

Library of Congress Cataloging-in-Publication Data is available on file.

Cover design by Rain Saukas
Cover photo: US Department of the Army

ISBN: 978-1-5107-1305-5

Printed in China

U.S. ARMY WEAPONS SYSTEMS 2016–2017

DEPARTMENT OF THE ARMY

Skyhorse Publishing

Introduction

The U.S. Army Acquisition Corps, with its 36,000 professionals, bears a unique responsibility for the oversight and systems management of the Army's acquisition lifecycle. With responsibility for hundreds of acquisition programs, civilian and military professionals collectively oversee research, development and acquisition activities totaling more than $20 billion in Fiscal Year 2016 alone.

With threat proliferation from the level of "lone wolf" terrorist to hostile nation-state, our country depends now more than ever on the capabilities placed into the hands of our men and women in uniform. Thankfully, Army systems and technologies—designed and developed under the auspices of our 12 Program Executive Offices and the Headquarters Staff—will ensure the defense of freedom for decades to come.

Advances in turbine engine technology will enable our Soldiers to fly for greater duration at high altitudes and in hot climates. New missile systems will operate with increased lethality and extended range. Next-generation ground vehicles will offer improved survivability and increased capabilities. Emerging infrared technologies will enable troops not only to "own the night" but also to overcome inclement conditions and "own the weather." These, and many more capabilities, continue to ensure that our warfighters maintain decisive overmatch in all contested environments.

The Army's Weapon Systems Handbook 2016 presents many of the acquisition programs currently fielded or in development. We hope that it provides a valuable resource, reminds us of our warfighters defending freedom around the globe, and motivates us to equip our Soldiers with the best materiel possible so that we can continue to maintain the decisive advantage in the fight!

Table of Contents

ACQUISITION CATEGORY II AND III

Table of Contents

ARMY SCIENCE AND TECHNOLOGY

APPENDICES

How to Use this Book

System name

PEO name and location

PEO logo

Foreign military sales

Contractor and location

ACAT level tabs
• ACAT I
• ACAT II and III

Highlighted tabs indicate warfighting function

Highlighted tabs indicate acquisition lifecycle phase

Highlighted tabs indicate milestone decision authority

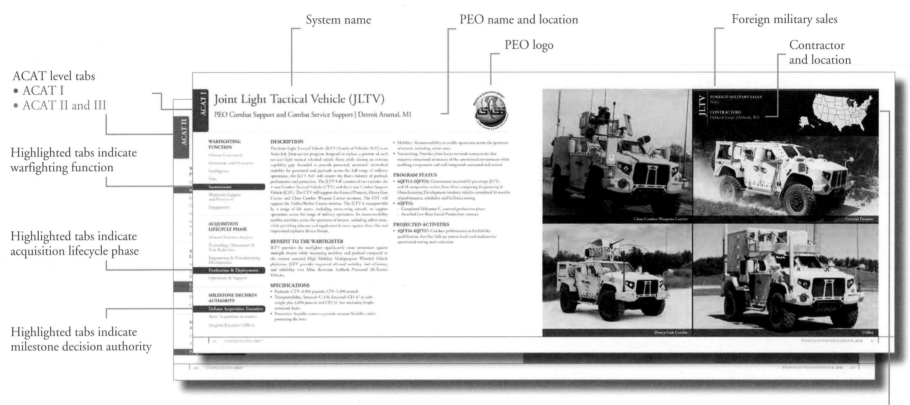

Contractor locations are highlighted

ACQUISITION CATEGORY (ACAT)

The tab in the top left corner indicates the program's Acquisition Category (ACAT). ACAT I programs have **dark green** tabs and all other programs (ACAT II and III) have **light green** tabs. A small number of programs have no ACAT designation and are shown as OTHER. The programs are arranged alphabetically within each ACAT section.

WARFIGHTING FUNCTION

This tab identifies the Warfighting Function(s) each program supports.

- **Mission Command** programs develop and integrate activities enabling a commander to balance the art of command and the science of control. This philosophy places people, rather than technology or systems, at the center.
- **Movement and Maneuver** programs move and employ forces to achieve a position of relative advantage over the enemy and other threats. Direct fire and close combat are inherent in this function.

- **Intelligence** programs facilitate understanding the enemy, terrain and civil considerations. This function synchronizes collection requirements with the execution of tactical tasks such as reconnaissance, surveillance and related intelligence operations.
- **Fires** programs provide collective and coordinated use of Army indirect fires, air and missile defense, and Joint fires through the targeting process.
- **Sustainment** programs provide support and services to ensure freedom of action, extend operational reach and prolong endurance. This function determines the depth and duration of Army operations, and is essential to retaining and exploiting the initiative.
- **Maneuver Support and Protection** programs preserve the force so the commander can apply maximum combat power to accomplish the mission. Preserving the force includes protecting personnel and physical assets of the United States, host-nation and multinational military and civilian partners.
- **Engagement** programs influence the behaviors of a people, security forces and governments.

ACQUISITION LIFECYCLE PHASE
This tab identifies the program's acquisition phase(s).
- **Materiel Solution Analysis** performs analysis needed to choose a product or system concept, identifies capability gaps, translates into system-specific requirements and conducts planning to support an acquisition strategy.
- **Technology Maturation & Risk Reduction** reduces technology risk, determines and matures the technologies to integrate into a full system, and demonstrates on prototypes. This is a continuous discovery and development process.
- **Engineering & Manufacturing Development** develops a system, completes full system integration, plans a feasible and affordable manufacturing process, and demonstrates system integration, interoperability and utility. This phase includes system integration, system demonstration and interim progress review.

- **Production & Deployment** achieves an operational capability that satisfies mission needs. Components of this phase include Low-Rate Initial Production, Full-Rate Production Decision Review, Full-Rate Production and Deployment, and Military Equipment Evaluation.
- **Operations & Support** executes a support program that meets materiel and performance requirements in the most cost-effective manner over the system's total lifecycle.

Because the Army is spiraling technology to its warfighters as soon as feasible, some programs and systems may be in all four acquisition lifecycle phases at the same time. Mature programs are often only in one phase, such as Operations & Support, while newer systems are usually only found in the Materiel Solutions Analysis or Technology Maturation & Risk Reduction phases.

MILESTONE DECISION AUTHORITY
This tab identifies the acquisition decision authority for each system.
- **Defense Acquisition Executive** is responsible for supervising the Defense Acquisition System and takes precedence on all acquisition matters after the Secretary of Defense and the Deputy Secretary of Defense.
- **Army Acquisition Executive** is responsible for acquisition matters within the Department of the Army and is the single decision authority for all Army acquisition matters.
- **Program Executive Officer** is responsible for ACAT I and IA and sensitive classified programs, or for any other program as needed.

For additional information and definitions of these categories and terms, please see the Glossary of Terms.

WEAPON SYSTEMS
ACAT I

Listed in alphabetical order

2.75 Inch Rocket Systems (Hydra-70)

PEO Missiles and Space | Redstone Arsenal, AL

WARFIGHTING FUNCTION

Mission Command

Movement and Maneuver

Intelligence

Fires

Sustainment

Maneuver Support and Protection

Engagement

ACQUISITION LIFECYCLE PHASE

Materiel Solution Analysis

Technology Maturation & Risk Reduction

Engineering & Manufacturing Development

Production & Deployment

Operations & Support

MILESTONE DECISION AUTHORITY

Defense Acquisition Executive

Army Acquisition Executive

Program Executive Officer

DESCRIPTION

The Hydra-70 Rocket System of 2.75-inch air-launched rockets is employed by tri-service and special operating forces on both fixed- and rotary-wing aircraft and is inherently immune to countermeasures. This highly modular rocket family incorporates several different mission-oriented warheads for the Hydra-70 variant, including high-explosive, anti-personnel, multipurpose submunition, red phosphorus smoke, flechette, training, visible-light illumination flare, and infrared illumination flare.

BENEFIT TO THE WARFIGHTER

Hydra-70 provides an air-to-ground suppression, smoke screening, illumination, and direct and indirect fires capability to defeat area, materiel and personnel targets at close and extended ranges. This Advanced Precision Kill Weapon System II guidance package will infuse precision into the current Hydra-70 weapon system by providing increased stowed kills and point target accuracy. It will also provide the capability for low collateral damage engagements against lightly armored and soft-point targets.

SPECIFICATIONS

- Diameter: 2.75 inches
- Weight: 23-27 pounds (depending on warhead)
- Length: 55-70 inches (depending on warhead)
- Range: 300-8,000 meters
- Velocity: 700-plus meters per second
- Area suppression: No precision

PROGRAM STATUS

- **Current:** Producing annual replenishment for training, theater combat expenditures and war reserve requirements

PROJECTED ACTIVITIES

- **FY16-17:** Continue Hydra-70 production, safety, reliability and producibility program activities; continue assessment of guided rocket inventory objective requirements

FOREIGN MILITARY SALES

Hydra-70: Colombia, Egypt, Japan, Jordan, Kuwait, the Netherlands, Saudi Arabia, Singapore, Thailand, Taiwan, Tunisia, United Arab Emirates and United Kingdom

CONTRACTORS

Prime System: General Dynamics (Burlington, VT)
Grain: BAE Systems (Radford, VA)
Warhead Fuses: Action Manufacturing (Philadelphia, PA)
Shipping Container (Fastpack): CONCO (Louisville, KY)
Fin and Nozzle: General Dynamics Ordnance and Tactical Systems (Anniston, AL)

Abrams Tank Upgrade

PEO Ground Combat Systems | Detroit Arsenal, MI

DESCRIPTION

The Abrams tank closes with and destroys enemy forces on the integrated battlefield using mobility, firepower and shock effect. The Abrams tank upgrade includes two powerful variants: the M1A1 SA (Situational Awareness) and the M1A2 SEP (System Enhancement Program) version 2. The 1,500-horsepower turbine engine, the 120 mm main gun and special armor make the Abrams tank particularly lethal against heavy armor forces.

M1A1 SA: Improvements include the Gunner's Primary Sight with enhanced thermal imaging capabilities of the new Block I 2nd generation forward-looking infrared (FLIR) technology. Lethality improvements include the Stabilized Commander's Weapon Station and ballistic solution upgrades for the M829A3 kinetic and the M1028 canister rounds. Modifications include Blue Force Tracking, a digital command and control system that gives commanders current information about their location relative to friendly forces, and the Power Train Improvement and Integration Optimization Program (Total InteGrated Engine Revitalization engine and improved transmission), which provides more reliability and durability. Survivability improvements include frontal armor and turret side-armor upgrades.

M1A2 SEPv2: Upgrades include improved survivability, automotive power pack, computer systems and night vision capabilities. Lethality improvements include Common Remotely Operated Weapon Station and ballistic solution upgrades for the M829A3 kinetic and the M1028 canister rounds. The M1A2 SEPv2 has improved microprocessors, color flat-panel displays, improved memory capacity, better Soldier-machine interface and a new open operating system designed to run the Common Operating Environment software. Both the Gunner's Primary Sight and the Commander's Independent Thermal Viewer tank include the improved thermal imaging capabilities of the new Block I 2nd generation FLIR technology.

M1A2 SEPv3: The next version of the Abrams tank is currently in development. Improvements will focus on increasing the electrical power margin; improving survivability with improved armor protection and advanced counter-improvised explosive device protection; integrating the new Army network; electronic component improvements; a new auxiliary power unit; and an ammunition data link.

BENEFIT TO THE WARFIGHTER

The Abrams tank upgrade ensures that the warfighter will continue to possess the lethality, survivability and fightability necessary to defeat advanced threats well into the future. The Abrams is the Army's primary ground combat system.

SPECIFICATIONS

- Combat weight: M1A1 SA – 67.6 tons; M1A2 SEPv2 – 71.2 tons
- Speed: 42 mph, 30 mph cross-country
- M1A1 SA – 120 mm/40 rounds; M1A2 SEPv2 – 120 mm/42 rounds
- Machine guns: .50 Caliber, 900 rounds, 7.62 mm 11,400 rounds

PROGRAM STATUS

- **FY13-FY15:** Abrams production of the M1A2 SEPv2 tank continued for both the Active Army and the Army National Guard
- **2QFY15:** Abrams program approved to add the next generation FLIR sensor to the Abrams tank fleet

PROJECTED ACTIVITIES

- **FY16-2QFY17:** Abrams production of the M1A2 SEPv2 tank will be complete
- **3QFY16:** Begin the development effort for the next generation FLIR for the Abrams tank
- **2QFY17-4QFY17:** Transitions production of M1A2 SEPv2 to M1A2 SEPv3 through a "Pilot" program
- **4QFY17:** M1A2 SEPv3 program production begins

M1A1 SA

FOREIGN MILITARY SALES
M1A1: Australia, Egypt, Iraq and Morocco
M1A2: Kuwait
M1A2/M1A2S: Saudi Arabia

CONTRACTORS
General Dynamics Land Systems
(Sterling Heights, MI)

M1A2 SEP v2

M1A2 SEP v3

AH-64D/E Apache

PEO Aviation | Redstone Arsenal, AL

WARFIGHTING FUNCTION

Mission Command

Movement and Maneuver

Intelligence

Fires

Sustainment

Maneuver Support and Protection

Engagement

ACQUISITION LIFECYCLE PHASE

Materiel Solution Analysis

Technology Maturation & Risk Reduction

Engineering & Manufacturing Development

Production & Deployment

Operations & Support

MILESTONE DECISION AUTHORITY

Defense Acquisition Executive

Army Acquisition Executive

Program Executive Officer

DESCRIPTION

The AH-64D/E Apache is the Army's only heavy attack helicopter for both the current and future force. It can destroy armor, personnel and materiel targets in obscured battlefield conditions. The Apache is a two-engine, four-bladed, tandem-seat attack helicopter with an M230 30 mm cannon, Hydra 70 2.75-inch rockets, laser and Radio Frequency HELLFIRE missiles. The current fleet consists of both D and E models. The Apache program is the second-time remanufacture of this combat system; D models are remanufactured into upgraded E models, which are designed and equipped with an open-systems architecture to incorporate the latest communications, navigation, sensor and weapon systems.

In the remanufacture process, the Apache receives modifications such as upgraded forward-looking infrared technology with the Modernized Target Acquisition Designation Sight/Pilot Night Vision Sensor (MTADS/PNVS) that provides blended infrared and night vision capability. The MTADS/PNVS upgrade is a major combat multiplier for the aircraft.

The MTADS/PNVS has a new integrated infrared laser allowing easier target designation. The E-model also has Link 16 capability supporting Joint communications. The updated Fire Control Radar will have the ability to operate in a maritime mode, enabling Apache to be integral in all environments. The Manned-Unmanned Teaming ability of the E model fleet provides Apache crews with the ability to receive unmanned aerial systems (UAS) video, control UAS sensors and direct UAS vehicles. The E-model meets all the requirements for Army and Joint interoperability goals for the future and will ensure the aircraft remains a viable combat multiplier beyond 2035.

BENEFIT TO THE WARFIGHTER

The Apache provides security to ground forces, fixed-based operations and aerial escorts. It can be used to conduct reconnaissance to provide situational awareness. The Apache decisively engages single or multiple enemy combatants to allow freedom of maneuver and protection.

SPECIFICATIONS

- Combat mission (maximum) speed: AH-64D – 145 knots; AH-64E – 164 knots
- Combat range: 260 nautical miles
- Combat endurance: 2.5 hours
- Maximum gross weight: 20,260 pounds
- Ordnance: 16 HELLFIRE missiles, 76 2.75-inch rockets, and 1,200 30 mm chain gun rounds
- Crew: Two (pilot and copilot gunner)
- Rate of Fire: 600-650 rounds per minute

PROGRAM STATUS

- **4QFY14:** Successfully completed Follow-on Test and Evaluation
- **1QFY15:** MTADS/PNVS Performance Based Logistics III Awarded
- **2QFY15:** Awarded Version 6 Development Contract

PROJECTED ACTIVITIES

- **2QFY16:**
  › Production Multiyear Contract Award
  › Version 4 Capability Aircraft Inspected Using Form DD250
- **4QFY17:** Follow-on Test and Evaluation II

Apache

FOREIGN MILITARY SALES
Egypt, Greece, Israel, Kuwait, Netherlands, Saudi Arabia, Singapore, United Arab Emirates, Indonesia, Korea, Taiwan, Qatar and Netherlands
Direct commercial sales: Greece, Japan and United Kingdom

CONTRACTORS
Airframe: Boeing (Mesa, AZ)
Major Components: Lockheed Martin (Orlando, FL), Northrop Grumman (Baltimore, MD), Longbow LLC (Orlando, FL)

Airborne and Maritime/Fixed Station (AMF)

PEO Command, Control and Communications – Tactical | Aberdeen Proving Ground, MD

DESCRIPTION

Airborne and Maritime/Fixed Station (AMF) radios, which are software programmable, multiband, multimode, mobile ad hoc networking radios, provide simultaneous voice, data and video communications. The radios support the Common Operating Picture, Situational Awareness and interoperability of Mission Command systems throughout the battlefield. Per Milestone Decision Authority direction, the redefined AMF Program will procure radios as Non-Developmental Items (NDI).

BENEFIT TO THE WARFIGHTER

AMF radios ensure the Soldier's ability to communicate both horizontally and vertically via voice and data within all mission areas. They also help close capability gaps by extending data networking to company-and-below echelons, enabling network services to the platform and connecting Army aviation platforms to Army ground and Joint air network domains.

SPECIFICATIONS

- Meets size, weight and power restrictions for Army rotary-wing platforms
- Small Airborne Networking Radio (SANR) provides a multi-channel networking radio capable of using Soldier Radio Waveform and Wideband Networking Waveform in addition to legacy Single Channel Ground and Airborne Radio System capability to interoperate with ground forces for seamless connectivity for combat operations
- SANR provides support to all Army rotary-wing platforms, as well as the Gray Eagle Unmanned Aircraft System

PROGRAM STATUS

- **3QFY12:** Received Under Secretary of Defense for Acquisition, Technology and Logistics (USD(AT&L)) direction to close out the AMF Joint Tactical Radio System Development and Demonstration contract
- **4QFY12:** Received USD(AT&L) direction to pursue an NDI acquisition approach to meet Army rotary-wing aircraft requirements
- **1QFY15:** AMF program split to reflect Small Airborne Link 16 Terminal and SANR subprograms
- **2QFY15:** President's FY16 Budget funds SANR development effort

PROJECTED ACTIVITIES

- **FY16:** Acquisition Strategy approved
- **3QFY16:** SANR Request for Proposal release
- **FY17:** Contract Award expected

FOREIGN MILITARY SALES
None

CONTRACTORS
TBD

WEAPON SYSTEMS HANDBOOK **2016**   17

Armored Multi-Purpose Vehicle (AMPV)

PEO Ground Combat Systems | Detroit Arsenal, MI

WARFIGHTING FUNCTION

Mission Command

Movement and Maneuver

Intelligence

Fires

Sustainment

Maneuver Support and Protection

Engagement

ACQUISITION LIFECYCLE PHASE

Materiel Solution Analysis

Technology Maturation & Risk Reduction

Engineering & Manufacturing Development

Production & Deployment

Operations & Support

MILESTONE DECISION AUTHORITY

Defense Acquisition Executive

Army Acquisition Executive

Program Executive Officer

DESCRIPTION

The Armored Multi-Purpose Vehicle (AMPV) is the replacement for the M113 Family of Vehicles (FoV) within the Armored Brigade Combat Team (ABCT), comprising approximately 30 percent of its tracked vehicle fleet.

The General Purpose variant accommodates two crew, six passengers, is reconfigurable to carry one litter, mount crew served weapon, integrates two Joint Tactical Radio System Handheld, Manpack and Small Form Fit (HMS) or two Single Channel Ground and Airborne Radio System (SINCGARS), Vehicle Intercom (VIC)-3, Driver's Vision Enhancer (DVE), Duke v3, and Force XXI Battle Command Brigade and Below (FBCB2)/Blue Force Tracker (BFT).

The Mortar Carrier variant accommodates two crew, two mortar crew, a mounted 120 mm mortar, 69 rounds of 120 mm ammunition, two HMS radios, a SINCGARS radio, VIC-3, DVE, Duke v3, FBCB2/BFT and M95 Mortar Fire Control System.

The Mission Command variant is the cornerstone of the Army's ABCT Network Modernization Strategy. It takes advantage of increased size, weight, power and cooling limitations and provides a significant increase in Command, Control, Communications and Computer capability. The variant accommodates a driver and commander and two workstation operators, and its red side Network provides full Tactical Command Post capabilities at brigade and battalion levels.

The Medical Evacuation variant includes room for three crew, six ambulatory patients or four litter patients or three ambulatory and two litter patients, two integrated HMS radios, VIC-3, DVE, DUKE v3, FBCB2/BFT and the storage for Medical Equipment Sets.

The Medical Treatment variant includes room for four crew, one litter patient, and a patient treatment table.

BENEFIT TO THE WARFIGHTER

The AMPV provides significant capability improvement over the M113 FoV in force protection, survivability, mobility and power generation to incorporate the Army's inbound network and other future technologies.

SPECIFICATIONS

- Weight: 75,000-80,000 pounds
- Sustained speed: 34-38 mph
- Acceleration (0-30 mph): 24 seconds
- Cruising range (at 30 mph): 225 miles
- Weapons: Hosts M249, M240, M2 or MK-19; 120 mm mortar

PROGRAM STATUS

- **1QFY13:** Engineering and Manufacturing (EMD) Development Requests for Proposal Defense Acquisition Board (DAB)
- **1QFY15:**
  › Milestone B DAB
  › EMD Contract Award
- **2QFY15:** System Requirements Review
- **3QFY15:** Preliminary Design Review
- **4QFY15:** Integrated Baseline Review

PROJECTED ACTIVITIES

- **3QFY16:** Critical Design Review
- **1QFY17:**
  › Coupon/Ballistic Hull Deliveries
  › First Prototype Delivery
- **3QFY17:** Production Prove Out and Live Fire Testing Initiated

FOREIGN MILITARY SALES
None

CONTRACTORS
Prime: BAE Systems (York, PA)

Army Integrated Air and Missile Defense (AIAMD)

PEO Missiles and Space | Redstone Arsenal, AL

WARFIGHTING FUNCTION

Mission Command

Movement and Maneuver

Intelligence

Fires

Sustainment

Maneuver Support and Protection

Engagement

ACQUISITION LIFECYCLE PHASE

Materiel Solution Analysis

Technology Maturation & Risk Reduction

Engineering & Manufacturing Development

Production & Deployment

Operations & Support

MILESTONE DECISION AUTHORITY

Defense Acquisition Executive

Army Acquisition Executive

Program Executive Officer

DESCRIPTION

The Army Integrated Air and Missile Defense (AIAMD) will enable the integration of modular components (current and future Air and Missile Defense (AMD) sensors, weapons and Mission Command (MC) technologies with a common MC capability in a networked and distributed plug-and-fight architecture. This common MC, called the Integrated AMD Battle Command System (IBCS), will provide standard configurations and capabilities at each echelon. This allows Joint, interagency, intergovernmental and multinational AMD forces to organize based on mission, enemy, terrain and weather, available time, troops and support available, and civil considerations. Shelters and vehicles may be added to enable broader missions and a wider span of control executed at higher echelons.

BENEFIT TO THE WARFIGHTER

The plug-and-fight architecture and common MC system will enable dynamic defense design for the warfighter and provide the capability for interdependent, network-centric operations to the supported force scheme of operations and maneuver. This architecture will enable extended range and nonline-of-sight engagements across the full spectrum of aerial threats. It will mitigate coverage gaps and single points of failure as well as reduce manpower, enhance training, and reduce operation and support costs.

SPECIFICATIONS

- Family of Medium Tactical Vehicles mounted MC shelter with Integrated Collaborative Environment Tent and trailer mounted support system

PROGRAM STATUS

- **1QFY13:** AIAMD Participation in Network Integration Evaluation 13.1
- **1QFY14:** AIAMD Demonstration
- **2QFY14:** IAMD Battle Command System Immersion Day at the Pentagon
- **1QFY15:** AIAMD Acquisition Program Baseline Update
- **3QFY15:** First Live Fire Flight Test
- **4QFY15:** New Equipment Training

PROJECTED ACTIVITIES

- **2QFY16:** Limited User Test
- **4QFY16:** Milestone C
- **3QFY17:** First Unit Equipped

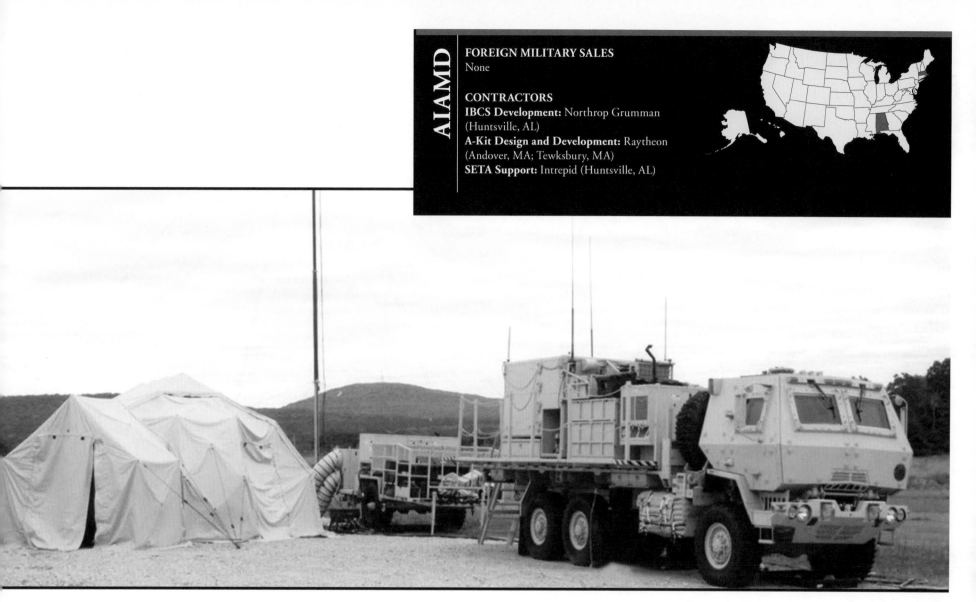

FOREIGN MILITARY SALES
None

CONTRACTORS
IBCS Development: Northrop Grumman
(Huntsville, AL)
A-Kit Design and Development: Raytheon
(Andover, MA; Tewksbury, MA)
SETA Support: Intrepid (Huntsville, AL)

Assembled Chemical Weapons Alternatives (ACWA)

PEO Assembled Chemical Weapons Alternatives | Aberdeen Proving Ground, MD

WARFIGHTING FUNCTION

Mission Command

Movement and Maneuver

Intelligence

Fires

Sustainment

Maneuver Support and Protection

Engagement

ACQUISITION LIFECYCLE PHASE

Materiel Solution Analysis

Technology Maturation & Risk Reduction

Engineering & Manufacturing Development

Production & Deployment

Operations & Support

MILESTONE DECISION AUTHORITY

Defense Acquisition Executive

Army Acquisition Executive

Program Executive Officer

DESCRIPTION

Assembled Chemical Weapons Alternatives (ACWA) enhances national security by destroying chemical weapons stockpiles in a safe and environmentally compliant manner at the U.S. Army Pueblo Chemical Depot (PCD) in Pueblo, CO, and Blue Grass Army Depot (BGAD) in Richmond, KY.

Established by Congressional legislation in 1996, Program Executive Office, Assembled Chemical Weapons Alternatives (PEO ACWA) reports directly to the Under Secretary of Defense for Acquisition, Technology and Logistics through the Assistant Secretary of Defense for Nuclear, Chemical and Biological Defense Programs. PEO ACWA is responsible for destruction of the chemical weapons stockpiles located at PCD and BGAD.

PEO ACWA is specifically responsible for managing the construction, systemization, operation and closure, and any contracting related to the Pueblo Chemical Agent-Destruction Pilot Plant (PCAPP) and the Blue Grass Chemical Agent-Destruction Pilot Plant (BGCAPP). The PCAPP is scheduled to begin main plant operations in 2016. A separate facility, the PCAPP Explosive Destruction System, is currently destroying a small quantity of munitions that cannot be processed by the plant's automated systems. Additionally, systemization is underway at the BGCAPP, where construction is substantially complete.

BENEFIT TO THE WARFIGHTER

ACWA eliminates stockpile storage costs and will allow for reallocation of funding to support high-priority programs that protect the warfighter.

SPECIFICATIONS

PCAPP:
- Destroys Mustard Agent in 4.2-inch mortar rounds and 105 mm and 155 mm projectiles
- Operational Concept: Neutralization followed by Biotreatment

BGCAPP:
- Destroys GB, VX and Mustard Agent in 8-inch and 155 mm projectiles and M55 rockets
- Operational Concept: Neutralization followed by Supercritical Water Oxidation

PROGRAM STATUS
- **1QFY13:** PCAPP construction complete
- **2QFY15:** PCAPP Explosive Destruction System Operations began
- **3QFY15:** BGCAPP Static Detonation Chamber (SDC) Factory Acceptance Test successfully completed

PROJECTED ACTIVITIES
- **3QFY16:** PCAPP Destruction Operations begin
- **4QFY17:** BGCAPP SDC Operations begin

BGCAPP

ACWA

FOREIGN MILITARY SALES
None

CONTRACTORS
PCAPP: Bechtel National, Inc. (Reston, VA)
BGCAPP: Bechtel Parsons Blue Grass, Joint
Venture (Richmond, KY)
Bechtel National, Inc. (Reston, VA)
Parsons Government Services, Inc. (Pasadena, CA)

PCAPP

Black Hawk UH/HH-60

PEO Aviation | Redstone Arsenal, AL

ACAT I

WARFIGHTING FUNCTION

Mission Command

Movement and Maneuver

Intelligence

Fires

Sustainment

Maneuver Support
and Protection

Engagement

ACQUISITION LIFECYCLE PHASE

Materiel Solution Analysis

Technology Maturation &
Risk Reduction

Engineering & Manufacturing Development

Production & Deployment

Operations & Support

MILESTONE DECISION AUTHORITY

Defense Acquisition Executive

Army Acquisition Executive

Program Executive Officer

DESCRIPTION

The Black Hawk UH/HH-60 is the Army's utility tactical transport helicopter. It provides air assault, general support, aeromedical evacuation, command and control, and special operations support to combat, stability and support operations. This versatile Black Hawk helicopter has enhanced the Army's overall mobility due to dramatic improvement in troop and cargo lift capacity. It will serve as the Army's utility helicopter in the Future Force. There are multiple versions of the UH-60 Black Hawk, including the UH-60M and the UH-60V.

The UH-60M includes the improved GE-701D engine and provides greater cruising speed, rate of climb and internal load than the UH-60A and UH-60L versions. The Medical Evacuation (MEDEVAC) version of the UH-60M, the HH-60M, includes an integrated MEDEVAC Mission Equipment Package kit, providing day, night and adverse weather emergency evacuation of casualties.

The UH-60V is designed to update the existing UH-60L analog architecture to a digital infrastructure, enabling the upgraded aircraft to have a similar Pilot-Vehicle Interface and commonality of training as the UH-60M.

BENEFIT TO THE WARFIGHTER

On the asymmetric battlefield, the Black Hawk enables commanders to get to the fight quicker and to mass effects throughout the battlespace across the full spectrum of conflict. A single Black Hawk can transport an entire 11-person, fully equipped infantry squad faster than a predecessor system in most weather conditions. The aircraft's critical components and systems are armored or redundant, and its airframe is designed to crush progressively on impact to protect crew and passengers. The UH-60M and the UH-60V are a digital networked platform with greater range and lift to support maneuver commanders through air assault, command and control, general support and aeromedical evacuation.

SPECIFICATIONS

	UH-60A	UH-60L/V	UH-60M
Max Gross Weight (Pounds)	20,250	22,000	22,000
Cruise Speed (Knots)	149	150	152
Rate of Climb (Feet/Minute)	814	1,315	1,646
Engines (Two each)	GE-700	GE-701C	GE-701D
External Load (Pounds)	8,000	8,000	9,000
Internal Load (Pounds)	2,640	2,640	3,190
Crew	Two pilots, two crew chiefs		
Armament	Two 7.62 mm machine guns		

PROGRAM STATUS

UH-60V:
- **3QFY13:** Materiel Development Decision
- **2QFY14:** Milestone B
- **4QFY14:** Engineering & Manufacturing Development Contract Award
- **3QFY15:** Preliminary Design Review
- **4QFY15:** Critical Design Review

UH/HH-60M:
- **Through FY15:** Fielded 691 UH-60M to Active Army, Reserve and the National Guard

PROJECTED ACTIVITIES

UH/HH-60M:
- **Current:** Multiyear IX Contract Award

UH-60V:
- **2QFY17:** First Flight

UH/HH-60

FOREIGN MILITARY SALES

UH-60L: Brazil, Colombia, Egypt, Saudi Arabia and Thailand

UH-60M: Bahrain, Jordan, Mexico, United Arab Emirates, Taiwan, Saudi Arabia and Thailand

CONTRACTORS

UH/HH-60M: Sikorsky (Stratford, CT)

701-Series Engine: General Electric (Lynn, MA)

UH-60V: U.S. Army Aviation and Missile Research Development and Engineering Center (AMRDEC) Prototype Integration Facility (PIF), Redstone Defense Systems (RDS) (Huntsville, AL)

Bradley Fighting Vehicle Systems (BFVS)

PEO Ground Combat Systems | Detroit Arsenal, MI

DESCRIPTION

The Bradley Fighting Vehicle Systems (BFVS) M2A3 Infantry Fighting Vehicle (IFV) features two second-generation, forward-looking infrared sensors, one in the Improved Bradley Acquisition Subsystem and another in the Commander's Independent Viewer. These provide "hunter-killer target handoff" capability with ballistic fire control. The Bradley A3 also has embedded diagnostics and an Integrated Combat Command and Control (IC3) digital communications suite hosting a Force XXI Battle Command Brigade-and-Below package with digital maps, messages and friend-or-foe information. These systems provide the vehicle with increased shared battlefield situational awareness. The Bradley's position navigation with Global Positioning Systems, inertial navigation and enhanced squad situational awareness includes a squad leader display integrated into vehicle digital images and IC3.

The Bradley Fire Support Team (BFIST) vehicle is the "Eyes of the Artillery." Using state-of-the-art long-range sensors, BFIST can acquire, identify, track and designate targets while mounted and under armor, enhancing crew survivability. BFIST is assigned to the Armored Reconnaissance Battalion and Combined Arms Battalions of the Armored Brigade Combat Team.

The M3A3 Cavalry Fighting Vehicle (CFV) is undergoing a conversion to the M2A3 IFV variant. This will reduce the sustainment footprint for the fleet and enhance Soldier proficiency and operational utility in the field.

BENEFIT TO THE WARFIGHTER

The Bradley Fighting vehicle ensures warfighters can continue to maintain combat overmatch capability.

SPECIFICATIONS

- Speed: 40 mph
- Range: 250 miles
- Payload: 6,000 pounds
- Vehicle Weapons: 25 mm, Tube-Launched, Optically Tracked, Wireless-Guided Missiles II, 7.62 mm
- M2/M3A3 mean miles between failure required/actual: 400/681 miles
- Deployable Aircraft: C-17, C-5

PROGRAM STATUS

- **2QFY15:** M3 to M2 conversions
- **3QFY15:** Engineering Change Proposal (ECP) 1 Suspension Upgrade in production

PROJECTED ACTIVITIES

- **3QFY16:** ECP2b Lethality Upgrade begins
- **4QFY16:** Establish Bradley M2 as baseline configuration for Infantry/Calvary Fighting Vehicle (IFV/CFV) roles
- **FY16-17:** ECP2 Network Upgrade Testing
- **2QFY17:** Completion of M3 to M2 conversion
- **FY17:** ECP2 Network Upgrade Production Decision planned
- **Through FY21:** ECP1 Suspension Upgrade continues

BFVS

FOREIGN MILITARY SALES
Saudi Arabia

CONTRACTORS
BAE Systems (York, PA; Santa Clara, CA)
L-3 Communications (Muskegon, MI)

CH-47F Chinook

PEO Aviation | Redstone Arsenal, AL

WARFIGHTING FUNCTION

Mission Command

Movement and Maneuver

Intelligence

Fires

Sustainment

Maneuver Support and Protection

Engagement

ACQUISITION LIFECYCLE PHASE

Materiel Solution Analysis

Technology Maturation & Risk Reduction

Engineering & Manufacturing Development

Production & Deployment

Operations & Support

MILESTONE DECISION AUTHORITY

Defense Acquisition Executive

Army Acquisition Executive

Program Executive Officer

DESCRIPTION

The CH-47F Chinook is the Army's only heavy-lift cargo helicopter supporting combat and other critical operations. The CH-47F has a suite of improved features such as an upgraded digital cockpit featuring the Common Avionics Architecture System, a new monolithic airframe with vibration reduction, and the Digital Automatic Flight Control System, which provides coupled controllability for operations in adverse environments (reduced visibility, brown out, high winds). The CH-47F's common cockpit enables multiservice digital compatibility and interoperability for improved situational awareness, mission performance and survivability, as well as future growth potential. The CH-47F can lift intra-theater payloads up to 16,000 pounds in high/hot environments.

BENEFIT TO THE WARFIGHTER

The CH-47F tactically transports forces and associated equipment and provides routine aerial sustainment of maneuver forces. Secondary missions the Chinook executes to support Soldiers and commanders include: medical evacuation, search and rescue, parachute drops, disaster relief and aircraft recovery.

SPECIFICATIONS

- Empty aircraft weight: 24,578 pounds
- Maximum gross weight: 50,000 pounds
- Maximum cruise speed: 160 knots
- Capacity: 36 (33 troops plus 3 crew)
- Litter capacity: 24
- Sling-load capacity: 26,000 pounds center hook; 17,000 pounds forward/aft hook; 25,000 pounds tandem
- Minimum crew: 3 (pilot, copilot and flight engineer)

PROGRAM STATUS

- **3QFY13:** Cargo On/Off Handling System (COOLS) Retrofit initiated
- **4QFY13:** Multiyear II contract award
- **4QFY14:**
  › COOLS delivered on production aircraft
  › Cargo Platform Health Environment delivered on production aircraft

PROJECTED ACTIVITIES

- **1QFY17:** Improved Vibration Control System delivered on production aircraft
- **4QFY17:** Delivery of 400th Chinook

CH-47F Chinook

FOREIGN MILITARY SALES
Australia, United Arab Emirates, Turkey and Netherlands

CONTRACTORS
Aircraft and Recap: Boeing (Philadelphia, PA)
Engine: Honeywell (Phoenix, AZ)
Software: Rockwell Collins (Cedar Rapids, IA)
Engine Controls: Goodrich (Danbury, CT)

Common Missile Warning System (CMWS), Laser Detection System (LDS), Radar Warning Receiver (RWR), Advanced Threat Infrared Countermeasures (ATIRCM) and Common Infrared Countermeasure (CIRCM) Programs

PEO Intelligence, Electronic Warfare and Sensors | Aberdeen Proving Ground, MD

WARFIGHTING FUNCTION

Mission Command

Movement and Maneuver

Intelligence

Fires

Sustainment

Maneuver Support and Protection

Engagement

ACQUISITION LIFECYCLE PHASE

Materiel Solution Analysis

Technology Maturation & Risk Reduction

Engineering & Manufacturing Development

Production & Deployment

Operations & Support

MILESTONE DECISION AUTHORITY

Defense Acquisition Executive

Army Acquisition Executive

Program Executive Officer

DESCRIPTION

The Common Missile Warning System (CMWS) and Advanced Threat Infrared Countermeasures (ATIRCM) system integrates defensive infrared (IR) countermeasures capabilities into existing, current-generation aircraft to engage and defeat IR-guided missile threats.

The Army operational requirements concept for IR countermeasures systems is the Suite of Integrated Infrared Countermeasures (SIIRCM). The CMWS and ATIRCM programs form the core element of SIIRCM. CMWS can function as a stand-alone system with the capability to detect missiles and provide audible and visual warnings to pilots. When installed with the Advanced IRCM Munitions and improved countermeasure dispensers, it activates expendables to decoy and defeat IR-guided missiles.

ATIRCM protects crews and aircraft from advanced threat Man Portable Air Defense Systems (MANPADS) until CIRCM is fielded.

The CIRCM program of record is entering Engineering & Manufacturing Development (EMD) and is being developed to replace ATIRCM. CIRCM will be lighter weight and more reliable, and have more affordable lifecycle costs. It is also designed to operate with CMWS and future missile warning systems to provide protection for rotary-wing, tiltrotor and small fixed-wing aircraft across DoD.

BENEFIT TO THE WARFIGHTER

MANPADS are proliferated worldwide and pose a strategic threat to all DoD rotary-wing and fixed-wing aircraft. Threat detection sensors are the first step in the detection-and-defeat engagement sequence. Improving sensor capability and exploiting new sensor technology translates into seeing the threat sooner and at greater distances, buying more time for the warfighter to successfully engage with an effective countermeasure solution. The combination of CIRCM and flares helps provide a tiered defense for DoD aircraft.

SPECIFICATIONS

Threat detection systems:

- CMWS detects threats in the ultraviolet spectrum, warns pilots and deploys flares to counter threat
- The Laser Detection System detects laser-guided threats and warns pilots
- The Radar Warning Receiver detects Radio Frequency (RF)-emitting and RF-guided threats, and warns pilots

Threat defeat systems:

- CIRCM system, the next generation lightweight laser-based system, defeats IR-guided MANPAD threats
- ATIRCM, the legacy laser-based infrared countermeasure system, is fielded only to the CH-47F fleet due to its size, weight and power requirements

PROGRAM STATUS

- **4QFY13:** Integrated onto select fixed-wing platforms
- **Current:** All aircraft deployed in support of contingency operations equipped with CMWS prior to deployment; now fielding Generation 3 Electronic Control Unit (ECU) and Missile Warning Algorithms for all aircraft

PROJECTED ACTIVITIES

- **FY16-FY17:**
  › CIRCM Milestone (MS) B Acquisition Decision Milestone signed and EMD contract awarded for the EMD phase effort
  › ATIRCM: Continue fielding to CH-47D/F; MS C re-approved; ATIRCM continues as the Army's most advanced Aircraft Survivability Equipment system designed to protect Army aircrews from advanced MANPADS
  › CMWS: Continue fielding Generation 3 ECU
- **2QFY18:** CIRCM: MS C

SENSORS

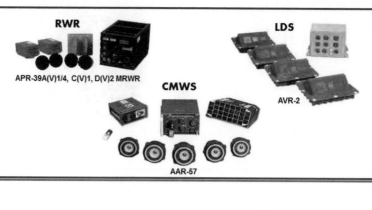

RWR

APR-39A(V)1/4, C(V)1, D(V)2 MRWR

LDS

AVR-2

CMWS

AAR-57

COUNTERMEASURE

CIRCM

ATIRCM

OT -225

CMWS, LDS, RWR, ATIRCM, CIRCM

FOREIGN MILITARY SALES
CMWS: United Kingdom, Egypt, Tunisia, Jordan, Korea, Qatar, Saudi Arabia and Indonesia

CONTRACTORS
ATIRCM and CMWS: BAE Systems (Nashua, NH)
CIRCM: Northrop Grumman (Rolling Meadows, IL)
Logistics Support: LogiCore (Huntsville, AL)
Programmatic Support: Wyle's CAS Group (Huntsville, AL)
System Engineering Support: Computer Sciences Corp. (CSC) (Huntsville, AL)
Software Configuration Management Support: CGI Federal (Huntsville, AL), Wavelink (Huntsville, AL)
CMWS-GTRI E2E Data Analysis/SIL Development: Georgia Tech Applied Research Corp. (Atlanta, GA)
Test Support Data Analysis: Penta Research, Inc. (Huntsville, AL)
UH-60A/L P31 Upgrade: Rockwell Collins (Cedar Rapids, IA)
Engineering/Tech Production Support: Intuitive Research and Technology Corp. (Huntsville, AL)
Open Architecture Translator System (OATS): David H. Pollock Consultants (Eatontown, NJ)

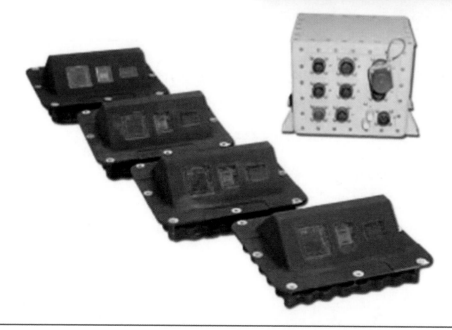

Common Remotely Operated Weapon Station (CROWS)

PEO Soldier | Fort Belvoir, VA

WARFIGHTING FUNCTION

Mission Command

Movement and Maneuver

Intelligence

Fires

Sustainment

Maneuver Support and Protection

Engagement

ACQUISITION LIFECYCLE PHASE

Materiel Solution Analysis

Technology Maturation & Risk Reduction

Engineering & Manufacturing Development

Production & Deployment

Operations & Support

MILESTONE DECISION AUTHORITY

Defense Acquisition Executive

Army Acquisition Executive

Program Executive Officer

DESCRIPTION

The Common Remotely Operated Weapon Station (CROWS) is a stabilized mount that contains a sensor suite and fire control software, allowing on-the-move target acquisition and first-burst target engagement. CROWS also features programmable target reference points for multiple locations, programmable sector surveillance scanning, automatic target ballistic lead, automatic target tracking, and programmable no-fire zones.

Future enhancements include integration of other weapons, escalation-of-force systems, sniper detection, integrated 360-degree situational awareness, increased weapon elevation and commander's display.

BENEFIT TO THE WARFIGHTER

CROWS allows the warfighter to remotely engage targets with precision fire while on the move or stationary to the maximum effective range of the weapon. Capable of target engagement under day and night conditions, the CROWS sensor suite includes a daytime video camera, thermal camera and laser rangefinder. CROWS is designed to mount on any tactical vehicle and supports the MK19 Grenade Machine Gun, M2 .50 Caliber Machine Gun, M240B Machine Gun and M249 Squad Automatic Weapon.

SPECIFICATIONS

- Interoperable with the MK19, M2, M240B, M249 and Javelin systems
- Camera: 27x zoom, 47-degree field of view (FOV) (day)
- Thermal: 2x zoom, 3 degrees and 11 degrees dual FOV (night)

PROGRAM STATUS

- **4QFY14:**
  › Full Materiel Release (FMR) for CROWS on Mine Resistant Ambush Protected All-Terrain Vehicle (M-ATV)
  › FMR for CROWS on Family of Medium Tactical Vehicles
  › Transition to Organic Field Support
- **2QFY15:** FMR on Special Operations Forces M-ATV
- **4QFY15:**
  › CROWS/Javelin Safety Confirmation approved
  › CROWS Low Profile testing conducted on M1A2
- **1QFY16:** CROWS Increment 2 Capability Development Document approved

PROJECTED ACTIVITIES

- **2QFY16:** Low Profile CROWS production decision
- **4QFY17:** Transition to organic depot support

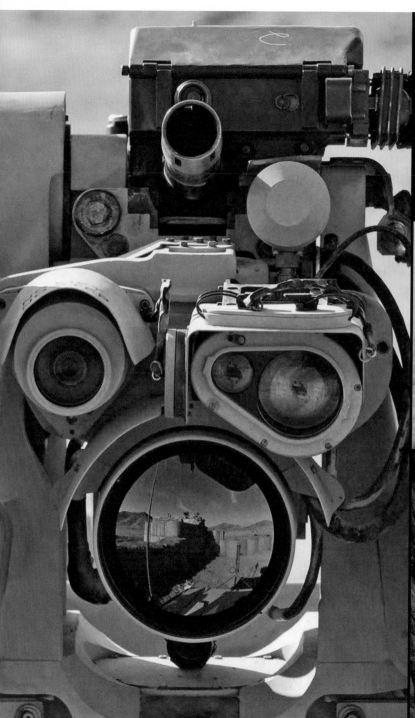

FOREIGN MILITARY SALES
None

CONTRACTORS
Kongsberg Defense & Aerospace (Johnstown, PA)

Distributed Common Ground System – Army (DCGS-A) Increment 1

PEO Intelligence, Electronic Warfare and Sensors | Aberdeen Proving Ground, MD

WARFIGHTING FUNCTION

Mission Command

Movement and Maneuver

Intelligence

Fires

Sustainment

Maneuver Support and Protection

Engagement

ACQUISITION LIFECYCLE PHASE

Materiel Solution Analysis

Technology Maturation & Risk Reduction

Engineering & Manufacturing Development

Production & Deployment

Operations & Support

MILESTONE DECISION AUTHORITY

Defense Acquisition Executive

Army Acquisition Executive

Program Executive Officer

DESCRIPTION

The Distributed Common Ground System – Army (DCGS-A) is a system of systems that integrated nine legacy stovepiped intelligence systems programs into one that gives commanders the ability to task battlespace sensors and receive intelligence information from multiple sources on the battlefield. DCGS-A contributes to visualization and situational awareness, thereby enhancing tactical maneuver, maximizing combat power and enhancing the ability to operate in an unpredictable and changing environment throughout the operational spectrum.

DCGS-A consists of both software and hardware. Hardware includes user laptops and desktops, fixed, portable and vehicle-mounted servers, and ground stations to receive, share and store collected intelligence. Software tools allow users to select and pull from DCGS-A's 700-plus data sources, perform analysis and share intelligence products generated from that analysis.

DCGS-A supports the intelligence warfighting function to assist the commander's visualization and understanding of the threat and other relevant aspects of the operational environment. The system assists in the application of the intelligence core competencies (intelligence synchronization, intelligence operations and intelligence analysis) through the ability to apply the intelligence process and to leverage the intelligence enterprise. DCGS-A is the Army's cornerstone intelligence system for sensor tasking, processing, exploitation and dissemination at all echelons, and provides unprecedented, timely, relevant and accurate data to Soldiers up to the TS/SCI level.

The Army produces and fields DCGS-A capability on various hardware platforms using consolidated releases. DCGS-A's modular, open systems architecture allows rapid adaptation to changing mission circumstances. As an analyst toolset, the system enables the user to collaborate, synchronize and integrate organic and nonorganic collection elements with operations; as the intelligence component supporting the operation, DCGS-A can discover and use all relevant threat, noncombatant,

weather, geospatial and space data, and evaluate technical data and information. DCGS-A leverages commercial products, creating a level playing field for industry through an open architecture design. DCGS-A is capable of multi-intelligence processing and is built to intelligence community framework standards.

BENEFIT TO THE WARFIGHTER

DCGS-A Increment 1 connects Soldiers to multiple Joint intelligence, surveillance and reconnaissance platforms and sensors, the Intelligence Community, and other services and Army Mission Command systems. It gives commanders the ability to view intelligence, surveillance and reconnaissance information in one place. It also integrates that information into tools that can support intelligence development.

SPECIFICATIONS

- Intelligence Fusion Server
- Portable Multifunctional Workstation
- Fixed Multifunctional Workstation
- Cross Domain Solution Suite
- Tactical Intelligence Ground Station
- Geospatial Intelligence Work Station
- Operational Intelligence Ground Station
- Intelligence Processing Center V1 and V2

PROGRAM STATUS

- **1QFY13:** DCGS-A Increment 1, Release 1 Full Deployment Decision
- **3QFY15:** DCGS-A Increment 1, Release 2 Follow on Test and Evaluation
- **1QFY16:** DCGS-A Increment 1, Release 2 Fielding Decision

PROJECTED ACTIVITIES

- **2QFY16:** Increment 1, Release 2 Fielding

DCGS-A Inc. I

FOREIGN MILITARY SALES
None

CONTRACTORS
Lockheed Martin (Denver, CO)
General Dynamics (Scottsdale, AZ)
ViaTech Systems, Inc. (Eatontown, NJ)
MITRE (Eatontown, NJ)
Textron/OverWatch Systems (Austin, TX)
Booz Allen Hamilton (Eatontown, NJ)
Raytheon (Garland, TX)
NetApp (Sunnyvale, CA)
VMware (Palo Alto, CA)
Esri (Redlands, CA)
Tucson Embedded Systems (Tucson, AZ)
L3 Communications (Tempe, AZ)
Dell (Austin, TX)
Potomac Fusion (Austin, TX)
Redhat (Raleigh, NC)
IBM (Armonk, NY)
HP (Palo Alto, CA)
Leidos (Reston, VA)
ManTech (Fairfax, VA)

Distributed Common Ground System – Army (DCGS-A) Increment 2

PEO Intelligence, Electronic Warfare and Sensors | Aberdeen Proving Ground, MD

WARFIGHTING FUNCTION

Mission Command

Movement and Maneuver

Intelligence

Fires

Sustainment

Maneuver Support and Protection

Engagement

ACQUISITION LIFECYCLE PHASE

Materiel Solution Analysis

Technology Maturation & Risk Reduction

Engineering & Manufacturing Development

Production & Deployment

Operations & Support

MILESTONE DECISION AUTHORITY

Defense Acquisition Executive

Army Acquisition Executive

Program Executive Officer

DESCRIPTION

The Distributed Common Ground System – Army (DCGS-A) Increment 2 gives commanders the ability to task battlespace sensors to receive intelligence information from multiple sources on the battlefield. DCGS-A contributes to visualization and situational awareness, thereby enhancing tactical maneuver, maximizing combat power and enhancing the ability to operate in an unpredictable and changing environment.

DCGS-A is the Army's cornerstone intelligence system for sensor Tasking, Processing, Exploitation and Dissemination. DCGS-A provides unprecedented timely, relevant and accurate data to Soldiers up to the Top Secret/Sensitive Compartmented Information level.

DCGS-A Increment 2 will deliver enhanced visualization, analytical tools and data integration, cyber analytics incorporation, and emerging cyber security considerations. It will also enable further compliance with common standards and environments across DoD and the Intelligence Community (IC).

BENEFIT TO THE WARFIGHTER

DCGS-A Increment 2 will continue to connect Soldiers to Army mission command systems, Joint intelligence, surveillance and reconnaissance capabilities (ISR), and the IC. It will give commanders the ability to view ISR information in one place. It will also improve integration of information into tools that can support the development of intelligence products.

SPECIFICATIONS

- Intelligence Fusion Server/Tactical Server Infrastructure
- Portable Multifunctional Workstation
- Fixed Multifunctional Workstation
- Cross Domain Solution Suite
- Tactical Intelligence Ground Station
- Geospatial Intelligence Work Station
- Intelligence Processing Center Versions 1, 2 and 3
- Operational Intelligence Ground Station

PROGRAM STATUS

- **FY15:** Program Initiation
- **3QFY15:** Materiel Development Decision
- **1QFY16:** Increment 2 Development Request for Proposal Release Decision Defense Acquisition Board

PROJECTED ACTIVITIES

- **4QFY16:**
  › Milestone B, Engineering & Manufacturing Development Decision
  › Increment 2 Contract Award

DCGS-A Inc. 2

FOREIGN MILITARY SALES
None

CONTRACTORS
TBD

Excalibur Precision 155 mm Projectiles

PEO Ammunition | Picatinny Arsenal, NJ

WARFIGHTING FUNCTION

Mission Command

Movement and Maneuver

Intelligence

Fires

Sustainment

Maneuver Support and Protection

Engagement

ACQUISITION LIFECYCLE PHASE

Materiel Solution Analysis

Technology Maturation & Risk Reduction

Engineering & Manufacturing Development

Production & Deployment

Operations & Support

MILESTONE DECISION AUTHORITY

Defense Acquisition Executive

Army Acquisition Executive

Program Executive Officer

DESCRIPTION

Excalibur (XM982, M982 and M982A1) is a 155 mm, Global Positioning System (GPS)-guided, extended-range artillery projectile in use as the Army's next-generation cannon artillery precision munition. It provides improved fire support to the maneuver force commander, increases lethality and reduces collateral damage. The target, platform location and GPS-specific data are entered into the projectile's mission computer through an Enhanced Portable Inductive Artillery Fuse Setter. Excalibur uses a jam-resistant internal GPS receiver to update the inertial navigation system, providing precision in-flight guidance and dramatically improving accuracy of less than 2 meters miss distance regardless of range. Excalibur has three fuse options (point-detonation, point-detonation-delay and height-of-burst) and is employable in all weather conditions and terrain. Excalibur's capability allows for first-round effects on target while simultaneously minimizing the number of rounds required to engage targets and minimizing collateral damage.

The program is using an incremental approach to provide a combat capability to the Soldier as quickly as possible, and to deliver advanced capabilities and lower costs as technology matures. The initial variant (XM982 Increment 1A-1) includes a unitary high-explosive warhead capable of penetrating urban structures and is also effective against personnel and light materiel targets. Increment 1A-2 (M982) provides increased range (up to 37.5 km) and reliability improvements. The third variant (M982A1 Increment 1B) maintains performance and capabilities while reducing unit cost and increasing reliability. Excalibur is designed for fielding to the Lightweight 155 mm Howitzer (M777A2), the 155 mm M109A6 Self-Propelled Howitzer (Paladin), M109A7 Paladin Integrated Management and the Swedish Archer Howitzer. Excalibur is an international cooperative program with Sweden, which contributes resources toward development in accordance with established cooperative development and production agreements.

The Army and Marine Corps are Excalibur-capable with Increments 1A-1 and 1A-2, and the Army is capable with Increment 1B as well. The system is proven compatible with M777, M109A6 and M109A7 Howitzers when firing Modular Artillery Charge System (MACS) propellant.

BENEFIT TO THE WARFIGHTER

The Excalibur projectile enables the Soldier to service a precisely located target with first-round effects, denying the enemy the ability to take protective measures or flee the area. Due to the precision achieved and relatively limited damage radius, Excalibur allows engagement of targets within close proximity.

SPECIFICATIONS

- Maximum range from U.S. 39 Caliber Howitzers with Zone 5 MACS: 39.3 km
- Minimum Range from U.S. 39 Caliber Howitzers with Zone 3 MACS: 8.7 km
- Precision achieved: less than 2 meters
- Fuse modes: point-detonation, point-detonation-delay, and height-of-burst

PROGRAM STATUS

- **2QFY15-4QFY15:** M982A1 (Increment 1B) in production; 1,388 items delivered to inventory

PROJECTED ACTIVITIES

- **1QFY16-3QFY16:** M982A1 (Increment 1B) in production; 1,052 items to be delivered to inventory
- **3QFY16:** M982A1 (Increment 1B) production completed

FOREIGN MILITARY SALES
Four countries—names for official use only and not for public disclosure

CONTRACTORS
Raytheon (Tucson, AZ with work also performed in Farmington, NM and Plymouth, UK)

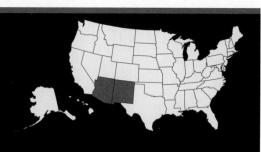

Family of Medium Tactical Vehicles (FMTV)

PEO Combat Support and Combat Service Support | Detroit Arsenal, MI

WARFIGHTING FUNCTION

Mission Command

Movement and Maneuver

Intelligence

Fires

Sustainment

Maneuver Support and Protection

Engagement

ACQUISITION LIFECYCLE PHASE

Materiel Solution Analysis

Technology Maturation & Risk Reduction

Engineering & Manufacturing Development

Production & Deployment

Operations & Support

MILESTONE DECISION AUTHORITY

Defense Acquisition Executive

Army Acquisition Executive

Program Executive Officer

DESCRIPTION

The Family of Medium Tactical Vehicles (FMTV) is a system of strategically deployable vehicles that performs general resupply, ammunition resupply, maintenance and recovery, and engineer support missions. It serves as weapon systems platforms for combat, combat support and combat service support units in a tactical environment.

The Light Medium Tactical Vehicle (LMTV) has a 2.5-ton capacity (cargo, van and chassis models) and a companion trailer. The Medium Tactical Vehicle (MTV) has a 5-ton capacity (cargo; long wheelbase cargo with and without materiel handling equipment; tractor; van; wrecker; 8.8-ton Load Handling System (LHS); 8.8-ton LHS trailer and 10-ton dump truck models). Three truck variants and two companion trailers, with the same payload capacity as their prime movers, provide airdrop capability. MTV also serves as the platform for the High Mobility Artillery Rocket System (HIMARS) and resupply vehicle for PATRIOT and HIMARS. MTV operates worldwide in all weather and terrain conditions.

FMTV incorporates a vehicle data bus and Class V interactive electronic technical manual, significantly lowering operating and support costs. Units are equipped with FMTV at more than 68 locations worldwide. The newest armored version, the Long Term Armor Strategy (LTAS) A-Cabs, are in production and being fielded. The LTAS B-Kit, modern armor designed to be installed on armor-capable vehicles, is also available.

BENEFIT TO THE WARFIGHTER

FMTV enhances crew survivability through the use of armor-capable cabs, three-point seat belts, automatic braking systems and central tire inflation capability. FMTV enhances tactical mobility and is strategically deployable in C-5, C-17 and C-130 aircraft. It reduces the Army's logistical footprint by providing commonality of parts and components, reduced maintenance downtime, high reliability and a high operational readiness rate for the warfighter.

SPECIFICATIONS

LMTV A1 Cargo
- Payload: 5,000 pounds
- Towed load: 12,000 pounds
- Engine: Caterpillar, 6-cylinder diesel, 275 horsepower
- Transmission: Automatic Allison Transmission
- Drive: 4x4 (4-wheel drive)

MTV A1 Cargo
- Payload: 10,000 pounds
- Towed load: 21,000 pounds
- Engine: Caterpillar, 6-cylinder diesel, 330 horsepower
- Transmission: Automatic Allison Transmission
- Drive: 4x4

PROGRAM STATUS
- **FY13-FY15:** Production and Deployment

PROJECTED ACTIVITIES
- **FY16-FY17:** Continue production and fielding to replace losses and modernize the fleet

FMTV

FOREIGN MILITARY SALES
Afghanistan, Canada, Djibouti, Greece, Iraq, Jordan, Macedonia, Saudi Arabia, Taiwan, Thailand and United Arab Emirates

CONTRACTORS
Prime: Oshkosh Corp. (Oshkosh, WI)
Axles: Meritor (Troy, MI)
Transmission: Allison Transmission (Indianapolis, IN)
Engine: Caterpillar Inc. (Greenville, SC)

General Fund Enterprise Business Systems (GFEBS)

PEO Enterprise Information Systems | Fort Belvoir, VA

WARFIGHTING FUNCTION

Mission Command

Movement and Maneuver

Intelligence

Fires

Sustainment

Maneuver Support and Protection

Engagement

ACQUISITION LIFECYCLE PHASE

Materiel Solution Analysis

Technology Maturation & Risk Reduction

Engineering & Manufacturing Development

Production & Deployment

Operations & Support

MILESTONE DECISION AUTHORITY

Defense Acquisition Executive

Army Acquisition Executive

Program Executive Officer

DESCRIPTION

General Fund Enterprise Business Systems (GFEBS), the Army's new Web-enabled financial, asset and accounting management system, was the first enterprise resource planning (ERP) structure to fully deploy within the Department of the Army. The system standardizes, streamlines and shares critical data across the Active Army, the Army National Guard and the Army Reserve. This commercial off-the-shelf ERP solution develops, acquires, integrates, deploys and sustains enterprisewide financial and procurement management capabilities to support the Army's current and future missions.

Moving forward, GFEBS plans on negotiating roles and responsibilities with the Assistant Secretary of the Army for Financial Management and Comptroller by identifying subject-matter experts on business-process-related issues; working with users to address issues; analyzing business processes, system or training problems; and proposing changes to Tier II Support. GFEBS will also review cost estimates to right-size sustainment and will support the maturation of the Functional Governance Board process.

BENEFIT TO THE WARFIGHTER

GFEBS provides financial, asset and accounting management across the Army.

SPECIFICATIONS

GFEBS Increment 2 will:
- Improve the Army's business processes, allow for full-cost reporting of the Army's outputs (products and services), and create an auditable trail
- Accommodate emerging requirements for enhanced financial integration, Army single-labor time tracking and environmental and integrated resource management
- Provide additional capability and improve automated integration of financial data, enhance business process efficiencies, increase interoperability and maintain auditability through these emerging requirements

PROGRAM STATUS
- **FY13-FY15:**
  › Quarterly releases and updates since Full Deployment in 2012
  › Ongoing audit readiness preparation
  › Maintained 98 percent availability
- **4QFY15:** Completed seventh successful year-end closeout

PROJECTED ACTIVITIES
- **3QFY16:** Recompete Increment 1 system integrator contract
- **TBD:** Increment 2 Materiel Development Decision

FOREIGN MILITARY SALES
None

CONTRACTORS
Accenture Federal Services (Reston, VA)
Connected Logistics, Inc. (Springfield, VA)
LMI Consulting (McLean, VA)
The MITRE Corp. (McLean, VA)

Global Combat Support System – Army (GCSS-Army)

PEO Enterprise Information Systems | Fort Belvoir, VA

WARFIGHTING FUNCTION

Mission Command

Movement and Maneuver

Intelligence

Fires

Sustainment

Maneuver Support and Protection

Engagement

ACQUISITION LIFECYCLE PHASE

Materiel Solution Analysis

Technology Maturation & Risk Reduction

Engineering & Manufacturing Development

Production & Deployment

Operations & Support

MILESTONE DECISION AUTHORITY

Defense Acquisition Executive

Army Acquisition Executive

Program Executive Officer

DESCRIPTION

Global Combat Support System – Army (GCSS-Army) is one program with two components. The first component, GCSS-Army Enterprise Resource Planning (ERP) Solution, is an automated information system that serves as the primary tactical logistics enabler supporting Army and Joint transformation for sustainment. The program re-engineers current business processes to achieve end-to-end logistics and integration with applicable command and control (C2) and Joint systems.

The second component, Army Enterprise Systems Integration Program (AESIP), formerly known as Product Lifecycle Management Plus, integrates Army business functions by providing a single source for enterprise hub services, master data and business intelligence. GCSS-Army uses commercial off-the-shelf ERP software products to support rapid force projection in the battlefield functional areas of arming, fixing, fueling, sustaining and tactical logistics financial processes.

BENEFIT TO THE WARFIGHTER

GCSS-Army will meet the Soldier's need for responsive support at the right place and time and improve the commander's situational awareness with accurate and responsive information.

SPECIFICATIONS

- Replaces five logistics Standard Army Management Information Systems in tactical units and will establish an interface/integration with applicable C2 and Joint systems
- Serves as the primary enabler to satisfy the Army's vision of a technologically advanced ERP that manages the flow of logistics, resources and information to meet the Army's modernization requirements
- AESIP integrates Army business functions by providing a single source for enterprise hub services, business intelligence and analytics, and centralized master data management across the business domain

PROGRAM STATUS

- **4QFY13:** Full Deployment Decision received
- **1QFY16:** Wave 1 fielding completed for 281 supply support activities and 20,000 Army users worldwide

PROJECTED ACTIVITIES

- **4QFY17:** Full Deployment

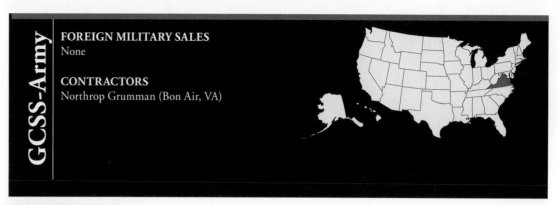

FOREIGN MILITARY SALES
None

CONTRACTORS
Northrop Grumman (Bon Air, VA)

Guided Multiple Launch Rocket System (GMLRS) DPICM/Unitary/Alternative Warhead

PEO Missiles and Space | Redstone Arsenal, AL

WARFIGHTING FUNCTION

Mission Command

Movement and Maneuver

Intelligence

Fires

Sustainment

Maneuver Support and Protection

Engagement

ACQUISITION LIFECYCLE PHASE

Materiel Solution Analysis

Technology Maturation & Risk Reduction

Engineering & Manufacturing Development

Production & Deployment

Operations & Support

MILESTONE DECISION AUTHORITY

Defense Acquisition Executive

Army Acquisition Executive

Program Executive Officer

DESCRIPTION

The Guided Multiple Launch Rocket System (GMLRS) is capable of producing precise, destructive and shaping fires against a variety of target sets. GMLRS is employed with the M270A1 upgraded MLRS tracked launcher and the M142 High Mobility Artillery Rocket System wheeled launcher. GMLRS munitions have greater accuracy than ballistic rockets with a resulting higher probability of kill and reduced logistics footprint.

There are two fielded variants of the GMLRS: Dual-Purpose Improved Conventional Munition (DPICM), designed to service area targets; and the Unitary variant with a single 200-pound-class high-explosive charge to service point targets with low collateral damage. Production of the Alternative Warhead (AW) began in 2015. AW will service area and imprecisely located targets without the risk of unexploded ordinance in compliance with the 2008 DoD Policy on Cluster Munitions and Unintended Harm to Civilians.

The original GMLRS development was an international cooperative program with the United Kingdom, Germany, France and Italy. More than 3,200 rockets have been used in overseas contingency operations through October 2015.

BENEFIT TO THE WARFIGHTER

GMLRS provides the warfighter the ability to engage both point and area targets with precision fires.

SPECIFICATIONS

- Length: 3,937 mm
- Diameter: 227 mm
- Reliability: 92 percent (threshold) and 95 percent (objective)
- Range: 15 to 70-plus km

PROGRAM STATUS

- **3QFY15:** AW combined Milestone C and Full-Rate Production Decision

PROJECTED ACTIVITIES

- **4QFY16:** GMLRS AW Initial Operational Capability

GMLRS

FOREIGN MILITARY SALES
United Kingdom, United Arab Emirates, Singapore, Bahrain, Italy, Japan, Canada, Jordan, Thailand, Finland, Germany and France

CONTRACTORS
Lockheed Martin (Camden, AR; Grand Prairie, TX)
Lockheed Martin Missiles and Fire Control (Las Cruces, NM)

Handheld, Manpack and Small Form Fit (HMS)

PEO Command, Control and Communications – Tactical | Aberdeen Proving Ground, MD

WARFIGHTING FUNCTION

Mission Command

Movement and Maneuver

Intelligence

Fires

Sustainment

Maneuver Support and Protection

Engagement

ACQUISITION LIFECYCLE PHASE

Materiel Solution Analysis

Technology Maturation & Risk Reduction

Engineering & Manufacturing Development

Production & Deployment

Operations & Support

MILESTONE DECISION AUTHORITY

Defense Acquisition Executive

Army Acquisition Executive

Program Executive Officer

DESCRIPTION

Handheld, Manpack and Small Form Fit (HMS) is a family of networking tactical radio systems that are interoperable with specified radios in the current forces. HMS provides Joint interoperable connectivity to the tactical edge and to the most disadvantaged warfighter with an on-the-move, at-the-halt and stationary line-of-sight and beyond-line-of-sight capability for both dismounted personnel and platforms. The radios are scalable and compliant with modular software communications architecture, enable net-centric operations, operate multiband and multimode, and deliver reliable, secure tactical communications.

The system is interoperable with currently fielded radios operating with Single Channel Ground and Airborne (SINCGARS) and Ultra High Frequency (UHF) Satellite Communications (SATCOM), as well as with new radios using Soldier Radio Waveform (SRW) and Mobile User Objective System (MUOS).

BENEFIT TO THE WARFIGHTER

HMS provides the warfighter with simultaneous voice, data and video communications with increased throughput using networking waveforms. It also offers routing and retransmission (cross-branding) and multichannel operations. A screen will be added for the Rifleman Radio (RR) that will reduce weight and provide additional waveforms (e.g., integrated waveform).

SPECIFICATIONS

- AN/PRC-154 RR Sensitive But Unclassified (1 Channel Type 2): Soldier Radio Waveform (SRW)
  › AN/PRC-154A RR Secret and Below (SAB) (1 Channel Type 1 Suite B): SRW
  › Full-Rate Production (FRP) Radios (1 Channel Type 1 Suite B): SRW
  › RF-330E-TR (Harris)
  › AN/PRC-154A (Thales)

- AN/PRC-155 Manpack SAB (2 Channel Type 1): SRW, SINCGARS, UHF SATCOM and MUOS
- Small Form Fit: SRW and various legacy waveform mixes

PROGRAM STATUS

- **FY15:**
  › FRP RR Vendor Selection
  › FRP RR Qualification Testing
  › Manpack FRP Request for Proposal Release
- **FY15-FY16:** Manpack FRP Vendor Source Selection

PROJECTED ACTIVITIES

- **1QFY16:** MUOS Multi-Service Operational Test and Evaluation
- **FY16:**
  › Manpack FRP Contract Award
  › RR Operational Test
- **FY16-FY17:** Manpack Qualification and Operational Testing
- **FY17:**
  › RR FRP Defense Acquisition Board (DAB)
  › Manpack FRP DAB

FOREIGN MILITARY SALES
None

CONTRACTORS
RR: Thales Defense & Security, Inc.
(Clarksburg, MD)
Harris Corp. (Rochester, NY)
Manpack: TBD

Heavy Expanded Mobility Tactical Truck (HEMTT)/ HEMTT Extended Service Program (ESP)

PEO Combat Support and Combat Service Support | Detroit Arsenal, MI

WARFIGHTING FUNCTION

Mission Command

Movement and Maneuver

Intelligence

Fires

Sustainment

Maneuver Support and Protection

Engagement

ACQUISITION LIFECYCLE PHASE

Materiel Solution Analysis

Technology Maturation & Risk Reduction

Engineering & Manufacturing Development

Production & Deployment

Operations & Support

MILESTONE DECISION AUTHORITY

Defense Acquisition Executive

Army Acquisition Executive

Program Executive Officer

DESCRIPTION

The Heavy Expanded Mobility Tactical Truck (HEMTT) is a 10-ton, 8-wheel drive vehicle designed for cross-country military missions, and can carry up to 11 tons of ammunition, petroleum, oils and lubricants. Vehicle variants include: M977, M978, M983, M984, M985 and M1120.

The HEMTT A4 began fielding in December 2008. Enhancements include a modern power train consisting of a Caterpillar C-15/500 horsepower engine and Allison transmission (4500 SP/5-speed automatic); anti-lock braking system and traction control; air-ride suspension; a J-1939 data-bus providing an updated electrical system; climate control; and a larger common cab.

The HEMTT Extended Service Program (ESP), also known as HEMTT RECAP, is a recapitalization program that converts high-mileage, older-version HEMTT trucks into the current A4 production configuration. Modernizing the fleet to one model reduces the logistics footprint and operational and sustainment costs of maintaining older vehicles.

BENEFIT TO THE WARFIGHTER

HEMTT variants provide comprehensive support to the warfighter in the delivery of general supplies, equipment and ammunition; refueling of ground vehicles and aircraft; and recovery and evacuation of heavy, wheeled vehicles and combat systems.

SPECIFICATIONS

- **M977 Cargo Truck:** equipped with light materiel handling crane (4,500-pound load capacity)
- **M978 Tanker:** 2,500-gallon fuel capacity for field refueling of ground vehicles and aircraft
- **M983 Tractor:** prime mover for the PATRIOT missile

- **M983 Light Equipment Transporter:** prime mover for tactical semitrailers in engineering units to include the M870 series, Intermediate Stryker Recovery System, and Mine Resistant Ambush Protected vehicles; fifth wheel vertical loading has winch with gross towing weight of 45.4 kilograms
- **M984 Wrecker:** equipped with crane and winch retrieval system; performs recovery and evacuation of heavy, wheeled vehicles and combat systems
- **M985 Cargo Truck:** equipped with heavy materiel handling crane (5,400-pound load capacity); primary transporter for Multiple Launch Rocket System ammunition
- **M1120 Load Handling System:** transports palletized materiel and International Standards Organization containers; provides NATO interoperability with standard flat-rack and mission modules for delivery of general supplies, equipment and ammunition with a Palletized Load System (PLS); compatible with the PLS trailer, which can carry a 26,000-pound payload

PROGRAM STATUS

- **FY13-FY15:** Continued to produce and field RECAP HEMTT to Active Army, National Guard, Reserve and Pre-Position Stocks

PROJECTED ACTIVITIES

- **FY16-FY17:** Continue to RECAP HEMTT to support the modernization of the HEMTT fleet

HELLFIRE Family of Missiles

PEO Missiles and Space | Redstone Arsenal, AL

WARFIGHTING FUNCTION

Mission Command

Movement and Maneuver

Intelligence

Fires

Sustainment

Maneuver Support and Protection

Engagement

ACQUISITION LIFECYCLE PHASE

Materiel Solution Analysis

Technology Maturation & Risk Reduction

Engineering & Manufacturing Development

Production & Deployment

Operations & Support

MILESTONE DECISION AUTHORITY

Defense Acquisition Executive

Army Acquisition Executive

Program Executive Officer

DESCRIPTION

The AGM-114 HELLFIRE Family of Missiles includes the HELLFIRE II and Longbow HELLFIRE Missiles. HELLFIRE II is a precision strike, Semi-Active Laser (SAL)-guided missile and is the principal air-to-ground weapon for the Army AH-64 Apache, OH-58 Kiowa Warrior, MQ-1C Gray Eagle Unmanned Aircraft System (UAS), Special Operations aircraft, Marine Corps AH-1W Super Cobra, and Air Force Predator and Reaper UAS.

The SAL HELLFIRE II missile is guided by laser energy reflected off the target. It has three warhead variants: a dual-warhead, shaped-charge, high-explosive anti-tank capability for armored targets (AGM-114K); a blast fragmentation warhead for urban, patrol boat and other "soft" targets (AGM-114M); and a metal-augmented charge warhead (AGM-114N) for urban structures, bunkers, radar sites, communications installations and bridges.

Beginning in 2012, a HELLFIRE II multipurpose warhead variant (AGM-114R) became available to the warfighter and allows selection of warhead effects corresponding to a specific target type. The AMG-114R is capable of being launched from Army rotary-wing and UAS platforms and provides the pilot increased operational flexibility.

The Longbow HELLFIRE (AGM-114L) is also a precision strike missile using millimeter wave (MMW) radar guidance instead of the HELLFIRE II's SAL. It is the principal anti-tank system for the AH-64D Apache Longbow helicopter and uses the same anti-armor warhead as the HELLFIRE II. The MMW seeker provides beyond-line-of-sight, fire-and-forget capability, as well as the ability to operate in adverse weather and battlefield obscurants.

BENEFIT TO THE WARFIGHTER

HELLFIRE provides the warfighter with an air-to-ground, point-target precision strike capability to defeat advanced armor and an array of traditional and nontraditional targets.

SPECIFICATIONS

- Diameter: 7 inches
- Weight: 99.8-107 pounds
- Length: 64-69 inches
- HELLFIRE II AGM-114R maximum range:
  › Direct fire: 7 km
  › Indirect fire: 8 km
  › Minimum range: 0.5-1.5 km

PROGRAM STATUS

- **FY13-FY15:** HELLFIRE II missiles procured annually to replace combat expenditures

PROJECTED ACTIVITIES

- **FY16-FY17:** Laser HELLFIRE to continue in production; Longbow HELLFIRE to continue sustainment activities

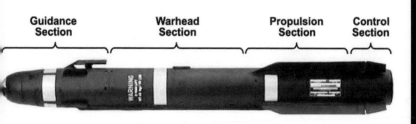

Guidance Section | Warhead Section | Propulsion Section | Control Section

FOREIGN MILITARY SALES
Laser HELLFIRE: Australia, Egypt, France, Greece, Israel, Japan, Kuwait, Netherlands, Saudi Arabia, Singapore, Spain, Taiwan, Sweden, United Arab Emirates and United Kingdom
Direct commercial sale: United Kingdom, Norway, Netherlands, Saudi Arabia and Turkey
Longbow HELLFIRE: Israel, Japan, Kuwait, Singapore, Taiwan and United Arab Emirates
Direct commercial sale: United Kingdom

CONTRACTORS
Lockheed Martin (Orlando, FL)

System Description	Production	Characteristics	Performance
AGM-114A, B, C, F, FA – HELLFIRE Weight = 45 kg Length = 163 cm	1982 – 1992	A, B, C have a Single Shaped-Charge Warhead; Analog Autopilot	• Not Capable Against Reactive Armor • Non-Programmable
		F has Tandem Warheads; Analog Autopilot	• Reactive Armor Capable • Non-Programmable
AGM-114K/K2/K2A – HELLFIRE II Weight = 45 kg Length = 163 cm	**1993 – Until Complete**	• Tandem Warheads • Electronic Safe & Arm Device • Digital Autopilot & Electronics • Improved Performance Software	• Capable Against 21st Century Armor • Hardened Against Countermeasures • K-2 adds Insensitive Munitions (IM) • K-2A adds Blast-Frag Sleeve
AGM-114L – HELLFIRE LONGBOW Weight = 49 kg Length = 180 cm	1995 – 2005	• Tandem Warheads • Digital Autopilot & Electronics • Millimeter-Wave (MMW) Seeker • IM Warheads	• Initiate on Contact • Hardened Against Countermeasures • Programmable Software • All-Weather
AGM-114M – HELLFIRE II (Blast Frag) Weight = 49 kg Length = 180 cm	1998 – 2010	• Blast-Frag Warhead • 4 Operating Modes • Digital Autopilot & Electronics • Delayed-Fuse Capability	• For Buildings, Soft-Skin Vehicles • Optimized for Low Cloud Ceilings • Hardened Against Countermeasures • WH Penetrates Target Before Detonation
AGM-114N – HELLFIRE II (MAC) Weight = 49 kg Length = 180 cm	**2003 – Until Complete**	• Metal-Augmented Charge – Sustained Pressure Wave • 4 Operating Modes • Delayed-Fuse Capability	• For Buildings, Soft-Skin Vehicles • Optimized for Low Cloud Ceilings • Hardened Against Countermeasures • WH Penetrates Target Before Detonation
AGM-114R – HELLFIRE II **(Bridge to JAGM – RW/UAS)** Weight = 49 kg Length = 180 cm	**2010 – Until Complete**	• Integratef Blast Frag Sleeve Warhead • Designed for all platforms • Health Monitoring	• For all Target Sets • Increased Lethality and Engagement Envelope

High Mobility Multipurpose Wheeled Vehicle (HMMWV)

PEO Combat Support and Combat Service Support | Detroit Arsenal, MI

WARFIGHTING FUNCTION

Mission Command

Movement and Maneuver

Intelligence

Fires

Sustainment

Maneuver Support and Protection

Engagement

ACQUISITION LIFECYCLE PHASE

Materiel Solution Analysis

Technology Maturation & Risk Reduction

Engineering & Manufacturing Development

Production & Deployment

Operations & Support

MILESTONE DECISION AUTHORITY

Defense Acquisition Executive

Army Acquisition Executive

Program Executive Officer

DESCRIPTION

The High Mobility Multipurpose Wheeled Vehicle (HMMWV) is a lightweight, highly mobile, high-performance, diesel-powered four-wheel drive, air-transportable and air-droppable family of tactical vehicles. The HMMWV supports combat and combat service support units with a versatile, mission-configurable, tactical wheeled vehicle.

The Army recognizes the tactical importance of the HMMWV fleet and the enduring requirement to maintain a relevant, capable fleet to support the Army enterprise. Congressional funding has enabled the modernization of the National Guard and Reserve HMMWV fleets.

The National Guard and Reserve modernization program consists of recapitalizing M1152A1 and M1165A1 Up-Armored HMMWV (UAH) Shelter and Troop Carriers; converting M1151A1 UAH Armament Carriers to M1167 UAH Tube-Launched, Optically Tracked, Wireless-Guided Missile Carriers; and purchasing new M997A3 ambulances. The recapitalization efforts involve a Public Private Partnership (PPP) between AM General and the Red River Army Depot (RRAD). The M997A3 effort is a joint effort with the chassis built by AM General and furnished to Rock Island Arsenal (RIA) for installation of an RIA-built box.

BENEFIT TO THE WARFIGHTER

Due to configurations for multiple mission types and roles, the HMMWV is well-suited to meet the needs of Soldiers on the battlefield. Its high power-to-weight ratio, high ground clearance and four-wheel drive make it agile in the most difficult terrain.

SPECIFICATIONS

- Gross vehicle weight: 11,500 pounds
- Wheelbase: 130 inches
- Engine: General Engine Products V8, 6.5-liter turbocharged diesel, 190 horsepower at 3,400 revolutions per minute
- Fuel Capacity: 25 gallons
- Payload: 3,350 pounds
- Maximum speed: 70 mph

PROGRAM STATUS

- **FY13:** HMMWV new production completed
- **2QFY13:** Began UAH Depot Recapitalization Automotive Improvement Program production at RRAD
- **1QFY14:** Began M997A3 ambulance production at RIA, projected through 1QFY18
- **4QFY14-3QFY15:** Began National Guard M1152 and M1165 modernization PPP between AM General and RRAD

PROJECTED ACTIVITIES

- **FY16:** Begin M1151A1-to-M1167 Conversion Recapitalization PPP between AM General and RRAD
- **FY16-FY17:** Sustainment; National Guard modernization to include M1151-to-M1167 conversion

FOREIGN MILITARY SALES

United Arab Emirates, Afghanistan, Argentina, Iraq, Ethiopia, Georgia, Kenya, Bahrain, Bulgaria, Chile, Colombia, Ecuador, Egypt, El Salvador, Czech Republic, Croatia, Hungary, Lebanon, Romania, Yemen, Tunisia, Mauritania, Burundi, Uganda, Israel, Jordan, Latvia, Macedonia, Mexico, Philippines, Slovenia, Nepal, Serbia and Saudi Arabia

CONTRACTORS

AM General (South Bend, IN)
New Production Ambulances: RIA-Joint Manufacturing & Technology Center (Rock Island, IL)
Lead Government Integrator: RRAD (Texarkana,TX)

Indirect Fire Protection Capability Increment 2 – Intercept Block 1

PEO Missiles and Space | Redstone Arsenal, AL

WARFIGHTING FUNCTION

Mission Command

Movement and Maneuver

Intelligence

Fires

Sustainment

Maneuver Support and Protection

Engagement

ACQUISITION LIFECYCLE PHASE

Materiel Solution Analysis

Technology Maturation & Risk Reduction

Engineering & Manufacturing Development

Production & Deployment

Operations & Support

MILESTONE DECISION AUTHORITY

Defense Acquisition Executive

Army Acquisition Executive

Program Executive Officer

DESCRIPTION

The Indirect Fire Protection Capability Increment 2 – Intercept (IFPC Increment 2-I) Block 1 System is a mobile, ground-based weapon system designed to defeat unmanned aircraft systems (UAS) and cruise missiles.

The Block 1 system will use an existing interceptor and sensor and will develop a Multi-Mission Launcher (MML) on an existing vehicle platform to support the Counter-UAS (C-UAS) and Cruise Missile Defense (CMD) missions. The system will use the Army Integrated Air and Missile Defense (AIAMD) open systems architecture, and will use the AIAMD Integrated Battle Command System as its mission command component.

BENEFIT TO THE WARFIGHTER

IFPC Increment 2-I Block 1 mitigates high priority capability gaps in two mission areas: CMD and C-UAS.

SPECIFICATIONS

- Provides 360-degree protection
- Provides ability to simultaneously engage threats arriving from different azimuths
- MML will use an open architecture that allows the employment of a variety of missiles

PROGRAM STATUS

- **2QFY14:** Milestone (MS) A, Acquisition Decision Memorandum (ADM)
- **1QFY15:** Completed Tube Demonstration
- **2QFY15:** Completed Launch Demonstration
- **4QFY15:**
  › Completed System Preliminary Design Review
  › Completed Assembly of MML Prototype 1
  › Delegation ADM designating program as ACAT 1C

PROJECTED ACTIVITIES

- **2QFY16:** Engineering Demonstration
- **3QFY16:** MS B Decision
- **2QFY17:** Critical Design Review

IFPC Increment 2-I

FOREIGN MILITARY SALES
None

CONTRACTORS
None—the IFPC Increment 2-I Block 1 system is composed of three existing major end items and one new major end item (MML; developed by the U.S. Army Aviation and Missile Research Development and Engineering Center, and Letterkenny Army Depot). The government is integrating the four major end items into this system.

Installation Information Infrastructure Modernization Program (I3MP)

PEO Enterprise Information Systems | Fort Belvoir, VA

US ARMY PE EIS PEO ENTERPRISE INFORMATION SYSTEMS

WARFIGHTING FUNCTION

Mission Command

Movement and Maneuver

Intelligence

Fires

Sustainment

Maneuver Support and Protection

Engagement

ACQUISITION LIFECYCLE PHASE

Materiel Solution Analysis

Technology Maturation & Risk Reduction

Engineering & Manufacturing Development

Production & Deployment

Operations & Support

MILESTONE DECISION AUTHORITY

Defense Acquisition Executive

Army Acquisition Executive

Program Executive Officer

DESCRIPTION

The Installation Information Infrastructure Modernization Program (I3MP) supports the warfighter through information technology, infrastructure modernization and lifecycle management of the Army's CONUS Installation Campus Area Networks (ICAN) and strategic command centers. It has no ACAT level because it is not executed as a Defense Acquisition Program. However, if it were, it would rival many ACAT I programs due to its overall lifecycle cost and the length of its mission.

I3MP provides a robust and scalable networked information infrastructure that allows migration to a network-centric, knowledge-based operation, and enhances connectivity between forward-deployed forces with CONUS installation infrastructure. It is a part of the Joint effort to improve and protect LandWarNet by enhancing the infrastructure for better efficiency and effectiveness of the network and Army interoperability across DoD. Ultimately the program builds network capacity, simplifies and standardizes ICAN, and establishes a foundation for new capabilities. This involves the conversion of base, post, camp and station voice circuits to Internet Protocol, transitioning from Time Distance Multiplexing to Voice over Internet Protocol (VoIP) technology, and a connection to the Defense Information Systems Agency's Enterprise VoIP architecture.

BENEFIT TO THE WARFIGHTER

I3MP provides the communications connectivity that allows the warfighter to access and utilize information technology applications.

SPECIFICATIONS

Designs are applicable to the specific site per the site's requirements.

PROGRAM STATUS

- **Current:** I3MP has more than 60 current contracting actions affecting, in turn, most of the Army's bases, each of which has some form of ICAN for communications; this year (2016) the base funding line for I3MP was in the $20 million range
- **2QFY15:** Modernized the information technology backbone at Fort Sill, OK and Fort Hood, TX
- **4QFY15:** Modernized the information technology backbone at White Sands Missile Range, NM

PROJECTED ACTIVITIES

- **3QFY16:** Modernize the information technology backbone at Fort Rucker, AL
- **3QFY16-4QFY18:** Initiate network standardizations at various Army posts, camps and stations
- **4QFY16:** Modernize the information technology backbone at Fort Myer, VA
- **4QFY16-4QFY18:** Initiate Home Station Mission Command Centers procurement and initial installation

FOREIGN MILITARY SALES
None

CONTRACTORS
AT&T (Dallas, TX)
Vision Ability Execution, Inc. (Reston, VA)
General Dynamics (Falls Church, VA)
Siemens (Washington, DC)

Integrated Personnel and Pay System – Army (IPPS-A)

PEO Enterprise Information Systems | Fort Belvoir, VA

WARFIGHTING FUNCTION

Mission Command

Movement and Maneuver

Intelligence

Fires

Sustainment

Maneuver Support and Protection

Engagement

ACQUISITION LIFECYCLE PHASE

Materiel Solution Analysis

Technology Maturation & Risk Reduction

Engineering & Manufacturing Development

Production & Deployment

Operations & Support

MILESTONE DECISION AUTHORITY

Defense Acquisition Executive

Army Acquisition Executive

Program Executive Officer

DESCRIPTION

The Integrated Personnel and Pay System – Army (IPPS-A) will provide the Army with an integrated, multicomponent personnel and pay system that streamlines Army human resources (HR), enhances the efficiency and accuracy of Army personnel and pay procedures, and supports Soldiers and their families. IPPS-A addresses major deficiencies in the delivery of military personnel and pay services, and provides internal controls and audit procedures that prevent erroneous payments and loss of funds.

BENEFIT TO THE WARFIGHTER

IPPS-A supports the Soldier in the core mission of conducting operations, promotes and maintains effective military personnel management, and ensures that accurate and timely military personnel data, including delivery of benefits, are available at all levels of management and oversight.

SPECIFICATIONS

- Will be Web-based
- Available 24/7
- Accessible to:
  › Solders
  › HR professionals
  › Combatant commanders
  › Personnel and pay managers
  › Other authorized users

PROGRAM STATUS

- **3QFY15:**
  › Deployed Release 1.2.3, implementing security and performance enhancements, predefined query updates, and improvements with data correctness and accuracy for all components
  › Deployed Release 1.2.4 implementing security and performance enhancements and improvements with data correctness and accuracy for all components
  › Full Deployment Acquisition Decision Memorandum signed; Increment 1 fully deployed and entered Operations and Sustainment
  › Received Army Test and Evaluation Command final test report completing the Adversarial Assessment for continuous evaluation
  › Increment 2 system integration services contract awarded
- **1QFY16:** Increment 2 System Readiness Review

PROJECTED ACTIVITIES

- **2QFY16:**
  › Increment 2 System Functional Review
  › Increment 2 Integrated Baseline Review

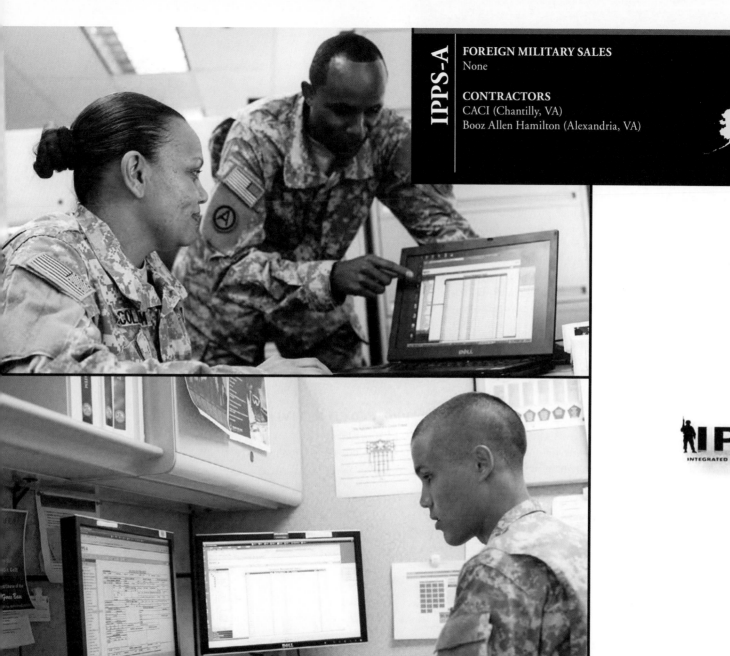

FOREIGN MILITARY SALES
None

CONTRACTORS
CACI (Chantilly, VA)
Booz Allen Hamilton (Alexandria, VA)

INTEGRATED PERSONNEL AND PAY SYSTEM – ARMY

Javelin

PEO Missiles and Space | Redstone Arsenal, AL

WARFIGHTING FUNCTION

Mission Command

Movement and Maneuver

Intelligence

Fires

Sustainment

Maneuver Support and Protection

Engagement

ACQUISITION LIFECYCLE PHASE

Materiel Solution Analysis

Technology Maturation & Risk Reduction

Engineering & Manufacturing Development

Production & Deployment

Operations & Support

MILESTONE DECISION AUTHORITY

Defense Acquisition Executive

Army Acquisition Executive

Program Executive Officer

DESCRIPTION

The Close Combat Missile System – Medium (CCMS-M) Javelin is a medium-range tactical missile with precision direct-fire effects to defeat armored vehicles as well as personnel and equipment in fortification or in the open. Javelin is highly effective against a variety of targets at extended ranges under day-and-night, battlefield obscurants, adverse weather and multiple countermeasure conditions. The system's soft-launch feature permits firing from enclosures commonly found in complex urban terrain, while its modular design allows the system to evolve to meet changing threats and requirements via both software and hardware upgrades. The system consists of a reusable command launch unit (CLU) and a modular missile encased in a disposable launch tube assembly. The CLU provides stand-alone, all-weather and day-and-night surveillance capability ideally suited for infantry operations in Afghanistan.

Javelin's fire-and-forget technology allows the gunner to fire and immediately take cover, move to another fighting position or reload. Javelin provides enhanced lethality through the use of a tandem warhead that defeats all known armor threats and is effective against stationary and moving targets. This system also provides defensive capability against attacking or hovering helicopters. A multipurpose warhead was added into FY 2015 procurement and provides improved lethality against secondary targets. A Lightweight CLU is being developed with the goal of reducing CLU size by 35 percent and weight by 50 percent. The Army is the lead for this Joint program with the Marine Corps.

BENEFIT TO THE WARFIGHTER

Javelin provides the Army, Marine Corps and our allies a man-portable, fire-and-forget missile system that is highly lethal against objects ranging from main battle tanks to fleeting targets of opportunity found in current threat environments.

SPECIFICATIONS

- Weight (Block 1 Javelin and CLU combined): 48.8 pounds (missile, 33.3 pounds; CLU, 15.5 pounds)
- Diameter: 127 mm
- Includes training devices for tactical and classroom training

PROGRAM STATUS

- **Current:**
  › Javelin has been fielded to the Active and Reserve fleet; Block I CLU retrofit kits continue to be fielded
- **FY15:**
  › Multipurpose warhead was integrated into Javelin missile procurement
  › First year of Javelin Lightweight CLU development

PROJECTED ACTIVITIES

- **FY16-FY17:**
  › Continue missile production for Army, Marine Corps and foreign military sales
  › Continue Lightweight CLU development
  › Modernization

FOREIGN MILITARY SALES

Australia, Czech Republic, France, Indonesia, Ireland, Jordan, Lithuania, New Zealand, Norway, Oman, Taiwan, United Arab Emirates, United Kingdom, Qatar and Estonia

CONTRACTORS

Javelin Joint Venture LLC—Raytheon and Lockheed Martin (Tucson, AZ; Goleta, CA; McKinney, TX; Dallas, TX; Sherman, TX; Orlando, FL; Ocala, FL; Troy, AL)

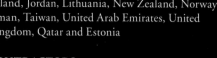

Joint Air-to-Ground Missile (JAGM)

PEO Missiles and Space | Redstone Arsenal, AL

WARFIGHTING FUNCTION

Mission Command

Movement and Maneuver

Intelligence

Fires

Sustainment

Maneuver Support and Protection

Engagement

ACQUISITION LIFECYCLE PHASE

Materiel Solution Analysis

Technology Maturation & Risk Reduction

Engineering & Manufacturing Development

Production & Deployment

Operations & Support

MILESTONE DECISION AUTHORITY

Defense Acquisition Executive

Army Acquisition Executive

Program Executive Officer

DESCRIPTION

The Joint Air-to-Ground Missile (JAGM) System will provide an air-to-surface, precision, standoff strike capability from the host platform. The adverse-weather-capable JAGM System will enable warfighters to attack critical, high-value, fixed and moving, and fleeting targets day or night in battlefield limited visibility conditions from significant standoff ranges while remaining fully effective against a variety of countermeasures. The standoff capability of the JAGM System enables the weapon to place high-value, heavily defended targets at risk while the aircrews remain outside the range of lethal point and area defenses. A terminal guidance capability enables the platform to launch the weapon and depart the launch area to enhance aircraft survivability. The precision accuracy enables the JAGM System to place point, moving and fleeting targets and target elements within a target complex at risk, and reduces the probability of collateral damage.

The JAGM is an Army program with Joint requirements from the Navy and Marine Corps. The threshold platforms for JAGM are the Army's Apache AH-64D and the Marine Corps' Super Cobra AH-1Z.

BENEFIT TO THE WARFIGHTER

The JAGM provides the warfighter the ability to destroy high-value stationary, moving, and relocatable land and naval targets from standoff range in day, night, adverse weather and obscured battlefield conditions.

SPECIFICATIONS

- Diameter: 7 inches
- Weight: 115 pounds
- Length: 70 inches
- Range: 500-8,000 meters

PROGRAM STATUS

- **1QFY13:** Delta Preliminary Design Review
- **1QFY14:** Critical Design Review (guidance section)
- **1QFY15:** Extended Technology Development Phase completed
- **3QFY15:** Milestone (MS) B

PROJECTED ACTIVITIES

- **2QFY16:**
  › System-level Critical Design Review
  › Initial Production Readiness Review
  › Ground-launched flight tests
- **4QFY17:**
  › MS C
  › Qualified production line

JAGM

FOREIGN MILITARY SALES
None

CONTRACTORS
Prime: Raytheon (Tucson, AZ)
Lockheed Martin (Orlando, FL)

Joint Light Tactical Vehicle (JLTV)

PEO Combat Support and Combat Service Support | Detroit Arsenal, MI

WARFIGHTING FUNCTION

Mission Command

Movement and Maneuver

Intelligence

Fires

Sustainment

Maneuver Support and Protection

Engagement

ACQUISITION LIFECYCLE PHASE

Materiel Solution Analysis

Technology Maturation & Risk Reduction

Engineering & Manufacturing Development

Production & Deployment

Operations & Support

MILESTONE DECISION AUTHORITY

Defense Acquisition Executive

Army Acquisition Executive

Program Executive Officer

DESCRIPTION

The Joint Light Tactical Vehicle (JLTV) Family of Vehicles (FoV) is an Army-led, Joint-service program designed to replace a portion of each service's light tactical wheeled vehicle fleets while closing an existing capability gap. Intended to provide protected, sustained, networked mobility for personnel and payloads across the full range of military operations, the JLTV FoV will restore the fleet's balance of payload, performance and protection. The JLTV FoV consists of two variants: the 4-seat Combat Tactical Vehicle (CTV) and the 2-seat Combat Support Vehicle (CSV). The CTV will support the General Purpose, Heavy Gun Carrier and Close Combat Weapon Carrier missions. The CSV will support the Utility/Shelter Carrier mission. The JLTV is transportable by a range of lift assets, including rotary-wing aircraft, to support operations across the range of military operations. Its maneuverability enables activities across the spectrum of terrain, including urban areas, while providing inherent and supplemental armor against direct fire and improvised explosive device threats.

BENEFIT TO THE WARFIGHTER

JLTV provides the warfighter significantly more protection against multiple threats while increasing mobility and payload compared to the current armored High Mobility Multipurpose Wheeled Vehicle platforms. JLTV provides improved off-road mobility, fuel efficiency and reliability over Mine Resistant Ambush Protected All-Terrain Vehicles.

SPECIFICATIONS

- Payloads: CTV–3,500 pounds; CSV–5,100 pounds
- Transportability: Internal–C-130, External–CH-47 at curb weight plus 2,000 pounds and CH-53, Sea–including height-restricted decks
- Protection: Scalable armor to provide mission flexibility while protecting the force

- Mobility: Maneuverability to enable operations across the spectrum of terrain, including urban areas
- Networking: Provides Joint forces network connectivity that improves situational awareness of the operational environment while enabling a responsive and well-integrated command and control

PROGRAM STATUS

- **4QFY13-2QFY15:** Government received 66 prototype JLTVs and 18 companion trailers from three competing Engineering & Manufacturing Development vendors; vehicles completed 14 months of performance, reliability and ballistics testing
- **4QFY15:**
  › Completed Milestone C, entered production phase
  › Awarded Low-Rate Initial Production contract

PROJECTED ACTIVITIES

- **1QFY16-4QFY17:** Conduct performance and reliability qualification, live fire (full-up system level) and multiservice operational testing and evaluation

Close Combat Weapons Carrier

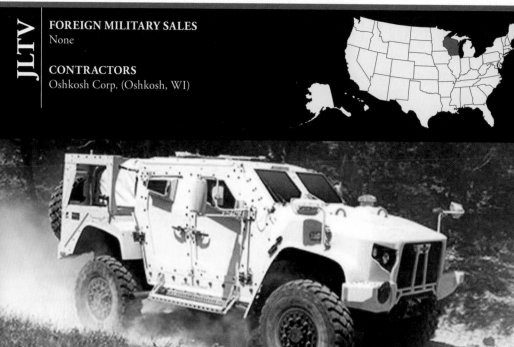

General Purpose

Heavy Gun Carrier

Utility

Lakota UH-72A Light Utility Helicopter (LUH)

PEO Aviation | Redstone Arsenal, AL

WARFIGHTING FUNCTION

Mission Command

Movement and Maneuver

Intelligence

Fires

Sustainment

Maneuver Support and Protection

Engagement

ACQUISITION LIFECYCLE PHASE

Materiel Solution Analysis

Technology Maturation & Risk Reduction

Engineering & Manufacturing Development

Production & Deployment

Operations & Support

MILESTONE DECISION AUTHORITY

Defense Acquisition Executive

Army Acquisition Executive

Program Executive Officer

DESCRIPTION

The UH-72A Light Utility Helicopter (LUH) is a Commercial/Non-Developmental-Item, twin-engine helicopter with seating for two pilots, capable of transporting up to six passengers. The medical evacuation (MEDEVAC) configuration is equipped with two NATO standard litters and seating for a medical attendant and crew chief. Visual and instrument flight certified, the UH-72A is equipped with a night-vision-compatible glass cockpit and modern communications and navigation avionics, including autopilot and dual Global Positioning Systems with Wide Area Augmentation System. Other aircraft configurations include Combat Training Center Opposing Forces and Observer/Controller, Security and Support, and VIP.

BENEFIT TO THE WARFIGHTER

Though not a warfighting aircraft, the UH-72A is an inexpensive light helicopter that operates in permissive environments to meet Homeland Defense and Security, general support, reconnaissance, command and control operations, search and rescue, and training requirements worldwide. Homeland Defense and Security missions include assistance to border patrol operations, terrorist incident response, counterdrug operations, and disaster relief missions, as well as Generating Force MEDEVAC capability for the Army National Guard.

SPECIFICATIONS

- Maximum speed: 145 knots
- Range: 370 nautical miles
- Endurance: 3.5 hours
- Maximum takeoff weight: 7,903 pounds

PROGRAM STATUS

- **3QFY14:** Began transfer and modification of UH-72As as the Army's training helicopter as part of the Aviation Restructure Initiative
- **1QFY15:** Fielded to Fort Rucker, AL, in the training configuration
- **2QFY15:** Completed fielding and training of Army National Guard fleet
- **1QFY16:** 412 aircraft on contract with 65 deliverable

PROJECTED ACTIVITIES

- **3QFY16:** Current production contract ends and award of new contract
- **1QFY17:** Current Logistics Support contract ends and award of new contract

Lakota UH-72A

FOREIGN MILITARY SALES
Thailand

CONTRACTORS
Airbus Defense and Space, Inc. (Herndon, VA)
Airbus Helicopter, Inc. (Grand Prairie, TX)

Long Range Precision Fires (LRPF)

PEO Missiles and Space | Redstone Arsenal, AL

WARFIGHTING FUNCTION

Mission Command

Movement and Maneuver

Intelligence

Fires

Sustainment

Maneuver Support and Protection

Engagement

ACQUISITION LIFECYCLE PHASE

Materiel Solution Analysis

Technology Maturation & Risk Reduction

Engineering & Manufacturing Development

Production & Deployment

Operations & Support

MILESTONE DECISION AUTHORITY

Defense Acquisition Executive

Army Acquisition Executive

Program Executive Officer

DESCRIPTION

The mission of the Long Range Precision Fires (LRPF) Missile is to attack, neutralize, suppress and destroy targets using missile-delivered indirect precision fires. LRPF provides field artillery units with long-range and deep-strike capability while supporting brigade, division, corps, Army, theater, Joint and Coalition forces and Marine Corps air-to-ground task forces in full, limited or expeditionary operations. The LRPF will replace the Army Tactical Missile System (ATACMS) capability, which is impacted by the age of the ATACMS inventory and the cluster munition policy that removes all M39 and M39A1 ATACMS from the inventory after 2018.

BENEFIT TO THE WARFIGHTER

LRPF will provide the warfighter with an all-weather, 24/7, precision surface-to-surface deep-strike capability.

SPECIFICATIONS

- Deep-strike capability will reach farther than 300 km
- Other specifications TBD

PROGRAM STATUS

- **1QFY14:** Materiel Development Decision
- **4QFY15:** Analysis of Alternatives Complete

PROJECTED ACTIVITIES

- **2QFY16:** Milestone A
- **1QFY17:** Technology Maturation & Risk Reduction Contract Award

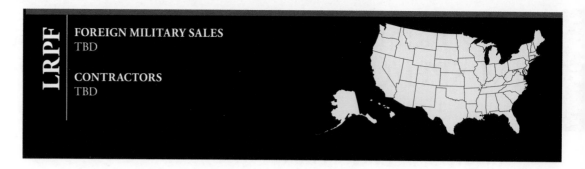

FOREIGN MILITARY SALES
TBD

CONTRACTORS
TBD

M109 Family of Vehicles (FOV) (Paladin/FAASV, PIM SPH/CAT)

PEO Ground Combat Systems | Detroit Arsenal, MI

DESCRIPTION

The M109A6 Paladin 155 mm Self-Propelled Howitzer (SPH) along with the M992A2 Field Artillery Ammunition Supply Vehicle (FAASV) provides the primary indirect-fire support to Armored Brigade Combat Teams (ABCT). Like the earlier M109 models, the M109A6 Paladin is a fully tracked, armored vehicle. The M109A6 Paladin configuration was achieved through modifications to earlier-built M109A2 and A3 vehicle hulls and the introduction of an entirely new cab and cannon assembly.

The M109A7 Self-Propelled Howitzer (SPH) and M992A3 Carrier Ammunition Tracked (CAT), formerly known as the Paladin Integrated Management (PIM) program, will replace the current M109A6 Paladin and the M992A2 FAASV respectively starting in FY17. The M109A7 SPH and M992A3 CAT vehicles are currently in Low-Rate Initial Production (LRIP). This next-generation Howitzer provides enhanced capabilities to maintain Army dominance on future battlefields, and is one of the most critical vehicle modernization programs.

The M109A7 SPH and M992A3 CAT comprise a modernization effort to improve size, weight, power, cooling, readiness, force protection and survivability, and to increase sustainability of the M109A6 Paladin and the M992A2 FAASV platforms through 2050. The platforms will also be fitted with Blue Force Tracker capability to ensure situational awareness with other friendly forces. The program has leveraged Bradley commonality for key components—engine, transmission, final drive, suspension—in a new hull. The new electric-gun drives and rammer components, as well as a microclimate air conditioning system, will be powered by the common modular power system utilizing a 600-volt onboard electrical system in the existing cab and cannon assembly.

BENEFIT TO THE WARFIGHTER

These upgrades and better communications technology will significantly improve the warfighter's battlespace awareness and reduce the logistics footprint within the ABCT. Once delivered to the field, the M109A7 SPH and M992A3 CAT will give ABCT commanders a more capable and sustainable vehicle, providing them with increased confidence in their artillery fleet.

SPECIFICATIONS

- Crew: Four (Paladin , SPH, FAASV and CAT)
- Combat loaded weight: Paladin – 34.25 tons, SPH – 39 tons, FAASV – 29.26 tons, CAT – 36 tons
- On-board ammunition: Paladin – 39 rounds, SPH – 42 rounds, FAASV – 95 rounds, CAT – 95 rounds
- Rates of fire: Four rounds per minute for first three minutes maximum; one round per minute sustained
- Maximum range: High-Explosive/Rocket Assisted Projectile, 22/30 km
- Cruising range: All – 180 miles
- Fire Support Network: Paladin Digital Fire Control System software supports Fire Support Network

PROGRAM STATUS

- **3QFY11–3QFY14:** Developmental Testing (DT)
- **3QFY13:** Milestone C
- **4QFY12-3QFY14:** Phase II Government DT
- **1QFY14:** Milestone C Decision; Low-Rate Initial Production (LRIP) Option 1 Award
- **3QFY15:** DT (Production Qualification Test)
- **4QFY15:** Full-Up System-Level
- **1QFY16:** LRIP Option 2 Award

PROJECTED ACTIVITIES

- **2QFY16:** Logistics Demonstration; Interactive Electronic Technical Manual Verification
- **2QFY17:** Full-Rate Production (FRP) Decision; First Unit Equipped
- **3QFY17:** FRP Contract Award

FOREIGN MILITARY SALES
None

CONTRACTORS
BAE Systems (York, PA)

M88A2 Improved Recovery Vehicle HERCULES (Heavy Equipment Recovery Combat Utility Lift and Evacuation System)

PEO Ground Combat Systems | Detroit Arsenal, MI

DESCRIPTION

The M88A2 Improved Recovery Vehicle HERCULES (Heavy Equipment Recovery Combat Utility Lift and Evacuation System) recovers tanks mired to different depths, removes and replaces tank turrets and power packs, and uprights overturned heavy combat vehicles. The main winch on the M88A2 is capable of a 70-ton, single-line recovery, allowing the HERCULES to provide recovery of the 70-ton M1A2 Abrams tank.

The A-frame boom and hoist winch of the M88A2 can lift 35 tons. The spade can be used to anchor the vehicle when using the main winch and can be used for light earth moving to prepare a recovery area. The M88A2 employs an auxiliary power unit to provide auxiliary electrical and hydraulic power when the main engine is not in operation. It can also be used to slave start other vehicles, as well as a means to refuel or defuel vehicles. The M88A2 can refuel Abrams tanks from its own fuel tanks.

The M88A2 HERCULES is the successor vehicle to the M88A1, which had only a recovery capability of 56 tons. The M88A1's mission was focused on the M60 Series tank while the M88A2 is focused on the Abrams tank.

BENEFIT TO THE WARFIGHTER

The HERCULES provides towing, winching and hoisting to support battlefield recovery operations and evacuation of heavy tanks and other tracked combat vehicles. As such, HERCULES is the recovery workhorse of the Armored Brigade Combat Team.

SPECIFICATIONS

- Crew: Three, plus space for four passengers
- Weight: 70 tons
- Length: 338 inches
- Width: 144 inches
- Height: 127 inches

- Speed (no load): 30 mph
- Speed (w/load): 26 mph with 70-ton load
- Cruising Range: 300 miles, 413 gallons
- Boom Lift Height: 25 feet
- Engine: 1,050 horsepower
- Armament: .50 Caliber M2

PROGRAM STATUS

- **FY13-FY15:** M88A2 production (converted from M88A1) continued at approximate rate of three vehicles per month at the BAE facility in York, PA; foreign military sales customers received completely new M88A2 vehicles
- **FY15:**
  › M88A2 HERCULES Fielding and New Equipment Training completed for Army units in Germany and Kuwait
  › Towing and evacuation tests completed at Aberdeen Proving Ground, MD; powertrain feasibility analysis completed by U.S. Army Tank Automotive Research, Development and Engineering Center, Warren, MI
- **Through 4QFY15:** 680 M88A2 vehicles produced against Army Acquisition Objective of 933 vehicles
- **Current:** Changes to M88A2 HERCULES to ensure single-vehicle recovery capability of modernized M1A2 Abrams and all other armored track vehicles

PROJECTED ACTIVITIES

- **FY16:** M88A2 Army Fielding and New Equipment Training will include Army units in Korea, Fort Hood, TX, Fort Bliss, TX, and Fort Riley, KS; Track and Suspension testing to be initiated and planning will begin for next version of the M88A2 Heavy Equipment Recovery vehicle; proposed upgrade will focus on single vehicle recovery of the modernized M1A2 Abrams tank

FOREIGN MILITARY SALES
Egypt, Kuwait, Australia, Iraq and Thailand

CONTRACTORS
BAE Systems, Inc. (York, PA)

Mid-Tier Networking Vehicular Radio (MNVR)

PEO Command, Control and Communications – Tactical | Aberdeen Proving Ground, MD

WARFIGHTING FUNCTION

Mission Command

Movement and Maneuver

Intelligence

Fires

Sustainment

Maneuver Support and Protection

Engagement

ACQUISITION LIFECYCLE PHASE

Materiel Solution Analysis

Technology Maturation & Risk Reduction

Engineering & Manufacturing Development

Production & Deployment

Operations & Support

MILESTONE DECISION AUTHORITY

Defense Acquisition Executive

Army Acquisition Executive

Program Executive Officer

DESCRIPTION

The Mid-Tier Networking Vehicular Radio (MNVR) system provides an extension of data services from the upper tactical network at brigade and battalion level to the lower tactical network at company and platoon echelons. The advanced network waveforms provide rapid distribution of data and imagery with increased information assurance protection and automatic routing across complex terrain. The MNVR capability consists of modular radios capable of running software-defined waveforms, which operate as nodes in a network to ensure secure wireless communication and networking services for mobile and stationary forces. This supports mission command, sensor-to-shooter, sustainment and survivability applications through the full range of military operations on tactical platforms.

BENEFIT TO THE WARFIGHTER

MNVR provides the warfighter with a dynamic, scalable, on-the-move voice and data network that connects company to brigade to support mission planning, command and control, and situational awareness.

SPECIFICATIONS

- Operates new Internet Protocol-based networking waveforms offering the warfighter increased data throughput through self-forming, self-healing and managed communications networks
- Dynamic, scalable, on-the-move network architecture connects the Soldier to the mission command network and enhances capability to exchange voice and data simultaneously and faster than current systems
- Advanced network waveforms provide rapid distribution of data and imagery with increased information assurance protection and automatic routing across complex terrain

PROGRAM STATUS

- **3QFY15:** Limited User Test

PROJECTED ACTIVITIES

- **2QFY16:** Milestone C Defense Acquisition Board
- **FY16:** Low-Rate Initial Production
- **FY17:**
  › Initial Operational Test & Evaluation
  › Production Decision

MNVR

FOREIGN MILITARY SALES
None

CONTRACTORS
Harris Radios Corporation (Rochester, NY)

Mine Resistant Ambush Protected Vehicles (MRAP), Army

PEO Combat Support and Combat Service Support | Detroit Arsenal, MI

WARFIGHTING FUNCTION

Mission Command

Movement and Maneuver

Intelligence

Fires

Sustainment

Maneuver Support and Protection

Engagement

ACQUISITION LIFECYCLE PHASE

Materiel Solution Analysis

Technology Maturation & Risk Reduction

Engineering & Manufacturing Development

Production & Deployment

Operations & Support

MILESTONE DECISION AUTHORITY

Defense Acquisition Executive

Army Acquisition Executive

Program Executive Officer

DESCRIPTION

The Mine Resistant Ambush Protected (MRAP) family of vehicles provides Soldiers with highly survivable multimission platforms capable of mitigating improvised explosive devices, rocket-propelled grenades, explosively formed penetrators, underbody mines and small arms fire threats which produce the greatest number of casualties in Overseas Contingency Operations.

Three variants comprise the Army MRAP enduring fleet: Mine Resistant Ambush Protected All-Terrain Vehicle (M-ATV), MaxxPro Dash with Independent Suspension System, and MaxxPro Long-Wheel-Based Ambulance. This versatile family of vehicles performs the mission roles of Armored Personnel Carrier, Weapons Carrier, Convoy Protection Platform, Key Leader Vehicle, Command Post and Armored Ambulance.

BENEFIT TO THE WARFIGHTER

MRAP provides light forces with protected mobility and mounted firepower to perform Wide Area Security while countering threats employing asymmetric tactics. They provide a rapid motorization capability for Brigade Combat Teams as the mission transitions from decisive operations to stability, or perform rear-area security during decisive operations.

SPECIFICATIONS

- Key components (transmissions, engines, etc.): Vary between vehicles and manufacturers; generally consist of common commercial and military parts
- Combat weight (fully loaded without add-on armor): 34,000-48,000 pounds
- Payloads: In the 8,000-pound range
- Engine: 370-375 horsepower
- Operational range: 300-370 miles

- Fuel tank capacity: 47-57 gallons
- Seats under armor protection: M1240A1, M-ATV-4 and M1235A4 MaxxPro Dash-6

PROGRAM STATUS

- **1QFY13:** Program designated ACAT IC (formerly ID)
- **2QFY13:** Army approved 8,585-vehicle MRAP enduring requirement
- **1QFY13-4QFY15:**
  › Continued support of MRAP vehicles fielded in response to urgent theater requirements
  › Continued RESET/standardization of MRAP vehicles returning from theater for enduring force requirements

PROJECTED ACTIVITIES

- **1QFY16-4QFY17:** Continue RESET/standardization activities of MRAP vehicles fielded in response to urgent theater requirements
- **4QFY17:**
  › Achieve Full Materiel Release for MaxxPro Dash and MaxxPro Long-Wheel-Based Ambulance variants
  › Begin transition to sustainment

FOREIGN MILITARY SALES
Afghanistan, Burundi, Croatia, Djibouti, Iraq, Jordan, Nigeria, Pakistan, Spain, Uganda and Uzbekistan

CONTRACTORS
Navistar Defense (Warrenville, IL)
Oshkosh Corp. (Oshkosh, WI)

MQ-1C Gray Eagle Unmanned Aircraft System (UAS)

PEO Aviation | Redstone Arsenal, AL

WARFIGHTING FUNCTION

Mission Command

Movement and Maneuver

Intelligence

Fires

Sustainment

Maneuver Support and Protection

Engagement

ACQUISITION LIFECYCLE PHASE

Materiel Solution Analysis

Technology Maturation & Risk Reduction

Engineering & Manufacturing Development

Production & Deployment

Operations & Support

MILESTONE DECISION AUTHORITY

Defense Acquisition Executive

Army Acquisition Executive

Program Executive Officer

DESCRIPTION

The MQ-1C Gray Eagle Unmanned Aircraft System (UAS) addresses the need for a long-endurance, armed, unmanned aircraft system that offers greater range, altitude and payload flexibility over earlier systems.

The Gray Eagle UAS is powered by a heavy fuel engine for higher performance, better fuel efficiency, common fuel on the battlefield and a longer lifetime.

The system is fielded in platoon sets consisting of four unmanned aircraft, two Universal Ground Control Stations, two Ground Data Terminals, one Portable Ground Control Station, one Portable Ground Data Terminal, one Satellite Ground Data Terminal, an automated takeoff and landing system, light medium tactical vehicles, and other ground-support equipment operated and maintained by a company of 128 Soldiers within the Combat Aviation Brigade.

BENEFIT TO THE WARFIGHTER

The MQ-1C provides the warfighter with dedicated, assured, multimission UAS capabilities across all 10 Army divisions to support commanders' combat operations.

SPECIFICATIONS

- Length: 28 feet
- Wingspan: 56 feet
- Gross takeoff weight: 3,600 pounds
- Maximum speed: 150 knots
- Ceiling: 25,000 feet
- Range: 2,500 nautical miles via satellite communications
- Endurance: 27-plus hours
- Payload: Up to four HELLFIRE missiles

PROGRAM STATUS

- **Current:** Full-Rate Production

PROJECTED ACTIVITIES

- **FY16-17:** Execute the Extended-Range Gray Eagle effort for the echelons-above-division units

MQ-1C Gray Eagle

FOREIGN MILITARY SALES
None

CONTRACTORS
General Atomics Aeronautical (San Diego, CA)

Multiple Launch Rocket System (MLRS) M270A1

PEO Missiles and Space | Redstone Arsenal, AL

WARFIGHTING FUNCTION

Mission Command

Movement and Maneuver

Intelligence

Fires

Sustainment

Maneuver Support and Protection

Engagement

ACQUISITION LIFECYCLE PHASE

Materiel Solution Analysis

Technology Maturation & Risk Reduction

Engineering & Manufacturing Development

Production & Deployment

Operations & Support

MILESTONE DECISION AUTHORITY

Defense Acquisition Executive

Army Acquisition Executive

Program Executive Officer

DESCRIPTION

The Multiple Launch Rocket System (MLRS) M270A1 is a combat-proven, mechanized artillery weapon system that provides the combat commander with highly lethal, all-weather, precise rocket and missile fires that defeat point and area targets in both urban/complex and open terrain. The system achieves these objectives for the Army, Marine Corps and coalition forces with minimal collateral damage via a highly mobile and responsive multiple launch system.

The M270A1 is an upgraded version of the M270 launcher. The program entailed the concurrent incorporation of the Improved Fire Control System and the Improved Launcher Mechanical System on a rebuilt M993 Carrier (derivative of the Bradley Fighting Vehicle). The M270A1 supports fires missions ranging from 15-300 km. The M270A1 can fire all munitions in the current and planned suite of the MLRS Family of Munitions, including Army Tactical Missile System missiles and Guided MLRS rockets. The M270A1 carries and fires two launch pods, each containing either six rockets or one missile. It operates with the same MLRS command, control and communications structure and three-man crew as the M142 High Mobility Artillery Rocket System. The Improved Armored Cab modification increases crew protection from small arms fire, artillery fragmentation and improvised explosive devices.

BENEFIT TO THE WARFIGHTER

The MLRS Launcher provides 24-hour, all-weather, lethal, close- and long-range precision rocket and missile fire support for Joint forces, early-entry expeditionary forces, contingency forces, and Modular Fire Brigades supporting Brigade Combat Teams.

SPECIFICATIONS

- Empty weight: 45,086 pounds
- Combat weight: 57,544 pounds
- Maximum speed: 64 kph
- Maximum cruising range: 483 km
- Ordnance options: All current and future MLRS rockets and Army Tactical Missile System missiles

PROGRAM STATUS

- **1QFY15:** Continued M270A1 launcher overhaul program at Red River Army Depot (RRAD)
- **3QFY15:**
  › Completed Improved Armor Cab (IAC) Product Manager's Enhanced Field Exercise
  › Delivery of Fire Control System – Update (FCS-U) hardware prototypes and first Software Engineering Release
- **4QFY15:** Completed IAC developmental testing
- **1QFY16:**
  › FCS-U Qualification Phase began
  › IAC Production Request For Proposal (RFP)

PROJECTED ACTIVITIES

- **Continue:**
  › M270A1 launcher overhaul program
  › Providing sustainment and support activities for MLRS strategic partners and foreign military sales customers
- **1QFY17:**
  › IAC Production Contract Award
  › FCS-U Production RFP
- **1QFY18:** FCS-U Production Contract Award; Modernization

MLRS M270A1

FOREIGN MILITARY SALES
M270 and M270A1: Bahrain, Egypt, Finland, France, Germany, Greece, Israel, Italy, Japan and Korea
M270 and M270B1: Norway, Turkey and United Kingdom

CONTRACTORS
Lockheed Martin (Grand Prairie, TX)

Palletized Load System (PLS) and PLS Extended Service Program (ESP)

PEO Combat Support and Combat Service Support | Detroit Arsenal, MI

WARFIGHTING FUNCTION

Mission Command

Movement and Maneuver

Intelligence

Fires

Sustainment

Maneuver Support and Protection

Engagement

ACQUISITION LIFECYCLE PHASE

Materiel Solution Analysis

Technology Maturation & Risk Reduction

Engineering & Manufacturing Development

Production & Deployment

Operations & Support

MILESTONE DECISION AUTHORITY

Defense Acquisition Executive

Army Acquisition Executive

Program Executive Officer

DESCRIPTION

The base Palletized Load System (PLS), initially fielded in 1994, consists of the PLS truck, PLS trailer and demountable flat racks. The PLS truck, commonly referred to simply as the PLS, is a 10x10 (10-wheel drive) truck with a 16.5-ton capacity that provides the timely delivery of high-tonnage cargo. This could include ammunition, unit equipment, International Organization for Standardization (ISO) containers and shelters, and all classes of supply and weapon systems. The PLS truck is equipped with an integral onboard load handling system that provides self-loading and unloading capability of flat racks, container roll-in and roll-out platforms and 20-foot ISO containers.

There are two PLS truck variants: The basic PLS truck (M1075) and the PLS truck with material handling crane (M1074). The system also includes the PLS trailer (M1076); optional truck-mounted container handling unit for transporting 20-foot ISO containers; the M3/M3A1 container roll-in and roll-out platform; and the M1/M1077A1 flat racks. The PLS trailer also has a payload capacity of 16.5 tons, which matches the payload capacity of the PLS truck.

The new PLSA1 truck model began fielding in 2011. It incorporates independent front suspension, a new Caterpillar C-15 engine, the Allison 4500SP 6-speed transmission, J-1939 data-bus and a cab that is common with the Heavy Expanded Mobility Tactical Truck A4 long-term, armor-strategy-compliant cab.

The PLS Extended Service Program (ESP) is a recapitalization program that converts high-mileage base PLS trucks to zero miles and zero hours and to the current A1 production truck configurations. The base PLS trucks are disassembled and rebuilt with improved technology such as an electronically controlled engine, electronic transmission, air ride seats, four-point seatbelts, bolted-together wheels, increased corrosion protection, enhanced electrical package and independent front suspension.

BENEFIT TO THE WARFIGHTER

The PLS supports Soldiers by performing cross country movement of configured loads of supplies on flat racks or in containers, while providing improved survivability.

PROGRAM STATUS

- **Current:** Fielded approximately 6,000 PLS trucks and 13,000 PLS trailers

PROJECTED ACTIVITIES

- **FY16-FY17:** Continued recapitalization efforts to modernize the fleet

FOREIGN MILITARY SALES
Turkey, Israel and Jordan

CONTRACTORS
Oshkosh Corp. (Oshkosh, WI)

SPECIFICATIONS

	PLS	PLSA1
Engine	DDC 8V92 - 500 horsepower	CAT C-15 - 600 hp @ 2100 RPM
Transmission	Allison CLT-755 - 5-Speed	Allison HD 4500 - 6-Speed
Transfer Case	Oshkosh 55,000 - 2-Speed	New Oshkosh - 2-Speed
Axles Front: Tandem	Rockwell SVI 5MR/Planetary Hub	Oshkosh TAK-4 with AxleTech carrier with differential lock and planetary wheelends
Axles: Rear Tridem	Rockwell SVI 5MR	AxleTech carrier with differential lock and planetary wheel ends
Suspension - Axles #1 & #2	Hendrickson RT-340 - Walking Beam	Oshkosh TAK 4 Steel Spring
Suspension - Axle #3	Hendrickson-Turner Air Ride	Hendrickson-Turner Air Ride
Suspension - Axles #4 & #5	Hendrickson RT-400 - Walking Beam	Hendrickson RT-400 - Walking Beam
Wheel Ends	Rockwell	Rockwell
Control Arms	N/A	Standard MTVR on Front Tandem
Steering Gears - Front	492 Master/M110 Slave	M110 Master/M110 Slave
Steering Gears - Rear	492	M110
Frame Rails	14-inch	14-inch
Cab	PLS	LTAS Compliant Common Cab
Radiator	Roof Mount	Side Mount
Muffler	PLS	New
Air Cleaner	United Air	United Air
LHS	Multilift MK V	Multilift MK V
Crane	Grove	Grove
Tires	Michelin 16.00 R20 XZLT	Michelin 16.00 R20 XZLT
Spare Tire	1 - Side Mounted	1 - Roof Mounted
CTI	CM Automotive	Dana
Air Compressor	1400 Bendix	922 Bendix
Starter	Prestolite	Prestolite
Alternator	12/24V	260 Amp Niehoff

PATRIOT Advanced Capability – 3 (PAC-3)

PEO Missiles and Space | Redstone Arsenal, AL

WARFIGHTING FUNCTION

Mission Command

Movement and Maneuver

Intelligence

Fires

Sustainment

Maneuver Support and Protection

Engagement

ACQUISITION LIFECYCLE PHASE

Materiel Solution Analysis

Technology Maturation & Risk Reduction

Engineering & Manufacturing Development

Production & Deployment

Operations & Support

MILESTONE DECISION AUTHORITY

Defense Acquisition Executive

Army Acquisition Executive

Program Executive Officer

DESCRIPTION

The Phased Array Tracking Radar to Intercept of Target (PATRIOT) Missile protects ground forces and critical assets at all echelons from advanced aircraft, cruise missiles and tactical ballistic missiles (TBM). The PATRIOT Advanced Capability – 3 (PAC-3) is the Army's premier guided air-and-missile defense (AMD) system providing highly reactive hit-to-kill capability in both range and altitude while operating in all environments.

The combat element of the PATRIOT system is the fire unit, primarily consisting of a radar set (RS), engagement control station (ECS) and launching stations (LS). The RS provides airspace surveillance, target detection, identification, classification, simultaneous tracking of targets, missile guidance and engagement support. The LS performs transport and missile launch functions remotely operated from the ECS, which provides command and control. The LS has a load-out capacity of between 12 and 16 PAC-3 missiles depending on configuration. The PAC-3 missile was initially fielded in 2001, introducing hit-to-kill technology for greater lethality against TBM, cruise missiles and aircraft carrying weapons of mass destruction. The combination of a highly responsive airframe and attitude control motors generates an angle of attack that would not be achievable with actuator-driven aerodynamic control surfaces alone.

The PAC-3 Missile Segment Enhancement (MSE), fielded in 2015, represents the next generation PAC-3 missile and provides expanded battlespace performance against complex threats. The PAC-3 MSE improves upon the original PAC-3 capability with a higher performance solid rocket motor, modified lethality enhancer, more responsive control surfaces, upgraded guidance software and insensitive munitions improvements.

PAC-3 milestone authority was assigned to the Army in 2004. The Army Acquisition Executive remains the Milestone Decision Authority (MDA) for the PAC-3 while the Defense Acquisition Executive is

the MDA for the PAC-3 MSE. The Army continues to modernize PATRIOT through phased efforts to maintain and improve system capabilities in the complex threat environment. This modernization provides greater resilience against advanced threats and leverages the enlarged engagement area afforded by the PAC-3 MSE interceptor. PATRIOT is transitioning to the Integrated Air and Missile Defense Battle Command System networked architecture.

BENEFIT TO THE WARFIGHTER

PATRIOT is a combat-proven ground-based AMD system that is providing critical AMD protection to the warfighter in 15 countries. Twelve foreign partners have PATRIOT in their inventories.

SPECIFICATIONS

- Advanced multifunction radar
- Engagement control operations
- Launcher capable of remote operations
- Deployed by fire units organized within a battalion
- Supported by ancillary communications and maintenance ground support equipment
- Designed to defend against current and emerging threats, including weapons of mass destruction

PROGRAM STATUS

- **FY13-FY15:** Post-Deployment Build-7 (PDB-7) fielding
- **2QFY14:** PAC-3 MSE Milestone C Defense Acquisition Board
- **1QFY16:** PAC-3 MSE First Unit Equipped

PROJECTED ACTIVITIES

- **1QFY17:** PAC-3 MSE Initial Operational Capability
- **3QFY17:** PDB-8 and PAC-3 MSE Initial Operational Test & Evaluation
- **1QFY18:** PAC-3 MSE Full-Rate Production

FOREIGN MILITARY SALES
PAC-3: Germany, Japan, Netherlands, Taiwan, United Arab Emirates, Kuwait, Qatar and Korea

CONTRACTORS
Missile Program Management Team: Lockheed Martin (Dallas, TX)
Missile Assembly: Lockheed Martin (Camden, AR)
System Integration/Ground Equipment: Raytheon (Andover, MA)

M902 LS with PAC-3 Load-out

RQ-7Bv2 Shadow Tactical Unmanned Aircraft System (TUAS)

PEO Aviation | Redstone Arsenal, AL

WARFIGHTING FUNCTION

Mission Command

Movement and Maneuver

Intelligence

Fires

Sustainment

Maneuver Support and Protection

Engagement

ACQUISITION LIFECYCLE PHASE

Materiel Solution Analysis

Technology Maturation & Risk Reduction

Engineering & Manufacturing Development

Production & Deployment

Operations & Support

MILESTONE DECISION AUTHORITY

Defense Acquisition Executive

Army Acquisition Executive

Program Executive Officer

DESCRIPTION

The RQ-7Bv2 Shadow Tactical Unmanned Aircraft System (TUAS) provides reconnaissance, surveillance, target acquisition and force protection for the Brigade Combat Team (BCT) in near-real-time during day, night and limited adverse weather conditions. The system is compatible with the All Source Analysis System, Advanced Field Artillery Tactical Data System, Joint Surveillance Target Attack Radar System Common Ground Station, Joint Technical Architecture – Army, the Defense Information Infrastructure Common Operating Environment and the Universal Ground Control Station (UGCS). The RQ-7Bv2 Shadow can be transported by six Air Force C-130 aircraft. It is currently operational in both the Army and Marine Corps.

The RQ-7Bv2 Shadow configuration, fielded in platoon sets, consists of:
- Four air vehicles with day and night electro-optical (EO) and infrared (IR) with laser designator (LD) and IR illuminator payloads
- Two UGCS on High Mobility Multipurpose Wheeled Vehicles
- Four One System Remote Video Transceivers
- One hydraulic launcher
- Two ground data terminals
- Associated trucks, trailers and support equipment

Shadow platoons are organic to the BCT. The Soldier platoon consists of a platoon leader, platoon sergeant, unmanned aerial vehicle warrant officer, 12 Air Vehicle Operators and Mission Payload Operators, 4 electronic warfare repair personnel, and 3 engine mechanics supporting launch and recovery. The Maintenance Section Multifunctional is manned by Soldiers who also transport spares and provide maintenance support. The Mobile Maintenance Facility is manned by contractor personnel located with the Shadow platoon to provide logistics support to include off-system support and maintenance-by-repair.

The Shadow also has an early entry configuration of 15 Soldiers, one Ground Control Station, the air vehicle transport High Mobility Multipurpose Wheeled Vehicle, and the launcher trailer, which can be transported in three C-130s. All components can be slung under a CH-47 or CH-53 helicopter for transport.

BENEFIT TO THE WARFIGHTER

The RQ-7Bv2 provides Army BCT, Aviation Brigades and Special Operation Units dedicated near-real-time reconnaissance, surveillance and target acquisition; intelligence; battle damage assessment; and Manned-Unmanned Teaming (MUM-T) capability. The RQ-7Bv2, teamed with the AH-64D/E, provides support and situational awareness to both the Soldier on the ground and warfighting leadership as they carry out operations in support of U.S. national interests.

SPECIFICATIONS
- Wingspan: 20 feet
- Gross takeoff weight: 440-plus pounds
- Payload capacity: 60 pounds
- Endurance: 8-plus hours on-station at a distance of 50 km
- Capable of cooperative engagements with AH-64E Apache for MUM-T

PROGRAM STATUS
- **Current:** In production and deployment with the V2 configuration; flown more than 960,000 hours, 90 percent of it in combat

PROJECTED ACTIVITIES
- **FY16-17:** Continue fielding v2 block upgrade to the Heavy Armed Reconnaissance Squadrons in accordance with the Aviation Restructure Initiative; procure second source EO, IR, and LD payloads and Block III engines

RQ-7Bv2 Shadow

FOREIGN MILITARY SALES
Australia

CONTRACTORS
Shadow System: AAI Corp. (Textron Systems)
(Hunt Valley, MD)

Stryker Family of Vehicles

PEO Ground Combat Systems | Detroit Arsenal, MI

DESCRIPTION

The National Military Strategy requires an Army that is rapidly deployable and strategically responsive across the full spectrum of operations. The Stryker Brigade Combat Team (SBCT) encompasses capabilities and characteristics that are needed but were not available until the first SBCT was declared operationally capable. As the primary combat and combat support platform of the SBCT, the Stryker Family of Vehicles fulfills an immediate requirement for a strategically deployable (C-130/C-17/C-5) brigade capable of rapid movement worldwide in a combat-ready configuration.

The Stryker Family of Vehicles is built on a common chassis, each with a different Mission Equipment Package. There are 17 variants: 10 flat-bottom variants that include the Infantry Carrier Vehicle (ICV), Mobile Gun System (MGS), Reconnaissance Vehicle (RV), Mortar Carrier (MC), Commander's Vehicle (CV), Fire Support Vehicle (FSV), Engineer Squad Vehicle (ESV), Medical Evacuation Vehicle (MEV), Anti-tank Guided Missile (ATGM) Vehicle and Nuclear Biological Chemical Reconnaissance Vehicle (NBCRV); and seven Double-V-Hull (DVH) variants for the following: ICV, CV, MEV, MC, ATGM, FSV and ESV.

The Stryker program leverages nondevelopmental items with common subsystems and components to allow rapid acquisition and fielding. Stryker integrates government-furnished materiel subsystems as required and stresses performance and commonality to reduce the logistics footprint and minimize costs. The 30 mm cannon was integrated on the Stryker platform to meet emerging operational requirements and to improve survivability. With the integration of Engineering Change Proposal 1 beginning 3QFY16 providing greater horsepower and electrical output, along with a more robust suspension and in-vehicle network, the Stryker will be an even more capable platform.

BENEFIT TO THE WARFIGHTER

Stryker vehicles provide the warfighter with a reliable, combat-tested platform that includes significant survivability and capability enhancements since the original fielding in 2002.

SPECIFICATIONS

- Built on a common chassis, with the exception of MGS and NBCRV, to reduce logistical footprint
- Certain variants, excluding the MEV, ATGM, FSV, RV, MC and MGS, armed with Remote Weapon Station supporting M2 .50 Caliber machine gun or MK19 grenade launcher
- Top speed: 60 mph
- Range: 330 miles
- Either 4x8 or 8x8 capability with run-flat tires, central tire inflation system and vehicle height management system

PROGRAM STATUS

- **3QFY13:** Army approves Prototype Build and Test for Engineering Change Proposal 1; Army approves procurement of Stryker DVH for 3rd DVH Brigade; Completion of Stryker fielding for SBCT 9
- **1QFY14:** Army directs fielding of DVH Strykers to SBCT, displacing flat-bottom Strykers
- **2QFY14:** Army begins first DVH Brigade fielding (1/4 SBCT, Fort Carson, CO)
- **4QFY14:** Army approves procurement of Stryker DVH for 4th DVH Brigade
- **3QFY15:** Army receives Operational Needs Statement for increased lethality and authorizes execution
- **4QFY15:** Completion of 2nd DVH Brigade fielding (3CR, Fort Hood, TX)

PROJECTED ACTIVITIES

- **3QFY16:** Army begins production of DVH Strykers for 4th DVH Brigade incorporating ECP1 technologies; Army completes fielding of 3rd DVH Brigade

Stryker FOV

FOREIGN MILITARY SALES
None

CONTRACTORS
General Dynamics Land Systems
(Sterling Heights, MI)

Tactical Mission Command (TMC)

PEO Command, Control and Communications – Tactical | Aberdeen Proving Ground, MD

WARFIGHTING FUNCTION

Mission Command

Movement and Maneuver

Intelligence

Fires

Sustainment

Maneuver Support and Protection

Engagement

ACQUISITION LIFECYCLE PHASE

Materiel Solution Analysis

Technology Maturation & Risk Reduction

Engineering & Manufacturing Development

Production & Deployment

Operations & Support

MILESTONE DECISION AUTHORITY

Defense Acquisition Executive

Army Acquisition Executive

Program Executive Officer

DESCRIPTION

Tactical Mission Command (TMC) is a suite of products and services that provides commanders and staffs with planning tools, common operational picture management, information and knowledge management, other maneuver functional tools, and executive decision making in a collaborative environment. Many TMC capabilities are transitioning to Web-based widgets that can be accessed via a secure Internet as part of the Army's Command Post Computing Environment (CP CE). The CP CE is consolidating and simplifying the separate capabilities that commanders use for missions related to all of the warfighting functions.

BENEFIT TO THE WARFIGHTER

TMC helps provide commanders with a consolidated readiness picture on a singular workstation, lessens the logistics trail for Soldiers and reduces the training burden.

SPECIFICATIONS

- Command Web provides modular software widgets served up over the Web, improved supportability, ease of use in robust network environments
- Command Post of the Future (CPOF) is the commander's situational awareness and decision support tool for the company level and above; integrates data feeds from other Army, Joint, Coalition systems into a tailorable operating picture
- Common Tactical Vision is an intuitive touch-screen situational awareness viewer with digital video recorder playback capability that provides Common Operational Picture data
- Battle Command Sustainment Support System (BCS3) provides supply visibility, logistics reporting, convoy tracking and alert reporting capabilities; includes the Logistics Reporting Tool, In-transit Visibility (ITV), Asset Visibility (AV) and Log View Web-apps

- Battle Command Sustainment Support System – Node Management (BCS3-NM) provides Web-based distribution management that integrates joint ITV and AV data sources focused on supply storage and distribution nodes

PROGRAM STATUS

- **1QFY13:** Quarterly release decision for MC13.0 baseline (Convergence)
- **2QFY13:** Certification Test for Command Post Web Engineer Mobility Services (EMS) and Obstacle and Hazard Services (OH) Widgets
- **3QFY13:**
  › CPOF next-generation architecture demonstration and Command Post Web demonstration of all Maneuver Function capabilities at Network Integration Evaluation (NIE) 13.2
  › Fielding decision for Command Post Web EMS and OH Widgets
- **2QFY13-3QFY13:** Common Operating Environment (COE)1.0 Integration and Interoperability Event (I2E) and Army Interoperability Certification (AIC) for CPOF and Command Post Web
- **3QFY14:** CPOF and Command Post Web demonstration and support for NIE 14.2
- **3QFY14-4QFY14:** COE2.0 I2E and AIC for CPOF and Command Post Web
- **1QFY15:**
  › COE2.0 Fielding Decision for CPOF and Command Post Web
  › Support for NIE 15.1
- **4QFY15:**
  › CPOF 13.2 Final Release
  › CP CE System Readiness Review

PROJECTED ACTIVITIES

- **2QFY16:**
  › Command Web Operational Test
  › NIE 16.2 CP CE Operational Assessment

TMC

FOREIGN MILITARY SALES
Canada

CONTRACTORS
General Dynamics (Taunton, MA; Fairfax, VA)
AASKI Technology (Ocean, NJ)
Computer Sciences Corporation (Belcamp, MD)
Future Skies (Aberdeen, MD)

Tube-Launched, Optically Tracked, Wireless-Guided (TOW) Missiles

PEO Missiles and Space | Redstone Arsenal, AL

WARFIGHTING FUNCTION

Mission Command

Movement and Maneuver

Intelligence

Fires

Sustainment

Maneuver Support and Protection

Engagement

ACQUISITION LIFECYCLE PHASE

Materiel Solution Analysis

Technology Maturation & Risk Reduction

Engineering & Manufacturing Development

Production & Deployment

Operations & Support

MILESTONE DECISION AUTHORITY

Defense Acquisition Executive

Army Acquisition Executive

Program Executive Officer

DESCRIPTION

The Close Combat Missile System – Heavy (CCMS-H) TOW (Tube-Launched, Optically Tracked, Wireless-Guided) Missile is a heavy anti-tank/precision assault weapon system consisting of a launcher and a missile. The gunner defines the aim point by maintaining the sight cross hairs on the target. The launcher automatically steers the missile along the line-of-sight toward the aim point via a one-way radio frequency link, which links the launcher and missile.

TOW missiles are employed on the High Mobility Multipurpose Wheeled Vehicle (HMMWV)-mounted Improved Target Acquisition System, HMMWV-mounted M220A4 launcher (TOW 2), Stryker Anti-Tank Guided Missile (ATGM) Vehicles, and Bradley Fighting Vehicles (A2/A2ODS/A2OIF/A3) within the Infantry, Stryker, and Armor Brigade Combat Teams, respectively. TOW missiles are also employed on the Marine HMMWV-mounted Saber, HMMWV-mounted M220A4 TOW 2, LAV-ATGM Vehicle and AH1W Cobra attack helicopter. TOW is also employed by allied nations on a variety of ground and airborne platforms.

The TOW 2B Aero is the most modern and capable missile in the TOW family, with an extended maximum range to 4,500 meters. The TOW 2B Aero has an advanced counteractive protection system capability and defeats all current and projected threat armor systems. The TOW 2B flies over the target (offset above the gunner's aim point) and uses a laser profilometer and magnetic sensor to detect and fire two downward-directed, explosively formed penetrator warheads into the target.

The TOW Bunker Buster (BB) is optimized for performance against urban structures, earthen bunkers, field fortifications and light-skinned armor threats. The missile impact is at the aim point. It has a 6.25-pound, 6-inch diameter high-explosive, bulk-charge warhead. The TOW BB has an impact sensor (crush switch) located in the main charge and gives a pyrotechnic detonation delay to enhance warhead effectiveness. The PBXN-109 explosive is housed in a thick casing for maximum performance. The TOW BB can produce a 21- to 24-inch-diameter hole in an 8-inch-thick, double reinforced concrete wall at a range of between 65 and 3,750 meters.

BENEFIT TO THE WARFIGHTER

The TOW Missile provides the warfighter with precise, lethal, direct fires against main battle tanks, field fortifications, heavy weapons teams, snipers and other targets of opportunity while minimizing collateral damage.

SPECIFICATIONS

- Weight: 49.8 pounds (65 pounds encased)
- Length: 49 inches
- Diameter: 6 inches (8.6 inches encased)
- Range: 4,500 meters (TOW 2B Aero)

PROGRAM STATUS

- **Current:** TOW missiles are procured via an FY12-FY16 TOW multiyear contract

PROJECTED ACTIVITIES

- **FY16-FY17:** Continue production and delivery

FOREIGN MILITARY SALES
The TOW weapon system has been sold to more than 43 allied nations over the life of the system.

CONTRACTORS
Raytheon Missile Systems (Tucson, AZ)

Warfighter Information Network – Tactical (WIN-T) Increment 1

PEO Command, Control and Communications – Tactical | Aberdeen Proving Ground, MD

WARFIGHTING FUNCTION

Mission Command

Movement and Maneuver

Intelligence

Fires

Sustainment

Maneuver Support and Protection

Engagement

ACQUISITION LIFECYCLE PHASE

Materiel Solution Analysis

Technology Maturation & Risk Reduction

Engineering & Manufacturing Development

Production & Deployment

Operations & Support

MILESTONE DECISION AUTHORITY

Defense Acquisition Executive

Army Acquisition Executive

Program Executive Officer

DESCRIPTION

The Army began fielding the Warfighter Information Network – Tactical (WIN-T) Increment 1, formerly known as the "Joint Network Node Network," in 2004 and completed fielding in 2012 to all units dedicated to receive the capability.

The WIN-T Increment 1 End Of Life Technical Refresh effort currently underway is one of four upgrades being made to WIN-T Increment 1. This effort advances capability while reducing equipment by one-third for increased unit agility. An ongoing enhanced networking upgrade, the WIN-T Increment 1B upgrade improves the efficiency, security and interoperability of the network. Other upgrades include the Network Operations Convergence Upgrade that simplifies and reduces the number of network management tools communications officers (S6s and G6s) use to manage the tactical communications network, and the High Capacity Line Of Sight Radio Upgrade that provides more than a fourfold increase in throughput.

BENEFIT TO THE WARFIGHTER

Similar to a home Internet connection, WIN-T Increment 1 provides a full range of at-the-halt data, voice and video communications, allowing Soldiers to simply pull over to the side of the road to communicate. WIN-T Increment 1 provides this networking capability to command posts and units at the battalion level and above.

SPECIFICATIONS

- High-speed, wide-area network capability for secure voice, video and data exchange from three types of transportable network nodes
  › Tactical Hub Node supports division headquarters
  › Joint Network Node supports brigade-level headquarters
  › Battalion Command Post Node supports battalion-level headquarters
- Regional Hub Node, a fourth and fixed-installation equivalent to three Tactical Hub Nodes, supports theater-level operations

- Satellite Transportable Terminal, a highly mobile satellite system operating with Joint Network Node and Battalion Command Post Node, establishes secure voice, video and data communications anytime, anywhere

PROGRAM STATUS

- **2QFY13-2QFY15:**
  › Increment 1B MWO fielding
  › Increment 1A End of Life Technical Refresh
- **FY15:** Continue fielding of Increment 1B colorless core and net centric waveform modem MWO
- **3QFY15:** Begin fielding new Increment 1B Upgraded baseline
- **4QFY15:** Fielding begins for next baseline of End of Life

PROJECTED ACTIVITIES

- **FY16-FY18:** Procuring and Fielding Wireless capability to Brigade, ESB and above

WIN-T Inc. 1

Warfighter Information Network – Tactical (WIN-T) Increment 2

PEO Command, Control and Communications – Tactical | Aberdeen Proving Ground, MD

WARFIGHTING FUNCTION

Mission Command

Movement and Maneuver

Intelligence

Fires

Sustainment

Maneuver Support and Protection

Engagement

ACQUISITION LIFECYCLE PHASE

Materiel Solution Analysis

Technology Maturation & Risk Reduction

Engineering & Manufacturing Development

Production & Deployment

Operations & Support

MILESTONE DECISION AUTHORITY

Defense Acquisition Executive

Army Acquisition Executive

Program Executive Officer

DESCRIPTION

The Warfighter Information Network – Tactical (WIN-T) Increment 2 began fielding in October 2012 and serves as the tactical network communications backbone of the Army's capability sets. With WIN-T Increment 2, Soldiers can utilize applications for maneuver, fires and intelligence from inside vehicles, enabling commanders to make decisions on-the-move rather than being tied down to a fixed command post. This ensures effective and unpredictable offensive and defensive operations.

The Tactical Communications Node (TCN) provides the principal backbone element and supports command post operations for the WIN-T Increment 2 network. It provides communication and networking equipment and allows the Soldier to access the network at a variety of security levels. While at-the-halt, the TCN is equipped with a 10-meter, extendable mast to improve line-of-sight connectivity and larger satellite assemblage for high throughput.

BENEFIT TO THE WARFIGHTER

Combat vehicles integrated with WIN-T Increment 2 provide the on-the-move communications, mission command and situational awareness that commanders need to lead from anywhere on the battlefield. WIN-T Increment 2 enables deployed Soldiers down to the company level operating in remote and challenging terrain to maintain voice, video and data communications while on patrol, with connectivity rivaling that found in a stationary command post.

SPECIFICATIONS

- Point of Presence installed on select platforms at division, brigade and battalion echelons, enabling mobile mission command by providing on-the-move network connectivity, including beyond-line-of-sight

- Soldier Network Extension (SNE) installed on select vehicles at the company echelon to extend network from brigade down to company level for the first time; on-the-move satellite communication systems enables SNE to heal and extend lower echelon tactical radio network for features blocked by terrain
- Vehicle Wireless Package (VWP) for non-WIN-T command and control (C2) vehicles provides remote connectivity to a TCN via a Local Access Waveform for C2 vehicles during at-the-halt and on-the-move operations
- NetOps and Security Center provides network management, enhanced tactical network planning, administration, monitoring and response capabilities

PROGRAM STATUS

- **3QFY13:** Initial Operational Capability
- **FY13-FY15:** Low-Rate Initial Production WIN-T Increment 2 fielding
- **FY14-FY15:** Successful completion Network Integration Evaluation 14.2 and 15.1 Operational Tests
- **2QFY15:** Successful Full-Rate Production decision
- **3QFY15:** Initial Full-Rate Production Contract Award

PROJECTED ACTIVITIES

- **FY16-FY17:**
  - › Full-Rate Production WIN-T Fielding
  - › WIN-T Increment 2 System Enhancement Integration
- **2QFY17:** TCN (Lite) and Network Operations Security Center (Lite) Operational Tests

FOREIGN MILITARY SALES
None

CONTRACTORS
General Dynamics (Taunton, MA)

Warfighter Information Network – Tactical (WIN-T) Increment 3

PEO Command, Control and Communications – Tactical | Aberdeen Proving Ground, MD

WARFIGHTING FUNCTION

Mission Command

Movement and Maneuver

Intelligence

Fires

Sustainment

Maneuver Support and Protection

Engagement

ACQUISITION LIFECYCLE PHASE

Materiel Solution Analysis

Technology Maturation & Risk Reduction

Engineering & Manufacturing Development

Production & Deployment

Operations & Support

MILESTONE DECISION AUTHORITY

Defense Acquisition Executive

Army Acquisition Executive

Program Executive Officer

DESCRIPTION

The Warfighter Information Network – Tactical (WIN-T) Increment 3 provides the fully integrated network operations (NetOps) capability to allow seamless integration of tactical network planning, management, monitoring and defense for the Signal Staff. NetOps will be provided as a technical insertion to WIN-T Increments 1 and 2 for fielding and support.

WIN-T Increment 3 provides enhanced NetOps software packages that support NetOps convergence activities across WIN-T and the Lower Tactical Internet to meet the Army's Convergence goals and Common Operating Environment interoperability. It also brings advancements in monitoring, control and planning tools to ensure effective management of emerging voice, data and internet transport networks, as well as improved information assurance and Network Centric Enterprise Services. Inherent software modernization occurs through ongoing technical refresh within the WIN-T family of programs.

WIN-T Increment 3 also provides waveform management and modernization with the new Highband Networking Waveform version 3.0 for line-of-sight communications, and the Net Centric Waveform version 10.x for increased throughput capability for beyond-line-of-sight satellite communications.

BENEFIT TO THE WARFIGHTER

These NetOps improvements simplify the management of the network, and increase the automation of tools and reporting. The effort will also increase visibility for the warfighter across the network to make communications systems easier to install, operate, maintain and defend — key elements to supporting an agile Future Force.

SPECIFICATIONS

- Improved beyond line-of-sight satellite communications via next generation Multi-Frequency Time Division Multiple Access Net-Centric Waveform supporting data rate increases for large terminals
- Next generation line-of-sight Highband Networking Waveform version 3.0 available to other programs via the Joint Tactical Networking Information Repository

PROGRAM STATUS

- **1QFY14:** Critical Design Review
- **4QFY14:** WIN-T Increment 3 restructure finalized
- **FY14-FY15:** Software development efforts

PROJECTED ACTIVITIES

- **2QFY16:** Network Integration Evaluation 16.2 Net Centric Waveform and NetOps Operational Tests
- **4QFY16:** Program development complete

FOREIGN MILITARY SALES
None

CONTRACTORS
Prime: General Dynamics (Taunton, MA, and Sunrise, FL)
Subcomponent: Lockheed Martin (Gaithersburg, MD)

WEAPON SYSTEMS
ACAT II and III

Listed in alphabetical order

120M Motor Grader

PEO Combat Support and Combat Service Support | Detroit Arsenal, MI

WARFIGHTING FUNCTION

Mission Command

Movement and Maneuver

Intelligence

Fires

Sustainment

Maneuver Support and Protection

Engagement

ACQUISITION LIFECYCLE PHASE

Materiel Solution Analysis

Technology Maturation & Risk Reduction

Engineering & Manufacturing Development

Production & Deployment

Operations & Support

MILESTONE DECISION AUTHORITY

Defense Acquisition Executive

Army Acquisition Executive

Program Executive Officer

DESCRIPTION

The 120M Motor Grader is a heavy-duty, pneumatic-tired commercial construction grader. It performs rough and fine grading, ditching, high-bank cutting and sloping and will serve the needs of Brigade Engineer Battalion, Infantry Brigade Combat Team and Equipment Support Company Airborne units employed and/or positioned throughout the entire range of military operations.

The 120M Motor Grader will be used along with other construction equipment to conduct general construction missions in support of repair, maintenance and construction of air and ground lines of communication, repair and restoration of infrastructure, and to enhance force and infrastructure protection. The Grader Type IA is air-droppable, commercial off-the-shelf construction equipment that is fully adaptable to military operations.

BENEFIT TO THE WARFIGHTER

The 120M Motor Grader improves and repairs air and ground lines of communication, such as airfields and main supply routes, which enhances infrastructure and force protection.

SPECIFICATIONS

- Six-wheeled, commercial, construction grader with all-wheel drive, articulated frame steer and pneumatic tires
- Electro-hydraulic joystick control operation
- Automatic power shift transmission with eight forward and six reverse speeds

PROGRAM STATUS

- **1QFY15:** Complete air drop testing for Type IA Airborne variant
- **2QFY15:** Completed Developmental Testing for Type IA Airborne variant
- **Through FY15:** 734 Type I systems fielded

PROJECTED ACTIVITIES

- **2QFY16:** Type IA Full Materiel Release, Full-Rate Production
- **3QFY16:** Type IA First Unit equipped
- **4QFY16:** Complete Type IA Army Acquisition Objective fielding of 20 systems
- **1QFY17:** Field 17 Type I Graders

120M Motor Grader

FOREIGN MILITARY SALES
Iraq and Afghanistan

CONTRACTORS
Caterpillar, Inc. (Peoria, IL)

621G Scraper

PEO Combat Support and Combat Service Support | Detroit Arsenal, MI

WARFIGHTING FUNCTION

Mission Command

Movement and Maneuver

Intelligence

Fires

Sustainment

Maneuver Support and Protection

Engagement

ACQUISITION LIFECYCLE PHASE

Materiel Solution Analysis

Technology Maturation & Risk Reduction

Engineering & Manufacturing Development

Production & Deployment

Operations & Support

MILESTONE DECISION AUTHORITY

Defense Acquisition Executive

Army Acquisition Executive

Program Executive Officer

DESCRIPTION

The 621G Scraper is a self-propelled, open-bowl, two-axle, single-diesel-engine-driven vehicle with pneumatic tires. It is capable of being push loaded with a T-9 Medium Dozer, reducing bowl loading times to less than one minute, and accepting the armor Crew Protection Kit. The 621G Scraper is used for cutting, scraping, self-loading, hauling, dumping and spreading of earth during earth-moving operations.

BENEFIT TO THE WARFIGHTER

The 621G Scraper provides cutting, dumping and spreading of soil in worldwide earth-moving and construction projects by Army forces in engineer troop support.

SPECIFICATIONS

- Payload capacity: 52,800 pounds and 22 loose cubic yards
- Cutting width: 119 inches
- Speed: 32 mph fully loaded

PROGRAM STATUS

- **3QFY13-4QFY15:** Fielded 362 621G Scrapers
- **3QFY13-4QFY15:** Trained 357 Soldiers from 60 different units

PROJECTED ACTIVITIES

- **FY16-FY20:** Continue 621G Scraper fielding and training

FOREIGN MILITARY SALES
Iraq and Afghanistan

CONTRACTORS
Caterpillar, Inc. (Peoria, IL)

Advanced Field Artillery Tactical Data System (AFATDS)

PEO Command, Control and Communications – Tactical | Aberdeen Proving Ground, MD

WARFIGHTING FUNCTION

Mission Command

Movement and Maneuver

Intelligence

Fires

Sustainment

Maneuver Support and Protection

Engagement

ACQUISITION LIFECYCLE PHASE

Materiel Solution Analysis

Technology Maturation & Risk Reduction

Engineering & Manufacturing Development

Production & Deployment

Operations & Support

MILESTONE DECISION AUTHORITY

Defense Acquisition Executive

Army Acquisition Executive

Program Executive Officer

DESCRIPTION

The Advanced Field Artillery Tactical Data System (AFATDS) software is used to plan, execute and deliver lethal and nonlethal effects within the overall Mission Command and Control Enterprise. AFATDS interoperates and integrates with more than 80 different battlefield systems, including Navy and Air Force command and control weapon systems and German, French, Turkish and Italian fire-support systems.

AFATDS fuses the essential situational awareness data, intelligence information and targeting data in near real-time to make effective targeting decisions that align with Mission Command guidance and priorities. It pairs targets to weapons to provide optimum use of fire-support assets and timely execution of fire missions. It also automates the planning, coordinating and controlling of all fire-support assets (field artillery, mortars, close air support, naval gunfire, attack helicopters, offensive electronic warfare, fire-support meteorological systems, forward observers and fire-support radars).

The Army Acquisition Executive redesignated AFATDS Increment 2 as a software modernization effort of the existing AFATDS program. AFATDS V7.0 will provide network-based capabilities to enable role- and duty-based functionality, and to establish an architecture for a future single integrated Fires Command and Control System.

BENEFIT TO THE WARFIGHTER

AFATDS provides the Army, Navy and Marine Corps with automated fires-support command, control and communications. It is used to plan, execute and deliver lethal and nonlethal effects. AFATDS also provides Joint/Coalition Situational Awareness for fires execution and mission management.

SPECIFICATIONS

• Windows software runs on ruggedized laptop computer

PROGRAM STATUS

• **3QFY15:** AFATDS V6.8.0.1 fielding complete
• **FY15:** AFATDS Increment 2 designated as Software Modernization effort and to be delivered as AFATDS 7.0
• **1QFY16:** AFATDS 7.0 Software Modernization Request for Proposal release

PROJECTED ACTIVITIES

• **3QFY16:** Network Integration Evaluation 16.2 AFATDS supports Command Post Computing Environment evaluation

AFATDS

FOREIGN MILITARY SALES
Australia, Bahrain, Egypt, Jordan, Portugal, Taiwan and Turkey

CONTRACTORS
Raytheon (Fort Wayne, IN)
General Dynamics (Taunton, MA)

Air and Missile Defense Planning and Control System (AMDPCS)

PEO Missiles and Space | Redstone Arsenal, AL

WARFIGHTING FUNCTION

Mission Command

Movement and Maneuver

Intelligence

Fires

Sustainment

Maneuver Support and Protection

Engagement

ACQUISITION LIFECYCLE PHASE

Materiel Solution Analysis

Technology Maturation & Risk Reduction

Engineering & Manufacturing Development

Production & Deployment

Operations & Support

MILESTONE DECISION AUTHORITY

Defense Acquisition Executive

Army Acquisition Executive

Program Executive Officer

DESCRIPTION

The Air and Missile Defense Planning and Control System (AMDPCS) provides an automated command and control system to integrate Air and Missile Defense planning and operations. There are two configurations of AMDPCS, which are deployed with Air Defense Artillery (ADA) units, including ADA Batteries, Battalions, Brigades and U.S. Army Air and Missile Defense Commands (AAMDC).

A third configuration, the Air Defense and Airspace Management (ADAM), is deployed with Army maneuver units, including Brigade Combat Teams, Functional Support Brigades, and Division and Corps Headquarters. ADAM provides collaboration and staff planning capabilities through Army Mission Command and operational links for airspace coordination with Joint, interagency, multinational and coalition forces.

BENEFIT TO THE WARFIGHTER

AMDPCS in ADA Brigades and AAMDC provides expanded staff planning and coordination capabilities for integrating defense of the air battlespace. ADAM provides maneuver units with collaboration and staff planning capabilities, and operational links for airspace coordination.

SPECIFICATIONS

- AMDPCS includes shelters, automated data processing equipment, tactical communications, standard vehicles, tactical power and two software systems for force and engagement operations:
  › Air and Missile Defense Workstation (AMDWS), a staff planning and battlespace situational awareness tool
  › Air Defense System Integrator (ADSI), a Joint multicommunications processor providing external Joint messages
- ADAM is a standard shelter mounted on a High Mobility Multipurpose Wheeled Vehicle with multiple radios, processors and servers

PROGRAM STATUS

- **FY15:** Production, overhaul and deployment

PROJECTED ACTIVITIES

- **3QFY16:** AMDWS Block V Contract Award
- **1QFY17:** ADAM Common Operating Environment projected for Army Warfighter Assessment 17.1
- **4QFY17:** Field AMDPCS configurations to 263rd AAMDC

FOREIGN MILITARY SALES
None

CONTRACTORS
Northrop Grumman (Huntsville, AL)

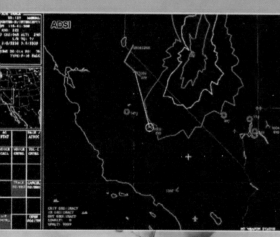

Air Defense Artillery (ADA) Targets

PEO Simulation, Training, and Instrumentation | Orlando, FL

STRI

WARFIGHTING FUNCTION

Mission Command

Movement and Maneuver

Intelligence

Fires

Sustainment

Maneuver Support and Protection

Engagement

ACQUISITION LIFECYCLE PHASE

Materiel Solution Analysis

Technology Maturation & Risk Reduction

Engineering & Manufacturing Development

Production & Deployment

Operations & Support

MILESTONE DECISION AUTHORITY

Defense Acquisition Executive

Army Acquisition Executive

Program Executive Officer

DESCRIPTION

The Air Defense Artillery (ADA) Targets program provides live targets and scoring systems in support of ADA Standards in Training Commission Department of Army Pamphlet 350-38 training and qualification tables. ADA Targets is comprised of three primary components: MQM-170 Remotely Piloted Vehicle Target (RPVT) Outlaw, MTR-15 Ballistic Aerial Target System (BATS) and Scoring Miss Distance Indicator (MDI) systems.

The MQM-170 RPVT Outlaw system and the scoring systems are government-owned/contractor-operated with target operations provided on unit training ranges. The MTR-15 BATS is a government-owned/government-operated system with targets provided to the unit for operation on their ranges. These systems are available for use on DoD test or training ranges within the continental United States and overseas, as well as in support of foreign military sales clients.

Crew-gunnery and live-fire training are conducted using various unmanned aerial targets. The targets are threat representative of real cruise missiles, unmanned aircraft systems and tactical fixed-wing aircraft currently being employed against U.S. forces. These targets must be capable of representing generic threat characteristics and must allow the ADA weapon systems crew to employ missile and gun systems to engage and destroy the target systems. ADA unit training programs must result in demonstrated tactical and technical competence, Soldier confidence in their weapon systems, and the abilities of our Soldiers to employ their weapon systems in a field environment.

BENEFIT TO THE WARFIGHTER

The ADA Targets program is an integral part of supporting ground combat readiness. ADA units cannot train or maintain certification for their wartime mission without enemy-representative targets supporting their live-fire training events.

SPECIFICATIONS

The ADA Targets program is composed of three primary components:
- MQM-170 RPVT Outlaw
- MTR-15 BATS
- Scoring MDI systems

PROGRAM STATUS
- **2QFY15:** Annual Gunnery Qualification Training for Avenger and Indirect Fire Protection Capability Army Air Defense units
- **3QFY15:** Marine Corps Stinger Training
- **4QFY15:** Navy Carrier fleet (surrogate threat Unmanned Aircraft Systems (UAS)) training and surrogate UAS joint testing requirements

PROJECTED ACTIVITIES
- **FY16-17:** Continued support for ADA Qualification Training, Black Dart Counter UAS demonstration support, National Training Center Surrogate Intelligence, Surveillance and Reconnaissance, UAS Opposing Force training with other Combat Training Center involvement, continued support for testing, and support for multiple Research, Development, Test & Evaluation activities for Army and other military services laboratories

FOREIGN MILITARY SALES
Israel, Japan, Portugal and NATO Support Agency

CONTRACTORS
Griffon Aerospace (Madison, AL)

Air Soldier System (Air SS)

PEO Soldier | Fort Belvoir, VA

DESCRIPTION

The Air Soldier System (Air SS) is flight crew life support equipment that improves mission effectiveness and duration by integrating protective clothing, personal electronics and survival equipment. Mission and survival gear sustains the aviation Soldier in water immersion, extreme heat and cold, and protects the Soldier from flash fire, crash impact, and chemical and ballistic threats. Air SS reduces body-worn bulk and weight and provides a helmet-mounted display with symbology to improve flight crew coordination and safety in all conditions, including Degraded Visual Environments (DVE).

BENEFIT TO THE WARFIGHTER

Air SS, through a Soldier-as-a-System approach, improves cockpit compatibility by reducing body-worn bulk and weight, enhances Situational Awareness (SA) and safety, including in DVE, and increases mission duration and effectiveness.

SPECIFICATIONS

- Mission Display Module and Soldier Computer Module for UH-60A/L aviators provides SA, mission planning and execution and command and control messaging
- Improved HGU-56/P Flight Helmet enhances SA and safety for aircrews
- Electronic Flight Bag tactical tablet replaces paper-based information in the cockpit
- Common Helmet Mounted Display offers digital, wide field of view, color flat-panel display for UH-60 and CH-47 aviators
- Helmet Head Tracking improves SA for UH-60 and CH-47 aviators
- Layered Clothing Ensemble (LCE) improves mission effectiveness and endurance
- 3D DVE conformal symbology improves SA and safety for UH-60 and CH-47 aviators
- 72-hour Survival Items reduce bulk and weight

- Aircrew Combat Ensemble reduces weight and bulk, integrates the Soldier Protection System modular ballistic system, and enhances compatibility and stowage interface for current and future clothing and individual equipment

PROGRAM STATUS

- **4QFY15:** Operational and Limited User Tests led by Operational Test Command; UH-60M and CH-47F aircrews from the 25th Combat Aviation Brigade evaluated the Air SS including:
  - › LCE
  - › Improved flight helmet
  - › Helmet Display and Tracking System
  - › Day/Night Helmet Mounted Displays
  - › Enhanced HMD Symbology

PROJECTED ACTIVITIES

- **3QFY16:** Capability Production Document approval/Milestone C
- **4QFY16:** Complete first follow-on Development Test/Operational Test

Air SS

FOREIGN MILITARY SALES
None

CONTRACTORS
Government is the prime integrator with various vendors providing components.

Platform-mounted **Mission Display Module (MDM)** and **Soldier Computer Module (SCM)** for UH-60A/L aviators; provides Situational Awareness, mission planning and execution, and C2 messaging

Helmet mounted components   Aircraft mounted components

Notional CHMD; material solution is TBD

Common Helmet Mounted Display (CHMD) Digital Wide FoV color flat-panel display for UH-60 and CH-47 aviators

Helmet Head Tracking improves SA for UH-60 and CH-47 aviators through other pilot Line of Sight capability; enables 3D DVE symbology; includes Soldier worn and aircraft mounted components

3D DVE conformal symbology displayed on the CHMD improves SA and safety for CH-47 and UH-60 aviators

Improved HGU-56/P Flight Helmet enhances SA and safety for aircrews on all platforms (except Apache) through improved Field Of View, energy absorbing liner, and retention assembly

Electronic Flight Bag (P3I) tactical tablet replaces paper-based Flight Information Publications in the cockpit

Layered Clothing Ensemble (LCE)

Lightweight Cooling Vest

Small Arms Ballisitc Insert (SABI)

Lightweight Immersion Suit for Aviation (LISA)

Lightweight JPACE

The **LCE** is integrated thermal, immersion, heat and flame, and Chem/Bio protection; also includes modifications to the AW survival vest to provide bulk and weight reduction, improves mission effectiveness and mission endurance

72 Hour Survival Items

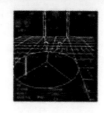

Standardized, integrated personal survival items reduce bulk and weight

Aircrew Combat Ensemble (P3I) reduces weight and bulk, integrates the Soldier Protection System modular ballistic system, and enhances capability and stowage interface for current and future clothing and individual equipment

Air Warrior (AW)

PEO Soldier | Fort Belvoir, VA

WARFIGHTING FUNCTION

Mission Command

Movement and Maneuver

Intelligence

Fires

Sustainment

Maneuver Support and Protection

Engagement

ACQUISITION LIFECYCLE PHASE

Materiel Solution Analysis

Technology Maturation & Risk Reduction

Engineering & Manufacturing Development

Production & Deployment

Operations & Support

MILESTONE DECISION AUTHORITY

Defense Acquisition Executive

Army Acquisition Executive

Program Executive Officer

DESCRIPTION

Air Warrior (AW) is a modular, integrated, rapidly reconfigurable combat aircrew ensemble that saves lives and maximizes Army aircrew mission performance. Previous aviation life-support equipment consisted of a nonintegrated assemblage of protective and survival gear. AW uses a systems approach to equip the aircrew and close the capability gap between human and machine. Fielded incrementally in blocks to rapidly provide enhanced capabilities to the warfighter, AW leverages and integrates clothing and equipment, such as the Army Aircrew Combat Uniform and ballistic protection from other product managers.

BENEFIT TO THE WARFIGHTER

AW provides enhanced mission effectiveness, leveraging clothing and equipment to maximize aircrew member survivability.

SPECIFICATIONS

AW Block I provides:
- Survival Equipment Subsystem that integrates first aid, survival, signaling and communications equipment with body armor and over-water survival subsystems
- Microclimate Cooling System that increases effective mission duration in heat-stress environments by more than 350 percent
- Aircrew Integrated Helmet System, a lighter helmet, which increases head and hearing protection

AW Increment 3 provides:
- Electronic Data Manager, a portable digital-mission planning device that provides over-the-horizon messaging and enhanced situational awareness capabilities through connectivity to Blue Force Tracking-Aviation
- Aircraft Wireless Intercom System that provides secure cordless, hands-free aircrew communications
- Survival Kit, Ready Access, Modular Go-Bag that delivers integrated hydration

- Portable Helicopter Oxygen Delivery System, which is a Soldier-worn supplemental breathing oxygen system for high-altitude operations
- Communication Enhancement and Protection System that allows for helmet hear-through capability

PROGRAM STATUS

- **Current:** Transitioned to Sustainment

PROJECTED ACTIVITIES

- None

FOREIGN MILITARY SALES
Australia, Bahrain, Canada and United
Arab Emirates

CONTRACTORS
**Government is the prime integrator with
various vendors providing components:**
Telephonics Corp. (Farmingdale, NY)
Carleton Technologies, Inc. (Orchard Park, NY)
Raytheon Technical Services (Indianapolis, IN)
Communications & Ear Protection (CEP), Inc. (Enterprise, AL)
Science and Engineering Services, Inc. (SESI) (Huntsville, AL)
Gibson & Barnes (Santa Clara, CA)
Gentex Corp. (Rancho Cucamonga, CA)
Rini Technologies (Oviedo, FL)
Switlik Parachute Co. (Trenton, NJ)

Airborne Reconnaissance Low (ARL)

ACAT II

PEO Aviation | Redstone Arsenal, AL

WARFIGHTING FUNCTION

Mission Command

Movement and Maneuver

Intelligence

Fires

Sustainment

Maneuver Support and Protection

Engagement

ACQUISITION LIFECYCLE PHASE

Materiel Solution Analysis

Technology Maturation & Risk Reduction

Engineering & Manufacturing Development

Production & Deployment

Operations & Support

MILESTONE DECISION AUTHORITY

Defense Acquisition Executive

Army Acquisition Executive

Program Executive Officer

DESCRIPTION

Airborne Reconnaissance Low (ARL) is a self-deploying, multisensor, day and night, all-weather reconnaissance and intelligence system. It consists of a modified DeHavilland Canada (DHC)-7 fixed-wing aircraft equipped with communications intelligence and imagery intelligence (COMINT/IMINT), Ground Moving Target Indicator/Synthetic Aperture Radar (SAR), and electro-optical and infrared full-motion video capability. The payloads are controlled and operated via onboard open-architecture, multifunction workstations. Intelligence collected on the ARL can be analyzed, recorded and disseminated on the aircraft workstations in real time and stored onboard for post-mission processing.

The ARL system includes a variety of communications subsystems to support near-real-time dissemination of intelligence and dynamic retasking of the aircraft. It provides real-time down-link of Moving Target Indicator (MTI) data to the Common Ground Station at the Brigade Combat Team through echelon-above-corps level. Seven aircraft are configured as ARL-Multifunction (ARL-M), equipped with a combination of IMINT, COMINT and SAR/MTI payload and demonstrated hyperspectral imager applications and multi-intelligence data fusion capabilities.

The ARL systems currently hosted on DHC-7 airframes will soon be replaced by more capable DHC-8-315 airframes. By leveraging existing DHC-8 platforms currently used within operational Quick Reaction Capability programs, the Army will meet the recently approved Capability Production Document requirements with added aircraft performance capabilities.

BENEFIT TO THE WARFIGHTER

ARL provides tactical commanders with day and night, near-all-weather, real-time airborne COMINT/IMINT collection and a designated area surveillance system. It can support collection requirements of Brigade Combat Teams and higher echelons across the full range of military operations, including coalition support processes.

SPECIFICATIONS

- Dual electro-optical Day and Night High-Definition Full Motion Video Sensors with Laser Range Finding and Target Designation Capability
- Tactical Signals and Communication Intelligence/Direction Finding Subsystems with Aerial Precision Geolocation and Theater Net-Centric Geolocation
- Synthetic Aperture Radar and Ground-Moving Target Indicator Radar

PROGRAM STATUS

- **3QFY13:** Workstation and Beyond-Line-of-Sight upgrades
- **FY13-FY14:** Continue imagery, radar, COMINT, system interoperability, and workstation architecture upgrades
- **3QFY14:** ARL-Enhanced (ARL-E) Capability Production Document was approved
- **3QFY15:** Aircraft Survivability Equipment (ASE) and cockpit updates began
- **4QFY15:** Army Acquisition Executive redesignated ARL as ACAT II program with PEO Aviation as the Milestone Decision Authority (MDA) and ARL Payloads as ACAT III with PEO Intelligence, Electronic Warfare and Sensors as the MDA
- **1QFY16:** Project Manager, Sensor-Aerial Intelligence (PM SAI) awards Mission Equipment Package (MEP) contract for the ARL-E program; MEP integration will fulfill the ARL-E CPD sensor requirements

PROJECTED ACTIVITIES

- **FY16:** PM Fixed Wing (FW) delivers two ARL-E Cockpit/ASE modified aircraft for induction into the ARL-E MEP integration effort
- **FY17:** PM FW delivers two ARL-E Cockpit/ASE modified aircraft for induction into the ARL-E MEP integration effort
- **FY18:** PM SAI performs Systems Integration Laboratory/aircraft MEP integration; Two systems fielded

FOREIGN MILITARY SALES
None

CONTRACTORS
King Aerospace, Inc. (Addison, TX)
Adams Communication and Engineering
Technology (Waldorf, MD)
Sierra Nevada Corp. (Hagerstown, MD)
Litton Advanced Systems (Gaithersburg, MD)
BAE Systems (Manchester, NH)
WESCAM (Hamilton, Ontario, Canada)
Lockheed Martin (Phoenix, AZ)
Leidos, Inc. (Reston, VA)

AN/MPQ-64 Sentinel

PEO Missiles and Space | Redstone Arsenal, AL

WARFIGHTING FUNCTION

Mission Command

Movement and Maneuver

Intelligence

Fires

Sustainment

Maneuver Support and Protection

Engagement

ACQUISITION LIFECYCLE PHASE

Materiel Solution Analysis

Technology Maturation & Risk Reduction

Engineering & Manufacturing Development

Production & Deployment

Operations & Support

MILESTONE DECISION AUTHORITY

Defense Acquisition Executive

Army Acquisition Executive

Program Executive Officer

DESCRIPTION

The AN/MPQ-64 Sentinel provides persistent air surveillance and fire control quality data through command and control systems to defeat unmanned aerial systems (UAS), cruise missiles and fixed- and rotary-wing aircraft threats.

The system features an X-Band, 360-degree phased array air defense radar with a 75-km instrumented range. It is equipped with Electronic Counter-Counter-Measure (ECCM) capabilities, a Mode 5 Identification Friend or Foe subsystem for positive identification of friendly aircraft, and Non-Cooperative Target Recognition capabilities to identify threat aircraft. Sentinel is trailer-mounted, pulled by either a High Mobility Multipurpose Wheeled Vehicle or an M1082 Family of Medium Tactical Vehicles (FMTV) truck. The system generator with a command and control interface is mounted on the vehicle.

Sentinel interfaces with the Integrated Air and Missile Defense (IAMD) Battle Command System architecture, the Forward Area Air Defense Command and Control System, and the National Capital Region Integrated Air Defense Command and Control System. Sentinel also interfaces with the Counter-Rocket, Artillery, Mortar (C-RAM) Increment 1 system to protect friendly aircraft during engagement of incoming indirect fire.

Sentinel is undergoing modifications to further enhance its UAS and cruise missile detection and tracking capability. Additional modifications are ongoing to convert all radars from the AN/MPQ-64A1 Improved Sentinel configuration to the AN/MPQ-64A3 Enhanced Sentinel. In addition to internal improvements, Enhanced Sentinel is integrated with the FMTV to enable additional vehicle cab armor protection for its two-man crew.

BENEFIT TO THE WARFIGHTER

Sentinel provides persistent air surveillance and fire control quality data to the warfighter through command and control systems to defeat unmanned aerial systems, cruise missiles and fixed- and rotary-wing aircraft threats.

SPECIFICATIONS

- All-weather, 360-degree capability
- Range: 75 km
- Three-dimensional X-Band radar
- Supports current AMD, C-RAM and Integrated Fire Protection Capability (IFPC) Block 1

PROGRAM STATUS

- **3QFY15-4QFY15:** Sentinel support to IAMD Flight Tests
- **3QFY15:** Begin full fleet upgrade to the FMTV platform
- **1QFY16:** Sentinel A3 Materiel Release

PROJECTED ACTIVITIES

- **1QFY16-2QFY16:** Sentinel support to IAMD Flight Tests and Limited User Test
- **2QFY17:** Sentinel Software Materiel Release supporting IAMD
- **2QFY18:** Sentinel software upgrade supporting IFPC Block 1 Limited User Test
- **1QFY19:** Sentinel Modernization Milestone B

AN/MPQ-64

FOREIGN MILITARY SALES
Egypt, Lithuania, Turkey, Latvia and Iraq
The Cruise Missile Defense Systems Project Office established a Sentinel Radar Software International Engineering Services Program with six partner nations: Oman, Egypt, Norway, Netherlands, Finland and Chile
Direct Commercial Sales (hardware) with classified software sold via foreign military sales (U.S. government controls Sentinel software): Norway, Netherlands, Spain, Mexico, Finland and Oman

CONTRACTORS
Thales Raytheon Systems (Fullerton, CA; El Paso, TX; Forest, MS; Largo, FL)
SETA Contract: IRTC (Huntsville, AL)

AN/TPQ-50 Lightweight Counter Mortar Radar (LCMR)

PEO Missiles and Space | Redstone Arsenal, AL

WARFIGHTING FUNCTION

Mission Command

Movement and Maneuver

Intelligence

Fires

Sustainment

Maneuver Support and Protection

Engagement

ACQUISITION LIFECYCLE PHASE

Materiel Solution Analysis

Technology Maturation & Risk Reduction

Engineering & Manufacturing Development

Production & Deployment

Operations & Support

MILESTONE DECISION AUTHORITY

Defense Acquisition Executive

Army Acquisition Executive

Program Executive Officer

DESCRIPTION

The AN/TPQ-50 Lightweight Counter Mortar Radar (LCMR) identifies indirect fire threats by providing the ability to rapidly locate rockets, artillery and mortar (RAM) firing positions automatically by detecting and tracking the shell and backtracking to the weapon position. The system provides observed fires (for friendly fires) and accurate "did hit" data of friendly fires, and detects and templates hostile locations.

BENEFIT TO THE WARFIGHTER

The AN/TPQ-50 provides continuous surveillance to indicate an incoming RAM round. The system consists of a laptop for man-machine interface and a radar processor with electronics housed inside a cylinder surrounded by antenna columns. It can be assembled and disassembled quickly by two Soldiers. The AN/TPQ-50 is a critical sensor to the Counter-Rocket, Artillery, Mortar (C-RAM) system of systems.

SPECIFICATIONS

- Provides continuous 360-degree battlefield surveillance coverage for mortars, artillery and rockets with an effective range out to 10 km
- Can be operated in a stand-alone or vehicle-mounted configuration
- Organic to Brigade Combat Teams and Fires Brigades
- Deployable with Indirect Fire Protection Capability

PROGRAM STATUS

- **3QFY13:** Full Rate Production (FRP) Decision Review
- **4QFY13:** FRP Contract Award
- **3QFY14:** Initial Operational Capability
- **1QFY15:** First FRP systems fielded
- **4QFY15:** Two systems provided to support Special Operations Command Operational Needs Statement

PROJECTED ACTIVITIES

- **2QFY16:** FRP Procurement of 39 AN/TPQ-50 systems
- **3QFY16:** Award of Research, Development, Test and Evaluation contract to develop enhanced Electronic Protect capability
- **4QFY16:** FRP Contract Extension Award
- **3QFY17:** Final procurement of 46 AN/TPQ-50 systems (for a total of 371 systems)
- **4QFY17:** Begin developmental testing on Pre-Planned Program Improvements upgrade (prototype) kits

AN/TPQ-53 Counterfire Target Acquisition Radar (formerly known as the Enhanced AN/TPQ-36)

PEO Missiles and Space | Redstone Arsenal, AL

WARFIGHTING FUNCTION

Mission Command

Movement and Maneuver

Intelligence

Fires

Sustainment

Maneuver Support and Protection

Engagement

ACQUISITION LIFECYCLE PHASE

Materiel Solution Analysis

Technology Maturation & Risk Reduction

Engineering & Manufacturing Development

Production & Deployment

Operations & Support

MILESTONE DECISION AUTHORITY

Defense Acquisition Executive

Army Acquisition Executive

Program Executive Officer

DESCRIPTION

AN/TPQ-53 Counterfire Target Acquisition Radar is a new generation of counterfire sensor. The AN/TPQ-53 detects, classifies, tracks, determines the location of, and provides accurate, targetable data regarding enemy mortars, cannon and rockets in either 360- or 90-degree modes. It replaces the current AN/TPQ-36 and AN/TPQ-37 Firefinder radar systems.

BENEFIT TO THE WARFIGHTER

Compared to current AN/TPQ-36 and AN/TPQ-37 Firefinder systems, AN/TPQ-53 offers enhanced performance, including greater mobility, increased reliability and supportability, lower lifecycle cost, reduced crew size, and the ability to track targets in a full-spectrum environment—a vital capability on today's battlefield.

SPECIFICATIONS

- Mounts on the 5-ton Family of Medium Tactical Vehicles prime mover
- Rapidly deployable to, and integrated into, the tactical battlefield with heavy, medium, light forces
- Mobile, maneuverable, fully supportable, easily maintained
- Target Acquisition Subsystem contains radar on a single prime mover and tows power generator; this package performs all essential missions of the Q-53 for short durations
- Second prime mover carries operations control shelter, backup power generator and two additional Soldiers to provide sustained operations capability

PROGRAM STATUS

- **2QFY13:** Limited User Test
- **1QFY14:** Initial Operational Test & Evaluation (IOT&E)
- **3QFY15:** Successful IOT&E 2 Completion
- **4QFY15:**
  › Retrofit 1 Contract Award
  › Full-Rate Production (FRP) Decision Review
  › Q-53 supporting Operation Inherent Resolve
  › Low-Rate Initial Production (LRIP) Lot 5 Contract Award
  › LRIP Contract Line Item Number 5002/5003 Contract Award
- **1QFY16:**
  › U.S. Army Test and Evaluation Command Operational Evaluation Report
  › Director Operational Test and Evaluation IOT&E Report
  › FRP Request for Proposal released
  › FRP Decision Memorandum signed

PROJECTED ACTIVITIES

- **2QFY16:** Conditional Materiel Release of AN/TPQ-53
- **3QFY16:** Fielding of AN/TPQ-53 begins
- **4QFY16:** FRP Contract Award

FOREIGN MILITARY SALES
Singapore

CONTRACTORS
Lockheed Martin (Syracuse, NY)

Army Key Management System (AKMS)

PEO Command, Control and Communications – Tactical | Aberdeen Proving Ground, MD

WARFIGHTING FUNCTION

Mission Command

Movement and Maneuver

Intelligence

Fires

Sustainment

Maneuver Support and Protection

Engagement

ACQUISITION LIFECYCLE PHASE

Materiel Solution Analysis

Technology Maturation & Risk Reduction

Engineering & Manufacturing Development

Production & Deployment

Operations & Support

MILESTONE DECISION AUTHORITY

Defense Acquisition Executive

Army Acquisition Executive

Program Executive Officer

DESCRIPTION

Under the umbrella of the National Security Agency Electronic Key Management System, the Army Key Management System (AKMS) provides tactical units and sustaining bases with an organic-key generation capability and an efficient, secure electronic key distribution means. AKMS consists of three subcomponents: Local Communications Security (COMSEC) Management Software (LCMS), Automated Communications Engineering Software (ACES) and Simple Key Loader (SKL). The system introduces capabilities and processes to transform operations from manual to secure automated distribution of keys and firmware directly to Information Assurance devices.

AKMS expands operations to DoD's unclassified network to reach a broader DoD customer base as well as to NATO and coalition users to support combatant commanders' needs. Additionally, the system offers flexibility and agility to support dynamic communities of interest.

BENEFIT TO THE WARFIGHTER

AKMS provides a system for distribution of COMSEC, electronic protection and Signal Operating Instructions (SOI) information from the planning level to the point of use in support of current, interim and objective forces at division and brigade levels.

SPECIFICATIONS

- Management Client Nodes (MGC): Automate COMSEC management and accounting; electronically generate and distributes keys; reduce hardcopy files use
- ACES and Joint Automated COMSEC System: Provides crypto network planning; generates SOI data and creates COMSEC key tags; supports emerging requirements
- Next Generation Load Device : Loads keys into End Cryptographic Units (ECU); small and ruggedized design allows easy key transfers; interface between LCMS and MGC (Key Generation), ACES and ECUs

PROGRAM STATUS

- **FY12-FY17:** Continue to procure and field SKLs for Air Force, Navy, Foreign Military Sales and other government organizations
- **3QFY12:** Key Management Infrastructure Initial Operational Capability
- **FY13:** ACES software upgrade version 3.2
- **FY14:**
  › SKL upgrade to SKLv3.1
  › ACES software upgrade version 3.3; SKL software upgrade version 9.0

PROJECTED ACTIVITIES

- **1QFY17:** SKL Next Generation Load Device Request for Proposal

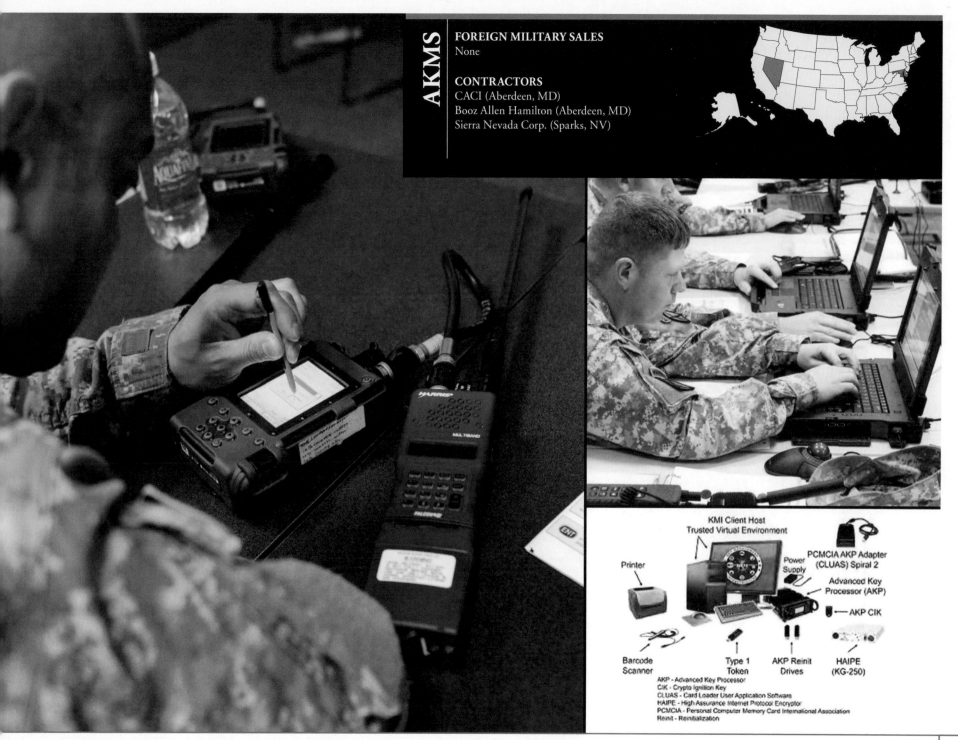

FOREIGN MILITARY SALES
None

CONTRACTORS
CACI (Aberdeen, MD)
Booz Allen Hamilton (Aberdeen, MD)
Sierra Nevada Corp. (Sparks, NV)

KMI Client Host
Trusted Virtual Environment

PCMCIA AKP Adapter
(CLUAS) Spiral 2

Power
Supply

Printer

Advanced Key
Processor (AKP)

AKP CIK

Barcode
Scanner

Type 1
Token

AKP Reinit
Drives

HAIPE
(KG-250)

AKP - Advanced Key Processor
CIK - Crypto Ignition Key
CLUAS - Card Loader User Application Software
HAIPE - High Assurance Internet Protocol Encryptor
PCMCIA - Personal Computer Memory Card International Association
Reinit - Reinitialization

Army Watercraft Systems (AWS)

PEO Combat Support and Combat Service Support | Detroit Arsenal, MI

DESCRIPTION

Army Watercraft Systems expand commanders' movement and maneuver options in support of unified land operations. The current fleet of 132 AWS enables commanders to operate through fixed, degraded and austere ports, conducting expeditionary sustainment and movement and maneuver of forces for missions across the spectrum of military operations. The vessels vary widely in age and do not have a single manufacturer.

BENEFIT TO THE WARFIGHTER

AWS deliver combat-configured equipment with personnel, vehicles and sustainment cargo to a wide variety of ports, providing commanders the ability to move strategic support and supplies within their respective areas of responsibility.

SPECIFICATIONS

Landing Craft: Provide inter- and intratheater transportation of personnel and materiel, delivering cargo from advanced bases and deep-draft strategic sealift ships to harbors, inland waterways, remote and unimproved beaches and coastlines, and denied or degraded ports
- Logistic Support Vessel
- Landing Craft Utility (LCU-2000)
- Landing Craft Mechanized (LCM-8) to be replaced by Maneuver Support Vessel (Light) (MSV(L))

Ship-to-Shore Enablers: Enable the discharge of strategic sealift ships when suitable ports are unavailable while at anchor or onto degraded ports or bare beaches; causeway systems enable Joint and Army forces to load, transload, and offload equipment, personnel and sustainment cargo during sea-based operations, operations in degraded or austere ports, and bare-beach, Joint logistics over-the-shore operations
- Modular Warping Tug
- Roll-on/Roll-off Discharge Facility
- Floating Causeway
- Causeway Ferry

Towing and Terminal Operations: Provide heavy lifting, ocean and port/harbor towing, and salvage operations in open, denied or degraded ports; used for general port management and husbandry duties (storing fuel, repositioning barges, firefighting, docking and undocking large ships); can clear and operate ports (fixed, degraded and austere) while providing coordinated, simultaneous support to multiple sustainment operations sites widely distributed throughout the area of operations
- Large Tug (LT-800)
- Small Tug (ST-900)
- Barge Derrick (BD 115-ton)

PROGRAM STATUS

LCU-2000 Command, Control, Communications, Computers, Intelligence, Surveillance and Reconnaissance (C4ISR) Modernization:
- **1QFY14:** Low-Rate Initial Production
- **1QFY15:** Full-Rate Production

LCU-2000 Service Life Extension Program (SLEP):
- **4QFY15:** Request for Proposal (RFP) for Phase (PH) I of the SLEP effort

PROJECTED ACTIVITIES

LCU-2000 C4ISR Modernization:
- **FY16-FY18:** Ongoing upgrades for LCU-2000 vessels

LCU-2000 SLEP:
- **3QFY16:** Contract Award for LCU SLEP PH I

MSV(L):
- **3QFY16:** RFP; Preparation for Milestone B
- **2QFY17:** Milestone B
- **3QFY17:** Contract Award

FOREIGN MILITARY SALES
None

CONTRACTORS
MSV(L): TBD
LCU SLEP: TBD
LCU-2000 C4ISR Modernization (Integrator):
SPAWAR Systems Center Atlantic (North
Charleston, SC)

Artillery Ammunition

PEO Ammunition | Picatinny Arsenal, NJ

WARFIGHTING FUNCTION

Mission Command

Movement and Maneuver

Intelligence

Fires

Sustainment

Maneuver Support and Protection

Engagement

ACQUISITION LIFECYCLE PHASE

Materiel Solution Analysis

Technology Maturation & Risk Reduction

Engineering & Manufacturing Development

Production & Deployment

Operations & Support

MILESTONE DECISION AUTHORITY

Defense Acquisition Executive

Army Acquisition Executive

Program Executive Officer

DESCRIPTION

The Army's artillery ammunition program includes 75 mm (used for ceremonies and simulated firing), 105 mm and 155 mm projectiles and their associated fuses and propelling charges.

Semifixed ammunition for short and intermediate ranges, used in 105 mm Howitzers, is characterized by adjusting the number of multiple propelling charges. Semifixed ammunition for long ranges contains a single bag of propellant optimized for obtaining high velocity, and is not adjustable. The primer is an integral part of the cartridge case, and is located in the base. The 105 mm cartridges are issued in a fused or unfused configuration. Both cartridge configurations are packaged with propellant.

Separate-loading ammunition, used in 155 mm Howitzers, has separately issued projectiles, fuses, propellant charges and primers. After installing the appropriate fuse on the projectile, the fused projectile is loaded into the cannon along with the appropriate amount of propellant charges and a primer.

The artillery ammunition program includes fuses for cargo-carrying projectiles, such as smoke and illumination, and bursting projectiles, such as high explosives. This program also includes bag propellant for the 105 mm semifixed cartridges and a modular artillery charge system for 155 mm Howitzers.

BENEFIT TO THE WARFIGHTER

The mission of the Field Artillery is to destroy, defeat or disrupt the enemy with integrated fires to enable maneuver commanders to dominate in unified land operations. Cannon-artillery-delivered munitions are a vital component of this mission.

SPECIFICATIONS

- Insensitive munitions (IM) fill is used in the following high explosive rounds, making the inventory safer: 105 mm M1; 105 mm M1130; 155 mm M1122; 155 mm M795
- Projectiles that utilize shell bodies obtained from 155 mm cluster munitions that have been demilitarized, significantly lowering unit cost: The M1122, 155 mm IM High-Explosive; M1123, 155 mm Infrared Illumination; M1124, 155 mm Visible Light Illumination; M110A3, 155 mm Spotting Smoke

PROGRAM STATUS

- **2QFY13:** Type Classified – Standard (TC-STD) achieved for the 155 mm Joint Extended-Range Illumination Projectiles M1123 and M1124, followed by Full Materiel Release in 3QFY14
- **3QFY13:** Commenced M739A1 fuse production to incorporate an enhanced safe-and-arm design to eliminate possibility of fuses inadvertently shipped in an armed condition
- **1QFY14:** M795 IM commenced Full-Rate Production (FRP); first 53,000 projectiles delivered to Army and Marine Corps customers in 2QFY15
- **3QFY15:** FRP of 155 mm M1122 commenced at McAlester Army Ammunition Plant, and Crane Army Ammunition Activity established as second source of 155 mm M1122
- **FY15:** Completed M82 155 mm primer design change for Paladin Integrated Management (PIM) Program

PROJECTED ACTIVITIES

- **FY16:** FRP for 155 mm Joint Extended-Range Illumination Projectiles M1123 and M1124 commences at Pine Bluff Arsenal
- **4QFY16:** Produce and deliver new production M82 primers in support of PIM Program Initial Operational Test & Evaluation
- **TBD:** Achieve TC-STD for Extended-Range Smoke 155 mm M110A2E1

FOREIGN MILITARY SALES

Fielded with multiple countries—names for official use only and not for public disclosure

CONTRACTORS

Action Manufacturing (Bristol, PA)
American Ordnance (Middletown, IA)
ARMTEC (Coachella, CA)
Bluegrass Army Depot (Lexington, KY)
Chemring Ordnance (Perry, FL)
Crane Army Ammunition Activity (Crane, IN)
Day & Zimmermann-Lone Star (Texarkana, TX)
General Dynamics Ordnance and Tactical Systems (Fort Lauderdale, FL; LeGardeur, Canada)
General Dynamics Ordnance and Tactical Systems-Scranton Operations (Scranton, PA)
Holston Army Ammunition Plant (Kingsport, TN)
McAlester Army Ammunition Plant (McAlester, OK)
Orbital ATK (Minneapolis, MN)
Pine Bluff Arsenal (Pine Bluff, AR)

Assault Breacher Vehicle (ABV)

PEO Combat Support and Combat Service Support | Detroit Arsenal, MI

WARFIGHTING FUNCTION

Mission Command

Movement and Maneuver

Intelligence

Fires

Sustainment

Maneuver Support and Protection

Engagement

ACQUISITION LIFECYCLE PHASE

Materiel Solution Analysis

Technology Maturation & Risk Reduction

Engineering & Manufacturing Development

Production & Deployment

Operations & Support

MILESTONE DECISION AUTHORITY

Defense Acquisition Executive

Army Acquisition Executive

Program Executive Officer

DESCRIPTION

The Assault Breacher Vehicle (ABV) is a highly mobile and heavily armored minefield and complex obstacle breaching system. It consists of an M1A1 Abrams tank hull; a unique turret with two Linear Demolition Charge Systems (employing two Mine Clearing Line Charges (MICLIC) and rockets); a Lane Marking System (LMS); Integrated Vision System; and a High Lift Adapter that interchangeably mounts a Full Width Mine Plow (FWMP) or a Combat Dozer Blade (CDB).

The ABV, which requires a crew of two Soldiers, improves the mobility and survivability of combat engineers while having the speed and ability to keep pace with the maneuver force. It creates a tank-width cleared lane through a minefield by launching and detonating one of its MICLIC systems across the minefield, then proofing the lane with its FWMP while marking the cleared lane with its LMS.

The ABV is fielded to the Combat Engineer Company organic to the Brigade Special Troops Battalion of Armored Brigade Combat Teams (ABCT). Each ABCT receives six ABV, four FWMP and two CDB. The ABV is air-transportable by C-17 and larger aircraft.

BENEFIT TO THE WARFIGHTER

The ABV provides crew protection and vehicle survivability while having the speed and mobility to keep pace with the maneuver force. Commonality of support (M1A1) is also a significant benefit to the Soldier.

SPECIFICATIONS

- ABV's M1A1 chassis is very similar to the Abrams in terms of size, weight, speed and range

PROGRAM STATUS

Fieldings:

- **2QFY13:** 1st Brigade (Bde), 34th Infantry Division (Div), MN Army National Guard (ARNG)
- **3QFY13:** 1st Bde 2d Infantry Div
- **4QFY13:** 155th Infantry Bde Separate (SEP) MS ARNG
- **1QFY14:** 1st Bde 1st Cavalry Div
- **2QFY14:** 3d Bde 1st Cavalry Div
- **3QFY14:** 2d Bde 1st Cavalry Div
- **1QFY15:** 4th Bde 1st Armored Div
- **2QFY15:**
  › 2d Bde 1st Infantry Div
  › 1st Bde 1st Infantry Div
- **3QFY15:** 2d Bde 1st Armored Div
- **1QFY16:** 3d Bde 4th Infantry Div

PROJECTED ACTIVITIES

Fieldings:

- **3QFY16:** 116th Infantry Bde SEP OR ARNG
- **3QFY17:** Army Preposition Stock

FOREIGN MILITARY SALES
None

CONTRACTORS
Integration: Anniston Army Depot
(Anniston, AL)
Front End Equipment: URS Corp.
(Albuquerque, NM)
Line Demolition Charge System: DRS
(Los Angeles, CA)
Technical Manuals: XMCO, Inc. (Warren, MI)

Autonomous Mine Detection System (AMDS)

PEO Ammunition | Picatinny Arsenal, NJ

WARFIGHTING FUNCTION

Mission Command

Movement and Maneuver

Intelligence

Fires

Sustainment

Maneuver Support and Protection

Engagement

ACQUISITION LIFECYCLE PHASE

Materiel Solution Analysis

Technology Maturation & Risk Reduction

Engineering & Manufacturing Development

Production & Deployment

Operations & Support

MILESTONE DECISION AUTHORITY

Defense Acquisition Executive

Army Acquisition Executive

Program Executive Officer

DESCRIPTION

Autonomous Mine Detection System (AMDS), a counter-improvised explosive device system, provides standoff detection, marking, and neutralizing capability of explosive hazards, booby-traps and unexploded ordnance in complex and urban terrain in support of route clearance operations. AMDS is a mission equipment package mounted on current and programmed man-portable unmanned ground vehicles organic to infantry and engineer units.

BENEFIT TO THE WARFIGHTER

AMDS detects, marks and neutralizes explosive hazards; operates in complex and urban terrain, including confined areas and subterranean environments; minimizes warfighter workload; enhances the rate of advance; and moves the warfighter out of the blast zone.

SPECIFICATIONS

- Scans a path with a ground penetrating radar and metal detector, marks the explosive hazards detected and neutralizes the explosive hazards while undercover

PROGRAM STATUS

- **1QFY14:** Milestone B, entering Engineering and Manufacturing Development
- **4QFY14:** Contract Award
- **1QFY15:** System Functional Review
- **2QFY15:**
  › Preliminary Design Review
  › Integrated Baseline Review
- **4QFY15:** Contractor Development Tests initiated
- **1QFY16:** Risk Reduction Test

PROJECTED ACTIVITIES

- **2QFY16:** Critical Design Review
- **3QFY16:** Developmental Test
- **4QFY16:** Logistics Demonstration
- **1QFY17:** Limited User Test
- **3QFY17:** Milestone C, entering Production and Deployment
- **4QFY17:** First Article Test

Aviation Combined Arms Tactical Trainer (AVCATT)

PEO Simulation, Training, and Instrumentation | Orlando, FL

WARFIGHTING FUNCTION

Mission Command

Movement and Maneuver

Intelligence

Fires

Sustainment

Maneuver Support and Protection

Engagement

ACQUISITION LIFECYCLE PHASE

Materiel Solution Analysis

Technology Maturation & Risk Reduction

Engineering & Manufacturing Development

Production & Deployment

Operations & Support

MILESTONE DECISION AUTHORITY

Defense Acquisition Executive

Army Acquisition Executive

Program Executive Officer

DESCRIPTION

The Aviation Combined Arms Tactical Trainer (AVCATT) is designed to enable unit collective and combined arms air-to-ground training for AH-64, UH-60, CH-47, UH-72 and OH-58 aircrews within the Live, Virtual and Constructive (LVC) Integrated Training Environment (ITE). It will support the training of nonrated crew members in crew coordination, flight, aerial gunnery, hoist and sling-load related tasks via the Non-Rated Crewmember Manned Module (NCM3).

AVCATT, the Army's only collective training system of record for Active, Reserve and Army National Guard aviation units, is a mobile multistation virtual simulation device that supports unit collective and combined arms training for helicopter aircrews. The trainer is composed of two trailers per suite with six reconfigurable modules for the Apache Longbow, Chinook, Kiowa Warrior, Lakota and Black Hawk. The NCM3 introduces a third trailer containing two reconfigurable modules that can be linked to AVCATT's UH-60 Black Hawk and CH-47 Chinook cockpit configurations to support a unit's specific mission training requirements. Both the AVCATT and NCM3 use Helmet Mounted Displays (HMD) for out-the-window scenes.

BENEFIT TO THE WARFIGHTER

AVCATT provides unit collective and combined arms air-to-ground training for AH-64, UH-60, CH-47, UH-72, and OH-58 aircrews within the LVC ITE. The AVCATT also supports the training of nonrated crew members in crew coordination, flight, aerial gunnery, hoist and sling-load related tasks via the NCM3.

SPECIFICATIONS

AVCATT:

- Consists of two wheel-mounted mobile trailers each measuring 53 feet long, 8.5 feet wide and 13.5 feet high
- Recommended improved surface area for setup is 70 feet long by 35 feet wide

NCM3:

- Consists of one wheel-mounted mobile trailer measuring 53 feet long, 8.5 feet wide and 13.5 feet high
- Recommended improved surface area for setup is 60 feet long by 25 feet wide
- Trailers are not self-propelled; they require external power and water hose connection; external shore power preferred
- Each device requires contracted personnel support provided through field operations program management office

PROGRAM STATUS

- **2QFY13:** Longbow lot 13.1 concurrency upgrade contract awarded
- **4QFY13:** Fielding of NCM3 #3-5
- **1QFY14-4QFY14:** Production and fielding of NCM3 #6-16
- **2QFY15:** Heating, ventilation and air conditioning (HVAC) replacement contract awarded
- **3QFY15:** Training Effectiveness Evaluation contract awarded
- **4QFY15:**
  › NCM3 #17 fielded
  › Post Deployment Software Support contract awarded

PROJECTED ACTIVITIES

- **1QFY16-2QFY16:** Fielding of software baseline 16.0 (UH-60M and Longbow lot 13.1 upgrades)
- **1QFY16-4QFY16:** HVAC upgrade production and fielding of 11 AVCATT suites
- **3QFY16:** Fielding of NCM3 #18
- **4QFY16:** Fielding of software baseline 17.0 (CH-47F and gunnery upgrades)
- **3QFY17:** HMD replacement contract award

AVCATT

FOREIGN MILITARY SALES
None

CONTRACTORS
AVCATT: AVT Simulation (Orlando, FL)
NCM3: CymSTAR LLC (Broken Arrow, OK)
Technology Refresh: Cole Engineering Services, Inc. (Orlando, FL)
HVAC Upgrades: Applied Companies (Valencia, CA)

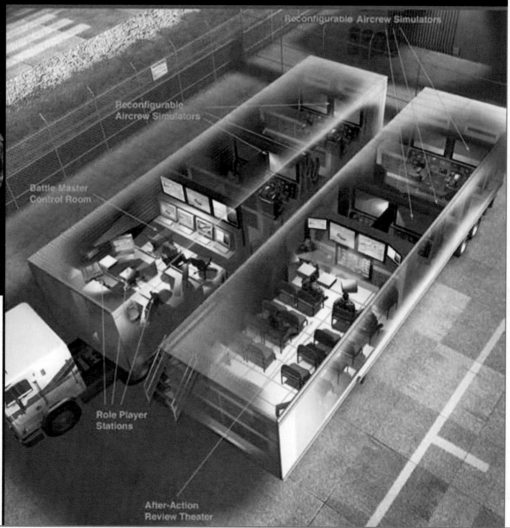

Reconfigurable Aircrew Simulators

Reconfigurable Aircrew Simulators

Battle Master Control Room

Role Player Stations

After-Action Review Theater

Battlefield Kitchen (BK)

PEO Combat Support and Combat Service Support | Detroit Arsenal, MI

WARFIGHTING FUNCTION

Mission Command

Movement and Maneuver

Intelligence

Fires

Sustainment

Maneuver Support and Protection

Engagement

ACQUISITION LIFECYCLE PHASE

Materiel Solution Analysis

Technology Maturation & Risk Reduction

Engineering & Manufacturing Development

Production & Deployment

Operations & Support

MILESTONE DECISION AUTHORITY

Defense Acquisition Executive

Army Acquisition Executive

Program Executive Officer

DESCRIPTION

The Battlefield Kitchen (BK) provides the capability to prepare meals to sustain 300 Soldiers with quality nutrition in a tactical environment. BK is a trailer-mounted, expandable platform towed by the Light Medium Tactical Vehicle. It will replace the Army's remaining Mobile Kitchen Trailers, primarily in echelon-above-brigade units.

BENEFIT TO THE WARFIGHTER

The BK will provide better meal quality, enhanced versatility and a healthier operator environment through the use of new thermostatically controlled, modular appliances. These energy efficient, quiet appliances will feature closed combustion to vent burner exhaust from the kitchen. The man-portable, modular appliances will also be reconfigurable within the kitchen or dismountable for use off the kitchen platform. This will provide the flexibility to adapt meal preparation to the mission scenario.

SPECIFICATIONS

- Capable of preparing rations for 300 personnel in 4 hours using any available military ration
- Projected to use standard military trailer (M1061A)
- Onboard 3kW military standard generator
- Modular appliances with a minimum of 20 percent less fuel consumption
- Onboard ventilation, running water and refrigeration
- Capable of rail, sea, road, variable and fixed wing transport
- Capable of being deployed and used worldwide in all conditions and environments
- Government-owned technical data for reprocurement and to provide complete lifecycle support

PROGRAM STATUS

- **1QFY16:** Request for Proposal Release Decision

PROJECTED ACTIVITIES

- **2QFY16:** Release Request for Proposal
- **3QFY16:** Award of development contract
- **3QFY17:** Complete component development phase

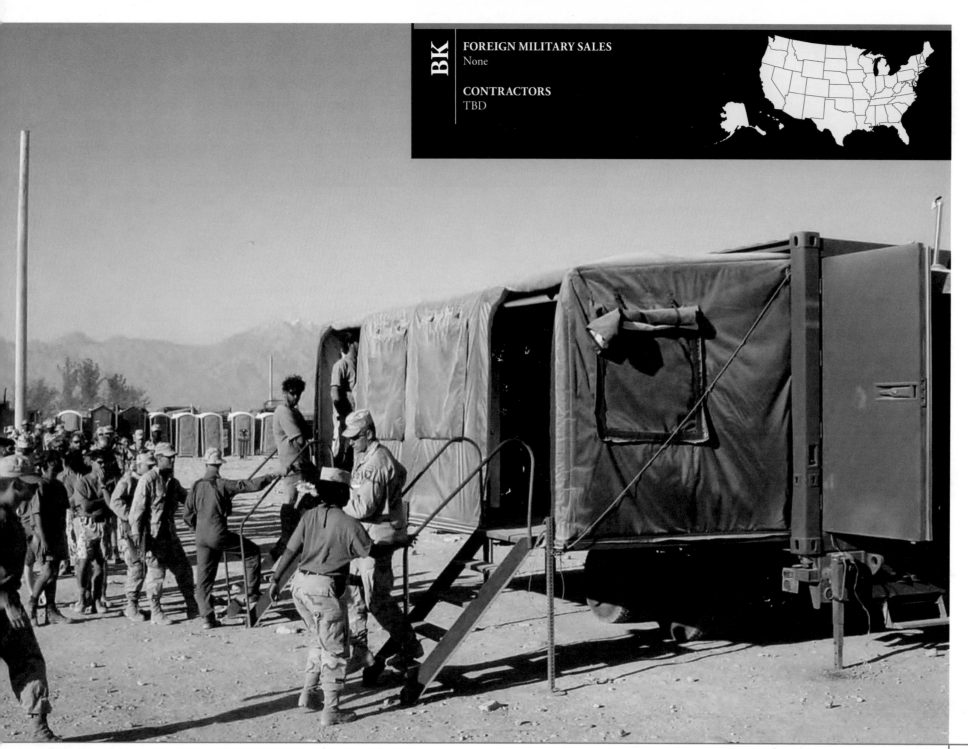

Biometric Enabling Capability (BEC)

PEO Enterprise Information Systems | Fort Belvoir, VA

WARFIGHTING FUNCTION

Mission Command

Movement and Maneuver

Intelligence

Fires

Sustainment

Maneuver Support and Protection

Engagement

ACQUISITION LIFECYCLE PHASE

Materiel Solution Analysis

Technology Maturation & Risk Reduction

Engineering & Manufacturing Development

Production & Deployment

Operations & Support

MILESTONE DECISION AUTHORITY

Defense Acquisition Executive

Army Acquisition Executive

Program Executive Officer

DESCRIPTION

The Biometric Enabling Capability (BEC) consists of the Next Generation Automated Biometric Identification System (ABIS), also known as the DoD ABIS. This central, authoritative, multimodal biometrics data repository is the enterprise-level authoritative data source for all DoD biometrics. DoD ABIS expands capabilities with multimodal (fingerprint, palm, iris and face) storage and matching, watch list capability, and improved integration with interagency repositories. It is based on adaptations of commercial off-the-shelf products, using open architecture to minimize development and speed deployment. The system takes advantage of low-risk, cost-effective blade hardware to optimize system availability and scalability, and to ensure continuity of operations.

DoD ABIS interfaces with numerous DoD and interagency biometrics systems, including FBI Next Generation IAFIS and Department of Homeland Security (DHS) Automated Biometric Identification System (IDENT), to store and match biometric data on non-U.S. persons of interest to DoD.

BENEFIT TO THE WARFIGHTER

BEC is a mission-enabler for force protection, intelligence, physical and logical access control, identity management/credentialing, detention and interception operations. The program supports overseas contingency operations, including counterintelligence; Iraqi and Afghan security force screening; detainee operations; cache and post-improvised explosive device incident exploitation; intelligence operations; presence operations; local population control; seizure operations; and base access control.

SPECIFICATIONS

- Multimodal storage and matching, including fingerprint, palm, iris and face
- Watch list capability
- Improved integration with interagency repositories, including the FBI Next Generation IAFIS and the DHS IDENT systems

PROGRAM STATUS

- **FY13:** Development of DoD ABIS 1.2
- **1QFY14:** Continued development of DoD ABIS 1.2
- **2QFY14-3QFY14:** Customer test overseen by Electronic Proving Ground (Fort Huachuca, AZ)
- **4QFY14:** Joint Interoperability Test Command interoperability assessment; Initial Operational Test & Evaluation (Phase II)
- **1QFY15:** DoD ABIS 1.2 operational (Go Live)
- **4QFY15-1QFY16:** Demonstration of the DoD ABIS Master Recovery System

PROJECTED ACTIVITIES

- **2QFY16:** DoD ABIS 1.2 Full Deployment Decision
- **FY17:** Operations and Support; service life extension

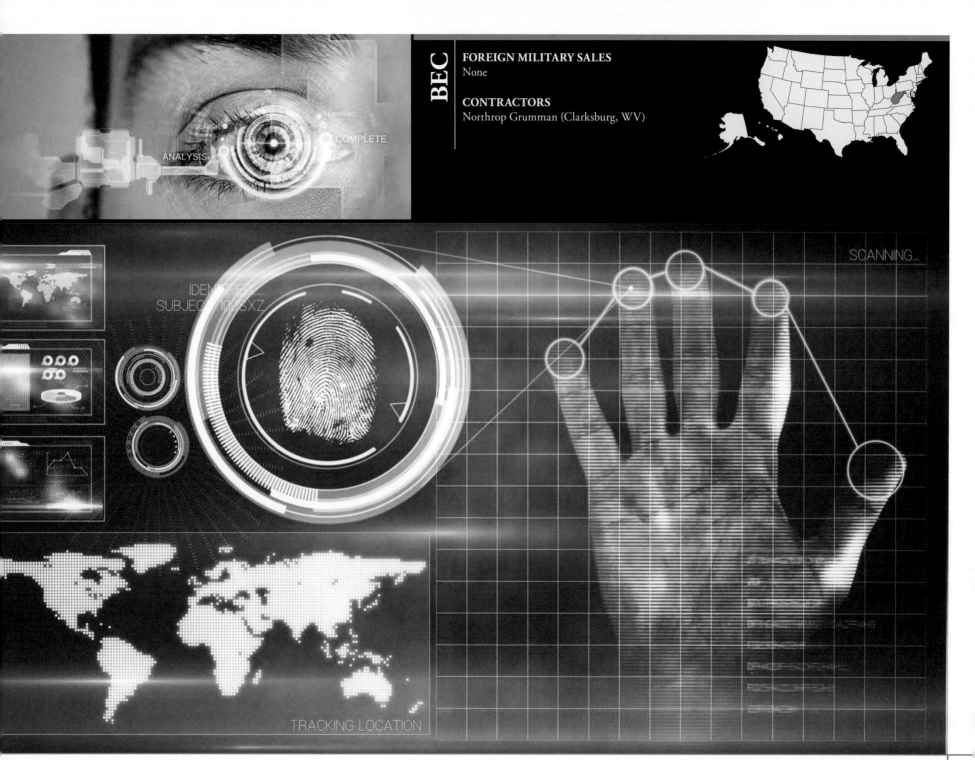

BEC

FOREIGN MILITARY SALES
None

CONTRACTORS
Northrop Grumman (Clarksburg, WV)

Calibration Sets Equipment (CALSETS)

PEO Combat Support and Combat Service Support | Detroit Arsenal, MI

WARFIGHTING FUNCTION

Mission Command

Movement and Maneuver

Intelligence

Fires

Sustainment

Maneuver Support and Protection

Engagement

ACQUISITION LIFECYCLE PHASE

Materiel Solution Analysis

Technology Maturation & Risk Reduction

Engineering & Manufacturing Development

Production & Deployment

Operations & Support

MILESTONE DECISION AUTHORITY

Defense Acquisition Executive

Army Acquisition Executive

Program Executive Officer

DESCRIPTION

Calibration Sets Equipment (CALSETS) consists of calibration instrumentation housed in fixed facilities or contained within tactical shelters with accompanying power generation equipment. CALSETS provides support to maintenance units and area support organizations from brigade to multitheater sustainment operations and ensures a cascading transfer of precision accuracy originating from the U.S. National Institute of Standards and Technology.

CALSETS tactical shelters, which are designed to plug into Army enterprise and battle networks, are 100 percent mobile and transportable by surface mode or aircraft (C-130, C-5 and C-17). They are configured in several set configurations and designed to calibrate 90 percent of the Army's test, measurement and diagnostic equipment workload with an objective of 98 percent.

- **Calibration Set, Secondary Transfer Standards Basic, AN/GSM-286:** This set consists of baseline instruments and components capable of supporting precision maintenance equipment in the physical, dimensional, electrical and electronic parameters.
- **Calibration Set, Secondary Transfer Standards Augmented, AN/GSM-287:** This set consists of baseline instruments and augmented components with expanded capability to support a wider variety of precision maintenance equipment. It is capable of supporting precision maintenance equipment in the physical, dimensional, electrical, electronic, radiological, electro-optical, and microwave frequency parameters.
- **Transfer Set, Standards, AN/GSM-439:** This set is a subset of the baseline instruments designed to support up to 70 percent of the Army's high-density precision measurement equipment in forward areas. The system is modular and configurable to meet mission requirements and can operate in a true extended range mission posture. Designed for rapid deployment by surface or air, AN/GSM-439 set is deployed in an AN/GSM-421A(V)2; a 20-foot ISO shelter

transported on an M1085A1P2 Medium Tactical Vehicle, an M1082 2.5-ton trailer and a 15kW power generator.

- **Transfer Set, Standards, AN/GSM-440:** This set configuration contains baseline instruments and augmented components designed for a tactical support mission. The platform applies a network-centric approach to precision maintenance support operations and data handling via an integrated data network, capable of sending calibration management system data to higher Army headquarters and obtaining calibration software updates. The set of instruments is deployed in an AN/GSM-705, 37-foot semitrailer with a M1088A1 Medium Tactical Vehicle Tractor with an integrated 15kW power generator.

BENEFIT TO THE WARFIGHTER

CALSETS provides warfighters with calibration and repair support capabilities for instrumentation and maintenance devices within a theater of operations.

SPECIFICATIONS

- Various dimensions depending on equipment

PROGRAM STATUS

- **Current:** Sustainment and modernization of Secondary Transfer Standards Basic, AN/GSM-286; Secondary Transfer Standards Augmented, AN/GSM-287; Transfer Set, Standards, AN/GSM-439 and AN/GSM-440; Production of Calibration Set, Secondary Transfer Standards, AN/GSM-421A(V)2; Fielding of Secondary Transfer Standards, AN/GSM-421A(V)2 to 12 Active Component and National Guard units

PROJECTED ACTIVITIES

- **2QFY16-2QFY17:** AN/GSM-421A(V)2 continue production and fielding

Call For Fire Trainer (CFFT) Immersive System

PEO Simulation, Training, and Instrumentation | Orlando, FL

WARFIGHTING FUNCTION

Mission Command

Movement and Maneuver

Intelligence

Fires

Sustainment

Maneuver Support and Protection

Engagement

ACQUISITION LIFECYCLE PHASE

Materiel Solution Analysis

Technology Maturation & Risk Reduction

Engineering & Manufacturing Development

Production & Deployment

Operations & Support

MILESTONE DECISION AUTHORITY

Defense Acquisition Executive

Army Acquisition Executive

Program Executive Officer

DESCRIPTION

The Call For Fire Trainer (CFFT) Immersive System is designed to provide realistic fire training in support of all indirect fire and close air support mission tasks at the Fires Center of Excellence, Fort Sill, OK.

The CFFT Immersive System augments the existing fire training capability of the base CFFT system. It provides a realistic virtual environment with Simulated Military Equipment (SME) to enhance the existing institutional training capability at the Fires Center of Excellence. Immersive systems train base fire support and close air support mission tasks, as well as advanced mission scenarios.

BENEFIT TO THE WARFIGHTER

CFFT provides an immersive, realistic, virtual environment with SME to augment the existing institutional training capability at the Fires Center of Excellence. It supports ground combat readiness with simulated battlefield training for Fire Support Specialists, Joint Fires Observers and other Soldiers. It ensures all fire support and close air mission tasks are discussed, and provides a realistic training environment using advanced firefighting techniques.

SPECIFICATIONS

The CFFT Immersive System is a collection of 15 immersive modules that realistically replicate 5 different environments. The modules in the complete system include:

- Four Adaptive Full Spectrum Modules for outdoor or rural scenarios
- Two Close Air Support Modules for learning close air support techniques
- Two Urban Terrain Modules for addressing generic, urban terrain scenarios
- Five Fire Effects and Cell Modules for chain-of-command coordination
- Two After Action Review Modules for enhanced learning and training

PROGRAM STATUS

- **1QFY15-3QFY15:** Government Acceptance Test of the CFFT III baseline

PROJECTED ACTIVITIES

- **2QFY16:** Test Readiness Review
- **2QFY16-3QFY16:** Technical Refresh of the Immersive System

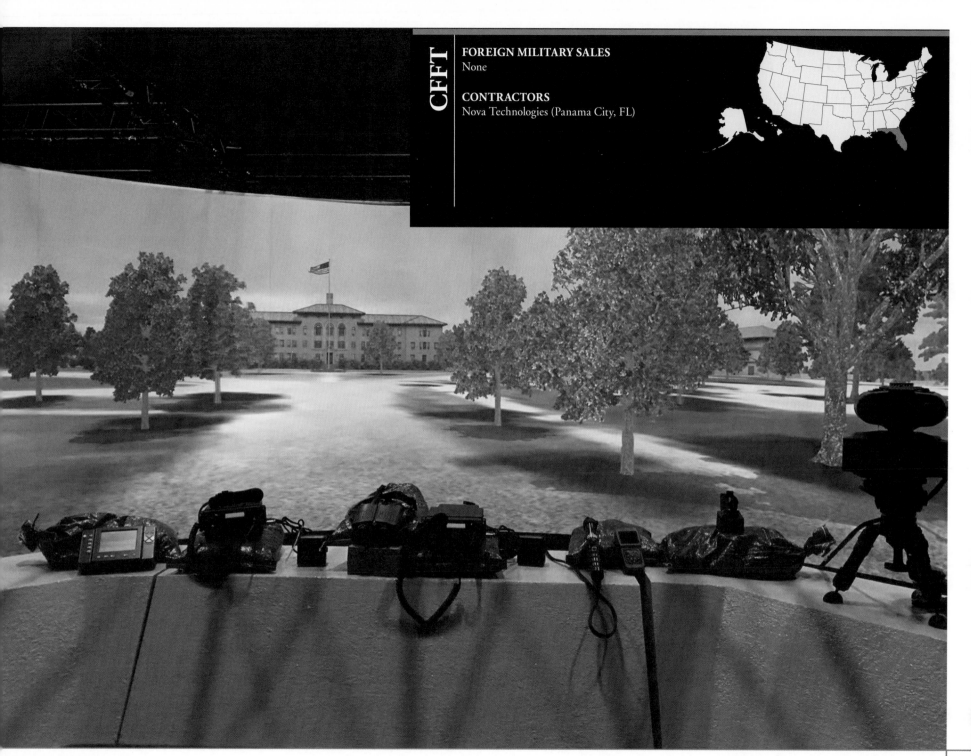

FOREIGN MILITARY SALES
None

CONTRACTORS
Nova Technologies (Panama City, FL)

Call For Fire Trainer Increment 3 (CFFT 3)

PEO Simulation, Training, and Instrumentation | Orlando, FL

WARFIGHTING FUNCTION

Mission Command

Movement and Maneuver

Intelligence

Fires

Sustainment

Maneuver Support and Protection

Engagement

ACQUISITION LIFECYCLE PHASE

Materiel Solution Analysis

Technology Maturation & Risk Reduction

Engineering & Manufacturing Development

Production & Deployment

Operations & Support

MILESTONE DECISION AUTHORITY

Defense Acquisition Executive

Army Acquisition Executive

Program Executive Officer

DESCRIPTION

Call For Fire Trainer Increment 3 (CFFT 3) is designed to provide realistic observed fire training in support of all indirect fire and close air support mission tasks. CFFT 3 upgrades the existing hardware and software of the CFFT 2. CFFT 3 is a lightweight, rapidly deployable, observed fire training system that provides simulated battlefield training for Fire Support Specialists (FSS), Joint Fires Observers (JFO) and other Soldiers. The system provides simulated battlefield training to conduct indirect fires, close air support, close combat attack and naval surface fire support. CFFT 3 utilizes the government-owned Joint Fires Product Line architecture, which is modular and scalable in design.

BENEFIT TO THE WARFIGHTER

CFFT 3 provides institutional and rapidly deployable virtual training capability for all fires and close air support tasks. It ensures ground combat readiness by providing simulated battlefield training for FSS, JFO and other Soldiers.

SPECIFICATIONS

- Two basic configurations:
  - › Classroom: 1 instructor to 30 students
  - › Transportable: 1 instructor to 4 students, and 1 instructor to 12 students
- Joint Close Air Support modification kit will substitute for two Live Type 1, 2 and 3 Day/Laser Close Air Support calls for Joint Terminal Attack Controller sustainment
- Modular system architecture allows for integration with other simulation systems
- Trains precision effects without the use of precision guided munitions
- Operates in stand-alone mode
- Network capable
- Supports classified training up to the secret level
- Provides virtual terrain databases including Fort Sill, OK, the National Training Center (NTC), Afghanistan and Korea

PROGRAM STATUS

- **1QFY15:** Test Readiness Review
- **1QFY15-3QFY15:** Government Acceptance Test of the CFFT 3 baseline
- **3QFY15:** Technical refresh of classroom systems
- **1QFY16:** Bold Quest 15.2, test interoperability with Joint fires simulators

PROJECTED ACTIVITIES

- **4QFY15-1QFY17:** Technical refresh classroom and transportable systems

FOREIGN MILITARY SALES
None

CONTRACTORS
Nova Technologies (Panama City, FL)

Chemical Biological Medical Systems – Therapeutics

JPEO for Chemical and Biological Defense | Aberdeen Proving Ground, MD

WARFIGHTING FUNCTION

Mission Command

Movement and Maneuver

Intelligence

Fires

Sustainment

Maneuver Support and Protection

Engagement

ACQUISITION LIFECYCLE PHASE

Materiel Solution Analysis

Technology Maturation & Risk Reduction

Engineering & Manufacturing Development

Production & Deployment

Operations & Support

MILESTONE DECISION AUTHORITY

Defense Acquisition Executive

Army Acquisition Executive

Program Executive Officer

DESCRIPTION

Chemical Biological Medical Systems – Therapeutics consists of the following components:

- **Improved Nerve Agent Treatment System (INATS):** This system is an enhanced treatment regimen to counter the effects of nerve agent poisoning. The new oxime component of INATS will replace 2-pyridine aldoxime methyl chloride in the Antidote Treatment Nerve Agent Autoinjector. In addition, U.S. Food and Drug Administration (FDA) approval will be obtained for use of pyridostigmine bromide (PB), the component of Soman Nerve Agent Pretreatment Pyridostigmine (SNAPP) to counter additional nerve agents. A third component to INATS is a centrally acting medical countermeasure designed to treat the nerve agent effects on the central nervous system.

- **Hemorrhagic Fever Viruses (HFV) medical countermeasures:** These countermeasures will mitigate the threat of illness or death, as well as lessen issues with performance degradation resulting from exposure to hemorrhagic fever viruses (Ebola and Marburg). Due to the severity of these diseases, HFV therapeutics will be administered to infected warfighters while under direct medical observation.

- **Emerging Infectious Disease Therapeutics (EID Tx):** These therapeutics will provide broad-spectrum medical countermeasures to protect against naturally occurring or biologically engineered influenza viruses. This therapeutic will mitigate the threat of pandemic- and drug-resistant influenza viruses and will mitigate performance degradation issues associated with exposure to this organism.

BENEFIT TO THE WARFIGHTER

Therapeutics play a critical and strategic role in chemical and biological defense by providing the warfighter with shield-and-sustain capabilities against known or novel threats.

SPECIFICATIONS

- System attributes established in requirements documentation

PROGRAM STATUS

- **1QFY13:** EID Flu Milestone (MS) B
- **3QFY13:** HFV MS B
- **3QFY14:** INATS initiated animal efficacy and clinical trials

PROJECTED ACTIVITIES

- **3QFY17:** EID Tx New Drug Application
- **1QFY18:** INATS MS B

FOREIGN MILITARY SALES
None

CONTRACTORS
INATS: Southwest Research Institute
(San Antonio, TX)
Battelle Memorial Institute (Columbus, OH)
HFV: Tekmira Pharmaceutical Corporation
(Burnaby, BC, Canada)
Sarepta Therapeutics (Cambridge, MA)
EID Tx: MediVector, Inc. (Boston, MA)

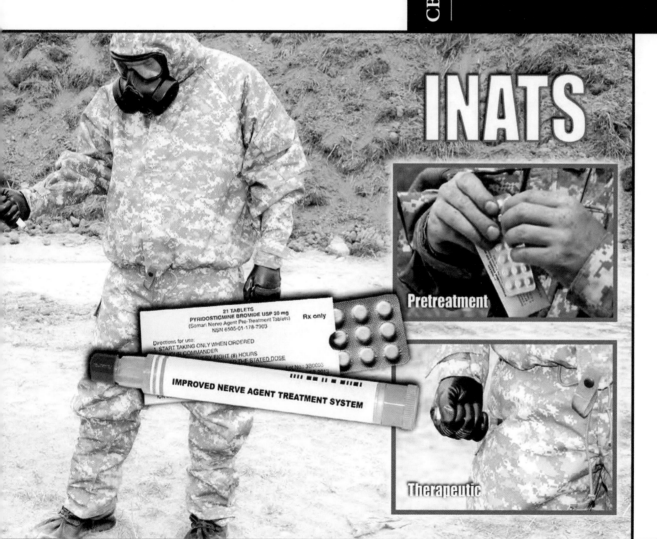

INATS

Pretreatment

Therapeutic

21 TABLETS
PYRIDOSTIGMINE BROMIDE USP 30 mg
(Soman Nerve Agent Pre-Treatment Tablets)
NSN 6505-01-178-7903   Rx only

Directions for use:
1. START TAKING ONLY WHEN ORDERED

IMPROVED NERVE AGENT TREATMENT SYSTEM

Chemical Biological Protective Shelter (CBPS) – M8E1

JPEO for Chemical and Biological Defense | Aberdeen Proving Ground, MD

WARFIGHTING FUNCTION

Mission Command

Movement and Maneuver

Intelligence

Fires

Sustainment

Maneuver Support and Protection

Engagement

ACQUISITION LIFECYCLE PHASE

Materiel Solution Analysis

Technology Maturation & Risk Reduction

Engineering & Manufacturing Development

Production & Deployment

Operations & Support

MILESTONE DECISION AUTHORITY

Defense Acquisition Executive

Army Acquisition Executive

Program Executive Officer

DESCRIPTION

The Chemical Biological Protective Shelter (CBPS) is a mobile, self-contained, rapidly deployable, chemically and biologically protected shelter system that provides a contamination-free, environmentally controlled medical treatment area. The CBPS is intended to be fielded to the Army, Army Reserves and Army National Guard.

BENEFIT TO THE WARFIGHTER

The CBPS provides medical treatment teams and squads, consisting of four medical personnel, with a contamination-free and environmentally controlled medical treatment area to treat up to eight litter and ambulatory patients without the encumbrance of individual protective clothing and equipment. The CBPS is capable of being transported by ground, rail, sea or air.

SPECIFICATIONS

- Rigid Wall Shelter
- Heating, ventilation and air conditioning system
- Nuclear, biological and chemical filtration system
- Onboard primary and auxiliary electric power sources
- Deployable chemical biological protective fabric shelter with ambulatory and litter airlocks
- Utilizes a Model M1085 Medium Tactical Vehicle to move the CBPS system as well as the medical treatment team's equipment

PROGRAM STATUS

- **1QFY15-4QFY15:** Produced CBPS units on existing contract
- **2QFY15:**
  › Army decision to provide a mix of armored and unarmored M1085 Medium Tactical Vehicles
  › Make-or-buy decision to transition production to Pine Bluff Arsenal in Arkansas

PROJECTED ACTIVITIES

- **2QFY16:** Pine Bluff Arsenal awards component supply contract
- **1QFY17:**
  › Type Classification/Materiel Release Decision
  › Pine Bluff Arsenal Production Readiness Review
  › First Article Test
- **2QFY17:** Fielding begins

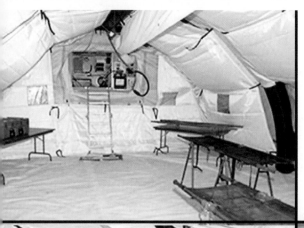

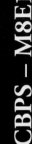

FOREIGN MILITARY SALES
None

CONTRACTORS
Smiths Detection, Inc. (Edgewood, MD)

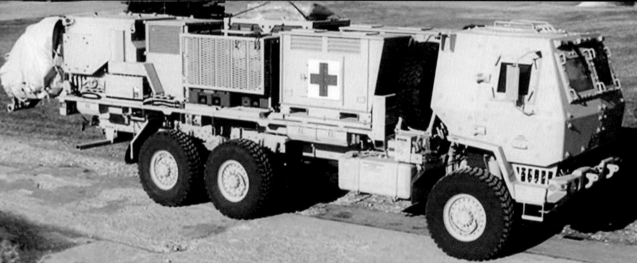

Chemical, Biological, Radiological, Nuclear Dismounted Reconnaissance Sets, Kits and Outfits (CBRN DR SKO)

ACAT III

JPEO for Chemical and Biological Defense | Aberdeen Proving Ground, MD

WARFIGHTING FUNCTION

Mission Command

Movement and Maneuver

Intelligence

Fires

Sustainment

Maneuver Support and Protection

Engagement

ACQUISITION LIFECYCLE PHASE

Materiel Solution Analysis

Technology Maturation & Risk Reduction

Engineering & Manufacturing Development

Production & Deployment

Operations & Support

MILESTONE DECISION AUTHORITY

Defense Acquisition Executive

Army Acquisition Executive

Program Executive Officer

DESCRIPTION

The Chemical, Biological, Radiological, Nuclear (CBRN) Dismounted Reconnaissance Sets, Kits, and Outfits (DR SKO) system will consist of commercial and government off-the-shelf equipment that will provide detection, identification, sample collection, decontamination, marking and hazard reporting of CBRN threats, as well as personnel protection from CBRN hazards.

CBRN DR SKO is composed of hand-held, man-portable detectors that identify potential weapons of mass destruction (WMD) and WMD precursors, and determine the levels of protection required to assess a sensitive site. The system supports dismounted reconnaissance, surveillance and CBRN site-assessment missions to enable more detailed CBRN information reports for commanders. These site locations may be enclosed or confined, and are therefore inaccessible by traditional CBRN reconnaissance-mounted platforms. CBRN site assessments help planners determine if more thorough analysis is required to mitigate risks or gather intelligence on adversaries' chemical warfare agents, biological warfare agents or toxic industrial material capabilities.

BENEFIT TO THE WARFIGHTER

CBRN DR SKO provides a comprehensive, all-hazards dismounted reconnaissance and site assessment capability to protect against, detect and decontaminate chemical warfare agents, biological warfare agents, toxic industrial chemicals and other hazards.

SPECIFICATIONS

- Commercial and government off-the-shelf equipment that will provide detection, identification, sample collection, decontamination, marking and hazard reporting of CBRN threats
- Supports dismounted reconnaissance, surveillance and CBRN site-assessment missions to enable more detailed CBRN information reports for commanders

PROGRAM STATUS

- **FY13-FY15:**
  › Milestone C Decision
  › Multi-Operational Test and Evaluation
  › Full-Rate Production Decision
  › Army Initial Operational Capability (IOC)
  › 76 systems fielded to 22 units
  › 326 warfighters trained to operate and maintain

PROJECTED ACTIVITIES

- **FY16-FY17:**
  › Marine Corps IOC

Dismounted Reconnaissance Sets, Kits and Outfits (DR SKO)

CBRN DR SKO

FOREIGN MILITARY SALES
None

CONTRACTORS
FLIR Systems, Inc. (Elkridge, MD)
Pine Bluff Arsenal (Pine Bluff, AR)

Close Combat Tactical Trainer (CCTT)

PEO Simulation, Training, and Instrumentation | Orlando, FL

WARFIGHTING FUNCTION

Mission Command

Movement and Maneuver

Intelligence

Fires

Sustainment

Maneuver Support and Protection

Engagement

ACQUISITION LIFECYCLE PHASE

Materiel Solution Analysis

Technology Maturation & Risk Reduction

Engineering & Manufacturing Development

Production & Deployment

Operations & Support

MILESTONE DECISION AUTHORITY

Defense Acquisition Executive

Army Acquisition Executive

Program Executive Officer

DESCRIPTION

Close Combat Tactical Trainer (CCTT) is designed to provide Armor, Mechanized Infantry, Cavalry, Infantry, and reconnaissance crews, units and staffs with a virtual, collective training capability that will increase and sustain readiness. The primary training audience operates from full-crew simulators, mock-up command posts, and live battalion command posts to train in combined arms maneuver and wide-area security tactical missions, conduct mission rehearsal and enhance live training.

The CCTT training program is composed of three subsystems: CCTT, Reconfigurable Vehicle Tactical Trainer (RVTT) and Dismounted Soldier Training Systems (DSTS). The CCTT system consists of computer-driven, manned-module simulators replicating the vehicles found in close combat units, including M1 Abrams tank; M2 Bradley Fighting Vehicle; M3 Cavalry Fighting Vehicle; Bradley Fire Support Team Vehicle (BFIST); M113 Armored Personnel Carrier; Heavy Expanded Mobility Tactical Truck; and High Mobility Multipurpose Wheeled Vehicle.

Semi-Automated Forces (SAF) populate the battlefield and function through emulators to work interactively with the manned modules. These simulators and SAF are connected via a local area network to provide real-time, fully interactive, collective task training on computer-generated terrain. The trainers are located in various-sized buildings in the fixed sites. Mobile sites are contained in a standard tractor-trailer.

BENEFIT TO THE WARFIGHTER

CCTT trainers allow inexperienced Soldiers to gain critical experience, confidence and tactical knowledge in a realistic but safe environment, which translates directly into increased effectiveness in live training and combat operations.

SPECIFICATIONS

- 7 CCTT/Reconfigurable Vehicle Simulator fixed sites
- 7 CCTT mobile sites
- 11 RVTT fixed sites
- 12 RVTT mobile sites

PROGRAM STATUS

- **3QFY15:** CCTT concurrency upgrades fielded to Fort Hood, TX, Los Alamitos, CA, and Gowen Field, ID; production and fielding of the DSTS to Gowen Field, ID
- **3QFY15-4QFY15:** Software upgrades fielded to all CCTT and RVTT sites
- **4QFY15:** CCTT concurrency upgrades fielded to Fort Riley, KS; Mobile CCTT M1 concurrency upgrades fielded to Fort Bragg, NC, and Camp Ripley, MN; M2A3 BFIST Critical Design Review
- **1QFY16:** Fielding of CCTT concurrency upgrades to Fort Stewart, GA; fielding of Mobile CCTT concurrency upgrades to Knoxville, TN; fielding of DSTS to Camp Butner, NC

PROJECTED ACTIVITIES

- **2QFY16:** Fielding of Mobile CCTT concurrency upgrades to Camp Casey, Korea, Los Alamitos, CA, and Camp Shelby, MS; First Unit Acceptance test for M2A3 BFIST
- **2QFY16-4QFY16:** Fielding of M2A3 BFIST
- **3QFY16:** Fielding of Mobile CCTT concurrency upgrades to Fort Indiantown Gap, PA, and Knoxville, TN; fielding of concurrency upgrades to Fort Carson, CO
- **4QFY16:** Concurrency upgrades to Camp Ripley, MN
- **FY17:** Fielding of concurrency upgrades at Fort Bliss, TX and Fort Benning, GA
- **2QFY17:** Post Deployment Software Support (PDSS) and Manned Module Modernization Contract Award

FOREIGN MILITARY SALES
None

CONTRACTORS
CCTT: Lockheed Martin Mission Systems and Training (Orlando, FL)
DSTS: Intelligent Decisions (Ashburn, VA)
PDSS: AVT Simulation (Orlando, FL)
Image Generator: Rockwell Collins (Cedar Rapids, IA)

Fixed Site CCTT Company/Battalion/Task Force

Operator Control

Dismounted Soldier

M2/M3

MIA2

MIA1

Commander's Station
Abrams Tank

RVS/RVTT

M113

Mobile CCTT Platoon Set

After Action Review

Driver's Station
Bradley Fighting Vehicle

Combat Service Support Communications (CSS Comms)

PEO Enterprise Information Systems | Fort Belvoir, VA

WARFIGHTING FUNCTION

Mission Command

Movement and Maneuver

Intelligence

Fires

Sustainment

Maneuver Support and Protection

Engagement

ACQUISITION LIFECYCLE PHASE

Materiel Solution Analysis

Technology Maturation & Risk Reduction

Engineering & Manufacturing Development

Production & Deployment

Operations & Support

MILESTONE DECISION AUTHORITY

Defense Acquisition Executive

Army Acquisition Executive

Program Executive Officer

DESCRIPTION

Combat Service Support Communications (CSS Comms) includes the Combat Service Support Automated Information Systems Interface (CAISI) and the CSS Satellite Communications (CSS SATCOM) system. CAISI allows current and emerging battlefield CSS automation devices to electronically exchange information via tactical networks. CAISI provides unit commanders and logistics managers an interface device to support CSS doctrine for full-spectrum operations. CAISI employs a deployable wireless local area network infrastructure linking Army logistics information system computers in a 7-square-km area. It is certified in accordance with Federal Information Processing Standards 140-2 Level 2. CSS SATCOM includes commercial-off-the-shelf, Ku-band, auto-acquire satellite terminals called CSS Very Small Aperture Terminals (CSS VSAT), repackaged in fly-away transit cases, along with a fixed infrastructure of four primary and three continuity of operations (COOP) teleports and high-speed terrestrial links that provide a highly effective, easy-to-use, transportable, SATCOM-based solution to CSS nodes. CSS SATCOM supports information exchange up to the sensitive level, is rapidly deployable anywhere in the world and is fully integrated into the Non-secure Internet Protocol Router Network (NIPRNet).

BENEFIT TO THE WARFIGHTER

CAISI allows deployed Soldiers to connect CSS automation devices to a secure wireless network and electronically exchange information via tactical or commercial communications. CSS SATCOM eliminates the often dangerous need for Soldiers to hand-deliver requisitions via convoys in combat areas.

SPECIFICATIONS

- 7-square-km wireless local area network infrastructure
- Federal Information Processing Standards 140-2 Level 2
- Ku-band
- Auto-acquire satellite terminals
- Fixed infrastructure of four primary and three COOP teleports and high-speed terrestrial links
- Supports information exchange up to the sensitive information level
- Fully integrated into NIPRNet

PROGRAM STATUS

- **FY13-FY15:** Conducted CSS VSAT Logistics Demonstration; completed Legacy Network deactivation; established Full Operational Capability (FOC) for Fucino, Italy and Napa, California teleports; supported major exercises for Network Integration Evaluation, Fort Bliss, TX

PROJECTED ACTIVITIES

- **FY16-FY17:** Modem Replacement FOC

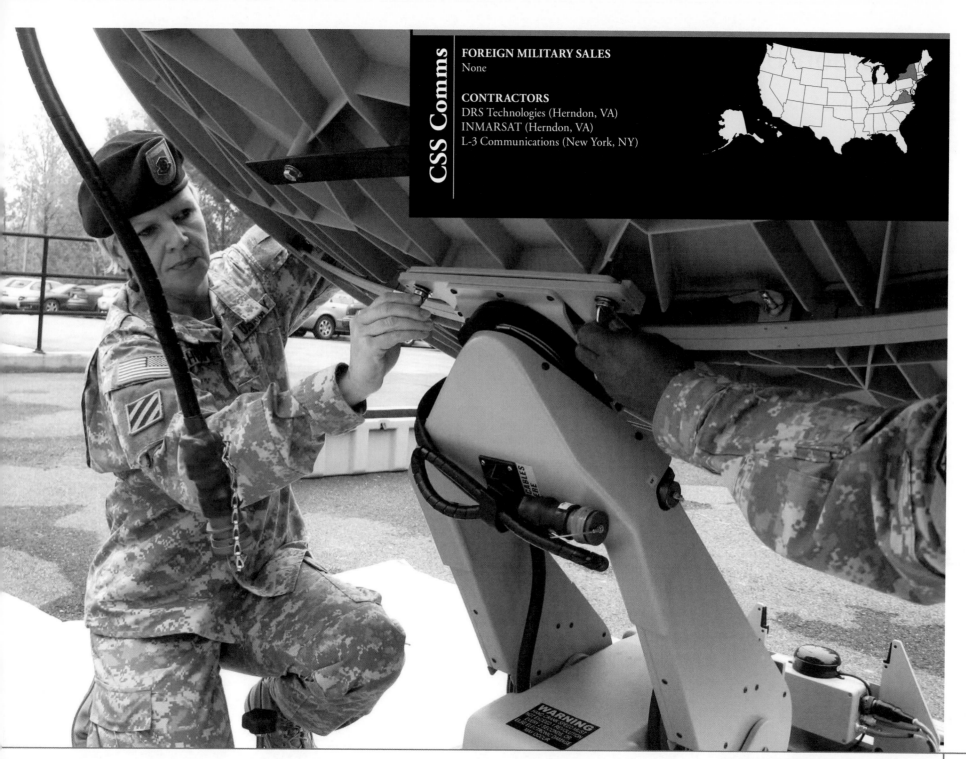

FOREIGN MILITARY SALES
None

CONTRACTORS
DRS Technologies (Herndon, VA)
INMARSAT (Herndon, VA)
L-3 Communications (New York, NY)

Common Bridge Transporter (CBT)

PEO Combat Support and Combat Service Support | Detroit Arsenal, MI

WARFIGHTING FUNCTION

Mission Command

Movement and Maneuver

Intelligence

Fires

Sustainment

Maneuver Support and Protection

Engagement

ACQUISITION LIFECYCLE PHASE

Materiel Solution Analysis

Technology Maturation & Risk Reduction

Engineering & Manufacturing Development

Production & Deployment

Operations & Support

MILESTONE DECISION AUTHORITY

Defense Acquisition Executive

Army Acquisition Executive

Program Executive Officer

DESCRIPTION

The M1977 Common Bridge Transporter (CBT) is a modified M977 Heavy Expanded Mobility Tactical Truck (HEMTT) cargo truck equipped with a Load Handling System. The M1977 CBT was designed to support the Engineer Corps in transporting all bridging assets. The M1977 CBT loads, launches and retrieves the Ribbon Bridge, Improved Ribbon Bridge and Heavy Dry Support Bridge utilizing the Bridge Adapter Pallet and associated legacy bridge erection boats. It is equipped with the Improved Boat Cradle and has a winch to assist in retrieving the deployed equipment.

BENEFIT TO THE WARFIGHTER

The CBT is an essential component of the Multi-Role Bridge Company (MRBC). The MRBC combines the roles of previous float- and fixed-bridge companies to perform their missions with less manpower and greater flexibility. The Army designed MRBC to give commanders a flexible and adaptable unit that can accomplish both float- and fixed-bridge missions. The MRBC are 100 percent mobile (every bridge load has a prime mover) and take advantage of product standardization.

SPECIFICATIONS

- Payload: 20,000 pounds
- Configuration: 8 feet by 8 feet
- Fording capability: 48 inches
- Grade: 60 percent

PROGRAM STATUS

- **3QFY15:** Contract Award

PROJECTED ACTIVITIES

- **Current:** Ongoing contract for recapitalization

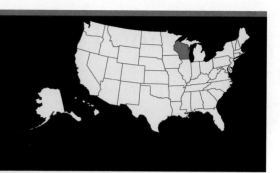

FOREIGN MILITARY SALES
None

CONTRACTORS
Oshkosh Corp. (Oshkosh, WI)

Common Hardware Systems (CHS)

PEO Command, Control and Communications – Tactical | Aberdeen Proving Ground, MD

WARFIGHTING FUNCTION

Mission Command

Movement and Maneuver

Intelligence

Fires

Sustainment

Maneuver Support and Protection

Engagement

ACQUISITION LIFECYCLE PHASE

Materiel Solution Analysis

Technology Maturation & Risk Reduction

Engineering & Manufacturing Development

Production & Deployment

Operations & Support

MILESTONE DECISION AUTHORITY

Defense Acquisition Executive

Army Acquisition Executive

Program Executive Officer

DESCRIPTION

The Common Hardware Systems (CHS) program office enables a holistic approach to acquiring common hardware across the battlespace by utilizing the most effective and efficient means to meet the unique fielding requirements of tactical program offices. CHS coordinates across tactical programs to provide consolidated procurement and sustainment of modified commercial off-the-shelf information technology (COTS IT) and to ensure configuration and obsolescence management. CHS also partners with industry to examine new and emerging technologies that meet operational needs. The CHS-4 contract provides a procurement mechanism to meet Army and DoD program requirements for COTS IT supplies and services.

BENEFIT TO THE WARFIGHTER

Procurement of common hardware provides the battlefield with a common look and feel across platforms and a reduced hardware footprint at a lower cost to the Army.

SPECIFICATIONS

- Streamlined Rapid Acquisition Process: CHS provides rapid acquisition capability for all requirements including engineering support, hardware, sustainment, services
- Rapid Execution: CHS works with stakeholders to facilitate the rapid execution of technology insertions, delivery orders, task orders
- Configuration Management: CHS-4 contract provides a mechanism to preserve hardware configurations, including designs for integrated solutions and kits to ensure interoperability with networked systems as well as continued information assurance compliance
- End of Life Management: CHS works with prime vendor and original equipment manufacturers (OEM) to manage technology obsolescence
- Replacement Configurations: CHS communicates with programs to identify next generation replacement configurations to ensure requirements continue to be met

- Emerging Technologies: CHS works with programs and industry to coordinate new commercial information technologies onto the Army's tactical network; CHS hosts industry roadmaps and technology demonstrations to facilitate collaboration between OEM and program offices

PROGRAM STATUS

- **FY13-FY15:** Managed acquisition and delivery of CHS equipment in support of customer requirements

PROJECTED ACTIVITIES

- **FY16-FY17:** Continue management and delivery of CHS equipment in support of customer requirements; CHS-5 Contract Acquisition Competition

FOREIGN MILITARY SALES
None

CONTRACTORS
CHS-4 production contract: General Dynamics
(Taunton, MA)
**Systems engineering, testing and
analysis support:** Booz Allen Hamilton
(Washington, DC)

Common Robotic System – Individual (CRS(I))

PEO Combat Support and Combat Service Support | Detroit Arsenal, MI

WARFIGHTING FUNCTION

Mission Command

Movement and Maneuver

Intelligence

Fires

Sustainment

Maneuver Support and Protection

Engagement

ACQUISITION LIFECYCLE PHASE

Materiel Solution Analysis

Technology Maturation & Risk Reduction

Engineering & Manufacturing Development

Production & Deployment

Operations & Support

MILESTONE DECISION AUTHORITY

Defense Acquisition Executive

Army Acquisition Executive

Program Executive Officer

DESCRIPTION

The Common Robotic System – Individual (CRS(I)) enables dismounted forces to individually provide a capability for lower-level Reconnaissance, Surveillance and Target Acquisition Units to enhance maneuvers and force protection.

CRS(I) establishes the Army's common small-base platform with a lightweight (less than 25 pounds), highly mobile, unmanned robotic system that includes standard payloads, advanced sensors and mission modules for dismounted forces. The system is designed to be quickly reconfigured for various missions by adding or removing modules or payloads.

The CRS(I) system includes a Universal Controller (UC) that has the ability to achieve and maintain active or passive control of any current Army or Marine Corps Program of Record (battalion and below), as well as any unmanned (air or ground) system or its respective payload. The UC will have the ability to control the Puma, Raven, Man Transportable Robot System Increment 2 and Ground Sensor System.

BENEFIT TO THE WARFIGHTER

CRS(I) is ideal for clearing buildings, caves and other restricted terrain where close-quarters combat is likely. CRS(I) identifies enemy positions, explosive hazards and civilians without exposing the warfighter.

SPECIFICATIONS

- Common small-base lightweight (less than 25 pounds) platform
- Highly mobile unmanned robotic system that includes standard payloads, advanced sensors and mission modules for dismounted forces

PROGRAM STATUS

- **1QFY16:** Materiel Development Decision

PROJECTED ACTIVITIES

- **2QFY17:**
  - › Milestone B
  - › Contract Award
- **4QFY19:** Milestone C

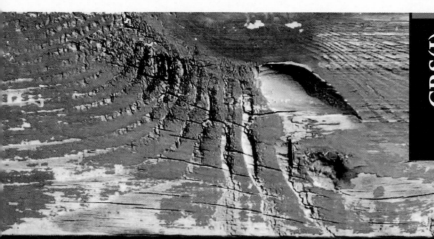

PROGRAM
UNDER DEVELOPMENT

Project Manager
Force Projection

PM Force Projection
PdM UGV

Counter Defilade Target Engagement (CDTE) – XM25

PEO Soldier | Fort Belvoir, VA

WARFIGHTING FUNCTION

Mission Command

Movement and Maneuver

Intelligence

Fires

Sustainment

Maneuver Support and Protection

Engagement

ACQUISITION LIFECYCLE PHASE

Materiel Solution Analysis

Technology Maturation & Risk Reduction

Engineering & Manufacturing Development

Production & Deployment

Operations & Support

MILESTONE DECISION AUTHORITY

Defense Acquisition Executive

Army Acquisition Executive

Program Executive Officer

DESCRIPTION

The Counter Defilade Target Engagement (CDTE) – XM25 System provides the Soldier with a smart revolutionary weapon system that breaks the current small-arms direct-fire parity. It dramatically increases Soldier lethality and range with a family of 25 mm programmable ammunition. The XM25 enables the small unit and individual Soldier to engage defilade targets by providing a 25 mm air bursting capability that can be used in all operational environments. The CDTE is an individually fired, semi-automatic, man-portable weapon system.

The CDTE System reduces the reliance of small units on nonorganic assets (mortars, artillery, and air support) and the need to compete for priority of fires when time is critical. In addition to air bursting ammunition, a family of ammunition is being developed to support other missions, which could include armor-piercing and nonlethal scenarios.

BENEFIT TO THE WARFIGHTER

XM25 allows the individual Soldier to quickly and accurately engage targets by producing an adjusted aim point based on range, environmental factors and user inputs. The target acquisition and fire control integrates thermal capability with direct-view optics, laser rangefinder, compass, fuse setter, ballistic computer and an internal display. An individual Soldier employing basic rifle marksmanship skills can effectively engage exposed or defilade targets in just seconds out to 800 meters.

SPECIFICATIONS

- Caliber: 25 mm
- Weight: 13.8 pounds (with target acquisition and fire control, unloaded)
- Length: 30 inches
- Range: 500 meters point target; 800 meters effective range for area target

PROGRAM STATUS

- **2QFY14-4QFY14:** Pre-Production Qualification Test 1
- **2QFY15-3QFY15:** Contractor Design Verification Test 1

PROJECTED ACTIVITIES

- **1QFY16-2QFY16:** Contractor Design Verification Test 2
- **2QFY16-4QFY16:** Pre-Production Qualification Test 2
- **1QFY17:**
  - › Conduct Limited User Test
  - › Milestone C decision and start of Low-Rate Initial Production

FOREIGN MILITARY SALES
None

CONTRACTORS
Orbital ATK (Plymouth, MN)

Counter-Rocket, Artillery, Mortar (C-RAM) Intercept Land-Based Phalanx Weapon System (LPWS)

PEO Missiles and Space | Redstone Arsenal, AL

MISSILES AND SPACE

WARFIGHTING FUNCTION

Mission Command

Movement and Maneuver

Intelligence

Fires

Sustainment

Maneuver Support and Protection

Engagement

ACQUISITION LIFECYCLE PHASE

Materiel Solution Analysis

Technology Maturation & Risk Reduction

Engineering & Manufacturing Development

Production & Deployment

Operations & Support

MILESTONE DECISION AUTHORITY

Defense Acquisition Executive

Army Acquisition Executive

Program Executive Officer

DESCRIPTION

The Counter-Rocket, Artillery, Mortar (C-RAM) Intercept evolved from the operational success of the C-RAM system-of-systems effort in theater. It transitioned to an acquisition program to provide counter-RAM protection to the Indirect Fire Protection Capability/Avenger Battalions, 5th Battalion 5th Air Defense Artillery (ADA) Regiment and 2nd Battalion 44th ADA Regiment, to defend against and defeat enduring indirect fire (IDF) threats. The C-RAM Intercept capability was originally deployed to forward operating bases in Iraq in support of Operation Iraqi Freedom, and some systems are currently deployed in Iraq and Afghanistan. In 2013, the Army Acquisition Executive designated C-RAM Intercept an Army acquisition program and authorized fielding of existing C-RAM Intercept assets and support equipment to ADA battalions. Fielding is ongoing and impacted by continued deployment of limited Land-Based Phalanx Weapon System (LPWS) assets in theater.

BENEFIT TO THE WARFIGHTER

C-RAM Intercept provides counter-RAM protection to warfighting personnel and high-value assets by detecting RAM launches and intercepting rounds in flight.

SPECIFICATIONS

- Primary component is the LPWS, a modified U.S. Navy Phalanx Close-In Weapon System mounted on a commercial 35-ton semitrailer for land-based operations
- M61A1 20 mm Gatling gun capable of onboard target acquisition and fire control
  - › Firing rate: 4,500 rounds per minute
- LPWS barrels optimized for use with M940 ammunition
  - › M940 designed to self-destruct beyond 2,000 meters to minimize collateral damage
- Integrated search-and-track radars detect and engage wide range of IDF threats
- C-RAM command and control system integrates sensors, weapons and warning systems

PROGRAM STATUS

- **4QFY13:**
  - › Capability Production Document approval
  - › Materiel Development Decision approval
- **1QFY15:** LPWS Operator New Equipment Training complete
- **2QFY15:** Operational Assessment

PROJECTED ACTIVITIES

- **2QFY16:** Conditional Materiel Release

C-RAM Intercept LPWS

FOREIGN MILITARY SALES
None

CONTRACTORS
Raytheon Missile Systems (Tucson, AZ)

Cryptographic Systems

PEO Command, Control and Communications – Tactical | Aberdeen Proving Ground, MD

WARFIGHTING FUNCTION

Mission Command

Movement and Maneuver

Intelligence

Fires

Sustainment

Maneuver Support and Protection

Engagement

ACQUISITION LIFECYCLE PHASE

Materiel Solution Analysis

Technology Maturation & Risk Reduction

Engineering & Manufacturing Development

Production & Deployment

Operations & Support

MILESTONE DECISION AUTHORITY

Defense Acquisition Executive

Army Acquisition Executive

Program Executive Officer

DESCRIPTION

The Communications Security (COMSEC) Cryptographic Systems Program procures, tests and fields COMSEC solutions to secure the Army's Tactical and Enterprise Networks. It is not a program of record, and therefore has no ACAT level; however, if it were, it would rival many ACAT III programs due to its overall lifecycle cost. New and emerging architectures, and DoD and Army policy, are driving the need to replace the current inventory with technologically advanced, network-centric, global-information-compliant devices. The new devices will incorporate Chairman of the Joint Chiefs of Staff and Joint Requirements Oversight Council-directed cryptographic standardization, advanced key management and network-centric performance capabilities.

BENEFIT TO THE WARFIGHTER

The Cryptographic Systems Program enables the Army to equip the force with critical cryptographic solutions and services during peacetime, wartime and contingency operations.

SPECIFICATIONS

- Inline Network Encryptor (INE) Family: Encryption systems that provide secure data and voice communications over Internet Protocol (IP) networks
- Link and Trunk Encryptor Family (LEF): Encryption systems that provide secure data and voice communication over point-to-point wideband data links
- Secure Voice Family: Encryption systems that provide secure voice and limited data communications over unsecured IP and public-switched telephone networks
- Inline Media Encryptor Family: Encryption systems that provide secure data encryption capabilities for data at rest

- Embedded Cryptographic Modernization Initiative: Retrofit of existing systems with embedded cryptographic capability ensures that they will be able to accept and utilize modern keying material; commercial solutions for classified commercially available products that when used together in a layered fashion are approved by the National Security Agency for protecting classified information

PROGRAM STATUS

- **FY13-FY14:** Pursued and executed upon the Army Airborne Secure Voice requirement
- **FY13-FY15:**
  › Continued modernization of INE, LEF and secure voice devices
  › Continuation of the Armywide Cryptographic Network Standardization effort

PROJECTED ACTIVITIES

- **1QFY17:**
  › Embedded COMSEC Modernization Production Request for Proposal (RFP)
  › KOV-21 Replacement Cryptographic Card Production and Support Services RFP
- **FY16-FY17:** Continued procurement and fielding of COMSEC Encryption Modernization Hardware

Cryptographic Systems

FOREIGN MILITARY SALES
None

CONTRACTORS
General Dynamics Communication Systems
(Needham, MA)
Harris Corp. (Palm Bay, FL)
L3 Communications (Camden, NJ)
SafeNet (Columbia, MD)
ViaSat, Inc. (Carlsbad, CA)

Defense Enterprise Wideband SATCOM System (DEWSS)

PEO Enterprise Information Systems | Fort Belvoir, VA

WARFIGHTING FUNCTION

Mission Command

Movement and Maneuver

Intelligence

Fires

Sustainment

Maneuver Support and Protection

Engagement

ACQUISITION LIFECYCLE PHASE

Materiel Solution Analysis

Technology Maturation & Risk Reduction

Engineering & Manufacturing Development

Production & Deployment

Operations & Support

MILESTONE DECISION AUTHORITY

Defense Acquisition Executive

Army Acquisition Executive

Program Executive Officer

DESCRIPTION

The Defense Enterprise Wideband SATCOM System (DEWSS) provides enterprise satellite communication systems and state-of-the-art satellite network control and planning systems for use with the Defense Satellite Communications Systems. DEWSS control systems, deployed worldwide at wideband satellite operation centers, also work with the Wideband Global Satellite and commercial satellite systems.

The DEWSS satellite communications portfolio includes terminal and baseband products that are integrated into a system-of-systems architecture supporting: strategic communications infrastructure; presidential communications; the Defense Information Systems Network; Army LandWarNet; the Ballistic Missile Defense System; and tactical reachback for deployed forces through DoD satellite communications gateways. The office provides comprehensive acquisition expertise, systems engineering and integration in support of other service program offices and Defense Agencies, including the DoD Teleport Program and the Missile Defense Agency.

BENEFIT TO THE WARFIGHTER

DEWSS provides critical satellite and terrestrial communication systems for the warfighter.

SPECIFICATIONS

DEWSS, which uses multiple hubs globally, is made up of three subproducts:

- Enterprise Terminal, an Army-developed system that communicates with satellites
- Wideband Control Facility, a primarily commercial off-the-shelf (COTS) product, which controls the information payload to the satellites and is scalable depending on user quantities
- Baseband Facility, also primarily COTS, which distributes transmissions to and from satellites and is scalable depending on user quantities

PROGRAM STATUS

- **FY13-FY15:**
  - › Completed fielding of Modernization of Enterprise Terminals (MET)/Army-Navy/GSC-52B Version 2 Large Fixed Terminal at Fort Buckner, Japan, and Ramstein Air Base, Germany
  - › Completed jackscrew replacement at Lago di Patria, Italy, supporting Ka-Band Satellite Transmit and Receive Systems
  - › Supported Senior National Leadership Communications Committee meeting in Moscow, Russia

PROJECTED ACTIVITIES

- **FY16-FY17:**
  - › Complete MET fielding at Forts Detrick and Meade, MD, and Fort Gordon, GA
  - › Complete Remote Monitoring Control Element installations at Forts Detrick and Meade; Camp Roberts, CA; Wahiawa, HI; Landstuhl, Germany; Lago di Patria, Italy; Fort Buckner, Japan; Arifjan, Kuwait; Harman, Australia; and Geraldton, Australia

Senior National Leadership Communications
Direct Communications Link
Fort Detrick, MD

Modernization of Enterprise Terminals
Installation of AN/GSC-52B(V)2
Satellite Terminal Antenna at Fort Detrick, MD

FOREIGN MILITARY SALES
None

CONTRACTORS
AASKI Technology, Inc. (Ocean, NJ)
Harris Corp. (Melbourne, FL)
Johns Hopkins University Applied Physics
Laboratory (Laurel, MD)
Northrop Grumman (Manassas, VA)

Early Entry Fluid Distribution System (E2FDS)

PEO Combat Support and Combat Service Support | Detroit Arsenal, MI

WARFIGHTING FUNCTION

Mission Command

Movement and Maneuver

Intelligence

Fires

Sustainment

Maneuver Support and Protection

Engagement

ACQUISITION LIFECYCLE PHASE

Materiel Solution Analysis

Technology Maturation & Risk Reduction

Engineering & Manufacturing Development

Production & Deployment

Operations & Support

MILESTONE DECISION AUTHORITY

Defense Acquisition Executive

Army Acquisition Executive

Program Executive Officer

DESCRIPTION

During the early phases of operations, the Early Entry Fluid Distribution System (E2FDS) is employed to throughput large quantities of petroleum or water while reducing the requirement for line-haul semitrailers, relieving main supply route congestion.

The E2FDS is a high-throughput flexible conduit system used for the transport of bulk petroleum or water on the modular battlefield. It is a rapidly emplaced conduit system capable of moving 850,000 gallons of fuel or 650,000 gallons of raw (nonpotable) water a distance of up to 50 miles in a 20-hour period. This new materiel system enhances the Inland Petroleum Distribution System (IPDS) by providing an early entry capability for petroleum throughput, as well as a means to rapidly extend existing pipeline traces or establish new traces during later phases of operations. The system is emplaced at a rate of 25 miles per day and retrieved at 10 miles per day.

The E2FDS is positioned and operated by Military Occupational Specialty 92F (petroleum supply specialist) and requires minimal engineering support to emplace the conduit or pump stations. Pump stations are centrally controlled to enable rapid and precise synchronization during pumping operations.

BENEFIT TO THE WARFIGHTER

The E2FDS enables a more rapid setup of the conduit trace, and the automation and centralized control enables greater precision of pipeline operations. Once IPDS pipeline is put in place, E2FDS can be used to extend the pipeline trace as a backup system or be moved to another location.

SPECIFICATIONS

- Comprised of flexible conduit, employment and retrieval systems
- Includes conduit support equipment (valves, couplings and joints), pump stations and a centralized control module
- Components are packed in International Standards Organization configuration for deployment and are Heavy Expanded Mobility Tactical Truck-Load Handling System, Palletized Load System (PLS) and PLS Trailer transportable

PROGRAM STATUS

- **FY15:** Request for proposal development
- **1QFY16:** Request for proposal release

PROJECTED ACTIVITIES

- **2QFY16:** Milestone (MS) B
- **3QFY16:** Contract Award
- **4QFY18:** MS C
- **4QFY20:** Full-Rate Production
- **4QFY21:** Full Materiel Release
- **3QFY22:** Full Operational Capability

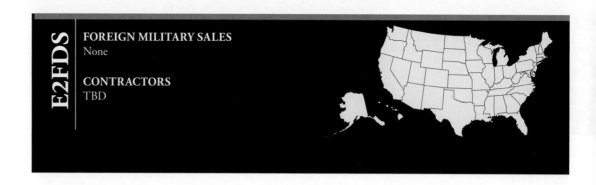

FOREIGN MILITARY SALES
None

CONTRACTORS
TBD

Engagement Skills Trainer (EST)

PEO Simulation, Training, and Instrumentation | Orlando, FL

WARFIGHTING FUNCTION

Mission Command

Movement and Maneuver

Intelligence

Fires

Sustainment

Maneuver Support and Protection

Engagement

ACQUISITION LIFECYCLE PHASE

Materiel Solution Analysis

Technology Maturation & Risk Reduction

Engineering & Manufacturing Development

Production & Deployment

Operations & Support

MILESTONE DECISION AUTHORITY

Defense Acquisition Executive

Army Acquisition Executive

Program Executive Officer

DESCRIPTION

The Engagement Skills Trainer (EST) is designed to simulate live weapon training events that directly support individual and crew-served weapons qualification, including collective and escalation-of-force exercises in a controlled environment. It provides detailed feedback to the individual fire team/squad that covers the fundamentals of marksmanship, fire control and distribution of fires.

EST provides the capability to build and sustain individual marksmanship, squad and team fire distribution, and control and judgmental use-of-force skills using computer-generated imagery and video. Home station and deploying units use EST to maintain skills when they are not able to conduct live-fire training. EST marksmanship qualification standards and collective scenarios are validated by the U.S. Army Training and Doctrine Command.

BENEFIT TO THE WARFIGHTER

EST supports ground combat readiness as the Army's virtual Basic Rifle Marksmanship training system. It provides individual marksmanship, small-unit (collective) gunnery, and tactical training and judgmental use of force (Shoot/Don't Shoot), which includes escalation-of-force/graduated response scenarios.

SPECIFICATIONS

Weapon system capabilities include:
- Small arms (pistol, rifle, carbine and grenade launcher) simulators
- Medium, crew-served weapons (M240B and M249 semi-automatic weapon) simulators
- Shoulder-fired munition (AT4 and M141 bunker-defeating munition) simulators
- Heavy machine gun (M2 and MK-19) simulators

The EST II system contract was recently awarded, and improved capabilities include:
- Moving-eye point (allows Soldiers to maneuver through a virtual battlespace scenario)

- Greater ballistic accuracy
- Higher quality 3D graphics
- 15 lanes (vs. 10 lanes)
- Tablets for roving intelligent tutoring and After Action Review capability

PROGRAM STATUS
- **3QFY14:** Base award
- **1QFY15:** System Readiness Review
- **3QFY15:** Preliminary Design Review
- **4QFY15:** Critical Design Review

PROJECTED ACTIVITIES
- **3QFY16:** Prototype evaluation
- **1QFY17-2QFY19:** Technical Refresh EST systems

FOREIGN MILITARY SALES
None

CONTRACTORS
EST II: Meggitt Training Systems (Suwanee, GA)
EST: Cubic Global Defense (San Diego, CA)

Enhanced Medium Altitude Reconnaissance and Surveillance System (EMARSS)

PEO Aviation | Redstone Arsenal, AL

WARFIGHTING FUNCTION

Mission Command

Movement and Maneuver

Intelligence

Fires

Sustainment

Maneuver Support and Protection

Engagement

ACQUISITION LIFECYCLE PHASE

Materiel Solution Analysis

Technology Maturation & Risk Reduction

Engineering & Manufacturing Development

Production & Deployment

Operations & Support

MILESTONE DECISION AUTHORITY

Defense Acquisition Executive

Army Acquisition Executive

Program Executive Officer

DESCRIPTION

The Enhanced Medium Altitude Reconnaissance and Surveillance System (EMARSS) provides a persistent Airborne Intelligence, Surveillance and Reconnaissance (AISR) capability to detect, locate, classify, identify and track surface targets with a high degree of timeliness and accuracy during the day, night and nearly all weather conditions. It enhances Brigade Combat Team effectiveness by defining and assessing the environment and providing surveillance, targeting support and threat warning.

EMARSS contains a tailored set of Distributed Common Ground System – A (DCGS-A) enabled software intelligence, surveillance and reconnaissance functionalities to process, exploit and rapidly disseminate the intelligence derived from the imagery sensor. Selected EMARSS imagery is immediately processed on the aircraft and forwarded to DCGS-A for further processing, analysis and reporting.

EMARSS complies with DoD Information Technology Standards Registry and Defense Information Systems Network. This architecture permits interoperability with any multiservice or Joint systems that comply with DoD standard formats for data transfer and dissemination.

BENEFIT TO THE WARFIGHTER

EMARSS, together with Aerial Exploitation Battalions within the Intelligence and Security Command, provides command and control, mission planning, sustainment support, and deployment packages to facilitate worldwide missions in accordance with standard Joint and Army tasking processes.

SPECIFICATIONS

- **EMARSS-S:** Multi-intelligence with Broad Spectrum Signals Intelligence and High Definition (HD) Full Motion Video (FMV)
- **EMARSS-G:** Geographical intelligence with Wide Area Surveillance, Light Imaging and Ranging, and HD FMV
- **EMARSS-M:** Multi-intelligence with Signals Intelligence and HD FMV

- **EMARSS-V:** Vehicle and Dismount Exploitation Radar (VADER) Moving Target Indication (MTI) with Vehicle and Dismount MTI, Signals Intelligence and HD FMV

PROGRAM STATUS

- **FY14:**
  › EMARSS: Capability Production Document approved; Milestone C Decision approved; authorized an acquisition strategy to leverage and incorporate Quick Reaction Capability (QRC) AISR systems into the EMARSS Program of Record (POR); transferred eight Liberty Project Aircraft from the Air Force to the Fixed Wing Project Office (FW PO) for future integration into the EMARSS-M variant; FW PO assumed overall program management responsibility for the ACAT II EMARSS Program of Record (POR)
- **FY15:**
  › Completed Limited User Test for EMARSS-S
  › Awarded Initial Variant Modification contract to initiate strategy to modify QRC aircraft to incorporate into the EMARSS POR
  › VADER: QRC – Divested two Twin Otter aircraft with VADER systems after two VADER systems (VADER 3 and 4) were fielded on King Air B300 platforms; VADER 3, 4 and 5 employed reachback control of VADER, FMV and signals intelligence via beyond-line-of-sight; VADER 5 was integrated under Rapid Acquisition Authority, completed under budget in 12 months and deployed in support of Operation Freedom Sentinel
- **1QFY16:**
  › Completion of New Equipment Training for EMARSS-S
  › Award Follow-on Variant Modification contract authorizing the modification of the remaining QRC aircraft to be incorporated into the EMARSS POR

PROJECTED ACTIVITIES

- **FY16:** Deploy and sustain OCONUS, three EMARSS-S aerial systems (MC-12S)

FOREIGN MILITARY SALES
None

CONTRACTORS
The Boeing Co. (Ridley Park, PA)
L-3 Communications Mission Integration
(Greenville, TX)
Sierra Nevada Corp. (Hagerstown, MD)
Adams Communication and Engineering
Technology, Inc. (Waldorf, MD)
Hawker Beechcraft Corp. (Wichita, KS)
L-3 Communication Systems-West (Salt Lake City, UT)
Rockwell Collins (Cedar Rapids, IA)
CACI (Arlington, VA)

Enhanced Night Vision Goggle (ENVG)

PEO Soldier | Fort Belvoir, VA

WARFIGHTING FUNCTION

Mission Command

Movement and Maneuver

Intelligence

Fires

Sustainment

Maneuver Support and Protection

Engagement

ACQUISITION LIFECYCLE PHASE

Materiel Solution Analysis

Technology Maturation & Risk Reduction

Engineering & Manufacturing Development

Production & Deployment

Operations & Support

MILESTONE DECISION AUTHORITY

Defense Acquisition Executive

Army Acquisition Executive

Program Executive Officer

DESCRIPTION

The AN/PSQ-20 Enhanced Night Vision Goggle (ENVG) provides dismounted Brigade Combat Team warfighters the capability to observe and maneuver in all weather conditions, through obscurants, during limited visibility and under all lighting conditions while enabling rapid detection and engagement with rifle-mounted aiming lasers. The ENVG uses both image intensification and infrared (thermal) sensors.

BENEFIT TO THE WARFIGHTER

The ENVG allows the individual Soldier to see, understand and act first during limited visibility conditions. It combines the visual detail in low light conditions that is provided by image intensification with the thermal sensor's ability to see through fog, dust and smoke. This thermal capability makes the ENVG useful during the day as well as at night, unlike earlier night vision devices.

SPECIFICATIONS

- Man-sized target recognition:
  › 80 percent probability at 150 meters (threshold) and 300 meters (objective)
  › 50 percent probability at 300 meters (threshold) and 550 meters (objective)
- Total system weight:
  › Less than 2 pounds (threshold) and 1.5 pounds (objective)
- Operating hours (continuous fusion):
  › Greater than 7.5 hours (threshold) and 15 hours (objective)

PROGRAM STATUS

- **2QFY15:** Contract awards to BAE Systems and DRS Technologies for ENVG III
- **3QFY15:** Critical Design Review (CDR) for DRS ENVG III design
- **4QFY15:**
  › CDR for BAE ENVG III design
  › Early User Assessment
- **1QFY16:** Production Qualification Test

PROJECTED ACTIVITIES

- **2QFY16:** Reliability Growth Test 1
- **3QFY16:** Reliability Growth Test 2
- **4QFY16:** Type Classification – Standard
- **1QFY17:**
  › ENVG III Full Materiel Release
  › ENVG III Full-Rate Production begins
- **2QFY17:** ENVG III Fieldings begin in accordance with Headquarters Department of the Army G-8 priorities

FOREIGN MILITARY SALES
None

CONTRACTORS
Harris Corp. (Roanoke, VA)
L-3 Warrior Systems (Londonderry, NH)
DRS Technologies (Melbourne, FL and Dallas, TX)
BAE Systems (Nashua, NH)

Expeditionary Water Packaging System (EWPS)

PEO Combat Support and Combat Service Support | Detroit Arsenal, MI

WARFIGHTING FUNCTION

Mission Command

Movement and Maneuver

Intelligence

Fires

Sustainment

Maneuver Support and Protection

Engagement

ACQUISITION LIFECYCLE PHASE

Materiel Solution Analysis

Technology Maturation & Risk Reduction

Engineering & Manufacturing Development

Production & Deployment

Operations & Support

MILESTONE DECISION AUTHORITY

Defense Acquisition Executive

Army Acquisition Executive

Program Executive Officer

DESCRIPTION

The Expeditionary Water Packaging System (EWPS) provides on-site water bottling capability, eliminating transportation requirements and risks. EWPS is a completely containerized, fully-automated water packaging system that fills and caps one-liter bottles with potable water for individual Soldier consumption. The EWPS features end-to-end automated production within a closed, hygienic environment.

BENEFIT TO THE WARFIGHTER

The EWPS reduces the distribution footprint for bottled water and the causalities associated with line-haul distribution. It provides inherent safety and health benefits by reducing Soldier contamination at bulk system fill points and minimizes the cost associated with procuring and transporting bottled water.

SPECIFICATIONS

- Fills 900 one-liter plastic bottles per hour, powered by standard military tactical generator sets
- Compatible with standard military Environmental Control Units

PROGRAM STATUS

- **2QFY16:** Request for Proposals released

PROJECTED ACTIVITIES

- **3QFY16:**
  › Milestone C
  › Award Production Contract
- **4QFY16:** Production and Fielding

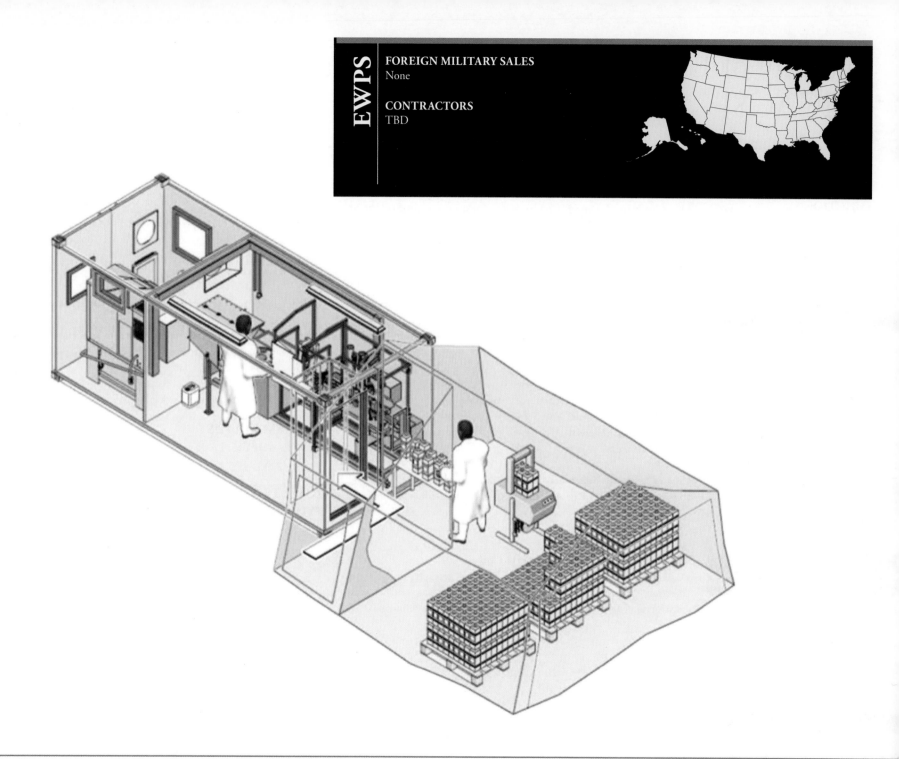

Family of Engineer Combat and Construction Sets (ECACS)

PEO Combat Support and Combat Service Support | Detroit Arsenal, MI

WARFIGHTING FUNCTION

Mission Command

Movement and Maneuver

Intelligence

Fires

Sustainment

Maneuver Support and Protection

Engagement

ACQUISITION LIFECYCLE PHASE

Materiel Solution Analysis

Technology Maturation & Risk Reduction

Engineering & Manufacturing Development

Production & Deployment

Operations & Support

MILESTONE DECISION AUTHORITY

Defense Acquisition Executive

Army Acquisition Executive

Program Executive Officer

DESCRIPTION

The Family of Engineer Combat and Construction Sets (ECACS) consists of engineer sets that aid in the detection, protection, surveillance, evacuation and clearance of buildings as well as facilities repair, road construction and other construction engineering tasks.

Hydraulic, Electric, Pneumatic, Operated Equipment (HEPPOE) provides engineer units with an effective means to operate hydraulic-electric-pneumatic tools in a non-power-sourced location while conducting theater-of-operation repair and construction tasks.

Urban Operations Platoon Set (UOpPS) provides the tools needed to mitigate gaps such as explosive detection and early and forcible entry, which enhances the engineer force's capability to rapidly shape the operational environment. The Soldier-portable tool load is composed of high-tech, commercial off-the-shelf (COTS) items contained in six ruggedized cases.

Urban Operations Squad Set (UOpSS) provides combat engineers the ability to operate in urban areas utilizing various breeching and marking techniques. The Soldier-portable tool load is composed of low-tech COTS items contained in four canvas bags.

BENEFIT TO THE WARFIGHTER

ECACS equips the warfighter with the tools necessary to perform detection, protection, surveillance and evacuation as well as any construction engineer task needed for urban and rural environments.

SPECIFICATIONS

HEPPOE:
- Includes 2 portable diesel-powered units and 13 lift cases of tools such as pavement breakers; concrete vibrators; concrete and wood chainsaws; sump pumps; various drills and saws; sanders and grinders; and post pullers

UOpPS:
- Includes vapor and trace explosives detector; Power Hawk rescue system; under-door remote-viewing instrument; articulating fiberscope; pole-mounted infrared camera; oxygen cutting torch; and portable hand-held welder

UOpSS:
- Includes urban assault ladder; breaching kit; rappelling kit; mechanical entry tools; and marker light sticks

PROGRAM STATUS
- **1QFY13-4QFY15:** Production and fielding for HEPPOE, UOpPS and UOpSS

PROJECTED ACTIVITIES
- **FY16-FY17:** Sustainment

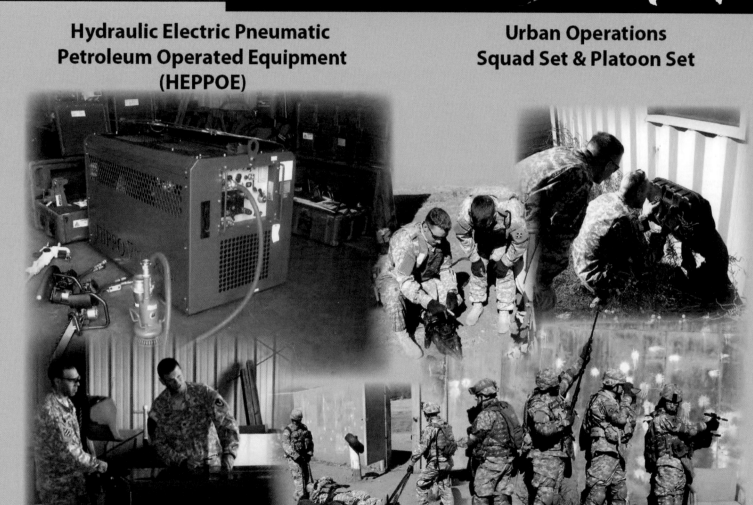

ECACS

FOREIGN MILITARY SALES
None

CONTRACTORS
Kipper Tool Company (Gainesville, GA)

Hydraulic Electric Pneumatic Petroleum Operated Equipment (HEPPOE)

Urban Operations Squad Set & Platoon Set

Family of Military Working Dogs Equipment and Kennel

PEO Ammunition | Picatinny Arsenal, NJ

WARFIGHTING FUNCTION

Mission Command

Movement and Maneuver

Intelligence

Fires

Sustainment

Maneuver Support and Protection

Engagement

ACQUISITION LIFECYCLE PHASE

Materiel Solution Analysis

Technology Maturation & Risk Reduction

Engineering & Manufacturing Development

Production & Deployment

Operations & Support

MILESTONE DECISION AUTHORITY

Defense Acquisition Executive

Army Acquisition Executive

Program Executive Officer

DESCRIPTION

Family of Military Working Dogs Equipment and Kennel provides dog handlers and kennel masters with equipment to maintain the health and well-being of the animals as well as to accomplish the missions assigned.

The program offers four equipment sets.
- **Handler Set:** Made up of leads, muzzles, collars and harnesses for management and control; bowls for feeding; tools for grooming; and a crate to ship the animal. Also includes equipment for deployments, a rappelling harness and a marking beacon.
- **Facility Set:** Consists of equipment used in a home station, including feeding and water pails, weight scales, a bite suit, tug toys and a starter pistol.
- **Obedience Course Set:** Contains the obstacles to conduct obedience training at the permanent kennel facilities.
- **Canine First-Aid Set:** Includes medical supplies such as bandages, medications, etc., to provide emergency care to the animals.

The Family of Military Working Dogs program allows military working dog handlers to deploy to a facility that will house and protect their dogs in a wide range of operational environments. Working dogs will be issued to authorized military police, provost marshal, and engineer units and activities.

BENEFIT TO THE WARFIGHTER

The kennel masters will have a consistent and common set of equipment at each facility to which they deploy.

SPECIFICATIONS

- Handler Set
- Facility Set
- Obedience Course Set
- Canine First-Aid Set
- Deployable Kennels

PROGRAM STATUS

- **3QFY14:** Milestone C for Equipment Sets, entered Production & Deployment
- **1QFY15:** First Unit Equipped for Equipment Sets
- **3QFY15:** Achieved Full Operational Capability
- **4QFY15:** Milestone C for Deployable Kennel, entered Production & Deployment
- **1QFY16:** Achieved First Unit Equipped for Deployable Kennel

PROJECTED ACTIVITIES

- **2QFY16:** Achieve Full Operational Capability

FOREIGN MILITARY SALES
None

CONTRACTORS
Equipment Sets: Garrett Container Systems, Inc.
(Accident, MD)
Deployable Kennel: Highland Engineering, Inc.
(Howell, MI)

Family of Weapon Sights – Crew Served (FWS-CS)

PEO Soldier | Fort Belvoir, VA

WARFIGHTING FUNCTION

Mission Command

Movement and Maneuver

Intelligence

Fires

Sustainment

Maneuver Support and Protection

Engagement

ACQUISITION LIFECYCLE PHASE

Materiel Solution Analysis

Technology Maturation & Risk Reduction

Engineering & Manufacturing Development

Production & Deployment

Operations & Support

MILESTONE DECISION AUTHORITY

Defense Acquisition Executive

Army Acquisition Executive

Program Executive Officer

DESCRIPTION

The Family of Weapon Sights – Crew Served (FWS-CS) will mount to the M240, M2 and Mk19 and will provide the Soldier with high-definition (HD) infrared (thermal) imagery in all weather conditions, through obscurants, and under all lighting conditions. The FWS-CS will also integrate an HD day camera, a laser rangefinder and a wireless Helmet Mounted Display.

BENEFIT TO THE WARFIGHTER

The FWS-CS HD thermal sensor and HD day camera will provide Soldiers with a long-range capability for crew-served weapons. The FWS-CS integrated laser rangefinder will support a ballistic crosshair that shifts based on the target range, enabling Soldiers to get first bursts on target. The FWS-CS wireless Helmet Mounted Display allows the Soldier to receive weapon sight imagery while behind protective armor and when using a weapon system with the Objective Gunners Protection Kit.

SPECIFICATIONS

- Man-sized target recognition at night:
  › 70 percent probability at 2,400 meters (threshold) and 2,600 meters (objective)
- Man-sized target recognition through smoke or other obscurants:
  › 90 percent probability at 500 meters (threshold) and 600 meters (objective)
- Total system weight:
  › Less than or equal to 3.25 pounds (threshold) and 2.5 pounds (objective)
- Field-of-view:
  › Greater than or equal to 9 degrees (threshold) and 18 degrees (objective)

PROGRAM STATUS

- **1QFY14:** FWS-CS Industry Days
- **2QFY15:** Draft Request for Proposal (RFP) released to industry
- **3QFY15:** Early User Assessment to influence Final RFP release
- **4QFY15:** Final RFP released to industry
- **1QFY16:** Source Selection Evaluation Board begins

PROJECTED ACTIVITIES

- **2QFY16:** Milestone B, entering Engineering & Manufacturing Development (EMD)
- **3QFY16:** EMD Contract Award
- **4QFY16:** Preliminary Design Review
- **2QFY17:** Critical Design Review
- **4QFY17:** Testing of EMD prototypes begins

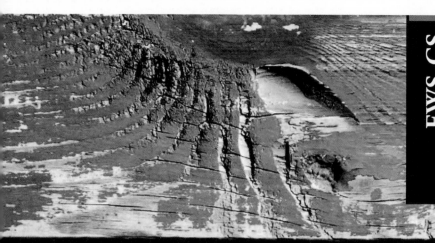

FOREIGN MILITARY SALES
None

CONTRACTORS
TBD (In Source Selection)

PENDING
CONTRACT AWARD

Family of Weapon Sights – Individual (FWS-I)

ACAT III

PEO Soldier | Fort Belvoir, VA

WARFIGHTING FUNCTION

Mission Command

Movement and Maneuver

Intelligence

Fires

Sustainment

Maneuver Support and Protection

Engagement

ACQUISITION LIFECYCLE PHASE

Materiel Solution Analysis

Technology Maturation & Risk Reduction

Engineering & Manufacturing Development

Production & Deployment

Operations & Support

MILESTONE DECISION AUTHORITY

Defense Acquisition Executive

Army Acquisition Executive

Program Executive Officer

DESCRIPTION

The Family of Weapon Sights – Individual (FWS-I) mounts to the M4 and M249 and provides the Soldier with infrared (thermal) imagery in all weather conditions, through obscurants and under all lighting conditions.

BENEFIT TO THE WARFIGHTER

The FWS-I wirelessly transmits the weapon sight crosshair and thermal imagery to the Enhanced Night Vision Goggle III providing a Rapid Target Acquisition (RTA) capability. RTA enables Soldiers to detect, recognize and engage targets accurately from any carry position and with significantly reduced exposure to enemy fire.

SPECIFICATIONS

- Man-sized target recognition at night:
  - › 70 percent probability at 960 meters (threshold) and 1,200 meters (objective)
- Man-sized target recognition through smoke or other obscurants:
  - › 90 percent probability at 300 meters (threshold) and 480 meters (objective)
- Total system weight:
  - › Less than or equal to 2 pounds (threshold) and 1.5 pounds (objective)
- Field-of-view:
  - › Greater than or equal to 18 degrees (threshold) and 26 degrees (objective)

PROGRAM STATUS

- **3QFY14:** Milestone B, entering Engineering & Manufacturing Development (EMD)
- **2QFY15:** EMD Contract Award to BAE Systems and DRS Technologies
- **1QFY16:** Reliability Growth Test 1

PROJECTED ACTIVITIES

- **2QFY16:** Developmental Testing
- **3QFY16:**
  - › Limited User Test
  - › Milestone C, Low-Rate Initial Production (LRIP) begins
- **2QFY17:** Qualification Testing of LRIP systems begins
- **3QFY17:** Reliability Growth Test 2

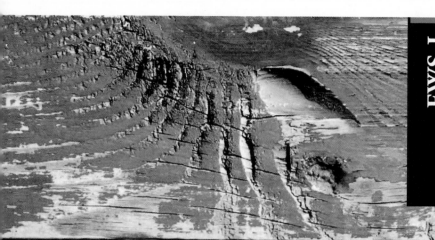

FOREIGN MILITARY SALES
None

CONTRACTORS
DRS Technologies (Melbourne, FL and Dallas, TX)
BAE Systems (Nashua, NH)

PROGRAM
UNDER DEVELOPMENT

Family of Weapon Sights – Sniper (FWS-S)

PEO Soldier | Fort Belvoir, VA

WARFIGHTING FUNCTION

Mission Command

Movement and Maneuver

Intelligence

Fires

Sustainment

Maneuver Support and Protection

Engagement

ACQUISITION LIFECYCLE PHASE

Materiel Solution Analysis

Technology Maturation & Risk Reduction

Engineering & Manufacturing Development

Production & Deployment

Operations & Support

MILESTONE DECISION AUTHORITY

Defense Acquisition Executive

Army Acquisition Executive

Program Executive Officer

DESCRIPTION

The Family of Weapon Sights – Sniper (FWS-S) will mount in-line with a sniper's day optic on the M110, M2010, M107, the Compact Semi-Automatic Sniper System and the Precision Sniper Rifle. The FWS-S will provide the Sniper with infrared (thermal) imagery in all weather conditions, through obscurants and under all lighting conditions. The FWS-S will also include a wired remote to adjust focus, a wired capability to the Small Tactical Optical Rifle Mounted (STORM) micro-Laser Rangefinder and a wireless capability to the STORM SLX (smaller, light, more cost effective).

BENEFIT TO THE WARFIGHTER

The FWS-S thermal sensor extends lethality for snipers to 1,800 meters, three times longer than the 600-meter capability provided by an image intensified system. The FWS-S will be the first clip-on thermal weapon sight specifically developed and fielded by the Army for the sniper community.

SPECIFICATIONS

- Man-sized target recognition at night:
  - › 70 percent probability at 1,800 meters (threshold) and 2,200 meters (objective)
- Man-sized target recognition through smoke or other obscurants:
  - › 90 percent probability at 600 meters (threshold) and 800 meters (objective)
- Total system weight:
  - › Less than or equal to 2 pounds (threshold) and 1.75 pounds (objective)
- Field-of-view:
  - › Greater than or equal to 4 degrees (threshold) and 9 degrees (objective)

PROGRAM STATUS

- **1QFY14:** FWS-S Industry Days
- **4QFY14:** Early User Assessment to influence Draft Request for Proposal (RFP) release
- **2QFY15:** Draft RFP released to industry
- **3QFY15:**
  - › Early User Assessment to influence final RFP release
  - › Final RFP released to industry
- **4QFY15:** Source Selection Evaluation Board begins

PROJECTED ACTIVITIES

- **2QFY16:** Milestone B, entering Engineering and Manufacturing Development (EMD)
- **3QFY16:** EMD Contract Award
- **4QFY16:** Preliminary Design Review
- **1QFY17:** Critical Design Review
- **2QFY17:** Testing of EMD prototypes begins

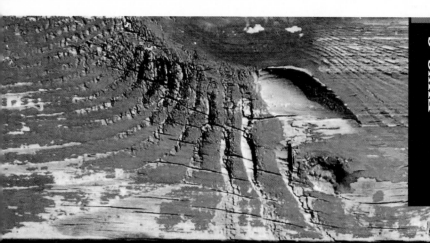

FOREIGN MILITARY SALES
None

CONTRACTORS
TBD (In Source Selection)

Fixed Wing

PEO Aviation | Redstone Arsenal, AL

WARFIGHTING FUNCTION

Mission Command

Movement and Maneuver

Intelligence

Fires

Sustainment

Maneuver Support and Protection

Engagement

ACQUISITION LIFECYCLE PHASE

Materiel Solution Analysis

Technology Maturation & Risk Reduction

Engineering & Manufacturing Development

Production & Deployment

Operations & Support

MILESTONE DECISION AUTHORITY

Defense Acquisition Executive

Army Acquisition Executive

Program Executive Officer

DESCRIPTION

Fixed Wing provides lifecycle acquisition management of the Army's fixed wing fleet of transport and manned intelligence, surveillance and reconnaissance aircraft.

Army fixed wing aviation units serve as intelligence and electronic warfare assets, provide timely movement of key personnel to critical locations throughout the theater of operations, and support worldwide peacetime contingencies and humanitarian relief efforts. The fixed wing fleet consists of 312 aircraft comprised of 8 missions, 16 designs and 35 series. All Army fixed wing aircraft are commercial derivative aircraft and are divided into three categories: Special Electronic Mission Aircraft, Transport Aircraft and Mission Support Aircraft.

The Fixed Wing Utility Aircraft (FUA), currently in development, is a retirement and replacement program for the aging and range-limited Operational Support Airlift aircraft (92 C-12 and C-26). The FUA will provide improved passenger and payload capability coupled with greater unrefueled range to support the needs of Army commanders. FUA will also integrate military communications, navigation, surveillance and survivability systems.

BENEFIT TO THE WARFIGHTER

Army fixed wing aviation units serve as intelligence and electronic warfare assets, and provide timely movement of key personnel to critical locations throughout the theater of operations.

SPECIFICATIONS

- The FUA program will have improved range, payload and high-hot performance along with the requisite aircraft survivability equipment, military multiband communication and onboard battlefield situational awareness to enable effective air movement of deployed forces.

PROGRAM STATUS

- **FY13-Current:** C-12, RC-12 and UC-35 aircraft sustained using Life Cycle Contractor Support (LCCS) Maintenance contract (L-3 Vertex); C-23 and C-26 aircraft sustained using LCCS maintenance contract (M-7 Aerospace); C-20 and C-37 aircraft sustained using LCCS maintenance contracts (Northrop Grumman Technical Services and Gulfstream)
- **FY14:** FUA Materiel Development Decision (MDD) Acquisition Decision Memorandum (ADM) signed by Army Acquisition Executive; ADM designated FUA as ACAT II program entering at Milestone C; MDD approved; FUA Milestone Decision Authority transferred to PEO Aviation; FUA is a retirement and replacement program for the Army's fleet of C-12 aircraft

PROJECTED ACTIVITIES

- **FY16:**
  - › In response to validated Operational Needs Statement 15-20470, Fixed Wing Project Office will award a contract to integrate the Communications Electronic Attack Surveillance and Reconnaissance Mission Equipment Package onto two C-12R aircraft, which will deliver in support of Overseas Contingency Operations
  - › Validation of the FUA Capability Production Document addressing capability gaps and sustainment issues with the legacy Operational Support Fleet
  - › In accordance with HQDA Execution Order 196-15, deliver 10 C-12Us to the U.S. Army Aviation Center of Excellence in Support of the Fixed Wing Transition Course; subsequently, divest 10 C-12Ds (from Fixed Wing Flight Training) by September 2016 along with four additional C-12C airplanes
- **4QFY17:** FUA Acquisition Milestone C and procurement contract award

FOREIGN MILITARY SALES
Greece

CONTRACTORS
L-3 Vertex (Madison, MS)
M-7 Aerospace (San Antonio, TX)
King Aerospace (Addison, TX)
Gulfstream (Savannah, GA)
Hawker Beechcraft Corp. (Wichita, KS)
Northrop Grumman Technical Services (Dallas, TX)
Boeing Defense, Space and Security (St. Louis, MO)
Leidos, Inc. (Reston, VA)
L-3 MID (Greenville, TX)
Sierra Nevada Corp. (Sparks, NV)
CACI International Inc. (Arlington, VA)
Adams Communication & Engineering Technology (Reston, VA)

Force Protection Systems

JPEO for Chemical and Biological Defense | Aberdeen Proving Ground, MD

WARFIGHTING FUNCTION

Mission Command

Movement and Maneuver

Intelligence

Fires

Sustainment

Maneuver Support and Protection

Engagement

ACQUISITION LIFECYCLE PHASE

Materiel Solution Analysis

Technology Maturation & Risk Reduction

Engineering & Manufacturing Development

Production & Deployment

Operations & Support

MILESTONE DECISION AUTHORITY

Defense Acquisition Executive

Army Acquisition Executive

Program Executive Officer

DESCRIPTION

Force Protection Systems consist of the following components:

- **Automated Installation Entry (AIE):** AIE is a software and hardware system that provides enhanced security through credential verification and authentication, personnel vetting and establishing permissions for Army installation access.

- **Battlefield Anti-Intrusion System (BAIS):** BAIS is a compact, modular, sensor-based warning system that can be used as a tactical stand-alone system for small units. It delivers early warning and situational awareness information based on proven, fielded, seismic and acoustic sensors and modified commercial off-the-shelf components; and classifies detections as personnel, vehicle, wheeled or tracked intrusions. BAIS provides a sizable increase in sensor density and depth to allow increased situational awareness.

- **The Lighting Kit, Motion Detector (LKMD):** LKMD is a simple, compact, modular, sensor-based early warning system that provides programmable responses of illumination and sound.

BENEFIT TO THE WARFIGHTER

AIE improves guard force efficiency by automating access control processes for personnel entering an installation and by increasing accuracy of credential vetting. BAIS and LKMD provide early detection and warning by enhancing force effectiveness as well as increasing situational awareness for small tactical units and bases.

SPECIFICATIONS

- **AIE:**
  - › System provides continuous vetting of credentials against federal data and interoperates with a defense enterprise capability to enable data sharing among Army installations, the Joint services and other agencies

  - › Can immediately adapt to threat condition changes and employ applicable restrictive entrance criteria
  - › Scalable architecture accommodates small, medium and large sites
  - › Autonomously reads and verifies personnel credentials
  - › Interfaces electronically with the Defense Enrollment Eligibility Reporting System
- **BAIS:**
  - › Consists of a hand-held monitor and three seismic/acoustic sensors
  - › Provides coverage across a platoon's defensive front (450 meters)
- **LKMD:**
  - › Modular, tactical ground sensor-based early warning system
  - › Enhances unit awareness and force effectiveness during all types of operations and environments, including small-scale contingencies and Military Operations in Urban Terrain as well as high-intensity combat

PROGRAM STATUS

AIE:
- **FY13-FY15:** Continued fielding and sustainment of existing systems

BAIS:
- **4QFY15:** Production and fielding completed

LKMD:
- **2QFY13-4QFY15:** Production completed

PROJECTED ACTIVITIES

AIE:
- **Through FY22:** Continued fielding and sustainment planned

BAIS:
- **FY16:** Complete fielding; sustainment CECOM Logistics and Readiness Center (LRC)

LKMD:
- **1QFY16 - 2QFY16:** Complete fielding; sustainment CECOM LRC begins in 1QFY16

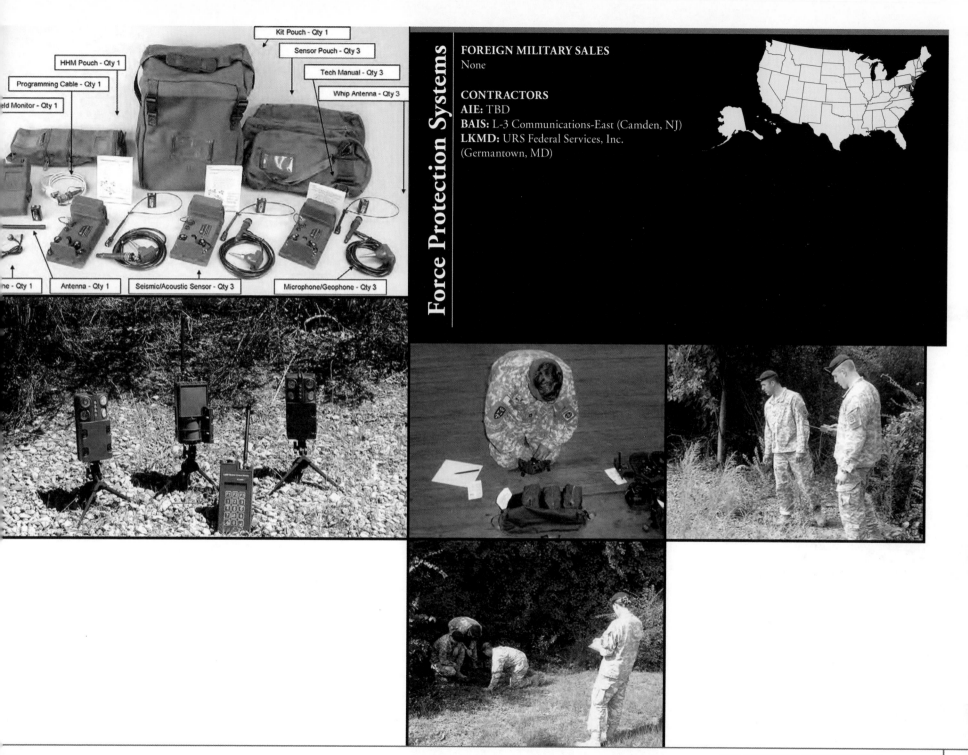

Kit Pouch - Qty 1

HHM Pouch - Qty 1

Sensor Pouch - Qty 3

Programming Cable - Qty 1

Tech Manual - Qty 3

eld Monitor - Qty 1

Whip Antenna - Qty 3

e - Qty 1

Antenna - Qty 1

Seismic/Acoustic Sensor - Qty 3

Microphone/Geophone - Qty 3

FOREIGN MILITARY SALES
None

CONTRACTORS
AIE: TBD
BAIS: L-3 Communications-East (Camden, NJ)
LKMD: URS Federal Services, Inc.
(Germantown, MD)

Force Provider (FP)

PEO Combat Support and Combat Service Support | Detroit Arsenal, MI

WARFIGHTING FUNCTION

Mission Command

Movement and Maneuver

Intelligence

Fires

Sustainment

Maneuver Support and Protection

Engagement

ACQUISITION LIFECYCLE PHASE

Materiel Solution Analysis

Technology Maturation & Risk Reduction

Engineering & Manufacturing Development

Production & Deployment

Operations & Support

MILESTONE DECISION AUTHORITY

Defense Acquisition Executive

Army Acquisition Executive

Program Executive Officer

DESCRIPTION

Each Force Provider (FP) is a high-quality deployable base camp that contains billeting, latrines, showers, laundry and kitchen facilities. The modules include fuel support, water and waste management, environmental control units, power generation and power distribution support ranging from 50- to 150-Soldier camps.

FP is staged in Army Prepositioned Stocks 1, 3 and 4 to support combatant commanders' requirements. All system components weigh less than 10,000 pounds and are prepackaged for rapid transport via air (C-130, C-141, C-5 and C-17), sea, road or rail.

Additional operational add-on kits include cold-weather kits, prime-power kits, large-scale electric kitchens, administration kits, and morale welfare and recreation kits. Resource efficiency add-ons include shower water reuse systems, energy saving shelter shades and insulating liner systems. New FP modules use AirBeam shelter technology, which reduces setup time from days to hours. These operational energy upgrades reduce fuel, power and water requirements.

BENEFIT TO THE WARFIGHTER

FP provides military personnel with configurable, containerized, expeditionary base camp modules designed to improve the warfighter's performance, morale, welfare and quality of life, while reducing fuel, power and water consumption rates.

SPECIFICATIONS

- A 150-Soldier FP set deploys via 18 triple container (TRICON) systems consisting of:
  › Eight latrine systems
  › Eight shower systems
  › One kitchen system
  › Containerized batch laundry systems
  › Fourteen TRICON refrigerated containers
  › Six 60-kW tactical quiet generators
  › 10 modular personnel tents (air supported)
  › Two 400,000 British-thermal-unit water heaters
  › One improved fuel distribution system
  › Six mobile electric power distribution replacement systems
  › 10 environmental control units
- All system components weigh less than 10,000 pounds

PROGRAM STATUS

- **FY14:** Preliminary Design Review for Rigid Wall configuration completed
- **FY14-FY15:** Energy efficiency testing of the Rigid Wall Shelter System

PROJECTED ACTIVITIES

- **2QFY16:** Integration of Rigid Wall Shelters and Full Materiel Release

FOREIGN MILITARY SALES
None

CONTRACTORS
Force Provider Assembly: Letterkenny Army Depot (Chambersburg, PA)
Expeditionary TRICON Kitchen System and Force Provider Electric Kitchen: Tri-Tech USA, Inc. (South Burlington, VT)
AirBeam TEMPER Tent: Vertigo, Inc. (Lake Elsinore, CA)
Environmental Control: Hunter Manufacturing Co. (Solon, OH)
TRICON Container: Charleston Marine Containers, Inc. (Charleston, SC)
Waste Water Evacuation Tank/Trailer: Marsh Industrial (Kalkaska, MI)
Cold Weather Kit Assembly: Berg Companies, Inc. (Spokane, WA)
Mobile Electric Power Distribution System Replacement: Lex Products Corp. (Stamford, CT)
Expeditionary TRICON Systems (shower, laundry and latrine): TBD

Global Command and Control System – Army (GCCS-A)

PEO Command, Control and Communications – Tactical | Aberdeen Proving Ground, MD

WARFIGHTING FUNCTION

Mission Command

Movement and Maneuver

Intelligence

Fires

Sustainment

Maneuver Support and Protection

Engagement

ACQUISITION LIFECYCLE PHASE

Materiel Solution Analysis

Technology Maturation & Risk Reduction

Engineering & Manufacturing Development

Production & Deployment

Operations & Support

MILESTONE DECISION AUTHORITY

Defense Acquisition Executive

Army Acquisition Executive

Program Executive Officer

DESCRIPTION

Global Command and Control System – Army (GCCS-A) is the Army's strategic, theater and tactical command, control and communications system. It provides a seamless link of operational information and critical data from the strategic GCCS – Joint (GCCS-J) to Army theater elements and below through a common picture of Army tactical operations to the Joint and Coalition communities.

GCCS-A strategic tools for readiness reporting were modernized and replaced with the Defense Readiness Reporting System – Army (DRRS-A), a suite of Web-based applications for Army Readiness, Force Registration and Force Projection.

BENEFIT TO THE WARFIGHTER

GCCS-A provides critical automated command and control tools for strategic Army Commands (division and above) to enhance the warfighter's ability to plan and execute missions throughout the spectrum of conflict during Joint and Combined operations and to provide interface between Joint and Combined Forces and tactical Army Mission Systems.

GCCS-A provides situational awareness to the operational and tactical levels throughout the Theater/Joint Task Force area of operations. The system also facilitates data exchange between Joint and Army systems.

SPECIFICATIONS

- Correlates Unique Identifier, Unique Reference Number and Unit Identification Code information to maintain persistent data across the forces
- Improves the Army's ability to analyze course of action, develop and manage Army forces and execute war plans
- Provides the Authoritative Army Common Operational Picture and links the strategic GCCS-Joint Common Operating Picture with the Army's Tactical Mission Command systems

PROGRAM STATUS

- **2QFY13-4QFY14:** Development of DRRS-A for continuing Global Force Management Data Initiative efforts
- **2QFY13-2QFY15:** Development of GCCS-A and DRRS-A software enhancements in support of the Command Post Computing Environment under the Common Operating Environment implementation plan
- **2QFY13–2QFY15:** Continued development in support of GCCS-A Modernization Bridge Effort and DRRS-A 2.4 requirements

PROJECTED ACTIVITIES

- **2QFY16:** Operational Test
- **3QFY16:** Network Integration Evaluation 16.2

FOREIGN MILITARY SALES
None

CONTRACTORS
System Hardware: General Dynamics
(Taunton, MA)
Systems Engineering and Support: Computer
Sciences Corporation (CSC) (Belcamp, MD)
Field Support Representatives (FSRs): AASKI Technology
(Ocean, NJ)

Guardrail Common Sensor (GR/CS)

PEO Aviation | Redstone Arsenal, AL

DESCRIPTION

Guardrail Common Sensor (GR/CS) provides signals intelligence (SIGINT) collection and precision targeting that intercepts, collects and precisely locates hostile communications intelligence radio frequency emitters and electronic intelligence (ELINT) threat radar emitters. It provides near-real-time information to tactical commanders in the Joint Task Force Area supporting a full spectrum of operations (close-in and deep-look collections) with emphasis on indications and warnings.

GR/CS is a fixed-wing, airborne, SIGINT-collection and precision targeting location system. It collects low-, mid- and high-band radio signals and ELINT signals; identifies and classifies them; determines source location; and provides near-real-time reporting, ensuring information dominance to commanders. GR/CS uses a Guardrail Mission Operations Facility (MOF) for the control, data processing and message center for the system.

A standard system has RC-12 aircraft flying operational missions in single-ship or multiship operations. Up to three aircraft and systems simultaneously collect communications and electronics emitter transmissions and gather lines of bearing and time-difference-of-arrival data, which is transmitted to the MOF, correlated and supplied to supported commands via National Security Agency Net.

BENEFIT TO THE WARFIGHTER

The warfighter will benefit from planned improvements through Guardrail modernization efforts, which support a full spectrum of operations, including:

- Full motion video (FMV), precision geolocation subsystem and the Communications High-Accuracy Location Subsystem – Compact with increased frequency coverage and a higher probability to collect targets
- Communications intelligence (COMINT) infrastructure and core COMINT subsystem provide a frequency extension and Enhanced Situational Awareness

- A capability to process special high-priority signals through the high-end COMINT subsystems High Band COMINT and X-Midas
- Ground processing software and hardware are being upgraded for interoperability with the Distributed Common Ground System – Army

SPECIFICATIONS

- Integrated COMINT and ELINT collection and reporting
- Enhanced signal classification and recognition and precision emitter geolocation
- Advanced integrated aircraft cockpit
- Tactical Satellite Remote Relay System

PROGRAM STATUS

- **FY13:** RC-12 fleet was reduced to 38 aircraft; three RC-12X mission aircraft were fielded bringing the total of the modernized Guardrail fleet to 14
- **FY14:** RC-12X FMV Prototype Flight Handling Qualities and Performance Flight Testing completed; eight RC-12 aircraft were deployed in support of Operation Enduring Freedom; these aircraft flew 6,721 hours and had an average mission-capable rate of 90.5 percent
- **FY15:** Four RC-12 aircraft remained deployed in support of operations in Afghanistan

PROJECTED ACTIVITIES

- **FY16:** RC-12 fleet will be reduced to 19 aircraft (14 operational and 5 trainers) with the divestment of 6 RC-12K aircraft in accordance with the Army 2020 Intelligence, Surveillance and Reconnaissance Plan; RC-12X Autopilot replacement program scheduled to begin with the induction of the prototype aircraft; continue to support contingency operations in Afghanistan with four RC-12X aircraft
- **FY17:** Field two FMV-capable systems and continue to support contingency operations

FOREIGN MILITARY SALES
None

CONTRACTORS
Northrop Grumman (Sacramento, CA)
L-3 Communications (Salt Lake City, UT)
Lockheed Martin (Owego, NY)
ArgonST (A Boeing Company) (Mountain View, CA)

Heavy Equipment Transporter System (HETS)

PEO Combat Support and Combat Service Support | Detroit Arsenal, MI

WARFIGHTING FUNCTION

Mission Command

Movement and Maneuver

Intelligence

Fires

Sustainment

Maneuver Support and Protection

Engagement

ACQUISITION LIFECYCLE PHASE

Materiel Solution Analysis

Technology Maturation & Risk Reduction

Engineering & Manufacturing Development

Production & Deployment

Operations & Support

MILESTONE DECISION AUTHORITY

Defense Acquisition Executive

Army Acquisition Executive

Program Executive Officer

DESCRIPTION

The Heavy Equipment Transporter System (HETS) consists of two pieces of equipment: the M1070 tractor and the M1000 semitrailer. The HETS tractor is used in combination with the M1000 trailer to transport the M1 Series Abrams tank and other heavy tracked and wheeled vehicles weighing up to 140,000 pounds during administrative and tactical operations. The HETS is capable of both on- and off-road operations over a variety of terrains and slopes, as well as temperature extremes from minus 50 degrees to 120 degrees Fahrenheit. Both tractors are capable of seating 6 occupants (driver, commander and 4-person tank crew) and have a heavy-duty, fully oscillating fifth wheel with a 3.5-inch kingpin and a central tire inflation system.

BENEFIT TO THE WARFIGHTER

HETS supports the warfighter with the capability to load, unload and transport the M1 Abrams tank and other heavy tracked and wheeled vehicles.

SPECIFICATIONS

Tractor:
- M1070A0
  › 2-cycle, V-8 engine, 500 horsepower
  › Automatic transmission, 5 forward and 1 reverse gears, 2-speed transfer case
- M1070A1
  › 4-cycle, in-line 6-cylinder engine, 700 horsepower
  › Automatic transmission, 7 forward and 1 reverse gears, single-speed transfer case
  › Anti-lock brakes
  › Integrated force protection

Trailer:
- M1000
  › Low-bed, fifth-wheel trailer that includes 5 axle rows
  › 4 hydraulically steered rows of bogie axles
  › 40 wheels
  › Operator-adjusted and -leveled hydraulic suspension
  › Single-cylinder, diesel engine auxiliary power unit to operate hydraulic suspension, gooseneck and steering systems

PROGRAM STATUS

- **FY13-FY15:**
  › Completed fielding of the M1070A1 tractor and M1000 trailers to Army Active Duty, Reserve and National Guard units
  › Transitioning to sustainment in FY16

PROJECTED ACTIVITIES

- **FY16-FY17:**
  › Working with European partners to coordinate administrative moves and public roadway permits in Europe
  › Updating capabilities documentation and acquisition strategies to support future weight growth of the primary HETS payloads and improve peacetime HETS operations on public roadways

FOREIGN MILITARY SALES
None

CONTRACTORS
Vehicle: Oshkosh Corp. (Oshkosh, WI)
Trailer: DRS Technologies (St. Louis, MO)

High Mobility Engineer Excavator (HMEE) I and III

PEO Combat Support and Combat Service Support | Detroit Arsenal, MI

WARFIGHTING FUNCTION

Mission Command

Movement and Maneuver

Intelligence

Fires

Sustainment

Maneuver Support and Protection

Engagement

ACQUISITION LIFECYCLE PHASE

Materiel Solution Analysis

Technology Maturation & Risk Reduction

Engineering & Manufacturing Development

Production & Deployment

Operations & Support

MILESTONE DECISION AUTHORITY

Defense Acquisition Executive

Army Acquisition Executive

Program Executive Officer

DESCRIPTION

The High Mobility Engineer Excavator Type I (HMEE-I) is a nondevelopmental military vehicle fielded to the Army's Brigade Combat Teams (BCT) and other selected engineering units. Tasks performed by the HMEE-I and III include repair and improvement of roads, trails, bridges and airfields.

The high mobility of the HMEE-I provides earth-moving machines capable of maintaining pace with the Army's current combat systems. All HMEE-I will be capable of accepting armor in the form of an armor cab (Crew Protection Kit), are C-130 transportable without armor, and diesel driven. HMEE-I replaces Small Emplacement Excavators in BCT and HMEE-I in Stryker BCT. The HMEE-I is employed in Infantry BCT, Armored BCT, Stryker BCT, Multi-Role Bridge Companies and Engineering Support Companies.

The HMEE-III Backhoe Loader is a commercial off-the-shelf backhoe loader with military modifications to include an armored cab designed for units that are relatively stationary and do not require speed and rapid deployability. The HMEE-III is used by Combat Support Brigades in general construction tasks. It is employed by Horizontal and Vertical Construction Units, and other nonengineering units such as Military Police and Quartermaster Units.

BENEFIT TO THE WARFIGHTER

The HMEE clears rubble and debris from routes and airfields. It provides survivability positions for critical assets like communication, control, radar and logistics, and improves ford sites.

SPECIFICATIONS

HMEE-I:
- Maximum speed: 60 mph on improved roads; 25 mph on secondary roads
- Lift and load: 1.5 cubic yards
- 13 total attachments

HMEE-III:
- Maximum speed: 60 mph on improved roads; 7 mph off roads
- Weight: approximately 18,700 pounds

PROGRAM STATUS

- **FY13-FY15:** HMEE-I fielding

PROJECTED ACTIVITIES

- **3QFY17:** HMEE-I fielding will be completed with the conclusion of the production contract

HMEE I and III

FOREIGN MILITARY SALES
HMEE-I: Israel and New Zealand
Original Equipment Manufacturer (OEM)
Direct Sales: United Kingdom, United Arab Emirates, Sweden, Australia and Germany

CONTRACTORS
HMEE-I OEM: JCB Inc. (Pooler, GA)
Armor: ADSI (Hicksville, NY); JCB Inc. (Pooler, GA)
Logistics: XMCO (Warren, MI)
HMEE-III Backhoe Loader OEM: Case New Holland (Racine, WI)
Armor: BAE Systems (Columbus, OH)
Logistics: XMCO (Warren, MI)

Home Station Instrumentation Training System (HITS)

PEO Simulation, Training, and Instrumentation | Orlando, FL

WARFIGHTING FUNCTION

Mission Command

Movement and Maneuver

Intelligence

Fires

Sustainment

Maneuver Support and Protection

Engagement

ACQUISITION LIFECYCLE PHASE

Materiel Solution Analysis

Technology Maturation & Risk Reduction

Engineering & Manufacturing Development

Production & Deployment

Operations & Support

MILESTONE DECISION AUTHORITY

Defense Acquisition Executive

Army Acquisition Executive

Program Executive Officer

DESCRIPTION

The Home Station Instrumentation Training System (HITS) is designed to enhance training at home stations by instrumenting force-on-force live training exercises for battalion-and-below units.

HITS includes automated tools to establish medium fidelity cause-and-effect analysis of battalion-and-below collective training performance in unified land operations. It is an integrated system of computer software and hardware; workstations; databases; voice, video, and data recording; production and presentation equipment; interface devices; and communication networks. It provides the tools for the Observer-Controller, Trainer and Operators to collect, analyze and present training performance feedback in the After Action Review (AAR) and a unit take-home package. HITS is a transportable system that can be rapidly deployed to support field training exercises. It operates at Mission Assurance Category III Sensitive, and produces Controlled Unclassified Information. HITS provides the live domain for the Live, Virtual, Constructive (LVC) Integrated Training Environment established by the LVC-Integrating Architecture Program. HITS is part of the Live Training Transformation – Family of Training Systems and is based on the Common Training Instrumentation Architecture.

BENEFIT TO THE WARFIGHTER

HITS tracks Soldiers and vehicles while collecting their real-time casualty assessment information during battalion level force-on-force collective training exercises. This allows the HITS Exercise Control to monitor and record the participant's position and the results of who shot whom, when, where and with what outcome.

SPECIFICATIONS

- Provides continuous support 24/7 during training
- Interoperates with up to 1,162 instrumented personnel and vehicles outfitted with the Instrumentable – Multiple Integrated Laser Engagement System
- HITS Battle Manager application allows operators to conduct fire missions and employ minefields and improvised explosive devices, allowing automatic adjudication of casualty and damage effects of these attacks
- Allows the operator to monitor and record training unit voice transmissions from up to four Single Channel Ground and Airborne Radio System channels
- Captures video that can be edited and embedded to display in an AAR

PROGRAM STATUS

- **FY13-FY15:** Fielded 12 systems to various home stations

PROJECTED ACTIVITIES

- **4QFY16:** Complete Basis of Issue Fielding

FOREIGN MILITARY SALES
None

CONTRACTORS
Cubic Global Defense (San Diego, CA)

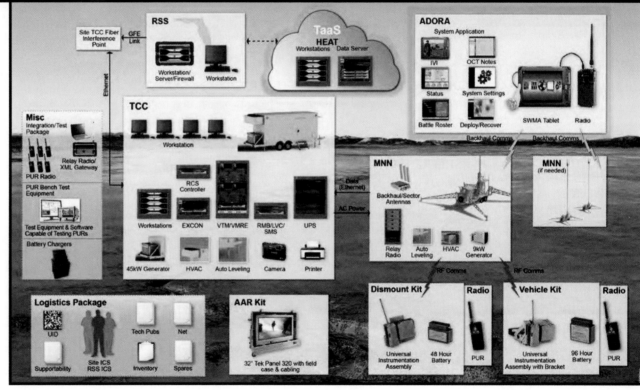

Husky Mounted Detection System (HMDS)

PEO Intelligence, Electronic Warfare and Sensors | Aberdeen Proving Ground, MD

WARFIGHTING FUNCTION

Mission Command

Movement and Maneuver

Intelligence

Fires

Sustainment

Maneuver Support and Protection

Engagement

ACQUISITION LIFECYCLE PHASE

Materiel Solution Analysis

Technology Maturation & Risk Reduction

Engineering & Manufacturing Development

Production & Deployment

Operations & Support

MILESTONE DECISION AUTHORITY

Defense Acquisition Executive

Army Acquisition Executive

Program Executive Officer

DESCRIPTION

The Husky Mounted Detection System (HMDS) is a counter-improvised explosive device system that provides stand-off detection and marking of surface-laid and buried explosive hazards, booby-traps and unexploded ordnance in complex and urban terrain in support of route clearance operations. HMDS is a mission equipment package mounted on current and programmed Husky vehicles organic to engineer units.

BENEFIT TO THE WARFIGHTER

HMDS will detect and mark explosive hazards, operate in complex and urban terrain, minimize warfighter workload, and move the warfighter out of the blast zone.

SPECIFICATIONS

HMDS will be developed in three increments:

- **Increment A1:** Ground Penetrating Radar (GPR) (variant used currently in theater) and stand-alone GPR V1 trainer
- **Increment A2:** GPR with an integrated Deep Buried Detection capability, Common Installation Kit and associated training devices
- **Increment B:** Semi-autonomous control of Husky vehicle and HMDS

PROGRAM STATUS

- **4QFY13:** Milestone (MS) B, entered Engineering & Manufacturing Development
- **3QFY14:** Increment A2 Contract Award
- **4QFY14:**
  - › Increment A1 Developmental Test
  - › Increment A2 System Functional Review
- **1QFY15:** Increment A2 Preliminary Design Review
- **2QFY15:** Increment A1 Limited User Test
- **3QFY15:** Integrated Baseline Review

PROJECTED ACTIVITIES

- **4QFY16:** MS C

Improved Environmental Control Units (IECU)

PEO Combat Support and Combat Service Support | Detroit Arsenal, MI

WARFIGHTING FUNCTION

Mission Command

Movement and Maneuver

Intelligence

Fires

Sustainment

Maneuver Support and Protection

Engagement

ACQUISITION LIFECYCLE PHASE

Materiel Solution Analysis

Technology Maturation & Risk Reduction

Engineering & Manufacturing Development

Production & Deployment

Operations & Support

MILESTONE DECISION AUTHORITY

Defense Acquisition Executive

Army Acquisition Executive

Program Executive Officer

DESCRIPTION

The Improved Environmental Control Unit (IECU) program consists of three standard shelter-mounted systems in the following sizes: 9,000 British thermal units per hour (Btuh); 18,000 Btuh; 36,000 Btuh; and one skid-mounted unit of 60,000 Btuh. The IECU systems provide critical cooling to vital military electronic and support systems and equipment for the Army and DoD.

BENEFIT TO THE WARFIGHTER

The IECU systems provide quality cooling, heating and dehumidification for command posts; command, control, communications, computers, intelligence, surveillance and reconnaissance systems; weapon systems; and other battlefield operating systems while using a non-ozone depleting refrigerant.

SPECIFICATIONS

- Form, fit and function replacement of military standard (MIL-STD) Environmental Control Units (ECU)
- Ruggedized for military environments
- Increased reliability over current MIL-STD ECU
- Reduced power consumption resulting in overall fuel savings
- Reduced weight: 10-25 percent lighter than current MIL-STD ECU
- Fully operable up to 125 degrees Fahrenheit
- Uses R-410A refrigerant, a commercial industry standard
- Compliant with all environmental legislative requirements
- Soft start, limited inrush current (no voltage drop or breaker trip due to compressor start-up)
- Electromagnetic interference and nuclear, biological and chemical-protected interface
- Remote control capability with automatic safety controls
- Organically supportable

PROGRAM STATUS

- **3QFY15:** Completed 60,000 Btuh IECU Full-Rate Production (FRP)
- **1QFY13-4QFY15:** Continued 9,000, 18,000, 36,000 Btuh IECU Engineering & Manufacturing Development (EMD) Phase II

PROJECTED ACTIVITIES

- **1QFY16-4QFY16:** 9,000, 18,000, 36,000 Btuh continue EMD
- **1QFY17:** 9,000, 18,000, 36,000 Btuh Milestone C, entering production

9k Btuh IECU

FOREIGN MILITARY SALES
None

CONTRACTORS
9,000, 18,000, 36,000 Btuh IECU: Mainstream
Engineering Corp. (Rockledge, FL)
60,000 Btuh IECU: DRS Environmental
Systems, Inc. (Florence, KY)

60k Btuh IECU

18k Btuh IECU

Improved Ribbon Bridge (IRB)

PEO Combat Support and Combat Service Support | Detroit Arsenal, MI

WARFIGHTING FUNCTION

Mission Command

Movement and Maneuver

Intelligence

Fires

Sustainment

Maneuver Support and Protection

Engagement

ACQUISITION LIFECYCLE PHASE

Materiel Solution Analysis

Technology Maturation & Risk Reduction

Engineering & Manufacturing Development

Production & Deployment

Operations & Support

MILESTONE DECISION AUTHORITY

Defense Acquisition Executive

Army Acquisition Executive

Program Executive Officer

DESCRIPTION

The Improved Ribbon Bridge (IRB) is used to transport weapon systems, troops and supplies over water when permanent bridges are not available, and thereby supports the Joint force commander's ability to employ and sustain forces worldwide.

The bridge system allows two-way traffic for High Mobility Multipurpose Wheeled Vehicle-width vehicles and increased Military Load Capacity at all water current speeds over those of the Standard Ribbon Bridge. It is usable on increased bank heights more than 2.2 meters and the improved folding and unfolding mechanism avoids cable breakage. Partially disassembled bays are C-130 transportable and externally transportable by CH-47 and CH-53 aircraft.

The Improved Ribbon Bridge Float Ribbon Bridge System is issued to the Multi-Role Bridge Company (MRBC). The Army Modified Table of Organization and Equipment authorizes MRBC to consist of: 42 IRB bridge bays (30 interior bays and 12 ramp bays); 42 Bridge Adapter Pallets; 14 Bridge Erection Boats (BEB); 14 Improved Boat Cradles; and 56 Common Bridge Transporters (CBT). These assets collectively address Tactical Float Ribbon Bridge "wet-gap" bridging. All components are required to transport, launch, erect and retrieve up to 210 meters of floating bridge per MRBC. The IRB can be configured as either a continuous full-closure bridge or assembled and used for rafting operations.

BENEFIT TO THE WARFIGHTER

The IRB allows for crossings of faster water with higher banks in contingency operations abroad and disaster relief and recovery efforts at home. It enables Soldiers to cross rivers, lakes, or other bodies of water in the absence of a means of crossing or in the event of an unreliable or damaged permanent bridge. The IRB provides commanders an important option to rapidly close distances and move critical capabilities and supplies by enabling formations to reliably cross gaps of still or moving water with currents of up to 10 feet per second.

SPECIFICATIONS

IRB Military Load Capacity:
- 105 wheeled or 85 tracked (normal)
- 110 wheeled or 90 tracked (caution crossing)

PROGRAM STATUS

IRB (BAYS):
- **3QFY13:** Fielding 310th MRBC
- **3QFY14:** Fielding Army Prepositioned Stocks

BEB:
- **1QFY15:** Milestone C
- **3QFY15:** Production Qualification Testing begins

PROJECTED ACTIVITIES

IRB (BAYS):
- **FY16-FY17:** Sustainment

BEB:
- **3QFY16:** Limited User Test
- **3QFY17:** Full-Rate Production Decision

FOREIGN MILITARY SALES
None

CONTRACTORS
General Dynamics European Land Systems –
Germany (GDELS-G) (Kaiserslautern, Germany)
Logistic support: AM General (Livonia, MI)
CBT manufacturer: Oshkosh Corp.
(Oshkosh, WI)
BEB manufacturer: Birdon Corporation (Denver, CO)

Improved Target Acquisition System (ITAS)

ACAT III

PEO Missiles and Space | Redstone Arsenal, AL

WARFIGHTING FUNCTION

Mission Command

Movement and Maneuver

Intelligence

Fires

Sustainment

Maneuver Support and Protection

Engagement

ACQUISITION LIFECYCLE PHASE

Materiel Solution Analysis

Technology Maturation & Risk Reduction

Engineering & Manufacturing Development

Production & Deployment

Operations & Support

MILESTONE DECISION AUTHORITY

Defense Acquisition Executive

Army Acquisition Executive

Program Executive Officer

DESCRIPTION

The Improved Target Acquisition System (ITAS) provides long-range sensor and anti-armor/precision assault fire capabilities, enabling the Soldier to shape the battlefield by detecting and engaging targets at long range with Tube-Launched, Optically Tracked, Wireless-Guided (TOW) Missiles; or directing the employment of other weapon systems to destroy those targets. ITAS is a multipurpose weapon system, used as a reconnaissance, surveillance and target acquisition sensor.

ITAS's second-generation forward-looking infrared sensors double the long-range surveillance of its predecessor, the M220 TOW system. ITAS offers improved hit probability with aided target tracking, improved missile flight software algorithms and an elevation brake to minimize launch transients. The system includes an integrated far-target location (FTL) capability (day-and-night sight with laser rangefinder), a position attitude determination subsystem, a fire-control subsystem, a lithium-ion battery power source and a modified traversing unit. Soldiers can also detect and engage long-range targets with TOW Missiles or, using the ITAS FTL enhancement, direct other fires to destroy them. The FTL enhancement consists of a position attitude determination subsystem that provides the gunner with his own Global Positioning System (GPS) location and a 10-digit grid location to his target through the use of differential GPS. With the PAQ-4/PEQ-2 Laser Pointer, ITAS can designate .50 Caliber or MK-19 grenade engagements. The ITAS can fire all versions of the TOW Family of Missiles.

The ITAS Image Enhancement Modification Kit reduces operator workload by optimizing the image presented to the gunner through electronic processing. Electronic focus, image stabilization, and other processing techniques ensure that the image presented is optimized for the environment without manual manipulation of the various adjustment settings. ITAS operates from the High Mobility Multipurpose Wheeled Vehicle, the dismount tripod platform and Stryker anti-tank guided missile vehicles. ITAS is the Infantry's precision weapon of choice in combat engagements.

BENEFIT TO THE WARFIGHTER

ITAS provides long-range anti-armor/precision assault fire capabilities to the Army's Infantry and Stryker Brigade Combat Teams as well as to the Marine Corps. ITAS is a major product upgrade that greatly reduces the number of components, minimizing logistics support and equipment requirements. Built-in diagnostics and improved interfaces enhance target engagement performance.

SPECIFICATIONS

- Superior long-range surveillance (second-generation forward-looking infrared)
- Long-range, lethal, heavy, close combat and precision assault fires
- Laser rangefinder (10 km)/Aided Target Tracker
- Fires all versions of TOW Missile
- Automatic boresight capability
- FTL capability
- Embedded training and Multiple Integrated Laser Engagement System
- 16-hour Silent Watch capability

PROGRAM STATUS

- **FY13-FY15:** Continued fielding of Image Enhancement modification kits to the fleet

PROJECTED ACTIVITIES

- **4QFY17:** Complete fielding of Image Enhancement modification kits to the fleet

FOREIGN MILITARY SALES
Canada and the NATO Support and
Procurement Agency

CONTRACTORS
Raytheon (McKinney, TX)

Instrumentable – Multiple Integrated Laser Engagement System (I-MILES)

PEO Simulation, Training, and Instrumentation | Orlando, FL

WARFIGHTING FUNCTION

Mission Command

Movement and Maneuver

Intelligence

Fires

Sustainment

Maneuver Support and Protection

Engagement

ACQUISITION LIFECYCLE PHASE

Materiel Solution Analysis

Technology Maturation & Risk Reduction

Engineering & Manufacturing Development

Production & Deployment

Operations & Support

MILESTONE DECISION AUTHORITY

Defense Acquisition Executive

Army Acquisition Executive

Program Executive Officer

DESCRIPTION

The Instrumentable – Multiple Integrated Laser Engagement System (I-MILES) is designed to simulate both the firing capabilities and the vulnerability of dismounted troops, tactical vehicles and combat vehicles and to objectively assess weapon effects during training. This provides unit commanders an integrated training system to use at the home station local training area and instrumented training areas. It will replace legacy systems at the End of Useful Life and in accordance with the Armywide distribution plan.

I-MILES is a laser-based training device used on Soldiers, small arms, tactical vehicles, tanks, Bradley Fighting Vehicles and opposing forces to provide real-time casualty effects. The I-MILES program is comprised of five product lines:
• Individual Weapon System
• Tactical Vehicle System
• Combat Vehicle System
• Shoulder Launched Munitions
• Universal Controller Device

Together, these provide the ability to adjudicate force-on-force training and provide data used in the After Action Review. It is an evolutionary approach to replace older I-MILES equipment with devices that provide better training fidelity. Use of the system, from squad-through-brigade-level exercises, reinforces good tactical maneuver skills by training Soldiers how to avoid direct fire as well as reward good target engagement ability. The system interfaces with instruments at both home stations and Combat Training Centers. The I-MILES modular design will accommodate new weapons, ammunition, vulnerabilities and vehicle types. The Army will use and field I-MILES worldwide.

BENEFIT TO THE WARFIGHTER

I-MILES allows soldiers to train as they fight using their tactical equipment and adding I-MILES equipment. Soldiers can function fully and operate as they would in a cooperative environment with other local units or multinational partners.

SPECIFICATIONS
• Works with a variety of weapon platforms
• Uses laser transmitter that sends simulated laser MILES code at laser detectors attached to Soldiers, vehicles, etc.
• Uses Class 1 and 3A lasers to replicate the engagement effects of line-of-sight weapon systems
• Capable of operating between 100 and 336 hours without power source replacement

PROGRAM STATUS
• **FY15:** Approximately 90,818 kits fielded

PROJECTED ACTIVITIES
• **4QFY16:**
  › Vehicle Tactical Engagement Simulation System (VTESS) award (568 kits)
  › Individual Weapon System (IWS) 27,994 kits
  › Combat VTESS 936 Basis of Issue plus 237 U.S. Army Europe for total of 1,173 kits (last year of procurement)
• **4QFY17:**
  › VTESS 2,440 kits
  › IWS 15,959 kits (last year of procurement)

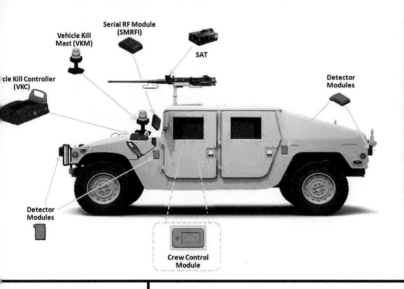

Serial RF Module (SMRFI)

Vehicle Kill Mast (VKM)

Vehicle Kill Controller (VKC)

SAT

Detector Modules

Detector Modules

Crew Control Module

FOREIGN MILITARY SALES
None

CONTRACTORS
Cubic Global Defense (San Diego, CA)
Saab Training USA, LLC (Orlando, FL)

Vehicle Kill Mast (VKM)

Vehicle Kill Controller (VKC)

Detector Modules (wireless)

Other Components - Not Visible in Image

Serial RF Module (SMRFI)

Crew Control Module (CCM)

Note: Not included but works with M2 or M240 Small Arms Transmitters (SATs)

Integrated Family of Test Equipment (IFTE)

PEO Combat Support and Combat Service Support | Detroit Arsenal, MI

WARFIGHTING FUNCTION

Mission Command

Movement and Maneuver

Intelligence

Fires

Sustainment

Maneuver Support and Protection

Engagement

ACQUISITION LIFECYCLE PHASE

Materiel Solution Analysis

Technology Maturation & Risk Reduction

Engineering & Manufacturing Development

Production & Deployment

Operations & Support

MILESTONE DECISION AUTHORITY

Defense Acquisition Executive

Army Acquisition Executive

Program Executive Officer

DESCRIPTION

The Integrated Family of Test Equipment (IFTE) consists of at- and off-platform automatic test systems. They provide electronic fault isolation as well as diagnostic and repair capabilities at all levels of maintenance more cost-effectively than system-specific testers. The IFTE, designed to support multiple weapon systems, includes:

Base Shop Test Facility – Version 3 (BSTF-V3):
The BSTF(V)3 is an off-platform automatic test system that tests electronic Line Replaceable Units and Shop Replaceable Units of ground and aviation systems.

Electro-Optics Test Facility (EOTF):
The EOTF tests the full range of Army electro-optical systems: laser transmitters, receivers, spot trackers, forward-looking infrared systems and television systems. It is fully mobile with Versa Module Europa eXtensions for Instrumentation, touch-screen operator interface and an optical disk system for test program software and electronic manuals.

Next Generation Automatic Test System (NGATS):
The NGATS is the follow-on reconfigurable, rapidly deployable, expeditionary interoperable tester and screener that supports Joint operations by reducing the logistics footprint. It replaces and consolidates obsolete, unsupportable test equipment in the Army's inventory.

Maintenance Support Device – Version 3 (MSD-V3):
The MSD-V3, a lightweight, rugged, compact, man-portable, general purpose tester, supports more than 50 weapon systems and is used by more than 40 military occupational specialties. It verifies the operational status of aviation, automotive, watercraft, electronic and missile weapon systems, and isolates faulty components for immediate repair or replacement. MSD-V3 hosts Interactive Electronic Technical Manuals, Aircraft Notebook software, and the Global Combat Support System – Army software enabling information entry into the logistics enterprise. It is used as a software uploader and verifier to provide or restore mission software to weapon systems, and is capable of supporting condition-based maintenance data collection and reporting.

BENEFIT TO THE WARFIGHTER

MSD-V3 provides an environmentally hardened tester capable of supporting multiple Army weapon systems and reduces the logistics footprint. NGATS provides the warfighter with automated test equipment that is significantly more reliable, offers increased mobility and provides substantially more capability than the obsolete legacy systems it replaces.

SPECIFICATIONS

- **MSD-V3:**
  › Dimensions: 11 inches wide, 10 inches deep and 4 inches high
  › Weight: 13 pounds (core and dock plus two batteries)
- **NGATS:**
  › Housed in a 20-foot International Organization for Standardization (ISO) shelter that uses a Heavy Expanded Mobility Tactical Truck as the prime mover as well as a 20-foot ISO shelter for storage of the accompanying Test Program Sets

PROGRAM STATUS

- **4QFY14:** NGATS Console contract awarded
- **4QFY15:** NGATS First Unit Acceptance Test conducted
- **Current:** MSD-V3 fielding; BSTF-V3/EOTF operations and support

PROJECTED ACTIVITIES

- **2QFY16:** NGATS Shelter contract award
- **1QFY17:**
  › NGATS Transportability Testing and Operational Assessment
  › MSD-V4 Rugged contract award (follow-on to MSD-V3)
- **2QFY17:** NGATS Type Classification-Standard; MSD-V4 Light contract award (follow-on to MSD-V3)
- **4QFY17:** NGATS First Unit Equipped

IFTE

FOREIGN MILITARY SALES
MSD: Afghanistan, Australia, Bahrain, Chile, Djibouti, Egypt, Ethiopia, Germany, Israel, Iraq, Jordan, Korea, Kuwait, Lithuania, Macedonia, Morocco, Netherlands, Oman, Poland, Portugal, Saudi Arabia, Taiwan, Turkey, United Arab Emirates, Uzbekistan and Yemen

CONTRACTORS
MSD-V3: Vision Technology Miltope Corp. (Hope Hull, AL)
BSTF-V3 and EOTF: Northrop Grumman (Rolling Meadows, IL)
NGATS: The Boeing Company (St. Louis, MO)

Intelligence Electronic Warfare Tactical Proficiency Trainer (IEWTPT)

PEO Simulation, Training, and Instrumentation | Orlando, FL

WARFIGHTING FUNCTION

Mission Command

Movement and Maneuver

Intelligence

Fires

Sustainment

Maneuver Support and Protection

Engagement

ACQUISITION LIFECYCLE PHASE

Materiel Solution Analysis

Technology Maturation & Risk Reduction

Engineering & Manufacturing Development

Production & Deployment

Operations & Support

MILESTONE DECISION AUTHORITY

Defense Acquisition Executive

Army Acquisition Executive

Program Executive Officer

DESCRIPTION

Intelligence Electronic Warfare Tactical Proficiency Trainer (IEWTPT) provides Military Intelligence (MI)-specific Warfighting-Function training at home stations to support the sustainment of critical individual and collective tasks, skills and Army Force Generation. IEWTPT fills critical intelligence warfighter training gaps at home stations for Human Intelligence (HUMINT), Signals Intelligence (SIGINT), Geospatial Intelligence (GEOINT) and All Source intelligence. It directly supports individual, crew and collective sustainment training in support of mission command and unified land operations. IEWTPT acts as the key enabler for military intelligence analyst and operator training in a live, virtual and constructive simulation environment. It supports the Intelligence Center of Excellence MI holistic training strategy for both stand-alone and network-enabled training.

The Technical Control Cell is the cornerstone training device of the IEWTPT. It powers SIGINT, GEOINT and All Source capabilities that enable individual and collective training, as well as the network interface to the exercise training environment.

The HUMINT Control Cell provides sustainment training for HUMINT and counterintelligence collectors in an immersive and virtual training environment.

BENEFIT TO THE WARFIGHTER

Intelligence is an essential enabler of ground combat readiness. The IEWTPT is the Army's only system that supports the sustainment of mission-essential and highly perishable skills of intelligence collectors and analysts. In addition to training individual measure-of-suitability skills, the IEWTPT facilitates collective training across the various intelligence disciplines.

SPECIFICATIONS

The IEWTPT technology is comprised of:

- Technical Control Cell (TCC), a server stack that includes exercise scenario development tools, management tools and an After Action Review capability
- HUMINT Control Cell, which consists of a 40-inch visual display, 3 laptop computers, a headset and 2 speakers

PROGRAM STATUS

- **3QFY15:** System certification inspections by Department of the Army Military Intelligence - G2, Fort Bragg, NC, Korea, Schofield Barracks, HI
- **3QFY15-4QFY15:** Competitive contract planning and execution
- **4QFY15:** SIGINT Exercise 2nd Brigade, 82nd Airborne Division

PROJECTED ACTIVITIES

- **2QFY16:**
  - › TCC fielding to Fort Stewart, GA
  - › Release Request for Proposal for IEWTPT recompete
- **3QFY16:** TCC fielding; TBD to Fort Gordon or Fort Gillem, GA

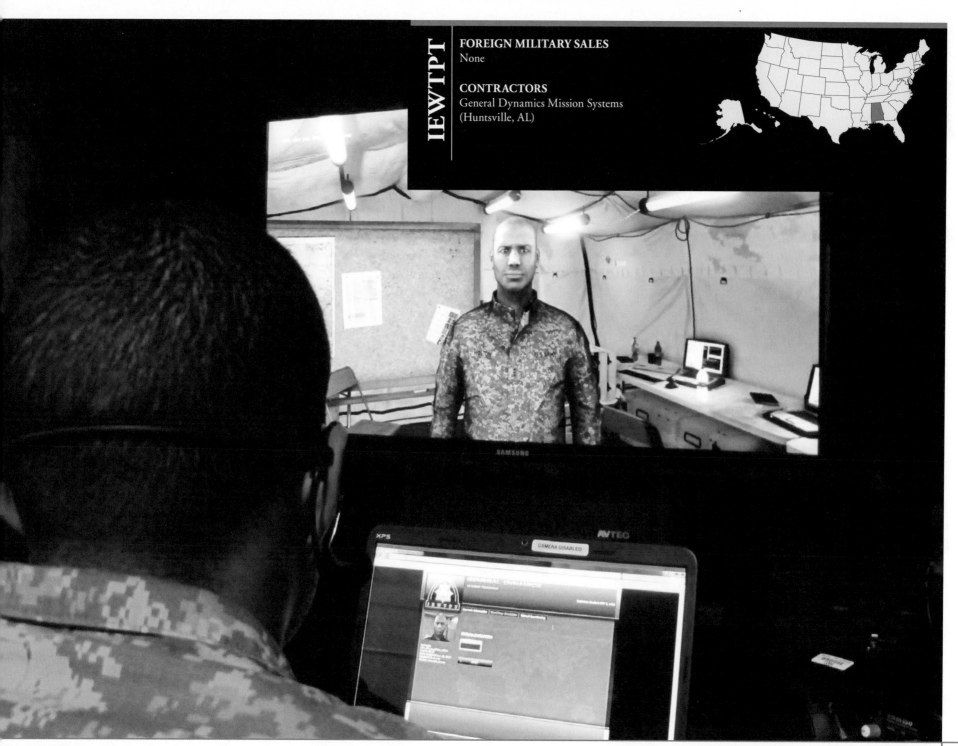

FOREIGN MILITARY SALES
None

CONTRACTORS
General Dynamics Mission Systems
(Huntsville, AL)

CAMERA DISABLED

Joint Assault Bridge (JAB)

PEO Combat Support and Combat Service Support | Detroit Arsenal, MI

WARFIGHTING FUNCTION

Mission Command

Movement and Maneuver

Intelligence

Fires

Sustainment

Maneuver Support and Protection

Engagement

ACQUISITION LIFECYCLE PHASE

Materiel Solution Analysis

Technology Maturation & Risk Reduction

Engineering & Manufacturing Development

Production & Deployment

Operations & Support

MILESTONE DECISION AUTHORITY

Defense Acquisition Executive

Army Acquisition Executive

Program Executive Officer

DESCRIPTION

The Joint Assault Bridge (JAB) provides the Army Mobility Augmentation Companies supporting Armored Brigade Combat Teams with a survivable, deployable and sustainable heavy-assault-bridging capability. The JAB will provide a gap-crossing capability to cross wet or dry gaps to provide freedom of maneuver on the battlefield and keep pace with Abrams Heavy Brigade Combat Team operations. The JAB is a M1A1 Abrams tank hull with heavy (M1A2) suspension integrated with a hydraulic bridge launcher system to launch the existing Armored Vehicle Launched Bridge (AVLB) Military Load Class 85 Scissor Bridge. The JAB improves force readiness, survivability, mobility and agility equal to the legacy force.

BENEFIT TO THE WARFIGHTER

The JAB provides survivability equal to the M1A1 chassis. It is the sustainable system designated to replace the AVLB system (chassis and launcher), which is mounted on an obsolete and unsupportable chassis. The M1A1 Abrams chassis base makes this system more affordable than the Wolverine (M1A2 System Enhancement Program-based). The JAB will replace the AVLB system (chassis and launcher) on a 1-for-1 basis up to 337 JAB systems.

SPECIFICATIONS

- Military load capacity: 85 tons
- Span: 19.19 meters
- Performance: Comparable to the M-1 Abrams and Assault Breacher Vehicle

PROGRAM STATUS

- **FY13:** Prototype fabrication
- **3QFY13:** Critical Design Review
- **FY14:** Prototype preproduction qualification testing
- **1QFY15:** Soldier feedback demonstration
- **3QFY15:** Request for Proposal release

PROJECTED ACTIVITIES

- **2QFY16:**
  › Milestone C
  › Low-Rate Initial Production contract award
- **2QFY17:** Initial Developmental/Operational Testing

FOREIGN MILITARY SALES
None

CONTRACTORS
TBD

Joint Battle Command – Platform (JBC-P)

PEO Command, Control and Communications – Tactical | Aberdeen Proving Ground, MD

WARFIGHTING FUNCTION

Mission Command

Movement and Maneuver

Intelligence

Fires

Sustainment

Maneuver Support and Protection

Engagement

ACQUISITION LIFECYCLE PHASE

Materiel Solution Analysis

Technology Maturation & Risk Reduction

Engineering & Manufacturing Development

Production & Deployment

Operations & Support

MILESTONE DECISION AUTHORITY

Defense Acquisition Executive

Army Acquisition Executive

Program Executive Officer

DESCRIPTION

The Joint Battle Command – Platform (JBC-P) is the Army's next-generation friendly-force tracking system, equipping Soldiers with a faster satellite network, secure data encryption and advanced logistics. JBC-P includes an intuitive interface with features like touch-to-zoom maps and drag-and-drop icons. JBC-P interoperates with the Nett Warrior hand-held device, managed by PEO Soldier, delivering situational awareness capabilities to dismounted Soldiers. JBC-P incorporates the common hardware solution known as the Mounted Family of Computer Systems (MFoCS), standardized tactical computers that are scalable and tailorable to the mission and vehicle. Encompassing options from a detachable tablet to a fully loaded, vehicle-mounted workstation, MFoCS runs not only JBC-P but other software applications, reducing size, weight and power demands. JBC-P builds on the situational awareness capability known as Force XXI Battle Command Brigade and Below/Blue Force Tracking, which is integrated on more than 120,000 platforms and is authorized and fielded to every Brigade Combat Team in the Army.

BENEFIT TO THE WARFIGHTER

JBC-P upgrades include a Soldier-friendly intuitive Google-Earth-like interface and real-time chat rooms so that Soldiers can now quickly zoom in to view precise locations and use icons on a universal map to pinpoint adversaries and other threats such as improvised explosive devices. Other benefits include instant message chat for functions such as call for medics. Lastly, JBC-P brings faster satellite networking, secure data encryption and Marine Corps interoperability.

SPECIFICATIONS

- Enables Soldiers to receive orders, graphical overlays, and situational awareness of friendly, hostile , neutral, unknown and noncombatant entities
- Allows communications between Soldiers including Free Draw, Free Text, chat and combat messages
- Provides capability to pinpoint locations through sensor integration
- Offers improved user interface

- Generates Electronic Casualty Report
- Facilitates improved route planning
- Utilizes universal hardware through the MFoCS
- Integrates with Nett Warrior hand-held devices hybrid network

PROGRAM STATUS

- **Continue:** JBC-P development and testing for Capability Sets 14 and 15
- **3QFY13:** Network Integration Evaluation 13.2: Operational Test
- **4QFY13:** Full-Rate Production Decision approved
- **1QFY14:** Initial Operating Concept
- **3QFY15:** First Unit Equipped
- **1QFY16:** Conditional Materiel Release for continued fielding

PROJECTED ACTIVITIES

- **FY16-17:** Continued JBC-P fielding
- **FY17:** Mounted Application Computing Environment – Tactical Apps Operational Assessment
- **1QFY17:** JBC-P Follow-on Test

FOREIGN MILITARY SALES
None

CONTRACTORS
Software Development (Government Performing): Software Engineering Directorate (SED), AMRDEC (Huntsville, AL)
MFoCS Hardware: DRS (Melbourne, FL)
Satellite Network Upgrade: VIASAT (Carlsbad, CA)

Joint Biological Tactical Detection System (JBTDS)

JPEO for Chemical and Biological Defense | Aberdeen Proving Ground, MD

WARFIGHTING FUNCTION

Mission Command

Movement and Maneuver

Intelligence

Fires

Sustainment

Maneuver Support and Protection

Engagement

ACQUISITION LIFECYCLE PHASE

Materiel Solution Analysis

Technology Maturation & Risk Reduction

Engineering & Manufacturing Development

Production & Deployment

Operations & Support

MILESTONE DECISION AUTHORITY

Defense Acquisition Executive

Army Acquisition Executive

Program Executive Officer

DESCRIPTION

The Joint Biological Tactical Detection System (JBTDS) will be a lightweight, man-portable, battery-operated system that detects the presence of, collects a sample of, and presumptively identifies biological warfare agents (BWA) to provide near real-time detection of biological attacks and hazards in the area of operation. It will have a local alarm and be networked to provide cooperative capability with reduced probability of false alarms. JBTDS will be employed organically at the battalion and lower levels by non-chemical, biological, radiological and nuclear personnel in tactical environments across multiple operational locations (e.g., forward operating bases, operationally engaged units, amphibious landing sites, air base operations, etc.).

JBTDS will ultimately support force protection and maximize combat effectiveness by enhancing medical response decision making. When networked, JBTDS will augment existing biological detection systems to provide a theaterwide, seamless array capability of detection and warning.

BENEFIT TO THE WARFIGHTER

JBTDS provides fully automated detection, collection and identification of BWA at very low concentrations.

SPECIFICATIONS

- TBD

PROGRAM STATUS

- **1QFY15:** Milestone B Decision
- **3QFY15:** Preliminary Design Review

PROJECTED ACTIVITIES

- **2QFY16:** Critical Design Review
- **2QFY16-4QFY17:** Developmental Testing
- **2QFY16-4QFY17:** Conduct Engineering and Manufacturing Development effort
- **4QFY17:** Operational Assessment
- **1QFY18:** Milestone C Decision

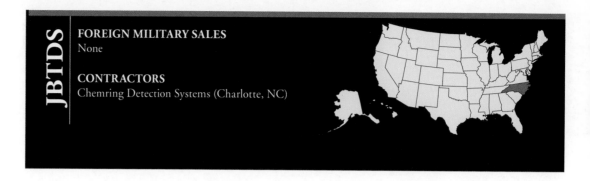

JBTDS Base Station

JBTDS Identifier

JBTDS Detector-Collector

Joint Chemical Agent Detector (JCAD) M4A1

JPEO for Chemical and Biological Defense | Aberdeen Proving Ground, MD

WARFIGHTING FUNCTION

Mission Command

Movement and Maneuver

Intelligence

Fires

Sustainment

Maneuver Support and Protection

Engagement

ACQUISITION LIFECYCLE PHASE

Materiel Solution Analysis

Technology Maturation & Risk Reduction

Engineering & Manufacturing Development

Production & Deployment

Operations & Support

MILESTONE DECISION AUTHORITY

Defense Acquisition Executive

Army Acquisition Executive

Program Executive Officer

DESCRIPTION

The Joint Chemical Agent Detector (JCAD) is a pocket-size, rugged hand-held detector that automatically detects, identifies and alarms to chemical warfare agents and toxic industrial chemical vapors.

The services can use the system on mobile platforms, at fixed sites and on individuals designated to operate in a chemical threat area. Additionally, the system can operate in a general chemical warfare environment as well as undergo conventional decontamination procedures by the warfighter.

The JCAD M4A1, which commenced production in FY11, will reduce operation and sustainment costs, has an improved user interface and is net ready.

The JCAD replaces the Automatic Chemical Agent Detector and Alarm, or M22, M90 and M8A1 systems. It may also replace the Chemical Agent Monitor and Improved Chemical Agent Monitor.

BENEFIT TO THE WARFIGHTER

JCAD M4A1 protects U.S. forces by detecting, identifying, alerting and reporting the presence of chemical warfare agents and toxic industrial chemical vapor.

SPECIFICATIONS

- Instant feedback of hazard (mask only or full Mission-Oriented Protective Posture)
- Real-time detection of nerve, blister and blood agents
- Stores up to 72 hours of detection data
- The M4A1 will be net-ready through implementation of the common chemical, biological, radiological and nuclear standard interface

PROGRAM STATUS

- **FY13-15:** Production and Deployment

PROJECTED ACTIVITIES

- **FY16-17:** Production and Deployment

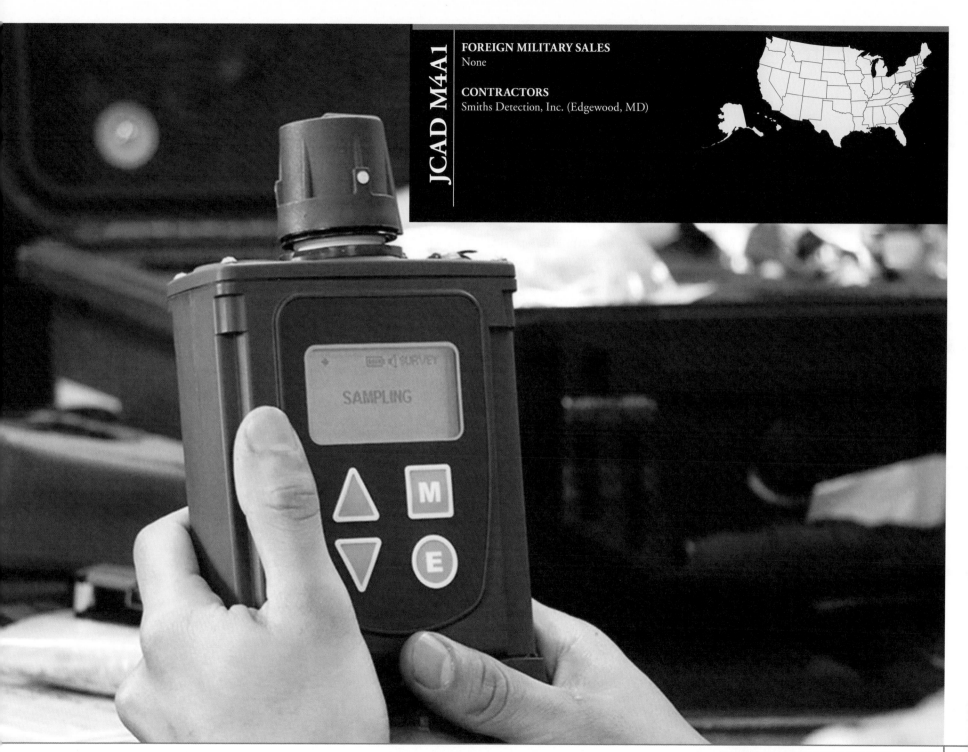

JCAD M4A1

FOREIGN MILITARY SALES
None

CONTRACTORS
Smiths Detection, Inc. (Edgewood, MD)

SAMPLING

Joint Effects Model (JEM)

JPEO for Chemical and Biological Defense | Aberdeen Proving Ground, MD

WARFIGHTING FUNCTION

Mission Command

Movement and Maneuver

Intelligence

Fires

Sustainment

Maneuver Support and Protection

Engagement

ACQUISITION LIFECYCLE PHASE

Materiel Solution Analysis

Technology Maturation & Risk Reduction

Engineering & Manufacturing Development

Production & Deployment

Operations & Support

MILESTONE DECISION AUTHORITY

Defense Acquisition Executive

Army Acquisition Executive

Program Executive Officer

DESCRIPTION

Joint Effects Model (JEM) is a Web-based software application that supplies the DoD with the one and only accredited tool to effectively model and simulate the effects of chemical, biological, radiological and nuclear (CBRN) weapon strikes and incidents. JEM can provide warfighters with the ability to accurately model and predict the time-phased impact of CBRN and Toxic Industrial Chemical/Material (TIC/TIM) events and effects. JEM supports planning to mitigate the effects of weapons of mass destruction and to provide rapid estimates of hazards and effects integrated into the Common Operational Picture (COP).

JEM Increment 2 is being developed to replace JEM Increment 1 and will use the agile development process to incrementally add capabilities.

BENEFIT TO THE WARFIGHTER

JEM provides warfighters with the only DoD-accredited modeling capability to predict high-fidelity downwind hazard areas and effects associated with the release of CBRN and Toxic Industrial Hazards (TIH) into the environment; incorporate the impacts of weather, terrain and material interactions into the downwind prediction; provide enhanced situational awareness of the battlespace; and deliver near real-time hazard information to influence and minimize CBRN and TIH effects on current operations, and to save lives.

SPECIFICATIONS

- Models CBRN hazards and resulting human physiological effects for chemical and biological weapon and facility strikes, nuclear weapon incidents and detonations, radiological weapon detonations, chemical weapon storage incidents, high-altitude releases and TIC/TIM releases
- Provides the ability to display to the COP and operates in an integrated fashion with operational and tactical command and control (C2) systems

- Interfaces and communicates with the Joint Warning and Reporting Network, associated weather systems, intelligence systems and various databases
- Supports multiple deployment strategies that operate on both UNIX and Windows systems, and is integrated into C2 systems across DoD
- Available as stand-alone, networked, distributed or Web access.
- Operationally supported, 24/7 reachback (call center and Web).
- Provides warfighters the best and most mature technology available to address a wide spectrum of threats

PROGRAM STATUS

- **FY13-FY15:** JEM Increment 1 continued in Sustainment
- **4QFY14:**
  › JEM Increment 2 Milestone B
  › JEM Increment 2 Build Decision 1
- **2QFY15:** Requirements Definition Package 2 and Build Decision 2
- **4QFY15:** Operational Assessment-1/Initial Operational Test & Evaluation 1 (National Guard Bureau)

PROJECTED ACTIVITIES

- **FY16-FY17:** JEM Increment 1 continued in Sustainment
- **1QFY16:** Fielding Decision 1
- **4QFY16:** Build Decision 2
- **1QFY17:** Build Decision 4

FOREIGN MILITARY SALES
Canada and Spain

CONTRACTORS
Increment 1: Northrop Grumman Mission Systems (San Diego, CA)
Increment 2: General Dynamics Information Technology (Middletown, RI; Buffalo, NY; and San Diego, CA)

Joint Effects Targeting System (JETS) Target Location Designation System (TLDS)

PEO Soldier | Fort Belvoir, VA

WARFIGHTING FUNCTION

Mission Command

Movement and Maneuver

Intelligence

Fires

Sustainment

Maneuver Support and Protection

Engagement

ACQUISITION LIFECYCLE PHASE

Materiel Solution Analysis

Technology Maturation & Risk Reduction

Engineering & Manufacturing Development

Production & Deployment

Operations & Support

MILESTONE DECISION AUTHORITY

Defense Acquisition Executive

Army Acquisition Executive

Program Executive Officer

DESCRIPTION

The Joint Effects Targeting System (JETS) Target Location Designation System (TLDS) is an Army-led, Joint-interest program with the Air Force and Marine Corps to develop and field a one-man-portable, hand-held capability to rapidly acquire, precisely locate, and engage targets with precision-guided munitions, and improves the effectiveness of engagement with unguided munitions.

BENEFIT TO THE WARFIGHTER

The JETS will answer the need for a lightweight, highly accurate targeting system that allows target engagements with precision munitions (e.g., Joint Direct Attack Munition, Excalibur and laser-guided weapons) and provide the warfighter with crucial digital connectivity to request and control indirect fires and close air support from all Joint assets. The JETS allows small units supported by Army forward observers or Joint Tactical Area Communications Systems to have access to precision targeting in all operational environments.

SPECIFICATIONS

- System weight: Less than or equal to 5.5 pounds (threshold) and 3.0 pounds (objective)
- Target Location Error: Less than or equal to 10 meters at 2.5 km (threshold) and 5 meters at 5 km (objective)

PROGRAM STATUS

- **2QFY13:**
  › Milestone B, entering Engineering and Manufacturing Development (EMD)
  › EMD contracts awarded to BAE Systems and DRS Technologies
- **1QFY16:** Contractor testing of JETS prototypes

PROJECTED ACTIVITIES

- **2QFY16:** Developmental testing of JETS prototypes
- **3QFY16:**
  › Milestone C, entering Production
  › Production Contract Award
- **4QFY17:** Initial Operational Test and Evaluation

FOREIGN MILITARY SALES
None

CONTRACTORS
BAE Systems (Nashua, NH)
DRS Technologies (Dallas, TX)

BAE

DRS

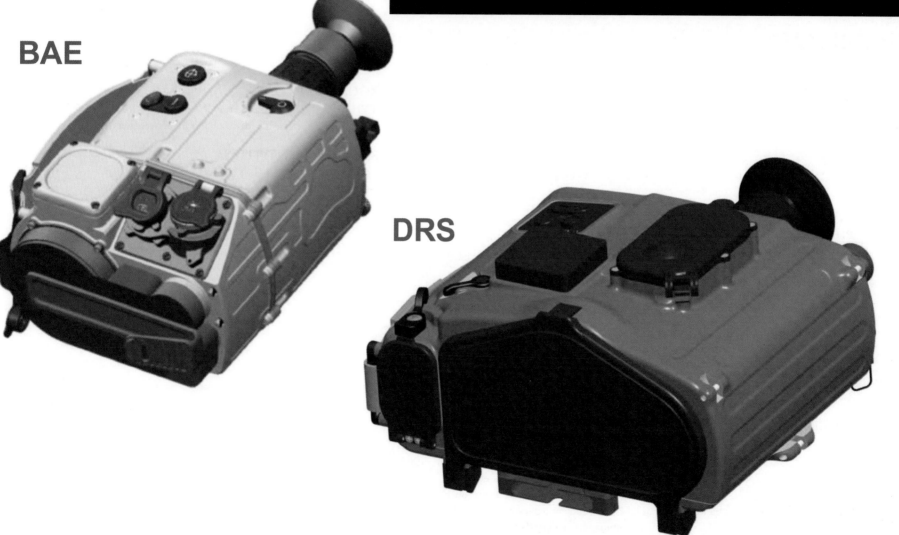

Joint Land Component Constructive Training Capability (JLCCTC)

PEO Simulation, Training, and Instrumentation | Orlando, FL

WARFIGHTING FUNCTION

Mission Command

Movement and Maneuver

Intelligence

Fires

Sustainment

Maneuver Support and Protection

Engagement

ACQUISITION LIFECYCLE PHASE

Materiel Solution Analysis

Technology Maturation & Risk Reduction

Engineering & Manufacturing Development

Production & Deployment

Operations & Support

MILESTONE DECISION AUTHORITY

Defense Acquisition Executive

Army Acquisition Executive

Program Executive Officer

DESCRIPTION

The Joint Land Component Constructive Training Capability (JLCCTC) is designed to provide Army commanders and their battle staffs the capability to train in an operationally relevant, constructive-simulation environment that mimics Army Decisive Action operations used for the Simulation/Stimulation (SIM/STIM) of collective digital mission command training.

The JLCCTC supports Army Title X training worldwide for Army commanders and their staffs at U.S. Army Mission Command Training Centers, U.S. Army Training and Doctrine Command facilities, and other customer locations. JLCCTC trains commanders and their staffs in offensive, defensive, stability and civil support operations. JLCCTC is composed of two separate federations: JLCCTC Multi-Resolution Federation (MRF) and JLCCTC Entity Resolution Federation (ERF). MRF is a set of constructive simulation software modules that support training of commanders and their staffs in maneuver, logistics, intelligence, air defense and artillery. System capabilities include:

- Stimulation of Mission Command systems
- Intelligence (human, imagery, electronics, communications, and measurement and signature intelligence)
- Irregular warfare
- Unmanned aerial vehicle visualization
- Logistics training
- Nonkinetic effects modeling
- After Action Review system
- Interface with the Air Force simulation and the Air and Space Cyber Constructive Environment

BENEFIT TO THE WARFIGHTER

JLCCTC enables commanders and their staffs to hone their warfighting skills and refine standard operating procedures for the effective operation of a tactical operations center. The wide spectrum of functional capabilities within JLCCTC accurately replicates real-world situations. JLCCTC will immerse commanders and staffs in the simulated fight.

SPECIFICATIONS

- Software-intensive
- Requires up to three server stacks
- Can accommodate hundreds of individual computers for role players
- Individual computers must meet certain processing standards
- Interoperable with mission command systems

PROGRAM STATUS

- **FY15:** Supported dozens of Army Warfighter Exercises (WFX) worldwide at the brigade, division and higher echelons

PROJECTED ACTIVITIES

- **1QFY16-4QFY16:** Support dozens of WFX worldwide
- **3QFY16:** Validate ERF v5.6 capabilities
- **3QFY16-4QFY16:** Validate MRF v7.1 and v8.0 capabilities

JLCCTC

FOREIGN MILITARY SALES
Japan

CONTRACTORS
Lockheed Martin Mission Systems and Training
(Orlando, FL)

Joint Personal Dosimeter (JPD)

JPEO for Chemical and Biological Defense | Aberdeen Proving Ground, MD

WARFIGHTING FUNCTION

Mission Command

Movement and Maneuver

Intelligence

Fires

Sustainment

Maneuver Support and Protection

Engagement

ACQUISITION LIFECYCLE PHASE

Materiel Solution Analysis

Technology Maturation & Risk Reduction

Engineering & Manufacturing Development

Production & Deployment

Operations & Support

MILESTONE DECISION AUTHORITY

Defense Acquisition Executive

Army Acquisition Executive

Program Executive Officer

DESCRIPTION

The Joint Personal Dosimeter (JPD) is intended to replace DoD's legacy dosimeters (the Navy's IM-270 and the Army's PDR-75 reader) with the DT-236 watch.

BENEFIT TO THE WARFIGHTER

The JPD will provide a sensor to record and retrieve the warfighter's radiation exposure from occupational to tactical levels. Acquisition strategy leverages the Navy's battlefield dosimeter to address interoperability lessons learned from Operation Tomadachi.

SPECIFICATIONS

- Weight: 2 ounces with batteries
- Power: Lithium coin cell, commercial off-the-shelf (COTS) model CR2450N and CR1216MFR
- Accurate and reliable Direct Ion Storage technology
- Hybrid device (active and passive)
- Self-reading for effective decision making
- Hands-free operation
- Programmable display
- Configurable operating parameters including dose alarm threshold
- Wrist-worn or clipped to lanyard or garment
- Field-replaceable batteries

PROGRAM STATUS

- **Current:** Pre-Milestone (MS) C (3QFY16 strategy is from Materiel Development Decision to MS C based on a COTS system)

PROJECTED ACTIVITIES

- **Mid-FY16:** MS C
- **1QFY17:** Production Qualification Testing
- **4QFY17:** Full-Rate Production Decision

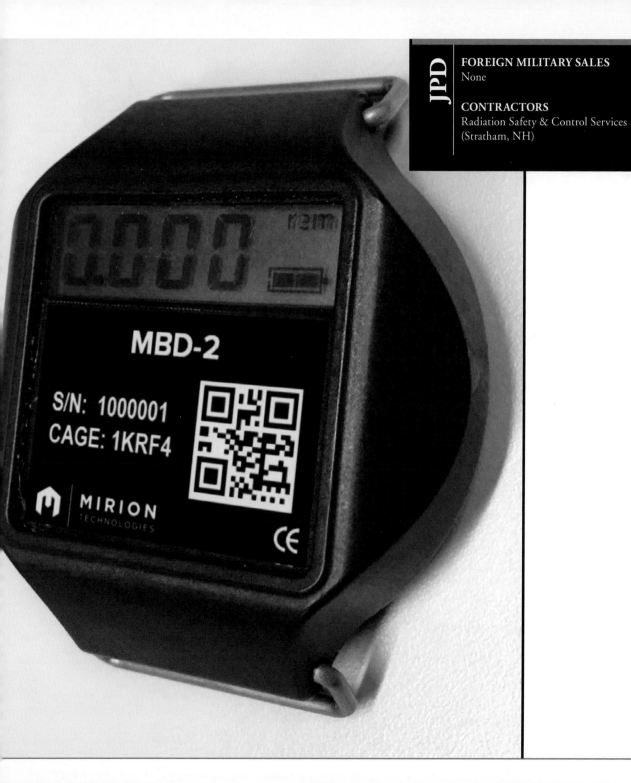

FOREIGN MILITARY SALES
None

CONTRACTORS
Radiation Safety & Control Services
(Stratham, NH)

Joint Precision Airdrop System (JPADS)

PEO Combat Support and Combat Service Support | Detroit Arsenal, MI

WARFIGHTING FUNCTION

Mission Command

Movement and Maneuver

Intelligence

Fires

Sustainment

Maneuver Support and Protection

Engagement

ACQUISITION LIFECYCLE PHASE

Materiel Solution Analysis

Technology Maturation & Risk Reduction

Engineering & Manufacturing Development

Production & Deployment

Operations & Support

MILESTONE DECISION AUTHORITY

Defense Acquisition Executive

Army Acquisition Executive

Program Executive Officer

DESCRIPTION

The Joint Precision Airdrop System (JPADS) provides rapid, precise, high-altitude delivery capabilities that do not rely on ground transportation. The system ensures accurate and timely delivery in support of operational missions, while providing aircraft with increased survivability.

JPADS integrates a parachute decelerator, an autonomous guidance unit and a load container or pallet to create a system that can accurately deliver critical supplies with great precision along a predetermined glide and flight path. The system consists of two weight classes: 2,000 pounds (2K) and 10,000 pounds (10K). The guidance system uses military Global Positioning System (GPS) data for precise navigation and interfaces with a wirelessly updatable mission planning module onboard the aircraft to receive real-time weather data and compute multiple aerial release points.

JPADS is designed for aircraft to drop cargo from altitudes of up to 24,500 feet mean sea level. It releases cargo from a minimum off-set of 8 km from the intended point of impact, with an objective capability of 25 km off-set. This off-set allows aircraft to stay out of range of many anti-aircraft systems. It also enables aircraft to drop systems from a single aerial release point and deliver them to multiple or single locations, thus reducing aircraft exposure time. Once on the ground, the precise placement of the loads greatly reduces the time needed to recover the load as well as minimize exposure to ground forces.

BENEFIT TO THE WARFIGHTER

JPADS increases aircraft and payload survivability and enables delivery of multiple loads to single or multiple drop zones in a single aircraft pass with accuracy better than 150 meters with 80 percent confidence.

SPECIFICATIONS

JPADS 2K includes:
- 1,025-square-foot ram air parafoil with a glide ratio of 3 to 1 coupled with a military GPS-based Autonomous Guidance Unit (AGU)

- Specially designed suspension sling is used to attach the AGU to the Container Delivery Systems payload
- Onboard Guidance, Navigation and Control software in the AGU autonomously steers the parafoil to the designated impact point

JPADS 10K includes:
- 3,500-square-foot ram air parafoil with a glide ratio of at least 3 to 1 coupled with a military GPS-based AGU
- Load is configured on a combat-expendable, 463L or Type V airdrop platform for gravity airdrop

PROGRAM STATUS

- **FY15:**
  › JPADS 2K transferred funding to Integrated Logistics Support Center (ILSC) sustainment contract
  › JPADS 10K fielding and delivery

PROJECTED ACTIVITIES

- **FY16:**
  › JPADS 2K ILSC sustainment and modernization via depot
  › JPADS 10K total package fielding and delivery continues

FOREIGN MILITARY SALES
None

CONTRACTORS
Airborne Systems North America
(Pennsauken, NJ)
Draper Laboratory, Inc. (Cambridge, MA)

Joint Service Aircrew Mask – Rotary Wing (JSAM RW) (MPU-5)

JPEO for Chemical and Biological Defense | Aberdeen Proving Ground, MD

WARFIGHTING FUNCTION

Mission Command

Movement and Maneuver

Intelligence

Fires

Sustainment

Maneuver Support and Protection

Engagement

ACQUISITION LIFECYCLE PHASE

Materiel Solution Analysis

Technology Maturation & Risk Reduction

Engineering & Manufacturing Development

Production & Deployment

Operations & Support

MILESTONE DECISION AUTHORITY

Defense Acquisition Executive

Army Acquisition Executive

Program Executive Officer

DESCRIPTION

The Joint Service Aircrew Mask – Rotary Wing (JSAM RW) is one of five variants in the JSAM Family of Systems that provides individual respiratory, eye and head protection against Chemical and Biological (CB) warfare agents and radiological particulates for aircrews of all rotary wing aircraft except Apache. JSAM RW decreases thermal burden as compared to legacy systems. It also provides CB protection during the full spectrum of rotary wing operations including flight, immediate maintenance operations, extended flight-related ground duties, and ground escape, as well as evasion operations.

BENEFIT TO THE WARFIGHTER

JSAM RW provides the warfighter with an above-the-neck CB protective respirator for general purpose rotary-wing aircrews. The mask is capable of being donned and doffed while in flight, provides greater comfort, less physiological burden and greater flexibility of use with man-mounted systems.

SPECIFICATIONS

- Protection against CB warfare agents and radiological particulate
- Compatible with appropriate life-support equipment across various aircraft platforms
- No aircraft modifications required

PROGRAM STATUS

- **2QFY15:** Achieved Milestone C and Low-Rate Initial Production (LRIP)
- **3QFY15:**
  › Army Operational Test (OT) Complete
  › Air Force OT Complete
- **4QFY15:** LRIP Contract Award

PROJECTED ACTIVITIES

- **2QFY16:** In-Progress Review with Milestone Decision Authority
- **4QFY16:** Initiate Navy and Marine Corps OT
- **2QFY17:** Indefinite Delivery, Indefinite Quantity Contract Award
- **4QFY17:** Full-Rate Production

JSAM RW MPU-5

FOREIGN MILITARY SALES
None

CONTRACTORS
Avox Systems (Lancaster, NY)

Joint Service Equipment Wipe (JSEW)

JPEO for Chemical and Biological Defense | Aberdeen Proving Ground, MD

WARFIGHTING FUNCTION

Mission Command

Movement and Maneuver

Intelligence

Fires

Sustainment

Maneuver Support and Protection

Engagement

ACQUISITION LIFECYCLE PHASE

Materiel Solution Analysis

Technology Maturation & Risk Reduction

Engineering & Manufacturing Development

Production & Deployment

Operations & Support

MILESTONE DECISION AUTHORITY

Defense Acquisition Executive

Army Acquisition Executive

Program Executive Officer

DESCRIPTION

Joint Service Equipment Wipe (JSEW) provides immediate operational decontamination capabilities for sensitive and nonsensitive equipment exposed to traditional and nontraditional chemical contamination. JSEW will be the first decontamination capability available to warfighters that is nondestructive to sensitive equipment. It will be applied directly to the contaminated surface and is capable of removing gross contamination and reducing contact hazard within five minutes of application.

BENEFIT TO THE WARFIGHTER

JSEW is sized for individuals to carry in the pocket of their overgarments. It is durable and allows for extended carry by individual users.

SPECIFICATIONS

- Decontaminate Nerve-G, Nerve-V, Blister-H and nontraditional agents of operational significance from a starting liquid challenge of 10 grams per square meter (5 grams per square meter for nontraditional agents) to 1 gram per square meter (threshold)
- Nondestructive to both sensitive and nonsensitive equipment
- Allows for decontamination of 1 gram per square meter of sensitive and nonsensitive equipment with a single kit (kit contains five individually packaged wipes)

PROGRAM STATUS

- **1QFY16:** Developmental Testing Complete

PROJECTED ACTIVITIES

- **2QFY16:** Milestone C approval
- **3QFY16:** Award Option 1
- **4QFY16:** Multiservice Operational Test & Evaluation

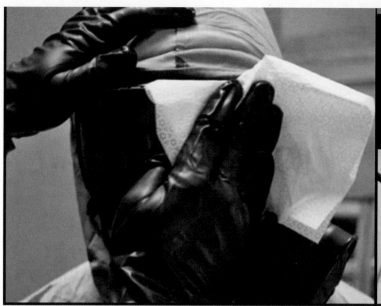

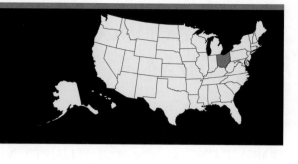

Joint Service General Purpose Mask (JSGPM) M-50/M-51

JPEO for Chemical and Biological Defense | Aberdeen Proving Ground, MD

WARFIGHTING
FUNCTION

Mission Command

Movement and Maneuver

Intelligence

Fires

Sustainment

**Maneuver Support
and Protection**

Engagement

ACQUISITION
LIFECYCLE PHASE

Materiel Solution Analysis

Technology Maturation &
Risk Reduction

Engineering & Manufacturing
Development

Production & Deployment

Operations & Support

MILESTONE DECISION
AUTHORITY

Defense Acquisition Executive

Army Acquisition Executive

Program Executive Officer

DESCRIPTION

The Joint Service General Purpose Mask (JSGPM) M50 and M51 is a lightweight, protective mask system consisting of mask, carrier and accessories that incorporates state-of-the-art technology to protect U.S. forces from anticipated threats. It is an above-the-neck, chemical-biological (CB) respirator that protects against battlefield concentrations of CB agents, toxins, toxic industrial materials and radioactive particulate matter. The mask components are designed to minimize impact on the wearer's performance.

This mask replaces the M40 and M42, MCU2/P series masks and the M45 in the Land Warrior Program. There are two mask variants: M50 (ground use) and M51 (ground vehicle use).

BENEFIT TO THE WARFIGHTER

JSGPM provides the warfighter with face, eye and respiratory protection from battlefield concentrations of CB agents, toxins, toxic industrial materials and radiological particulate matter.

SPECIFICATIONS

- Overall field-of-view is greater than or equal to 80 percent
- Improved compatibility with current and emerging CB garments
- Improvements over the MCU2/P, M40/M42 and M45:
  › Reduced weight, bulk and lower breathing resistance
  › Increased drinking capability
  › Improved mask carrier system
  › Filter service life indicator capability
  › Flame resistant hood for combat vehicle version
  › Improved reliability; and improved comfort
- Filter change-out in a contaminated environment (self-sealing valve)
- More than 24 hours of above-the-neck protection from CB agents and radioactive particles
- More than 50 percent improvement in breathing resistance compared to legacy masks

PROGRAM STATUS

- **1QFY13-4QFY15:** Ongoing production
- **2QFY14:** Began fielding to Army warfighters
- **1QFY16:** Completed fieldings to Army units in Europe and Hawaii

PROJECTED ACTIVITIES

- **2QFY16:**
  › Complete fielding to Army units in Middle East
  › Begin fielding to Army units in Washington state

FOREIGN MILITARY SALES
M50: Iraq
M51: Australia

CONTRACTORS
Avon Protection Systems (Cadillac, MI)

M50
Ground Variant

M51
Combat Vehicle Variant

Joint Service Transportable Decontaminating System Small Scale (JSTDS-SS) M26

JPEO for Chemical and Biological Defense | Aberdeen Proving Ground, MD

WARFIGHTING FUNCTION

Mission Command

Movement and Maneuver

Intelligence

Fires

Sustainment

Maneuver Support and Protection

Engagement

ACQUISITION LIFECYCLE PHASE

Materiel Solution Analysis

Technology Maturation & Risk Reduction

Engineering & Manufacturing Development

Production & Deployment

Operations & Support

MILESTONE DECISION AUTHORITY

Defense Acquisition Executive

Army Acquisition Executive

Program Executive Officer

DESCRIPTION

The Joint Service Transportable Decontaminating System Small Scale (JSTDS-SS) M26 provides the military and first responders with a lightweight, transportable decontamination system. It uses water from any source—fresh, still or salt—and offers variable-pressure and high-pressure operating modes. The JSTDS-SS can be used to decontaminate people or equipment; for cleaning, personnel showers and laundries; and for field hospital use. Weighing only 560 pounds, the JSTDS-SS can fit in a standard truck bed and requires minimal operator training. Two people can set it up in less than 15 minutes.

BENEFIT TO THE WARFIGHTER

The JSTDS-SS M26 supports the warfighter by sustaining a system to decontaminate current and emerging threats.

SPECIFICATIONS

- System will be transportable by a nondedicated platform (i.e., High Mobility Multipurpose Wheeled Vehicle and Trailer, Family of Medium Tactical Vehicles and Trailer) off-road over any terrain
- Decontaminate Chemical Warfare Agents (i.e., Nerve-G, Nerve-V and Blister-H) on tactical vehicles and crew-served weapons below detection levels of M8 detector papers within five minutes of contact time after exposure to a 10-grams-per-square-meter challenge-level attack
- Will have a reliability of greater than or equal to 89 percent

PROGRAM STATUS

- **4QFY13:** Fielding completed

PROJECTED ACTIVITIES

- None

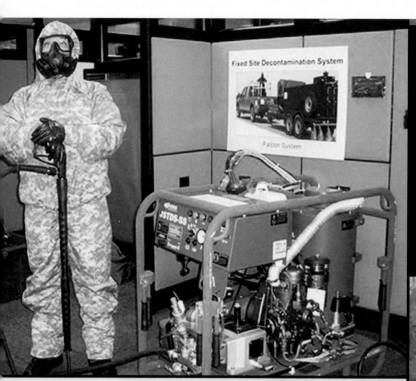

FOREIGN MILITARY SALES
None

CONTRACTORS
DRS Technologies (Florence, KY)

Joint Tactical Ground Station (JTAGS)

PEO Missiles and Space | Redstone Arsenal, AL

WARFIGHTING FUNCTION

Mission Command

Movement and Maneuver

Intelligence

Fires

Sustainment

Maneuver Support and Protection

Engagement

ACQUISITION LIFECYCLE PHASE

Materiel Solution Analysis

Technology Maturation & Risk Reduction

Engineering & Manufacturing Development

Production & Deployment

Operations & Support

MILESTONE DECISION AUTHORITY

Defense Acquisition Executive

Army Acquisition Executive

Program Executive Officer

DESCRIPTION

Joint Tactical Ground Stations (JTAGS) are forward-deployed, echelon-above-corps, transportable systems designed to receive, process and disseminate direct down-linked infrared data from space-based sensors. They provide commanders with real-time warning, alerting and cueing information on ballistic missile launches.

Ongoing product improvement efforts will integrate JTAGS with the next-generation Space Based Infrared System (SBIRS) satellites. Five JTAGS are deployed worldwide as part of the U.S. Strategic Command's Tactical Event System. Army Space and Missile Defense Command Soldiers operate JTAGS to provide 24/7 support to theater operations.

BENEFIT TO THE WARFIGHTER

JTAGS processes satellite data and disseminates ballistic missile warning or special event messages to warfighters in support of regional combatant commanders over multiple theater communication systems.

SPECIFICATIONS

- SBIRS sensors significantly improve theater missile warning parameters
- Expected improvements:
  › Higher quality cueing of active defense systems
  › Decreased missile launch search area
  › Faster initial report times
  › Improved impact ellipse prediction

PROGRAM STATUS

- **1QFY13-4QFY15:** Contractor logistics support continues in support of JTAGS legacy (Block 1) system
- **3QFY13:** Conducted Preliminary Design Review/Critical Design Review for new contract, JTAGS Pre-Planned Product Improvement (Block 2), which includes development of SBIRS geosynchronous satellite integration, desheltering, improved cyber posture, improved human factors and user interface, new mission processing and operating system and new log support system
- **3QFY15:** Conducted initial JTAGS P3I Developmental Test and Train-the-Trainers

PROJECTED ACTIVITIES

- **4QFY16:** Conduct JTAGS P3I Operator Limited User Test
- **2QFY17-3QFY17:** Field JTAGS P3I (Block 2) Trainer and OCONUS-1

FOREIGN MILITARY SALES
None

CONTRACTORS
Northrop Grumman Electronic Systems
(Colorado Springs, CO)
Sigmatech, Inc. (Huntsville, AL)

Joint Warning and Reporting Network (JWARN)

JPEO for Chemical and Biological Defense | Aberdeen Proving Ground, MD

WARFIGHTING FUNCTION

Mission Command

Movement and Maneuver

Intelligence

Fires

Sustainment

Maneuver Support and Protection

Engagement

ACQUISITION LIFECYCLE PHASE

Materiel Solution Analysis

Technology Maturation & Risk Reduction

Engineering & Manufacturing Development

Production & Deployment

Operations & Support

MILESTONE DECISION AUTHORITY

Defense Acquisition Executive

Army Acquisition Executive

Program Executive Officer

DESCRIPTION

The Joint Warning and Reporting Network (JWARN) provides Joint Forces with a capability to report, analyze and disseminate detection, identification, location and warning information to accelerate the warfighter's response to a chemical, biological, radiological and nuclear (CBRN) attack.

JWARN is a computer-based application integrating CBRN data and facilitates sensor information into Joint and service command and control systems for battlespace situational awareness. JWARN replaces the manual processes of incident reporting, hazard plot generation and warning affected forces.

BENEFIT TO THE WARFIGHTER

JWARN reduces the time from incident observation to warning to less than two minutes, enhances situational awareness throughout the area of operations and supports warfighter battle management tasks.

SPECIFICATIONS

- Incorporates sensor alert information and CBRN observation reports from the field
- Makes a plot of the hazard area
- Provides overlays for display on the Common Operational Picture
- Generates warning message to units

PROGRAM STATUS

- **4QFY14:** Full Operational Test of Army JWARN Increment 1 software modernization to a Web-based services application
- **3QFY15:** Approval of JWARN Increment 2
- **4QFY15:** JWARN Increment 2 Web Application hosted on the CBRN Information Systems MilCloud for demonstration purposes; facilitates warfighter feedback for future JWARN capabilities

PROJECTED ACTIVITIES

- **3QFY16:** JWARN Increment 2 Operational Test
- **4QFY16:** JWARN Increment 2 Fielding Decision

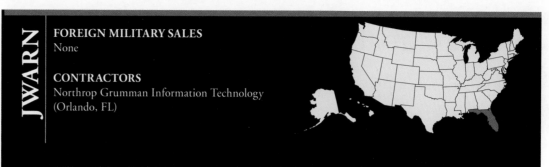

JWARN

FOREIGN MILITARY SALES
None

CONTRACTORS
Northrop Grumman Information Technology
(Orlando, FL)

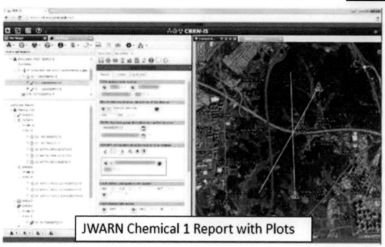

JWARN Chemical 1 Report with Plots

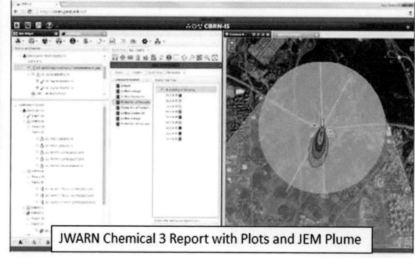

JWARN Chemical 3 Report with Plots and JEM Plume

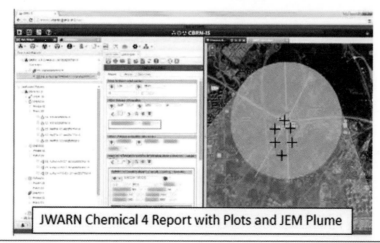

JWARN Chemical 4 Report with Plots and JEM Plume

Light Capability Rough Terrain Forklift (LCRTF)

PEO Combat Support and Combat Service Support | Detroit Arsenal, MI

WARFIGHTING FUNCTION

Mission Command

Movement and Maneuver

Intelligence

Fires

Sustainment

Maneuver Support and Protection

Engagement

ACQUISITION LIFECYCLE PHASE

Materiel Solution Analysis

Technology Maturation & Risk Reduction

Engineering & Manufacturing Development

Production & Deployment

Operations & Support

MILESTONE DECISION AUTHORITY

Defense Acquisition Executive

Army Acquisition Executive

Program Executive Officer

DESCRIPTION

The Light Capability Rough Terrain Forklift (LCRTF) is a C-130 and CH-47 sling load transportable, 5,000-pound capacity, variable-reach, rough-terrain forklift with fork tine oscillation and side-shift cab controls. The LCRTF enters, loads and unloads Army International Organization for Standardization (ISO) containers. The extendable boom fork carriage removes pallets from ISO containers on trucks. The LCRTF is a significant improvement over the existing 4,000-pound capacity fleet because of its enclosed air conditioned cab, moveable tines and improved helicopter lift.

BENEFIT TO THE WARFIGHTER

LCRTF provides a safe and efficient way to load and unload Army cargo in unimproved and improved areas. The new LCRTF is more reliable, available and maintainable than the system it replaces.

SPECIFICATIONS

* 5,000-pound lift capacity
* 36-inch fording
* 20-mph traverse speed

PROGRAM STATUS

* **FY13-FY15:** Fielded 831 systems

PROJECTED ACTIVITIES

* **FY16-2QFY17:** Continue production and fielding to units; 336 systems projected to be fielded
* **3QFY16:** Award follow-on LCRTF production contract
* **4QFY16:** Start Technical Manual/Log Development
* **4QFY16-3QFY17:** Start/Complete First Article Testing

FOREIGN MILITARY SALES
None

CONTRACTORS
Kalmar RT Center LLC (Cibolo, TX)

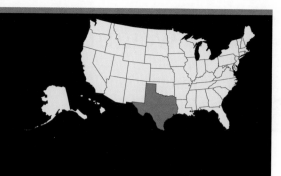

Lightweight 155 mm Howitzer System (LW155)

PEO Ammunition | Picatinny Arsenal, NJ

WARFIGHTING FUNCTION

Mission Command

Movement and Maneuver

Intelligence

Fires

Sustainment

Maneuver Support and Protection

Engagement

ACQUISITION LIFECYCLE PHASE

Materiel Solution Analysis

Technology Maturation & Risk Reduction

Engineering & Manufacturing Development

Production & Deployment

Operations & Support

MILESTONE DECISION AUTHORITY

Defense Acquisition Executive

Army Acquisition Executive

Program Executive Officer

DESCRIPTION

The Lightweight 155 mm Howitzer System (LW155) provides direct, reinforcing and general artillery fire support to maneuver forces. The M777A2 is a towed 155 mm Howitzer jointly developed by the Army and Marine Corps to replace the M198 Howitzer. The extensive use of titanium in all its major structures makes it 7,000 pounds lighter than the M198 with no sacrifice in range, stability, accuracy or durability. The M777A2's independent suspension, smaller footprint and lower profile increase strategic deployability and tactical mobility. The system uses numerous improvements to enhance reliability and accuracy, and significantly increase system survivability. The system has a Digital Fire Control System (DFCS) that includes an inertial navigation unit with Global Positioning System backup to allow it to self-locate. The DFCS also includes a mission computer, displays and digital communications. Software upgrades incorporating the Enhanced Portable Inductive Artillery Fuse Setter and the Excalibur Platform Integration Kit hardware give the M777A2 the capability to program and fire the Excalibur precision-guided munition.

BENEFIT TO THE WARFIGHTER

The LW155 offers the warfighter improved survivability, lethality, deployability and mobility to counter threat forces.

SPECIFICATIONS

- Weight: 10,000 pounds
- Emplace: Less than three minutes
- Displace: Less than three minutes
- Maximum range: 30 km (rocket assisted round)
- Rate-of-fire: Up to four rounds per minute
- Ground mobility: Family of Medium Tactical Vehicles, Medium Tactical Vehicle Replacement, 5-ton trucks
- Air mobility: CH-53D/E; CH-47D; MV-22; C-130; C-17; C-5
- 155 mm compatibility: All fielded and developmental NATO munitions

- Digital and optical fire control: Self-locating and pointing; digital and voice communications; self-contained power supply

PROGRAM STATUS

- **3QFY13:** Competitive Award for Long-Term Performance-Based Sustainment
- **2QFY14:**
  - › Final U.S. production gun delivered
  - › Completed fielding to Army Stryker Brigade Combat Teams
  - › Commenced fielding to Army Infantry Brigade Combat Teams
  - › Initiated Tri-Lateral Sustainment discussions with Foreign Military Sales (FMS) customers Australia and Canada
- **1QFY16:** Continue Infantry Brigade Combat Team (IBCT) fielding

PROJECTED ACTIVITIES

- **2QFY16:** Performance-Based Lifecycle Support Contract Award
- **3QFY16-4QFY18:**
  - › Continue IBCT fielding
  - › DFCS refresh and modernization
  - › Fielding of training devices
  - › Support FMS customers Australia and Canada

FOREIGN MILITARY SALES
Australia, Canada and potentially India

CONTRACTORS
BAE Systems (Hattiesburg, MS; Barrow-in-Furness, United Kingdom)

Lightweight Laser Designator Rangefinder (LLDR) AN/PED-1 and AN/PED-1A

PEO Soldier | Fort Belvoir, VA

WARFIGHTING FUNCTION

Mission Command

Movement and Maneuver

Intelligence

Fires

Sustainment

Maneuver Support and Protection

Engagement

ACQUISITION LIFECYCLE PHASE

Materiel Solution Analysis

Technology Maturation & Risk Reduction

Engineering & Manufacturing Development

Production & Deployment

Operations & Support

MILESTONE DECISION AUTHORITY

Defense Acquisition Executive

Army Acquisition Executive

Program Executive Officer

DESCRIPTION

The Lightweight Laser Designator Rangefinder (LLDR) is a crew-served, long-range modular system designed for man-portable, day-and-night, all-weather use. Warfighters use the LLDR to acquire, precisely locate and engage targets with precision Global Position System (GPS)-guided and laser-guided munitions, and improve the effectiveness of engagement with unguided munitions. The LLDR 2H (AN/PED-1A) integrates a celestial navigation system with a digital magnetic compass, providing highly accurate target coordinates to allow the Soldier to call for fire with precision GPS-guided munitions. A Modification of In-Service Equipment program is ongoing that retrofits fielded LLDR 1 and 2 systems with the LLDR 2H precision targeting capability.

BENEFIT TO THE WARFIGHTER

Planned improvements to the system will provide 24/7 all-weather precision targeting and increased target-acquisition range, and support mounted operations to increase warfighter effectiveness.

SPECIFICATIONS

- Target Designation:
  - › Moving, day: Greater than or equal to 3 km (threshold) and 5 km (objective)
  - › Moving, night: Greater than or equal to 2 km (threshold) and 5 km (objective)
  - › Stationary, day: Greater than or equal to 5 km (threshold) and 7 km (objective)
  - › Stationary, night: Greater than or equal to 2 km (threshold) and 5 km (objective)
- Target Location Error:
  - › Less than or equal to 10 meters at 2.5 km (threshold) and 10 meters at 10 km (objective)
- Total System Weight:
  - › Less than or equal to 35.3 pounds (threshold) and 30 pounds (objective)

PROGRAM STATUS

- **2QFY13:** LLDR 2H Type Classification Standard
- **1QFY14:** LLDR 2H Full Materiel Release
- **2QFY14:** LLDR 2H Initial Operating Capability
- **1QFY16:** Initiating Engineering Change Proposal (ECP) to incorporate Precision Azimuth and Vertical Angle Module (PAVAM) capability

PROJECTED ACTIVITIES

- **3QFY16:** Conduct PAVAM ECP Critical Design Review
- **3QFY17:** PAVAM ECP Developmental Testing begins

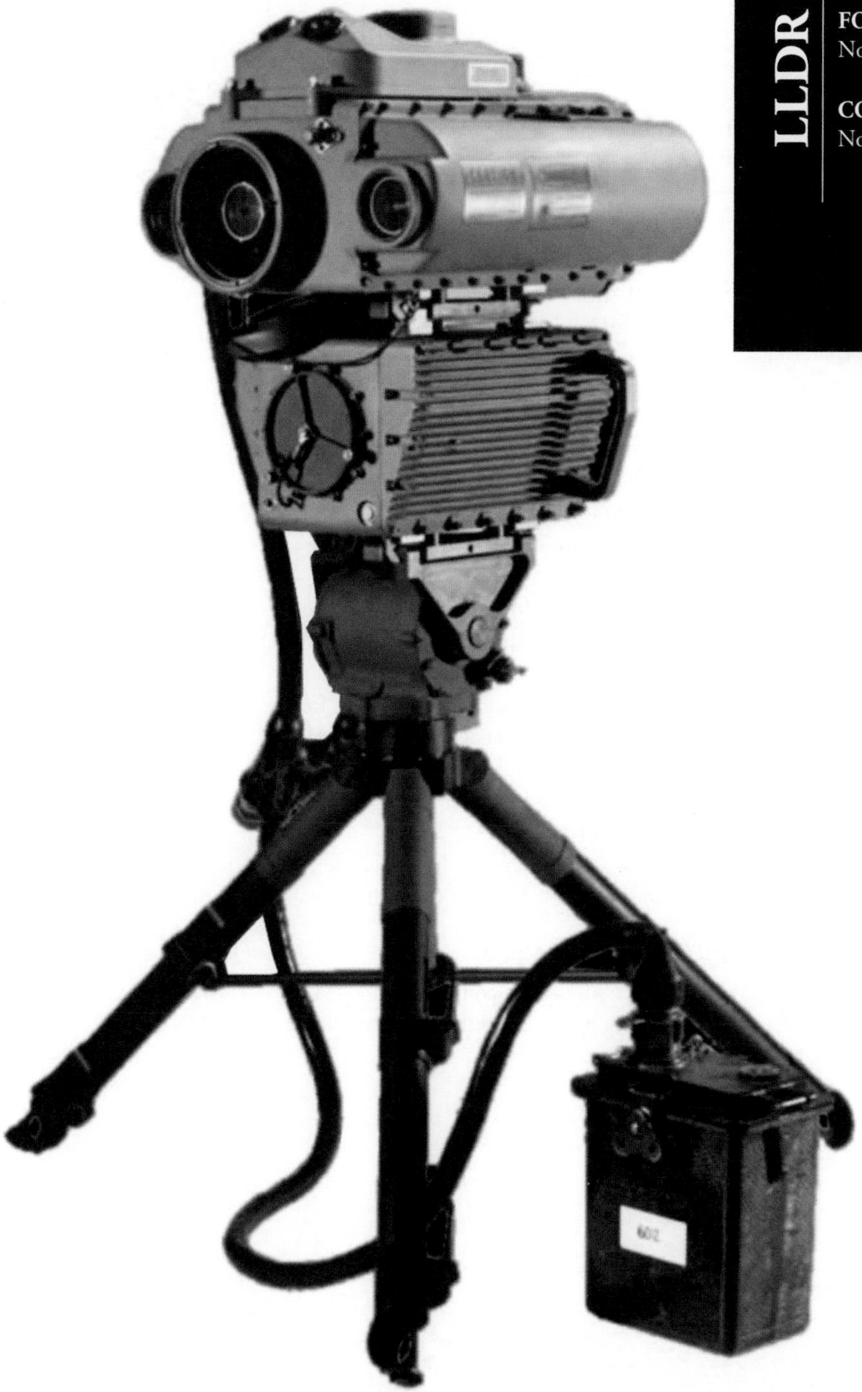

LLDR

FOREIGN MILITARY SALES
None

CONTRACTORS
Northrop Grumman Laser Systems (Apopka, FL)

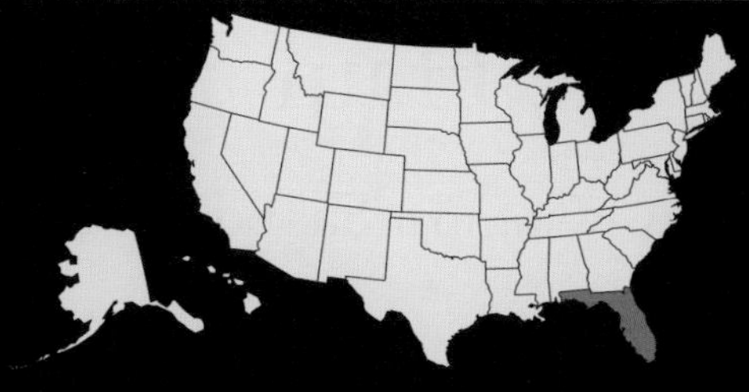

Line Haul Tractor

PEO Combat Support and Combat Service Support | Detroit Arsenal, MI

ACAT III

WARFIGHTING FUNCTION

Mission Command

Movement and Maneuver

Intelligence

Fires

Sustainment

Maneuver Support and Protection

Engagement

ACQUISITION LIFECYCLE PHASE

Materiel Solution Analysis

Technology Maturation & Risk Reduction

Engineering & Manufacturing Development

Production & Deployment

Operations & Support

MILESTONE DECISION AUTHORITY

Defense Acquisition Executive

Army Acquisition Executive

Program Executive Officer

DESCRIPTION

The M915A5 Truck Tractor is used to perform line haul missions. The M915A5 is a block upgrade of the M915A3 system, incorporating enhanced suspension and power train components. This block upgrade allows the M915A5 to readily accept armor packages without reducing mission capability. The M915A5 truck is equipped with a two-passenger cab and has an updated power distribution module, upgraded wiring harnesses, and a roll stability control system. Auxiliary power connections have been added to supply emerging systems and added command, control, communications, computers and intelligence communication systems.

The M915A3 Line Haul Tractor is the Army's key line haul distribution platform. The M916A3 Light Equipment Transport is used primarily to transport the M870 40-ton low-bed semitrailer. The M917A2 Truck Chassis Dump Truck Vehicle is authorized for Corps units, primarily the Construction and Combat Support Companies and the Combat Heavy Battalions.

BENEFIT TO THE WARFIGHTER
The M915A5 offers increased crew protection, improved range and fuel efficiency, and has better reliability due to onboard diagnostics.

SPECIFICATIONS
Line Haul Tractor (M915A5):
- Size: 6x4 (6-wheeled vehicle with 4-wheel drive) semi-tractor
- Gross vehicle weight rating (maximum haul weight): 120,000 pounds
- Engine: Detroit Diesel S60 (500 horsepower, 1,650 foot-pounds torque, Detroit Diesel Electronic Control (DDEC) IV engine controller)
- Transmission: Allison HD4500SP (6-speed automatic)
- Maximum towing speed: 65 mph with full payload on flat terrain

Line Haul Tractor (M915A3):
- Size: 6x4 tractor with a 2-inch kingpin
- Gross vehicle weight rating: 105,000 pounds
- Engine: Detroit Diesel S60 (430 horsepower, 1,450 foot-pounds torque, DDEC IV engine controller)
- Transmission: Allison HD5460P (6-speed automatic) with power take-off
- Maximum towing speed: 65 mph with full payload on flat terrain

Light Equipment Transport (M916A3):
- Size: 6x6 tractor
- Gross vehicle weight rating: 130,000 pounds
- Engine: Electronic diesel
- Transmission: Automatic electronic
- Maximum towing speed: 60 mph with full payload on flat terrain

Truck Chassis Dump Truck Vehicle (M917A2):
- Size: 8x6 for 20-ton dump truck
- Gross vehicle weight rating: 115,000 pounds
- Engine: Electronic diesel
- Transmission: Automatic electronic
- Maximum speed: 55 mph with full payload on flat terrain

PROGRAM STATUS
- **Current:** Production completed of all M915A5 currently on contract, 220 produced; fielding completed to all CONUS-based units

PROJECTED ACTIVITIES
- **FY16-FY17:**
  › Continued divestment of older M915 variants (A0, A1, A2, A4)
  › Development of M915A3, M915A5, and M916A3 C-Kit armor

Line Haul Tractor

FOREIGN MILITARY SALES
Afghanistan

CONTRACTORS
Prime: Daimler Trucks North America LLC/
Freightliner (Portland, OR and Cleveland, NC)
Engine: Detroit Diesel (Detroit, MI)
ABS Brakes: Meritor (Troy, MI)
Dump body: Casteel Manufacturing
(San Antonio, TX)

Line of Communications Bridge (LOCB)

PEO Combat Support and Combat Service Support | Detroit Arsenal, MI

WARFIGHTING FUNCTION

Mission Command

Movement and Maneuver

Intelligence

Fires

Sustainment

Maneuver Support and Protection

Engagement

ACQUISITION LIFECYCLE PHASE

Materiel Solution Analysis

Technology Maturation & Risk Reduction

Engineering & Manufacturing Development

Production & Deployment

Operations & Support

MILESTONE DECISION AUTHORITY

Defense Acquisition Executive

Army Acquisition Executive

Program Executive Officer

DESCRIPTION

The Line of Communications Bridge (LOCB) restores and maintains line of communication routes in theater, supporting both civilian and military traffic. Intended for long-term emplacement, it consists of mission-configurable ramp and span segments. LOCB comes in two military configurations: 50-meter fixed and 280-meter float. Launch time requires up to 8 hours with 29 Soldiers.

BENEFIT TO THE WARFIGHTER

LOCB bridging is focused on sustainment of the force. LOCB supports the focused logistics concept by its ability to facilitate sustainment of widely dispersed forces over a large area of operation. As such, the LOCB facilitates the uninterrupted flow of forces, equipment, personnel and supplies for sustained ground operations for the warfighter, Allied, Coalition and host nation forces, and displaced civilians.

SPECIFICATIONS

- Maximum load capacity: 120 wheeled or 100 tracked vehicles
- Roadway width: 4.5 meters
- Assembled length: Spans gaps up to 300 meters

PROGRAM STATUS

- **2QFY13:** Milestone B

PROJECTED ACTIVITIES

- **2QFY16:** Milestone C
- **4QFY18:** Full-Rate Production Decision
- **2QFY19:** First Unit Equipped

FOREIGN MILITARY SALES
None

CONTRACTORS
Rock Island Arsenal (Rock Island, IL)

Load Handling System Compatible Water Tank Rack (Hippo)

PEO Combat Support and Combat Service Support | Detroit Arsenal, MI

WARFIGHTING FUNCTION

Mission Command

Movement and Maneuver

Intelligence

Fires

Sustainment

Maneuver Support and Protection

Engagement

ACQUISITION LIFECYCLE PHASE

Materiel Solution Analysis

Technology Maturation & Risk Reduction

Engineering & Manufacturing Development

Production & Deployment

Operations & Support

MILESTONE DECISION AUTHORITY

Defense Acquisition Executive

Army Acquisition Executive

Program Executive Officer

DESCRIPTION

The Load Handling System Compatible Water Tank Rack (Hippo) enhances and expedites the delivery of bulk potable water into the division and brigade areas. It represents the latest in bulk water distribution technology and replaces the 3,000 and 5,000 semitrailer-mounted fabric tanks.

The Hippo is fully functional, mounted or dismounted, and is air- and ground-transportable when full, partially full or empty. It is Heavy Expanded Mobility Tactical Truck Palletized Load System (PLS) and PLS trailer compatible. The Hippo can be moved and set up rapidly using minimal assets and personnel. No site preparation is required and its modular configuration supports expeditionary Joint forces operations.

BENEFIT TO THE WARFIGHTER

Hippo provides the Army with the capability to receive, store and distribute potable water to warfighting units deployed throughout the battlefield.

SPECIFICATIONS

- Consists of a 2,000-gallon potable-water tank in an International Organization for Standardization frame
- Employs integrated pump, engine, alternator, filling stand and 70-foot hose reel with bulk suction and discharge hoses
- Pumps 125 gallons of water per minute
- Prevents water from freezing in cold weather environments down to minus 25 degrees Fahrenheit

PROGRAM STATUS

- **Current:** Low-Rate Initial Production; continue RESET Program to reset system to required capability

PROJECTED ACTIVITIES

- **3QFY16:** Full-Rate Production

FOREIGN MILITARY SALES
None

CONTRACTORS
Mil-Mar Century, Inc. (Miamisburg, OH)
Entwistle (Danville, VA)

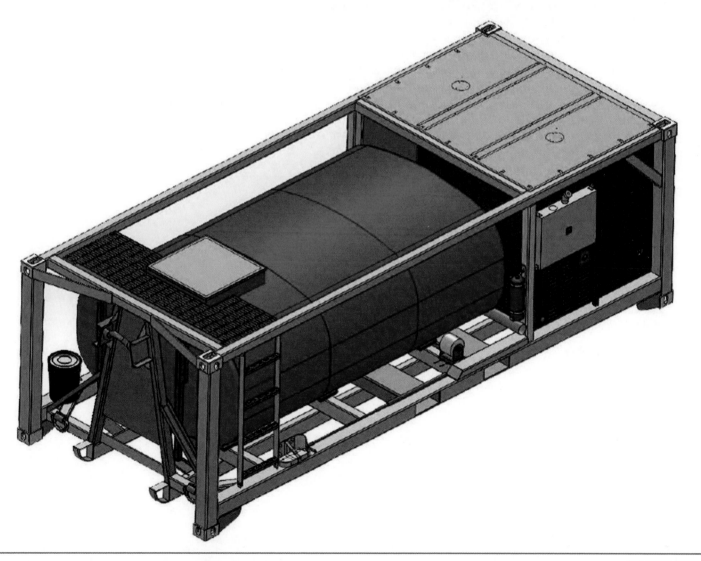

M160 Robotic Mine Flail

PEO Combat Support and Combat Service Support | Detroit Arsenal, MI

WARFIGHTING FUNCTION

Mission Command

Movement and Maneuver

Intelligence

Fires

Sustainment

Maneuver Support and Protection

Engagement

ACQUISITION LIFECYCLE PHASE

Materiel Solution Analysis

Technology Maturation & Risk Reduction

Engineering & Manufacturing Development

Production & Deployment

Operations & Support

MILESTONE DECISION AUTHORITY

Defense Acquisition Executive

Army Acquisition Executive

Program Executive Officer

DESCRIPTION

The M160 Robotic Mine Flail is used to clear areas infested with land mines and counter the effects of mines that could impede the mobility of friendly forces, destroy systems or cause personnel casualties. It is designed to be protected against mine explosion fragments. Mine clearing is conducted using the flailing motion of high-speed, rotating chained hammers. The machine digs and pounds the soil, which results in the detonation or shattering of anti-personnel (AP) mines.

The system, an improved version of the basic commercial off-the-shelf DOK-ING MV-4 Mechanical Anti-Personnel Mine Clearing System. The remote control system provides real-time control of the mine-clearing vehicle and allows the operator to control the vehicle from either a mounted or stand-off dismounted position.

The M160 is also equipped with a communication system that transfers operating status and video feedback to the operator. The M160's hand-held, stand-off, remote control feature allows the operator to remain outside the range of exploding mines during the clearing process. Additionally, the engine and vital components of the machine are protected by steel armor plates. Mine rollers and earth-moving blades will be fielded to units after being reset to a desired level of combat capability.

BENEFIT TO THE WARFIGHTER

The M160 provides stand-off protection to Soldiers while they clear areas of AP mines.

SPECIFICATIONS

Major components:

- Engine
- Hydraulic system
- Flail head assembly
- Remote control system
- Drive train

PROGRAM STATUS

- **Current:** Completing reset to desired level of combat capability; updating technical manuals and incorporating Engineering Change Proposals

PROJECTED ACTIVITIES

- **2QFY17:** Begin fielding
- **4QFY21:** Fielding complete

Man Transportable Robot System (MTRS) Increment 2

PEO Combat Support and Combat Service Support | Detroit Arsenal, MI

WARFIGHTING FUNCTION

Mission Command

Movement and Maneuver

Intelligence

Fires

Sustainment

Maneuver Support and Protection

Engagement

ACQUISITION LIFECYCLE PHASE

Materiel Solution Analysis

Technology Maturation & Risk Reduction

Engineering & Manufacturing Development

Production & Deployment

Operations & Support

MILESTONE DECISION AUTHORITY

Defense Acquisition Executive

Army Acquisition Executive

Program Executive Officer

DESCRIPTION

The Man Transportable Robot System (MTRS) Increment 2 is a remotely operated, man-transportable robotic system that provides a stand-off capability to detect and confirm the presence of, identify the disposition of, and counter hazards by carrying various platform payloads in support of current and future missions. MTRS Increment 2 supports engineers, chemical, biological, radiological, and nuclear (CBRN) Soldiers, and Special Operations forces.

BENEFIT TO THE WARFIGHTER

The MTRS provides the warfighter with a stand-off ability to locate, identify and clear landmines, unexploded ordnance and improvised explosive devices in the path of maneuvering Army or Joint forces. It also provides CBRN Soldiers with the capability to employ CBRN sensors from a distance.

SPECIFICATIONS

• Hand-held controller allows operator a stand-off capability to operate MTRS Increment 2 from a mounted or dismounted location and receive video and vehicle control data
• Allows multiple payload platforms to improve support to Soldiers in current and future operating environments

PROGRAM STATUS

• **Current:** Request for Proposal development

PROJECTED ACTIVITIES

• **2QFY16:** Request for Proposal release
• **4QFY16:** Milestones B and C
• **1QFY17:** Contract award

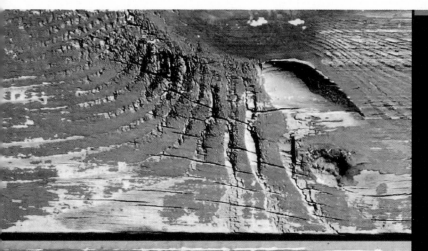

FOREIGN MILITARY SALES
None

CONTRACTORS
TBD

PROGRAM
UNDER DEVELOPMENT

**Project Manager
Force Projection**

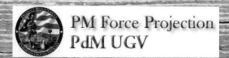

PM Force Projection
PdM UGV

Medical Communications for Combat Casualty Care (MC4)

PEO Enterprise Information Systems | Fort Belvoir, VA

DESCRIPTION

Medical Communications for Combat Casualty Care (MC4) is a ruggedized system of systems containing medical software packages fielded to operational medical forces worldwide. The system is comprised of joint software, commercial and government off-the-shelf products including Theater Medical Information Program – Joint (TMIP-J) applications provided by Defense Health Clinical Systems. MC4 provides the tools needed to digitally record and transfer critical medical data from the foxhole to medical treatment facilities around the world. With more than a decade of experience managing the Army's deployable medical recording system, MC4 remains the most widely used, comprehensive information management medical system on the battlefield.

BENEFIT TO THE WARFIGHTER

Deployable medical forces use the MC4 system to gain quick, accurate access to patient histories and forward casualty resuscitation information. The system also provides units with automated tools facilitating patient and item tracking, blood management, medical reporting and medical logistical support.

SPECIFICATIONS

The TMIP-J applications include:
- Software for electronic medical record (EMR) documentation
- A Web-based application that serves as a deployed EMR repository
- A Web-based application for conducting battlefield surveillance

PROGRAM STATUS

- **2QFY13:**
  - › Completed v2.2.0.0 Site Acceptance Test
  - › Completed 2.1.3.1 Update 3 and data-at-rest-compliant hard drive upgrade to 2,400-plus systems across 493 locations
- **4QFY13:** Conducted Operational Readiness Review of v2.2.0.0
- **3QFY14:** Supported establishment of the Combat Support Hospital in Kabul, Afghanistan

- **4QFY14:** Supported Operation United Assistance Ebola medical task force deployment
- **FY15:**
  - › Upgraded 3,486 systems to v2.2.0.0, including 563 units in 16 countries
  - › Supported operations in theater and multiple OCONUS locations while deploying system upgrade version 2.2.0.0 Update 2 worldwide; v2.2.0.0 includes Block 2, Release 2 upgrade to TMIP-J software; deployment to active users completed; initiated deployment to other Army units based on Army Resourcing Priority List
- **4QFY15:** Completed Multiservice Operational Test and Evaluation of v2.3.1.0., which includes final upgrade of TMIP-J software (Block 2, Release 3)

PROJECTED ACTIVITIES

- **FY16:**
  - › Identify and pilot emerging technologies to enhance system capability
  - › Initiate deployment (training and fielding) of v2.3.1.0 to active users; initiate delivery of upgraded hardware
- **FY17:**
  - › Finalize technology transfer agreements for promising new technologies and incorporate selected technologies
  - › Initiate planning for new commercial off-the-shelf software to modernize the Joint Service Electronic Health Record System to incrementally replace TMIP-J beginning in FY18; TMIP-J will remain operational until the new system attains full deployment

Medical Countermeasure Systems (MCS) – Diagnostics

JPEO for Chemical and Biological Defense | Aberdeen Proving Ground, MD

WARFIGHTING FUNCTION

Mission Command

Movement and Maneuver

Intelligence

Fires

Sustainment

Maneuver Support and Protection

Engagement

ACQUISITION LIFECYCLE PHASE

Materiel Solution Analysis

Technology Maturation & Risk Reduction

Engineering & Manufacturing Development

Production & Deployment

Operations & Support

MILESTONE DECISION AUTHORITY

Defense Acquisition Executive

Army Acquisition Executive

Program Executive Officer

DESCRIPTION

Medical Countermeasure Systems (MCS) – Diagnostics provides technologies and Food and Drug Administration (FDA)-cleared devices intended for Service members to aid in early diagnosis, prevention and treatment of the effects of exposure to chemical, biological and radiological agents. The Diagnostics portfolio consists of:

- The Joint Biological Agent Identification and Diagnostic System (JBAIDS), which is capable of rapid, reliable and simultaneous identification of biological agents and other pathogens of operational concern in environmental or clinical sample matrices. The JBAIDS is an FDA-cleared device for Anthrax, Tularemia, Plague, Q-Fever, H5 Avian Flu, Influenza A/B typing and Influenza A subtyping. The system also includes environmental assays for 16 different pathogens. Assay consumables are freeze-dried reagents that are necessary for DNA/RNA amplification and fluorescence detection.
- The Next Generation Diagnostic System (NGDS) Increment 1, which will be deployed to roles 2 and 3 of combat health support units for clinical diagnostics and environmental analysis. NGDS Increment 1 is intended to mitigate the effects of exposure to biological warfare agents (BWA) and endemic diseases of military relevance through rapid diagnostics and detection.

BENEFIT TO THE WARFIGHTER

MCS – Diagnostics provides improved patient outcomes to biological warfare and endemic disease infections and informs force health protection and force protection decision making.

SPECIFICATIONS

- **Application:** *In vitro* diagnostic or environmental sample (i.e., blood, nasal, urine, soil)

PROGRAM STATUS

JBAIDS:
- **FY14:** Emergency Use Authorization for Ebola Zaire real-time reverse transcription polymerase chain reaction (TaqMan®) Diagnostic Assay Kits
- **4QFY15:**
  › Submitted special 510(k) package for H7N9 subtype avian influenza virus detection with existing influenza kits
  › Food and water color compensation calibration completed
- **4QFY15-2QFY16:** Laptop replacement fielding; all JBAIDS laptops meet Army requirement to utilize Windows 7 operating system

NGDS Increment 1:
- **1QFY15:**
  › Emergency Use Authorization for Ebola virus diagnostic
  › Urgent Materiel Release of systems and Ebola virus diagnostics (CONUS and OCONUS)
- **2QFY15:** Revised Acquisition Strategy (Consolidated Capability Development Strategy and Schedule Revision)

PROJECTED ACTIVITIES

JBAIDS:
- **1QFY16:** Clinical studies initiated for six-agent BWA diagnostic
- **4QFY16:** FDA clearance (whole blood and blood culture)
- **FY17:** Begin transition of NGDS Increment 1 systems to JBAIDS users

NGDS Increment 1:
- **3QFY17:** FDA clearance of sputum samples for assays
- **4QFY17:** Full-Rate Production for Army

FOREIGN MILITARY SALES
None

CONTRACTORS
BioFire Defense, LLC (Salt Lake City, UT)

Medical Countermeasure Systems (MCS) – Joint Vaccine Acquisition Program (JVAP) and Bioscavenger

JPEO for Chemical and Biological Defense | Aberdeen Proving Ground, MD

WARFIGHTING FUNCTION

Mission Command

Movement and Maneuver

Intelligence

Fires

Sustainment

Maneuver Support and Protection

Engagement

ACQUISITION LIFECYCLE PHASE

Materiel Solution Analysis

Technology Maturation & Risk Reduction

Engineering & Manufacturing Development

Production & Deployment

Operations & Support

MILESTONE DECISION AUTHORITY

Defense Acquisition Executive

Army Acquisition Executive

Program Executive Officer

DESCRIPTION

The Joint Vaccine Acquisition Program (JVAP) consists of seven components:

- Anthrax Vaccine Absorbed (AVA): Sustainment
  › The Anthrax Vaccine Absorbed is the only Food and Drug Administration (FDA)-licensed anthrax vaccine in the United States that provides protection against cutaneous, gastrointestinal and aerosol infection by battlefield exposure to Bacillus anthracis.
- Recombinant Plague Vaccine (PLG VAC): ACAT II
  › The Recombinant Plague Vaccine is a highly purified polypeptide produced from bacterial cells transfected with a recombinant vector from the Yersinia pestis bacterium to prevent pneumonic plague.
- Recombinant Botulinum Toxin Vaccine A/B (BOT VAC A/B): ACAT II
  › The Recombinant Botulinum Bivalent Vaccine is comprised of nontoxic botulinum toxin heavy chain fragments of serotypes A and B formulated with an aluminum hydroxide adjuvant and delivered intramuscularly prior to potential exposure to botulinum toxin.
- Smallpox Vaccine System (SVS): Sustainment
  › The Smallpox Vaccine System provides both the ACAM2000™ smallpox vaccine and the Vaccinia Immune Globulin, Intravenous (VIGIV) to vaccinate and protect the warfighter from potential exposure to smallpox. Both products are FDA-approved.
- Filovirus Vaccine (FILO VAC):
  › The Filovirus Vaccine program addresses an essential capability gap for protecting warfighters against aerosolized filovirus for which there is no current therapeutic. Target filovirus strains include Ebola Sudan, Ebola Zaire and Marburg.
- Ricin Vaccine (RIC VAC):
  › The Ricin Vaccine program will develop a vaccine against the A and B chains of this threat agent and validate performance against aerosolized material.

- Western, Eastern Venezuelan Equine Encephalitis Vaccine (WEVEE VAC):
  › The WEVEE VAC program will develop a vaccine against three arboviruses with the goal of a single product protecting against all three threats.

The Bioscavenger program fills an urgent capability gap in the warfighter's defense against nerve agents by development of a nerve agent prophylactic that significantly reduces or eliminates the need for postexposure antidotal therapy.

BENEFIT TO THE WARFIGHTER

JVAP and Bioscavenger provide protection to the warfighter against aerosolized biological warfare agents and a broad spectrum of nerve agents.

SPECIFICATIONS

- System attributes established in requirements documentation

PROGRAM STATUS

BOT VAC
- **FY14:** Technology transfer process development work initiated

FILO VAC
- **FY15:** Ebola response efforts

WEVEE VAC
- **FY13:** Milestone A

RIC VAC
- **FY13:** Milestone A

PROJECTED ACTIVITIES

BOT VAC
- **FY17:** Chemistry Manufacturing Control submission to FDA

FILO VAC
- **FY17:** Milestone B

MCS - JVAP

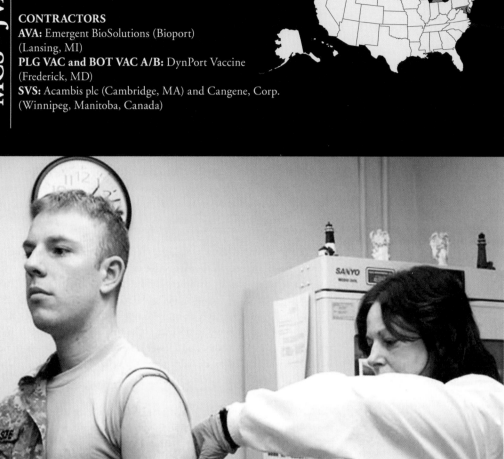

FOREIGN MILITARY SALES
Canada, United Kingdom

CONTRACTORS
AVA: Emergent BioSolutions (Bioport)
(Lansing, MI)
PLG VAC and BOT VAC A/B: DynPort Vaccine
(Frederick, MD)
SVS: Acambis plc (Cambridge, MA) and Cangene, Corp.
(Winnipeg, Manitoba, Canada)

Medical Simulation Training Center (MSTC)

PEO Simulation, Training, and Instrumentation | Orlando, FL

WARFIGHTING FUNCTION

Mission Command

Movement and Maneuver

Intelligence

Fires

Sustainment

Maneuver Support and Protection

Engagement

ACQUISITION LIFECYCLE PHASE

Materiel Solution Analysis

Technology Maturation & Risk Reduction

Engineering & Manufacturing Development

Production & Deployment

Operations & Support

MILESTONE DECISION AUTHORITY

Defense Acquisition Executive

Army Acquisition Executive

Program Executive Officer

DESCRIPTION

The Medical Simulation Training Center (MSTC) conducts sustainment and enhanced medical training for combat medics and combat lifesavers in support of unified land operations. MSTC provide hands-on instruction in the latest battlefield trauma and critical care techniques based on U.S. Army Medical Department-approved performance-oriented training curricula. Medical treatment validation exercises simulate the high stress of performing medical interventions in combat.

MSTC Increment 1 provides realistic medical training to both medical and nonmedical Soldiers in the Army, Reserve and National Guard. MSTC supports unit medical readiness by validating Combat Medic (68W) Emergency Medical Technician biennial recertification requirements and providing combat lifesaver training to nonmedical Soldiers. Increment 2 will focus on improving health care at the first responder, combat medic, special operations medic, and forward deployed surgical levels to better meet the commander's casualty response system needs now and in the Force 2025 operating environment.

The MSTC mannequin provides realistic trauma treatment practice opportunities for self and buddy rescue performance in the Squad Overmatch Study – Tactical Combat Casualty Care (SOvM-TC3) study. Implementing the MSTC in the integrated SOvM-TC3 increased the squads' training experience because of the realism that was applied across the gaming and live environments.

BENEFIT TO THE WARFIGHTER

The MSTC saves Soldiers through enhanced hands-on medical training, which is provided and taught under realistic battlefield conditions. From this sustainment and validation medical training, first responders are able to provide emergency medical treatment for the three main preventable causes of death on the battlefield (hemorrhage, airway compromise and tension pneumothorax).

SPECIFICATIONS

MTSC consists of:
- A 7,000-square-foot structure
- Virtual Patient System
- Instructor Support System
- Medical Training Evaluation System
- Medical Training Command and Control
- Professional instruction and administrative support

PROGRAM STATUS

- **4QFY15:** Sustainment and maintenance, technical refresh and concurrency on medical training aids, devices, simulators and simulations

PROJECTED ACTIVITIES

- **1QFY17:** Award of the Virtual Patient Simulation Systems contract

MSTC

FOREIGN MILITARY SALES
Uruguay and Serbia

CONTRACTORS
Computer Science Corp. (Orlando, FL)
Laerdal (Wappingers Falls, NY)
Simetri, Inc. (Winter Park, FL)
Optimal Technologies International (Orlando, FL)
PULAU Corp. (Orlando, FL)
Kforce Government Solutions, Inc. (Fairfax, VA)
SKEDCO, Inc. (Tualatin, OR)

Medium Caliber Ammunition (MCA)

PEO Ammunition | Picatinny Arsenal, NJ

WARFIGHTING FUNCTION

Mission Command

Movement and Maneuver

Intelligence

Fires

Sustainment

Maneuver Support and Protection

Engagement

ACQUISITION LIFECYCLE PHASE

Materiel Solution Analysis

Technology Maturation & Risk Reduction

Engineering & Manufacturing Development

Production & Deployment

Operations & Support

MILESTONE DECISION AUTHORITY

Defense Acquisition Executive

Army Acquisition Executive

Program Executive Officer

DESCRIPTION

Medium Caliber Ammunition (MCA) includes 20 mm, 25 mm, 30 mm, and 40 mm armor-piercing, high-explosive, smoke, illumination, training and antipersonnel cartridges with the capability to defeat light armor, materiel and personnel targets. These munitions provide overwhelming lethality in MCA and point- and area-target engagement via medium hand-held and crew-served weapons.

BENEFIT TO THE WARFIGHTER

Standard ammunition provides the warfighter with the necessary lethality needed to defeat the enemy. Specialty 40 mm rounds provide specific tools for the warfighter (e.g. illumination). The Counter-Rocket, Artillery, and Mortar (C-RAM) defends against enemy rocket, mortar and artillery fires.

SPECIFICATIONS

Various specifications used are dependent on weapon platform, caliber and target set and effect.

- 20 mm cartridge is a multipurpose tracer with self-destruct, used in the C-RAM weapon system
- 25 mm target practice (TP), high-explosive incendiary and armor-piercing cartridges are fired from the M242 Bushmaster Cannon from the Bradley Fighting Vehicle
- 30 mm TP and High Explosive-Dual Purpose (HEDP) cartridges are fired from the M230 chain gun mounted on the Apache and Blackhawk helicopters
- Varieties of 40 mm TP, HEDP and specialty cartridges are designed for use in the M203 Grenade Launcher, M320 Grenade Launcher and the MK19 Grenade Machine Gun

PROGRAM STATUS

- **Current:** Production and sustainment

PROJECTED ACTIVITIES

- **FY16:**
  › Cannon-caliber and 40 mm legacy production and sustainment
  › New multiyear 40 mm production contract
  › Develop 40 mm day, night and thermal cartridges
  › Qualify 30 mm ammunition for Stryker Infantry Combat Vehicle 2nd Cavalry Regiment lethality upgrade

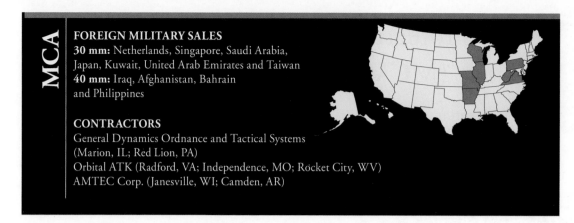

Medium Caliber Ammunition Family

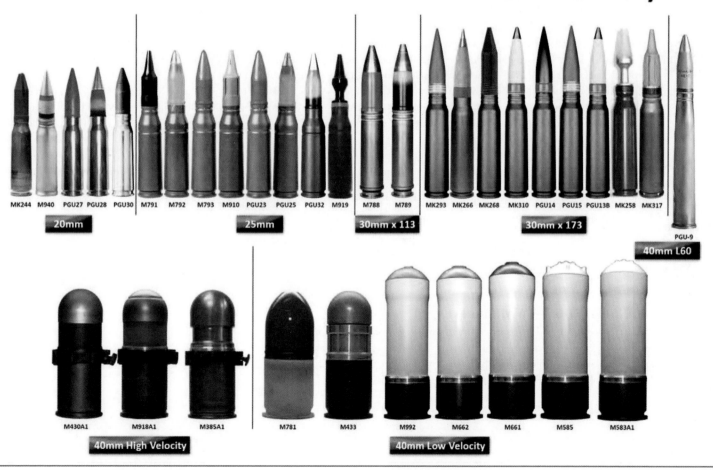

MK244 M940 PGU27 PGU28 PGU30 **20mm**

M791 M792 M793 M910 PGU23 PGU25 PGU32 M919 **25mm**

M788 M789 **30mm x 113**

MK293 MK266 MK268 MK310 PGU14 PGU15 PGU13B MK258 MK317 **30mm x 173**

PGU-9 **40mm L60**

M430A1 M918A1 M385A1 **40mm High Velocity**

M781 M433 M992 M662 M661 M585 M583A1 **40mm Low Velocity**

Mine Protection Vehicle Family (MPVF), Mine Clearing Vehicle (MCV), Explosive Hazard Pre-Detonation (EHP)

PEO Combat Support and Combat Service Support | Detroit Arsenal, MI

WARFIGHTING FUNCTION

Mission Command

Movement and Maneuver

Intelligence

Fires

Sustainment

Maneuver Support and Protection

Engagement

ACQUISITION LIFECYCLE PHASE

Materiel Solution Analysis

Technology Maturation & Risk Reduction

Engineering & Manufacturing Development

Production & Deployment

Operations & Support

MILESTONE DECISION AUTHORITY

Defense Acquisition Executive

Army Acquisition Executive

Program Executive Officer

DESCRIPTION

The Mine Protection Vehicle Family (MPVF) consists of the Medium Mine Protected Vehicle (MMPV) Type I and II, the Husky Vehicle Mounted Mine Detection (VMMD) system, and the Buffalo Mine Protected Clearance Vehicle (MPCV). All are blast-protected with a V-shaped hull. The MMPV Type I (Panther) will support Explosive Ordnance Disposal Companies and Chemical Biological Response Teams. The MMPV Type II (RG-31) will support Engineer Units in route and area clearance operations. The VMMD is a vehicle-mounted mine-detection and lane-proofing system capable of finding and marking metallic explosive hazards, including metallic-encased improvised explosive devices (IED). The MPCV is capable of interrogating and classifying suspected explosive hazards, including IED. The MPCV has an articulating arm with a digging and lifting attachment and camera to remotely interrogate a suspected explosive hazard and allow the crew to confirm, deny and classify the hazard.

The MCV is a vehicle designed to clear large areas of anti-tank and anti-personnel mines by means of a rotating flail.

The EHP capabilities will counter the full spectrum of conventional and asymmetric explosive hazards including surface-laid, buried and concealed landmines, IED, Explosively Formed Penetrators, Unexploded Ordnance, battlefield munitions and booby traps to include associated trigger mechanisms.

BENEFIT TO THE WARFIGHTER

These systems provide the warfighter with effective, reliable and affordable blast protection by interrogating and classifying suspected explosive hazards while providing force protection to defeat the full spectrum of worldwide explosive hazards.

PROGRAM STATUS

- **2QFY15:** MMPV Type II Production Qualification Testing complete; EHP Wire Neutralization System (WNS) Prototype Production
- **2QFY15-4QFY15:** EHP Testing, Prototype Production and Logistics Development (all EHP systems)
- **3QFY15:** MMPV Type I achieved Conditional Materiel Release, with First Unit Equipped

PROJECTED ACTIVITIES

- **FY16:** MMPV Type II RESET/RECAP ongoing at Letterkenny Army Depot
- **3QFY16:** EHP Blower Milestone C; MCV complete fielding and transition to Organic Support; MMPV Type I obtain Organic Maintenance Capability; MMPV Type II obtain Conditional Materiel Release
- **4QFY16:** MMPV Type II begins fielding
- **3QFY17:** MPCV Logistics and Technical Manual revisions complete
- **4QFY17:** EHP Blower obtain Full Materiel Release and begin fielding

FOREIGN MILITARY SALES
MPCV: United Kingdom
VMMD: Canada, Kenya and Australia
MCV: Austria

CONTRACTORS
MMPV Type I (Panther): BAE Systems (York, PA)
MMPV Type II (RG-31): General Dynamics Land Systems-Canada (Ontario, Canada)
MPCV: General Dynamics Land Systems (Sterling Heights, MI)
VMMD: Critical Solutions International, Inc. (Charleston, SC)
M1271 MCV: Hydrema (Støvring, Denmark)
EHP Debris Blower: Buffalo Turbine (Springville, NY)
EHP WNS (Prototype): Anniston Army Depot (Anniston, AL)
EHP Mine Roller (Prototype): Anniston Army Depot (Anniston, AL)

SPECIFICATIONS

	MMPV Type I	MMPV Type II	MPCV Buffalo	VMMD Husky	MCV
Personnel Capacity	5	4	6	1	2
Operational Length	349 inches	276.8 inches	323 inches	291.6 inches	392.4 inches
Operational Width	124 inches	107.1 inches	106 inches	100.8 inches	189.5 inches
Operational Height	136 inches	141.4 inches	156 inches	122 inches	99.3 inches
Gross Vehicle Weight	74,000 pounds	35,000 pounds	48,500 pounds	15,240 pounds	42,628 pounds

Mobile Maintenance Equipment Systems (MMES)

PEO Combat Support and Combat Service Support | Detroit Arsenal, MI

WARFIGHTING FUNCTION

Mission Command

Movement and Maneuver

Intelligence

Fires

Sustainment

Maneuver Support and Protection

Engagement

ACQUISITION LIFECYCLE PHASE

Materiel Solution Analysis

Technology Maturation & Risk Reduction

Engineering & Manufacturing Development

Production & Deployment

Operations & Support

MILESTONE DECISION AUTHORITY

Defense Acquisition Executive

Army Acquisition Executive

Program Executive Officer

DESCRIPTION

Mobile Maintenance Equipment Systems (MMES) provide two-level maintenance capability to the warfighter. Eight interconnected maintenance systems are distributed throughout the Army at multiple levels and provide a holistic repair capability in all environments. This approach meets the Army's two-level maintenance philosophy and supports the current force while also providing modular configurations to meet the specific needs of the Army in today's transforming environment.

BENEFIT TO THE WARFIGHTER

The MMES provides technological advancements and professional-grade tools with lifetime warranties that will save the Army money for years to come. This integrated maintenance system serves to consolidate Line Item Numbers to one and equips our forces with the most current and accurate tools to complete the mission while performing maintenance on the latest technologically advanced equipment and weaponry.

SPECIFICATIONS

MMES family of systems includes:

- Metal Working and Machining Shop Set (MWMSS)
- Fire Suppression Refill System (FSRS)
- Armament Repair Shop Set (ARSS)
- The Hydraulic Systems Test and Repair Unit (HSTRU)
- Shop Equipment, Welding Trailer (SEW)
- Shop Equipment Contact Maintenance (SECM)
- Forward Repair System (FRS)
- Standard Automotive Tool Set (SATS)

PROGRAM STATUS

3QFY14:
- › MWMSS, Milestone (MS) C
- › ARSS, MS C

1QFY16:
- › FSRS, MS C
- › FSRS, First Unit Equipped

PROJECTED ACTIVITIES

- **4QFY16:** Load Banks, MS C
- **2QFY17:** Refrigeration Took Kit, MS C

Fire Suppression Refill System (FSRS)

Armament Repair Shop Set (ARSS)

Hydraulic System Test & Repair Unit MX3 (HSTRU)

Metal Working & Machine Shop Set (MWMSS)

Modular Fuel System (MFS)

PEO Combat Support and Combat Service Support | Detroit Arsenal, MI

WARFIGHTING FUNCTION

Mission Command

Movement and Maneuver

Intelligence

Fires

Sustainment

Maneuver Support and Protection

Engagement

ACQUISITION LIFECYCLE PHASE

Materiel Solution Analysis

Technology Maturation & Risk Reduction

Engineering & Manufacturing Development

Production & Deployment

Operations & Support

MILESTONE DECISION AUTHORITY

Defense Acquisition Executive

Army Acquisition Executive

Program Executive Officer

DESCRIPTION

The Modular Fuel System (MFS) rapidly establishes fuel distribution and storage capability at any location regardless of material handling equipment availability. The MFS performs both retail and bulk fueling operations, and is capable of receiving, storing, filtering and issuing all kerosene-based fuels.

The MFS is composed of 14 Tank Rack Modules (TRM) and one of the pump and filtration modules, commonly known as Pump Rack Modules (PRM). The TRM can be used with the PRM, the Heavy Expanded Mobility Tactical Truck (HEMTT) tankers or as a stand-alone system. When used with the HEMTT tanker, the TRM doubles the HEMTT tanker capacity to 5,000 gallons of fuel. The MFS is transported by the HEMTT Load Handling System and the Palletized Load System.

The PRM has an evacuation capability that allows the hoses in the system to be purged of fuel prior to recovery, and is capable of refueling both ground vehicles and aircraft.

BENEFIT TO THE WARFIGHTER

The MFS enables retail operation for the warfighter by storing, transporting and issuing fuel.

SPECIFICATIONS

- TRM includes continuous duty retail pump, flow meter, filter separator and 2,500-gallon tank
- PRM includes self-priming, 600-gallons-per-minute diesel-engine-driven centrifugal pump; filter separator; valves; fittings; hoses; refueling nozzles; aviation fuel test kits; fire extinguishers; grounding rods; flow meter and NATO connectors

PROGRAM STATUS

- **1QFY16:** TRM I Full Materiel Release

PROJECTED ACTIVITIES

- **1QFY17:** TRM II Full Materiel Release
- **2QFY17:**
  › PRM Full Materiel Release
  › PRM Production Contract Award

Mortar Systems

PEO Ammunition | Picatinny Arsenal, NJ

DESCRIPTION

The family of mortar systems provides organic, indirect fire support to the maneuver unit commander and is employed in all combat formations. The Army uses three variants of 120 mm mortar systems. The two mounted variants are the M121 120 mm mortar, used on the M1064A3 Mortar Carrier, and the 120 mm Recoiling Mortar System, used on the M1129 and M1252 Stryker Mortar Carriers. The M120A1 120 mm Towed Mortar System is the dismounted variant. The Mortar Fire Control System (MFCS) provides the warfighter improvements in command and control of mortar fires and the speed of employment, accuracy and survivability of mortars. The M95/M96 MFCS – Mounted (MFCS-M), used on the M1064A3, M1129 and M1252, and the M150/M151 MFCS – Dismounted (MFCS-D), used with the M120A1, combine a fire control computer with an inertial navigation and pointing system, allowing crews to fire in less than a minute and greatly improving mortar lethality and accuracy, and crew survivability. The Lightweight M252A1 81 mm Mortar System and Lightweight M224A1 60 mm Mortar System have been qualified and are in production and fielding. The M252A1 weighs 20 percent less and the M224A1 weighs 13 percent less than their legacy counterparts, yet maintain the same capability. All of the mortar systems fire a full family of ammunition including high-explosive, infrared and visible light illumination, smoke, and training.

The M32 and M32A1 Lightweight Handheld Mortar Ballistic Computers (LHMBC) have a tactical modem and embedded Global Positioning System, allowing mortar crews to send and receive digital call-for-fire messages, calculate ballistic solutions and navigate. The next-generation Android-based M32A2 is under development.

The XM395 Accelerated Precision Mortar Initiative (APMI) achieved an Urgent Materiel Release in March 2011. APMI has been deployed and used in combat since June 2011. Based on the success of the APMI program, the Army is moving forward with the High Explosive Guided Mortar (HEGM) and in February 2015 validated the Capability Development Document.

BENEFIT TO THE WARFIGHTER

Mortar Systems provide the maneuver commander rapid, responsive, hip-pocket indirect fires in support of combat operations.

PROGRAM STATUS

- **1QFY13-4QFY15:** 1,540 Mortar Weapon Systems (Lightweight 60 mm, 81 mm, 120 mm) fielded to numerous Infantry Brigade Combat Teams (IBCT), Heavy Brigade Combat Teams, Stryker Brigade Combat Teams and Special Forces groups; 295 M150/M151 Mortar Fire Control Systems and 268 Mortar Stowage Kits (MSK) fielded to 15 IBCT, 14 Infantry Battalions, and the Ranger Regiment; continued production of MFCS-D
- **3QFY13:** M32 Software Version 4.1 Materiel Release (MR) (Common Operating Environment Version 1.0); TC-STD 60 mm HE Mortar M1061 Enhanced Fragmentation Cartridge
- **3QFY13-4QFY15:** 228 LHMBC fielded to 4 IBCT, 1 Special Forces Group and 10 IBCT Battalions
- **1QFY15:** Completed production of the M120A1 MSK
- **1QFY16:** M32 Software Version 5.0 MR for M32A1 variant

PROJECTED ACTIVITIES

- **1QFY16-4QFY16:** Continue fielding of the 60 mm Lightweight Mortar (M224A1) and product improvements
- **1QFY16-4QFY17:** Continue fielding of the 81 mm Lightweight Mortar (M252A1) and product improvements; continue production and fielding of MFCS-D and product improvements
- **2QFY16:** Begin production of M32A1; Materiel Development Decision on HEGM
- **2QFY16-4QFY17:** Software integration for Android-based M32A2
- **3QFY16:** Selection of new Mortar Weapon Systems, Mortar Weapon Components and Mortar Fire Control System prime contractors; conduct 60 mm M1061 mortar Full Materiel Release
- **1QFY17-4QFY17:** Begin fielding M32A1
- **2QFY17:** Achieve Milestone B and begin HEGM Engineering & Manufacturing Development

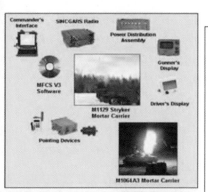

Commander's Interface | SINCGARS Radio | Power Distribution Assembly | MFCS V3 Software | Gunner's Display | M1129 Stryker Mortar Carrier | Driver's Display | Pointing Devices | M1064A3 Mortar Carrier

Mortar Fire Control System (MFCS-Mounted)

Electronics Rack w/ FCC, Portable Universal Battery Supply, DAGR, and Enhanced Power Distribution Assembly

Talin Pointing Device Mounted on Cannon

Motar Fire Control System (MFCS-Dismounted)

Lightweight Handheld Mortar Ballistic Computer (LHMBC)

Mounted Weapon System Production

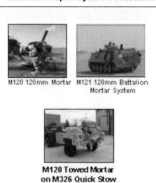

M120 120mm Mortar | M121 120mm Battalion Mortar System

M120 Towed Mortar on M326 Quick Stow Mount

60mm Lightweight Mortar System | 81mm Lightweight Mortar System

M1064A3 Motar Carrier

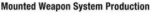

Mortar Systems

FOREIGN MILITARY SALES
Fielded with multiple countries—names for official use only and not for public disclosure

CONTRACTORS
60 mm and 81 mm mortar bipod production: MaTech (Salisbury, MD)
60 mm and 81 mm baseplate production: AMT (Fairfield, NJ)
MFCS-D and MFCS-M production, fielding and installation: Elbit Systems of America (Fort Worth, TX)
M32A1 LHMBC (RTHD-2): VT Miltope (Hope Hull, AL)
M32A2 (Nett Warrior): PM Ground Soldier (Ft. Belvoir, VA)
120 mm, 81 mm, and 60 mm cannons: Watervliet Arsenal (Watervliet, NY)
Mortar ignition cartridge: POCAL Industries, Inc. (Scranton, PA)
Mortar cartridge load, assemble, package: Pine Bluff Arsenal (Pine Bluff, AR)
Mortar fuses: L3 Fuzing and Ordnance Systems (Cincinnati, OH)

SPECIFICATIONS

Mortar	Range (meters)	Weight (pounds)	Rate of Fire (rounds per minute)	Crew	Ammunition
M120/ M121 120mm	7240	319	16 for the first minute 4 sustained	4 M121 carrier-mounted 5 M120 towed	High-explosive (HE) (M934A1), white phosphorus (WP) smoke (M929), illumination (visible light, M930 and infrared [IR], M983), M933A1 (operational training), and full-range practice (FRP) (M931)
M252 81mm	5935	90	30 for the first 2 minutes 15 sustained	3	HE (M821A2), red phosphorus smoke (M819), illumination (visible light, M853A1 and IR, M816), M889A2 (operational training), and FRP (M879)
M224 60mm	3489	46.5 (conventional), 18.0 (handheld)	30 for the first 4 minutes 20 sustained	3	HE (M720A1), WP smoke (M722A1), illumination (visible light, M721 and IR, M767), M768 (operational training), and FRP (M769)

NAVSTAR Global Positioning System (GPS)

PEO Intelligence, Electronic Warfare and Sensors | Aberdeen Proving Ground, MD

DESCRIPTION

The NAVSTAR Global Positioning System (GPS) is a space-based, Joint-service program led by the Air Force that distributes Positioning, Navigation and Timing (PNT) data to tactical and strategic organizations. The GPS has three segments: A space segment (nominally 24 satellites), a ground control segment, and a user equipment segment consisting of receivers configured for hand-held, ground, aircraft and watercraft applications.

Military GPS receivers utilize the Selective Availability Anti-Spoofing Module (SAASM) to access the Precise Positioning Service signal for enhanced accuracy and signal protection not available to commercial equipment. The two highest density GPS receivers in the Army today are the Defense Advanced GPS Receiver (DAGR) and the Ground-Based GPS Receiver Applications Module (GB-GRAM). Approximately 331,000 DAGR were fielded through 2012 for dismounted use and platform installations. More than 125,000 GB-GRAM have been procured to date through a still-active Army contract to equip a wide array of weapon systems. In addition, the DAGR Distributed Device (D3) will provide a distributed PNT capability to selected platforms in FY16.

BENEFIT TO THE WARFIGHTER

When operated in keyed mode, SAASM-based GPS receivers provide warfighters with enhanced positional accuracy and signal protection.

SPECIFICATIONS

DAGR:
- Size: 6.37 x 3.4 x 1.56 inches
- Weight: 1 pound; fits in a two-clip carrying case that attaches to load-bearing equipment
- Frequency: Dual (L1/L2)
- Battery Life: 19 hours (4 AA batteries)
- Satellites: All-in-view

GB-GRAM:
- Size: 0.6 x 2.45 x 3.4 inches
- Weight: 3.5 ounces
- Frequency: Dual (L1/L2)
- Satellites: All-in-view

D3:
- Size: 6.37x 3.74 x 1.64 inches
- Weight: 1 pound
- Frequency: Dual (L1/L2)
- Satellites: All-in-view

PROGRAM STATUS
- **Through FY17:** DAGR hardware retrofit process continues
- **4QFY14:**
  › DAGR sustainment management transitioned to U.S. Army Communications-Electronics Command Logistics and Readiness Center
  › New operating software issued for field reprogramming
- **FY15:** D3/Stryker was designated as Army-led platform for Military GPS User Equipment (MGUE) integration

PROJECTED ACTIVITIES
- **2QFY16-4QFY17:**
  › Field D3 to Armored Knight vehicles
  › D3/Stryker support for evaluation of MGUE prototypes through FY19
  › Resiliency Software Assurance modification for DAGR with Modification Working Order field reprogramming in FY18
  › Completion of DAGR 3.2 retrofit and retirement of DAGR 3.1 to standardize DAGR configuration in field Army
  › Award production contract for embeddable Military-code (M-code)
  › Mitigate gap between GB-GRAM (SAASM) production contract and initial availability of successor M-code product
  › Program Management Office and System Engineering support for modernization of DAGR, GB-GRAM and D3

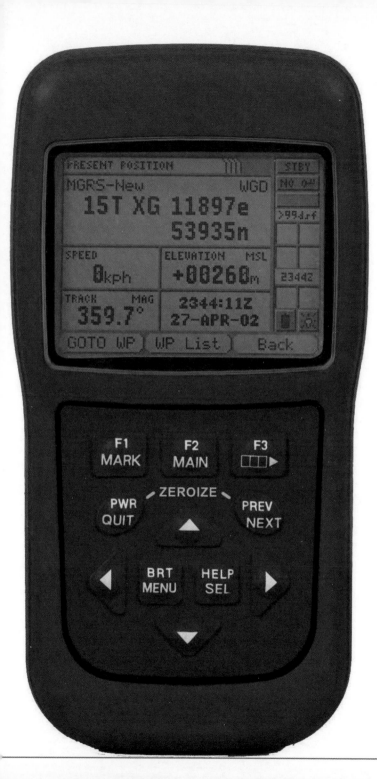

FOREIGN MILITARY SALES
Pulse-per-second-capable GPS receivers have been
sold to 41 authorized countries

CONTRACTORS
DAGR/GB-GRAM acquisition and support:
Rockwell Collins (Cedar Rapids, IA)
D3 acquisition: GPS Source, Inc. (Pueblo, CO)

Nett Warrior (NW)

PEO Soldier | Fort Belvoir, VA

WARFIGHTING FUNCTION

Mission Command

Movement and Maneuver

Intelligence

Fires

Sustainment

Maneuver Support and Protection

Engagement

ACQUISITION LIFECYCLE PHASE

Materiel Solution Analysis

Technology Maturation & Risk Reduction

Engineering & Manufacturing Development

Production & Deployment

Operations & Support

MILESTONE DECISION AUTHORITY

Defense Acquisition Executive

Army Acquisition Executive

Program Executive Officer

DESCRIPTION

Nett Warrior (NW) is an integrated dismounted leader Situational Awareness (SA) system used during combat operations. The system provides unparalleled SA to the dismounted leader, allowing for faster and more accurate decisions in the tactical fight. With advanced navigation, SA and information-sharing capabilities, leaders are able to avoid fratricide and are more effective and lethal in the execution of their combat missions.

The NW program focuses on the development of the SA system, which has the ability to graphically display the location of an individual leader's location on a digital georeferenced map image. The system is connected through a secure radio that sends and receives information from one NW to another, thus connecting the dismounted leader to the network. Additional Soldier and leader locations are displayed on the smart device digital display.

These radios also connect the equipped leader to higher-echelon data and information products to assist in decision making and situational understanding. Soldier position location information will be added to the network via interoperability with the Army's Joint Tactical Radio System capability. All of this will allow the leader to easily see, understand and interact in the method best suited to the user and the particular mission.

BENEFIT TO THE WARFIGHTER

NW employs a system-of-systems approach, optimizing and integrating capabilities while reducing the Soldier's combat load and logistical footprint. It also provides overmatch operational capabilities to all ground combat leaders and small-unit operations.

SPECIFICATIONS

- Off-the-shelf smartphone end-user device with cable (less than 2 pounds) for connection to a radio running Soldier Radio Waveform. The system can operate 8 to 24 hours depending on power-source connection configuration.

- NW, U.S. government-owned open architecture software, has published a Software Development Kit that permits rapid application development and integration. The software also enables the expansion of this platform to other warfighting functions and/or handheld requirements.

PROGRAM STATUS

- **2QFY13:** Favorable NW Operational Assessment from DoD; First unit equipped
- **3QFY13:** NW participation in Network Integration Evaluation (NIE) 13.2 at Fort Bliss, TX
- **4QFY13:** Army Acquisition Executive approved Additional Low-Rate Initial Production #2
- **3QFY14:** NW at NIE 14.2 (Initial Operational Test & Evaluation (IOT&E) Phase I)
- **1QFY15:** NW at Fort Polk, LA (IOT&E Phase II)
- **2QFY15:** NW at Army Expeditionary Warfighting Experiment Spiral J at Fort Benning, GA; 3/10 Mountain Division (MTN DIV) New Equipment Training (NET) at Fort Polk
- **3QFY15:** 3/101st Airborne Division (ABN DIV) Air Assault (AASLT) (NET); Support to 3/10th MTN DIV at JRTC
- **4QFY15:** 2/82nd ABN DIV NET
- **4QFY15-1QFY16:** NW-UK test in Warminster, England; Army Warfighting Assessment 16.1; Support to 1/10th MTN (Operation Inherent Resolve), 2/10th MTN and 3/10th MTN (Operation Freedom's Sentinel)
- **1QFY16:** Support to 1/101st ABN DIV at JRTC

PROJECTED ACTIVITIES

- **2QFY16:** NW at Army Expeditionary Warrior Experiment 2016
- **3QFY17:** Full-Rate Production Decision

FOREIGN MILITARY SALES
None

CONTRACTORS
Government is the prime integrator with various
vendors providing components.

Next Generation Chemical Detector (NGCD)

JPEO for Chemical and Biological Defense | Aberdeen Proving Ground, MD

WARFIGHTING FUNCTION

Mission Command

Movement and Maneuver

Intelligence

Fires

Sustainment

Maneuver Support and Protection

Engagement

ACQUISITION LIFECYCLE PHASE

Materiel Solution Analysis

Technology Maturation & Risk Reduction

Engineering & Manufacturing Development

Production & Deployment

Operations & Support

MILESTONE DECISION AUTHORITY

Defense Acquisition Executive

Army Acquisition Executive

Program Executive Officer

DESCRIPTION

The Next Generation Chemical Detector (NGCD) will detect and identify nontraditional agents (NTA), chemical warfare agents (CWA), toxic industrial chemicals (TIC) and other hazards in the air and on surfaces. NGCD will improve CWA/TIC selectivity and sensitivity in multiple environments. NGCD will sample, detect, identify and quantify traditional and nontraditional chemical and TIC vapor, liquid, solid and aerosol hazards. The warfighter will be able to characterize chemical, biological, radiological and nuclear (CBRN) environment in air and water as well as on land, personnel, equipment and facilities. The NGCD will support manned and unmanned platform integration and the following combat weapons of mass destruction (WMD) military mission areas: CBRN passive defense; WMD interdiction; WMD elimination; and WMD consequence management.

NGCD will provide four capabilities or systems: NGCD-1, Detector Alarm; NGCD-2, Survey Detector; NGCD-3, Sample Analysis; and NGCD-4, Individual Detector.

BENEFIT TO THE WARFIGHTER

The NGCD capabilities and sensors will provide the warfighter with improved detection, consequence management and reconnaissance, and WMD interdiction.

SPECIFICATIONS

- NGCD-1: Man-portable, battery-operated, aerosol and vapor detection
- NGCD-2: Man-portable, battery-operated, surface detection
- NGCD-3: Two-man-portable, shore-and-battery-powered, very low detection levels
- NGCD-4: Wearable
- All detect NTA, CWA, TIC

PROGRAM STATUS

- **2QFY14:** Milestone A Approved, Prototyping and Testing

PROJECTED ACTIVITIES

- **FY16-FY17:** Final Prototype Testing
- **FY17:** Early Operational Assessment
- **3QFY17:** Milestone B

NGCD-1

Differential Mobility Spectroscopy (DMS)

Rapid Thermal Modulation Ion Spectrometry

Compact Ion Trap Mass Spec

NGCD-2

Short Wave IR (SWIR)
Hyperspectral Imagery (HSI)

Long Wave IR (LWIR) HSI
and Raman (785 nm)

LWIR HSI, and Raman (1064 nm),
Quantum Cascade Laser (QCL) IR

NGCD-3

Ion Trap Mass Spec

Triple Quad Mass Spec

GC-DMS and Raman (1064 nm)

NGCD-4

*Colorimetric
Nano-Electrochemical
Resistive Sensing
Metal Organic Framework*

Non-Intrusive Inspection Systems (NIIS)

JPEO for Chemical and Biological Defense | Aberdeen Proving Ground, MD

DESCRIPTION

The Non-Intrusive Inspection Systems (NIIS) program consists of commercial off-the-shelf products that utilize nuclear source and X-ray technologies to scan vehicles, cargo and personnel for detection of explosives and other contraband. These systems are employed within a layered force protection system that includes security personnel trained to maintain situational awareness, aided by a range of other products including military working dogs, under-vehicle scanning mirrors and hand-held or desktop trace explosive detectors.

NIIS includes a variety of products with differing characteristics that are added to the Army commander's tool box. They include mobile, rail-mounted but relocatable, and fixed-site characteristics.

BENEFIT TO THE WARFIGHTER

NIIS provides critical force protection measures to safeguard secure areas and protect Soldiers from hidden improvised explosive devices and other contraband not visible to the naked eye.

SPECIFICATIONS

- **Mobile Vehicle and Cargo Inspection System (MVACIS):** Truck-mounted system that uses a nuclear source that can penetrate approximately 6.5 inches of steel
- **Relocatable Vehicle and Cargo Inspection System:** Rail-mounted system that uses the same nuclear source as the MVACIS; operates on rails and is employed in static locations or moved within 24 hours to locations where prepared use of rail system eliminates requirement to maintain truck platform
- **Militarized MVACIS:** Uses same gamma source as other VACIS products, but it is mounted on a High Mobility Multipurpose Wheeled Vehicle
- **Militarized MVACIS (ZBV):** Van-mounted system that uses backscatter X-ray technology; penetrates approximately one-quarter inch of steel and can be employed in static locations where room is limited

- **Backscatter Vehicle Mounted Trailer (BVMT):** Mobile inspection system for vehicles and cargo that uses same backscatter X-ray technology as the ZBV; BVMT trailer contains the X-ray source and backscatter detectors while the forward scatter trailer contains forward scatter detectors
- **Personnel Scanners:** Use backscatter X-ray technology to nonintrusively scan people for the presence of explosives, weapons or other contraband and are American National Standards Institute compliant; depending on the model, these systems can scan between 140 and 240 people per hour
- **T-10 Trailer:** High-energy gantry vehicle and cargo scanner that uses a 1-Megavolt Liner Accelerator that penetrates up to 4 inches of steel while scanning

PROGRAM STATUS

- **1QFY13-4QFY13:** Replaced obsolete systems that reached their useful life and did not provide stand-off capabilities

PROJECTED ACTIVITIES

- **FY16-FY17:** Continue in sustainment

ZBV BACKSCATTER

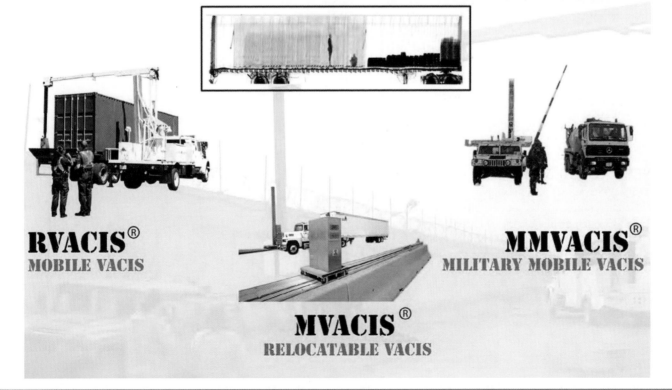

RVACIS®
MOBILE VACIS

MVACIS®
RELOCATABLE VACIS

MMVACIS®
MILITARY MOBILE VACIS

Nuclear Biological Chemical Reconnaissance Vehicle (NBCRV) – Stryker Sensor Suites

JPEO for Chemical and Biological Defense | Aberdeen Proving Ground, MD

WARFIGHTING FUNCTION

Mission Command

Movement and Maneuver

Intelligence

Fires

Sustainment

Maneuver Support and Protection

Engagement

ACQUISITION LIFECYCLE PHASE

Materiel Solution Analysis

Technology Maturation & Risk Reduction

Engineering & Manufacturing Development

Production & Deployment

Operations & Support

MILESTONE DECISION AUTHORITY

Defense Acquisition Executive

Army Acquisition Executive

Program Executive Officer

DESCRIPTION

The Nuclear Biological Chemical Reconnaissance Vehicle (NBCRV) – Stryker Sensor Suites is the chemical, biological, radiological and nuclear (CBRN) reconnaissance configuration of the Infantry Carrier Vehicle in the Stryker Brigade Combat Teams (SBCT), Heavy Brigade Combat Teams (HBCT) and Chemical Companies (CC).

The NBCRV-Stryker Sensor Suite consists of a dedicated system of CBRN detection, warning and biological-sampling equipment on a Stryker vehicle (high-speed, high-mobility, armored carrier). The NBCRV detects chemical, radiological and biological contamination in its immediate environment through the Chemical Biological Mass Spectrometer, Automatic Chemical Agent Detector Alarm, AN/VDR-2 Radiac Detector, AN/UDR-13 Radiac Detector and Joint Biological Point Detection System, and, at a distance, through the use of the Joint Service Lightweight Standoff Chemical Agent Detector. It automatically integrates contamination information from detectors with input from onboard navigation and meteorological systems, and transmits digital nuclear, biological and chemical (NBC) warning messages through the vehicle's command and control equipment to warn follow-on forces. The NBCRV can also collect samples for analysis.

BENEFIT TO THE WARFIGHTER

The NBCRV-Stryker Sensor Suite supports the warfighter by performing NBC reconnaissance. It also locates, identifies, marks, samples and reports NBC contamination on the battlefield.

SPECIFICATIONS

- Stryker variant with multiple unique sensors.

PROGRAM STATUS

- **FY13-FY15:** Full-Rate Production; fielding to SBCT, select Active Component HBCT and CC

PROJECTED ACTIVITIES

- **FY16-FY17:** Fielding to select Active Component and Reserve Component HBCT and CC
- **1QFY18:** Full Operational Capability and Initiate Sensor Suite Enhancement Program

JOINT PROJECT MANAGER, NBC CONTAMINATION AVOIDANCE

Stryker Nuclear, Biological, Chemical Reconnaissance Vehicle

Laptops

Joint Biological Point Detection System

Joint Service Lightweight Standoff Chemical Agent Detector

Force XXI Battle Command, Brigade-and-Below CECOM-Managed

Laser Printer

AN/UDR-13 RADIAC

AN/VDR-2 RADIAC

Automatic Chemical Agent Alarm

Inertial Reference Unit GDLS-Managed

METSMAN Meterological Sensor

Chemical Vapor Sampling System

Chemical Biological Mass Spectrometer

Double Wheel Sampling System GDLS-Managed

NBCRV-Stryker Sensor Suites

FOREIGN MILITARY SALES
None

CONTRACTORS
Prime Vehicle: General Dynamics Land Systems
(Sterling Heights, MI)
Sensor Software Integrator: CACI Technologies
(Lorton, VA)

One Semi-Automated Force (OneSAF)

PEO Simulation, Training, and Instrumentation | Orlando, FL

WARFIGHTING FUNCTION

Mission Command

Movement and Maneuver

Intelligence

Fires

Sustainment

Maneuver Support and Protection

Engagement

ACQUISITION LIFECYCLE PHASE

Materiel Solution Analysis

Technology Maturation & Risk Reduction

Engineering & Manufacturing Development

Production & Deployment

Operations & Support

MILESTONE DECISION AUTHORITY

Defense Acquisition Executive

Army Acquisition Executive

Program Executive Officer

DESCRIPTION

One Semi-Automated Force (OneSAF) is a computer generated forces simulation that provides entity-level models and behaviors that are both semi-automated and fully automated applications designed to achieve Army readiness. As a cross-domain simulation, OneSAF supports the training, test and evaluation, analysis, intelligence, acquisition and experimentation communities by providing the latest physics-based modeling and data, enhanced data collection, and reporting capabilities. OneSAF models real-world representations of platforms, Soldiers, equipment, logistical supplies, communications systems and networks, emerging threats, and aviation assets to achieve the level of fidelity required for a particular application or scenario.

OneSAF was created to be uniquely capable of simulating aspects of the urban operating environment and its effects on simulated activities and behaviors. OneSAF is unique in its ability to model unit behaviors from fire team to company level for all units in both combat and noncombat operations. Intelligent, doctrinally correct behaviors and a range of constructive, gaming and virtually based user interfaces are provided to increase the span of control for workstation operators.

BENEFIT TO THE WARFIGHTER

OneSAF provides a transparent training environment for today's commanders and their battle staffs by utilizing current Mission Command Systems, and eliminates the need for multiple simulation tools across analysis, experimentation, test and evaluation, training, intelligence and acquisition.

SPECIFICATIONS

- Software-only program
- Uses controlled unclassified information
- Computer generated forces simulation
- Standards-based architecture

PROGRAM STATUS

- **FY15:**
  › New releases: Version 8.0 and 8.5 released
  › Training and events: Network Integration Evaluation (NIE) 15.1 and 15.2 support (Fort Bliss, TX); NIE 16.1 (Fort Bliss)

PROJECTED ACTIVITIES

- **FY16:**
  › Version 8.6 release
  › NIE 16.1 support (Fort Bliss)

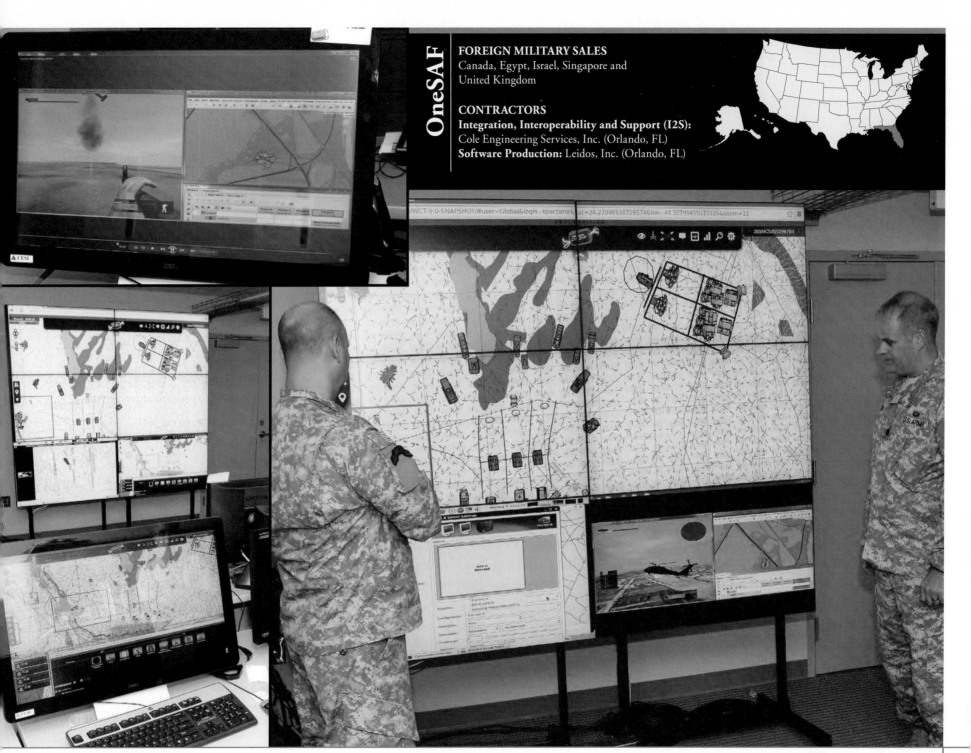

OneSAF

FOREIGN MILITARY SALES
Canada, Egypt, Israel, Singapore and
United Kingdom

CONTRACTORS
Integration, Interoperability and Support (I2S):
Cole Engineering Services, Inc. (Orlando, FL)
Software Production: Leidos, Inc. (Orlando, FL)

Precision Guidance Kit (PGK)

PEO Ammunition | Picatinny Arsenal, NJ

WARFIGHTING FUNCTION

Mission Command

Movement and Maneuver

Intelligence

Fires

Sustainment

Maneuver Support and Protection

Engagement

ACQUISITION LIFECYCLE PHASE

Materiel Solution Analysis

Technology Maturation & Risk Reduction

Engineering & Manufacturing Development

Production & Deployment

Operations & Support

MILESTONE DECISION AUTHORITY

Defense Acquisition Executive

Army Acquisition Executive

Program Executive Officer

DESCRIPTION

Precision Guidance Kit (PGK) technology is state-of-the-art and provides a first-of-its-kind capability. PGK contains a Global Positioning System (GPS) guidance kit with fusing functions and an integrated GPS receiver to correct the inherent errors associated with ballistic firing solutions, reducing the number of artillery projectiles required to attack targets. The increase in efficiency that PGK's "near-precision" capability provides allows operational commanders to engage assigned targets and rapidly achieve desired effects while minimizing collateral damage. The PGK currently has two DoD Identification Codes (DoDIC), NA28 and NA29. The 2,399 kits that were procured for early fielding under an Urgent Material Release to Operation Enduring Freedom have the NA28 DoDIC. The PGK currently being procured in Low-Rate Initial Production (LRIP) has the NA29 DoDIC. PGK is also developing an increased capability to operate in a GPS-degraded environment and to be compatible with the future M-Code GPS architecture.

BENEFIT TO THE WARFIGHTER

PGK provides improved fire support to the maneuver force commander through effectively reducing target delivery error of conventional artillery munitions, and reduces the number of projectiles required to execute a fire mission.

SPECIFICATIONS

- Demonstrated accuracy: Less than 30 meters circular error probable
- Compatible with the M795 and M549A1 155 mm high-explosive (HE) projectiles
- Mission-critical flight data is inductively loaded into PGK using the Enhanced Portable Inductive Artillery Fuse Setter

PROGRAM STATUS

- **2QFY13:** Milestone C, entering LRIP
- **1QFY15:** Successfully completed First Article Acceptance Testing
- **3QFY15:** Successfully completed Initial Operational Test & Evaluation
- **1QFY16:**
  › Successfully completed the first five lot acceptance tests
  › Achieved Type Classification – Standard
  › Full Materiel Release

PROJECTED ACTIVITIES

- **2QFY16:** Full-Rate Production Decision

FOREIGN MILITARY SALES
Fielded with multiple countries—names for official use only and not for public disclosure

CONTRACTORS
Orbital ATK (Plymouth, MN)

PGK
Precision Guidance Kit

Paladin 155mm
Self-Propelled Howitzer   Light Weight 155mm
Towed Howitzer

M549A1

M795

Prophet

PEO Intelligence, Electronic Warfare and Sensors | Aberdeen Proving Ground, MD

WARFIGHTING FUNCTION

Mission Command

Movement and Maneuver

Intelligence

Fires

Sustainment

Maneuver Support and Protection

Engagement

ACQUISITION LIFECYCLE PHASE

Materiel Solution Analysis

Technology Maturation & Risk Reduction

Engineering & Manufacturing Development

Production & Deployment

Operations & Support

MILESTONE DECISION AUTHORITY

Defense Acquisition Executive

Army Acquisition Executive

Program Executive Officer

DESCRIPTION

The latest version of Prophet, called Prophet Enhanced, is a dedicated all-weather, 24-hour, near-real-time, ground-based tactical signals intelligence and electronic warfare system that provides force protection and situational awareness through technologically advanced intelligence support to U.S. Army Brigade Combat Team (BCT) and Expeditionary – Military Intelligence Brigade (E-MIB) commanders. Prophet is fielded with three sensors to BCT and Multifunctional Teams and eight sensors to E-MIB. Prophet Enhanced systems provide commanders flexible, modular components for their mission.

Prophet Enhanced is a non-platform-dependent, modular system that will allow easy integration onto a vehicle. Each sensor supports stationary, dismounted, on-the-move (mobile) and man-pack operations. Prophet's mobility and modularity allows supported units to easily reposition its collection capability based on evolving tactical situations.

Prophet Enhanced has a common wide-band beyond-line-of-site capability, which is based on the Project Manager Warfighter Information Network – Tactical. This capability allows the vehicles to operate at extended distances from each other or from other nodes on the battlefield. Prophet Enhanced also has a common server, processing architecture, encryption devices, etc., that currently support operations on three classification networks and domains.

Prophet Enhanced is interoperable on the Global Signals Intelligence Enterprise, delivering collected data to common databases for access by the intelligence community.

BENEFIT TO THE WARFIGHTER

Prophet Enhanced provides the warfighter with critical situational awareness on the availability and synergy of objective intelligence data access and processing. It also provides high-value individual targeting through precision geolocation. Prophet Enhanced mobility and multimode employment (dismounted, mounted on-the-move and man-pack) enables commander flexibility in a dynamic threat environment.

SPECIFICATIONS

- Classified

PROGRAM STATUS

- **1QFY13-4QFY14:** Continue production and fielding of Prophet Enhanced Systems
- **2QFY15:** Acquisition Decision Memorandum to initiate Prophet Enhanced Quick Reaction Capability modernization

PROJECTED ACTIVITIES

- **1QFY16-4QFY16:** Complete modernization of the Prophet Enhanced quick reaction capability
- **2QFY16-4QFY17:** Continue modernization

FOREIGN MILITARY SALES
None

CONTRACTORS
General Dynamics Mission Systems (GD-MS)
(Scottsdale, AZ)

Radiological Detection System (RDS)

JPEO for Chemical and Biological Defense | Aberdeen Proving Ground, MD

WARFIGHTING FUNCTION

Mission Command

Movement and Maneuver

Intelligence

Fires

Sustainment

Maneuver Support and Protection

Engagement

ACQUISITION LIFECYCLE PHASE

Materiel Solution Analysis

Technology Maturation & Risk Reduction

Engineering & Manufacturing Development

Production & Deployment

Operations & Support

MILESTONE DECISION AUTHORITY

Defense Acquisition Executive

Army Acquisition Executive

Program Executive Officer

DESCRIPTION

The Radiological Detection System (RDS) is intended to replace DoD's legacy Radiation Detection, Indication and Computation (RADIAC) survey meters (PDR-77, MFR Suite and ADM-300).

The RDS will provide warfighters with the capability to measure alpha, beta, gamma, neutron and low-energy X-rays. It is the first Joint Rad/Nuc detector solution to increase capability and reduce lifecycle costs, as well as address Operation TOMODACHI Lessons Learned for common, interoperable equipment with adequate sensitivity and common units of measure.

Additional capabilities beyond that of legacy RADIAC include Net-Readiness, incorporation of Global Positioning System data, and use of both conventional and international system measurement units.

BENEFIT TO THE WARFIGHTER

The RDS will provide warfighters with the capability to measure alpha, beta, gamma, neutron and low-energy X-rays.

SPECIFICATIONS

- Requirements Basis: Capability Development Document, Jan. 2015
- Performance Specification: Amendment 2, dated April 27, 2015
- Contract Type: Cost Plus Fixed Fee (development)/Fixed Price Incentive (Successive Targets) (production)

PROGRAM STATUS

- **Current:** Pre-Milestone (MS) C (projected 4QFY19); in Source Selection

PROJECTED ACTIVITIES

- **4QFY16:** Contract Award
- **4QFY17:** Critical Design Review
- **1QFY18:** Test Article Delivery
- **4QFY19:** MS C

FOREIGN MILITARY SALES
None

CONTRACTORS
TBD

Rocket, Artillery, Mortar (RAM) Warn

PEO Missiles and Space | Redstone Arsenal, AL

WARFIGHTING FUNCTION

Mission Command

Movement and Maneuver

Intelligence

Fires

Sustainment

Maneuver Support and Protection

Engagement

ACQUISITION LIFECYCLE PHASE

Materiel Solution Analysis

Technology Maturation & Risk Reduction

Engineering & Manufacturing Development

Production & Deployment

Operations & Support

MILESTONE DECISION AUTHORITY

Defense Acquisition Executive

Army Acquisition Executive

Program Executive Officer

DESCRIPTION

Rocket, Artillery, Mortar (RAM) Warn provides early, localized warning of indirect fire (IDF) threats to all Maneuver Brigade Combat Teams (BCT). The RAM Warn program evolved from the operational success of the Counter-Rocket, Artillery, Mortar (C-RAM) Program and is a horizontal technology insertion using current C-RAM warning capability. Integration of RAM Warn equipment provides a warn capability to BCT for detection of threat RAM rounds and transmission of the detection data to the command and control (C2) element for correlation and determination of a predicted point of impact (POI). Based on the POI, the C2 then determines which warning nodes should send "incoming" warning alarms and transmits this information to the appropriate warning nodes.

BENEFIT TO THE WARFIGHTER

Timely warning enables those BCT personnel in the hazard area of an inbound IDF threat to seek cover or a prone position prior to impact, thus reducing casualties for the warfighter.

SPECIFICATIONS

- Employs the Air Defense Airspace Management (ADAM) Cell already resident in the BCT Headquarters as the C2 element
- Networks existing radars in the Target Acquisition Platoon of the Fires Battalion as the sense element
- Adds enhanced C2 warning devices, controllers and dedicated communications between the existing radars, the ADAM Cell and warning systems

PROGRAM STATUS

- **1QFY13:** Milestone C, Low-Rate Initial Production approval
- **2QFY14:**
  › Full Materiel Release
  › Initial Operational Capability
- **3QFY14:** Full-Rate Production Decision Review

PROJECTED ACTIVITIES

- **FY16-FY18:** RAM Warn production and fielding continues

RAM Warn

FOREIGN MILITARY SALES
None

CONTRACTORS
Northrop Grumman (Huntsville, AL)

Route Clearance Interrogation System (RCIS) Type I

PEO Combat Support and Combat Service Support | Detroit Arsenal, MI

WARFIGHTING FUNCTION

Mission Command

Movement and Maneuver

Intelligence

Fires

Sustainment

Maneuver Support and Protection

Engagement

ACQUISITION LIFECYCLE PHASE

Materiel Solution Analysis

Technology Maturation & Risk Reduction

Engineering & Manufacturing Development

Production & Deployment

Operations & Support

MILESTONE DECISION AUTHORITY

Defense Acquisition Executive

Army Acquisition Executive

Program Executive Officer

DESCRIPTION

Route Clearance Interrogation System (RCIS) Type I detects, interrogates and neutralizes the full spectrum of Explosive Hazards (EH) while on the move and takes the Soldier out of the EH Kill Zone during Route Clearance Operations.

The RCIS Type I will allow for the semi-autonomous control of a Mobile Base Unit equipped High-Mobility Engineer Excavator (HMEE) and its capabilities from an Operator Control Unit (OCU) inside a Mine Protected Clearance Vehicle (MPCV). This capability will enable Soldiers to interrogate, classify and excavate deep-buried explosive hazards, improvised explosive devices and caches in a wide range of road surfaces and soil conditions. This capability is designed to remove Soldiers, other route clearance vehicles and equipment from the blast effects of EH.

BENEFIT TO THE WARFIGHTER

RCIS Type I removes Soldiers from the blast effects of EH.

SPECIFICATIONS

- Modified HMEE base platform will:
  › Provide by-wire control of the vehicle's automotive and interrogation functions
  › Add boom arm attachments (air spade, rake and spork, and clamshell bucket) to expand RCIS Type I interrogation capabilities
  › Integration of a Semi-Autonomous Control System, consisting of wireless communications equipment, cables, brackets, cameras and other equipment as necessary, will allow vehicle control from an MPCV in a stand-off position
- MPCV platform will be enhanced to include wireless communications equipment, OCU controls, video display, head-aimed control viewer, cables, bracketry and other equipment as necessary to control the HMEE from a stand-off position

PROGRAM STATUS

- **Current:** Pre-Milestone B – on schedule to enter the Engineering & Manufacturing Development (EMD) phase in FY17

PROJECTED ACTIVITIES

- **2QFY17:** Milestone B
- **FY17-FY19:** EMD
- **2QFY19:** Low-Rate Initial Production
- **2QFY21:** Full-Rate Production and fielding of 266 RCIS Type I

FOREIGN MILITARY SALES
None

CONTRACTORS
TBD

RQ-11B Raven Small Unmanned Aircraft System (SUAS)

PEO Aviation | Redstone Arsenal, AL

WARFIGHTING FUNCTION

Mission Command

Movement and Maneuver

Intelligence

Fires

Sustainment

Maneuver Support and Protection

Engagement

ACQUISITION LIFECYCLE PHASE

Materiel Solution Analysis

Technology Maturation & Risk Reduction

Engineering & Manufacturing Development

Production & Deployment

Operations & Support

MILESTONE DECISION AUTHORITY

Defense Acquisition Executive

Army Acquisition Executive

Program Executive Officer

DESCRIPTION

The RQ-11B Raven is a Small Unmanned Aircraft System (SUAS). The SUAS provides reconnaissance, surveillance, target acquisition and force protection for the battalion commander and below during day and night operations. The Raven and its larger SUAS counterpart, the RQ-20 Puma, make up a formidable SUAS team. The SUAS is comprised of three air vehicles, a ground control station (GCS), a remote video terminal (identical to GCS), electro-optical (EO) and infrared (IR) payloads, aircraft and GCS batteries, a field repair kit and a spares package. Normal operational altitude is 500 feet or lower. The system, aircraft and ground control station are assembled by operators in approximately five minutes. Both color EO sensors and infrared IR sensors are fielded for day and night capabilities with each system. A hand controller displays live video and aircraft status.

Mission planning is performed on the hand controller or ruggedized laptop running Portable Flight Planning Software/Falcon View Flight Planning Software. Aircraft flight modes include fully autonomous navigation, altitude hold, loiter and return home. In-flight retasking and auto-loiter at sensor payload point of interest are also available. Raven incorporates secure Global Positioning System navigation. The digital data link incorporates encryption, improves spectrum management allowing more air vehicles to be flown in an operational area, and provides range extension via data relay between two SUAS aircraft.

The SUAS is operated by two Soldiers and has a rucksack-portable design. No specific military occupational specialty is required. Operator training requires 10 days.

BENEFIT TO THE WARFIGHTER

The SUAS provides the battalion-and-below ground-maneuver elements with an organic, on-demand asset to develop situational awareness, enhance force protection and secure routes, points and areas. The system provides the small unit commander a responsive tactical Reconnaissance, Surveillance and Target Acquisition capability through real-time, full-motion video and sensor data via the hand controller.

SPECIFICATIONS

Raven:
- Wingspan: 4.5 feet
- Weight: 4.2 pounds
- Range: 10 km
- Endurance: 90 minutes at 300 feet above ground level (AGL) or higher

Puma:
- Wingspan: 9.2 feet
- Weight: 12.9 pounds
- Range: 10 km
- Endurance: 120 minutes at 500 feet AGL or higher

PROGRAM STATUS

- **Current:** In Production and Deployment

PROJECTED ACTIVITIES

- **FY16-FY17:** Complete fielding of the gimbaled payload upgrade and Tactical Open Government Architecture controller

FOREIGN MILITARY SALES
Denmark, Estonia, Lebanon and Uganda

CONTRACTORS
Aerovironment, Inc. (Simi Valley, CA)

Secure Mobile Anti-Jam Reliable Tactical Terminal (SMART-T)

PEO Command, Control and Communications – Tactical | Aberdeen Proving Ground, MD

WARFIGHTING FUNCTION

Mission Command

Movement and Maneuver

Intelligence

Fires

Sustainment

Maneuver Support and Protection

Engagement

ACQUISITION LIFECYCLE PHASE

Materiel Solution Analysis

Technology Maturation & Risk Reduction

Engineering & Manufacturing Development

Production & Deployment

Operations & Support

MILESTONE DECISION AUTHORITY

Defense Acquisition Executive

Army Acquisition Executive

Program Executive Officer

DESCRIPTION

Secure Mobile Anti-Jam Reliable Tactical Terminal (SMART-T) is the Army's protected satellite communications (SATCOM) system that enables commanders at brigade-and-higher levels to operate in an electronic warfare threat environment that includes radio frequency signal interference (jamming), signal detection and geographic location of threats. Additionally, SMART-T can survive the effects of a high-altitude electromagnetic pulse (EMP) produced by nuclear detonations, and can operate and survive in a biological and chemical environment.

BENEFIT TO THE WARFIGHTER

SMART-T provides the warfighter with worldwide protected SATCOM capability immediately following an EMP event where other systems may experience a high degree of degradation or complete failure. Additionally, it provides range extension to the Army's tactical communications networks.

SPECIFICATIONS

- Interoperable with advanced extremely high-frequency (AEHF) satellite constellation
- Enhanced system interfaces
- Low and Medium Data Rate (LDR/MDR) capability for voice and data transmission
- Interoperable with Milstar, Ultra High-Frequency Follow-On, Extremely High-Frequency (EHF) Military-Standard (MIL-STD) 1582D and MIL-STD 188-136 compatible payloads
- Anti-jam and anti-scintillation (nuclear environment) communications
- Palletized Platform
- High Mobility Multipurpose Wheeled Vehicle-mounted
- EHF data rates
  › MDR up to 1.544 megabits per second (Mbps) (T1)
  › LDR 75-2400 bits per second
- AEHF data rates up to 8.192 Mbps

PROGRAM STATUS

- **FY13-FY15:** Conducted new equipment training at the fielding and training facility in Largo, FL
- **2QFY13:** SMART-T participated in Air Force AEHF multiservice operational test and evaluation
- **4QFY15:** Completed upgrades of SMART-T terminals to AEHF-capable

PROJECTED ACTIVITIES

- **Through FY18:** Perform sustainment planning activities and task execution in preparation of transitioning SMART-T to sustainment in FY18

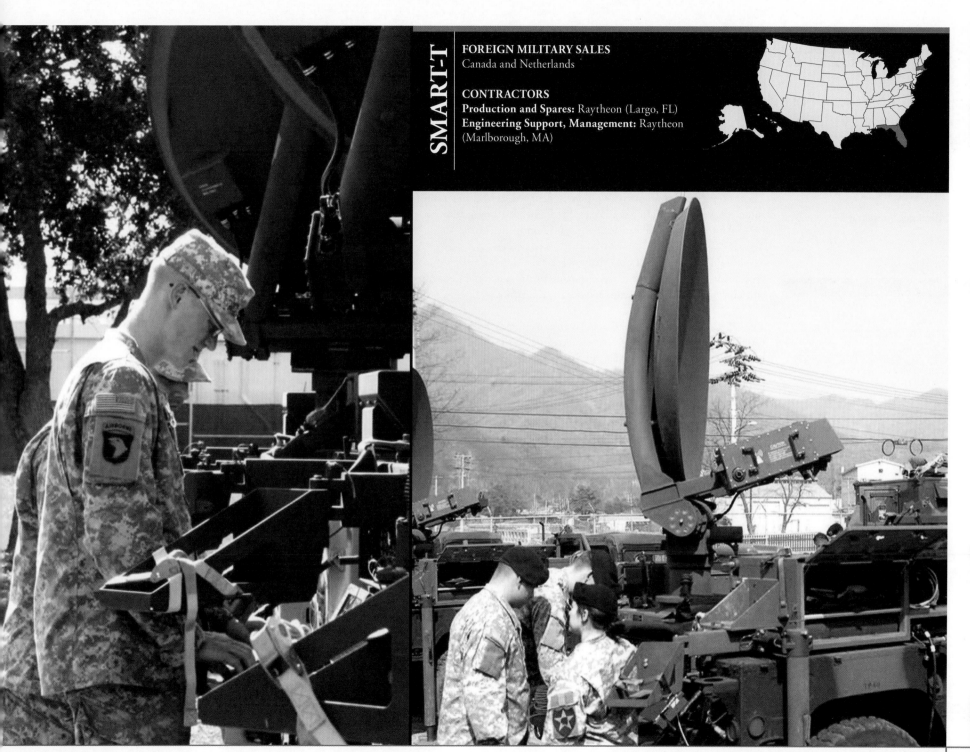

FOREIGN MILITARY SALES
Canada and Netherlands

CONTRACTORS
Production and Spares: Raytheon (Largo, FL)
Engineering Support, Management: Raytheon
(Marlborough, MA)

Small Arms – Crew Served Weapons

PEO Soldier | Fort Belvoir, VA

DESCRIPTION

The M249 Squad Automatic Weapon is designed as the fire team automatic weapon providing suppressive fire at extended ranges, allowing fire and movement to make contact with and destroy the enemy.

The M240B and 240L 7.62 mm Medium Machine Guns are designed to provide the platoon with accurate, continuous fires to suppress the enemy and allow maneuver to close with and destroy the enemy.

The M2A1 with Quick Change Barrel is an enhancement to the M2 .50 Caliber Machine Gun offering Soldiers increased performance as well as new features and design improvements that make it easier and safer to use. The M2A1 provides a fixed headspace and timing configuration, flash hider and removable carrying handle, which increase the performance of the battle-proven M2. It mounts on the M3 tripod and on most vehicles while also serving as an anti-personnel and anti-aircraft weapon. It is capable of single-shot and automatic fire, can defeat lightly armored vehicles and provides indirect fires from defilade position.

The MK19 Grenade Machine Gun supports the Soldier by delivering heavy, accurate and continuous firepower against enemy personnel and lightly armored vehicles. The MK19 can be mounted on a tripod or on multiple vehicle platforms and is the primary suppression weapon for combat support and combat service support units.

BENEFIT TO THE WARFIGHTER

The M249 allows the warfighter improved weapon control, egress and maneuver in close-quarter combat due to a collapsible buttstock and a new, short barrel. An improved bipod provides Soldiers with increased reliability and weapon accuracy. The M240L is a lightweight variant of the M240B Machine Gun and reduces the Soldier's combat load while allowing easier handling and movement. The M2A1 speeds target engagement and improves survivability and safety by reducing the time required to change the barrel and eliminating the timely procedure of setting headspace and timing. The MK19 supports the warfighter in both the offense and defense by providing the unit the capability of laying down a heavy volume of close, accurate and continuous 40 mm grenade fire.

PROGRAM STATUS

M249:
- **Current:** In sustainment, Army Acquisition Objective (AAO) met

M240B:
- **Current:** Product qualification and verification activities ongoing for the Colt M240B Weapons

M240L:
- **Current:** Through FY15, issued 8,721 240L

M2/M2A1:
- **As of 1QFY16:** Issued 23,354 M2A1, recovered 19,362 M2 for conversion

MK19:
- **Current:**
  › In Sustainment, AAO met
  › Supporting foreign military sales requirements

PROJECTED ACTIVITIES

M249:
- Modification kit under development to enhance performance, reliability and durability

M240B/M240L:
- Continue fielding to National Guard and Reserve units
- Conducting engineering study to improve barrel design to increase performance

M2/M2A1:
- **4QFY16:** Anticipated award for procurement of requirements of M2/M2A1 for all services and foreign military sales

MK19:
- Introducing a MOD kit which improves reliability, rate of fire, range and accuracy
- Will introduce improved optics and fire control system

M249

M2A1

FOREIGN MILITARY SALES

M249: Afghanistan, Iraq and Pakistan
M240B: Iraq, Afghanistan, Jordan, Morocco, Brazil, Kenya, Tunisia, Philippines, Barbados, Belize, Yemen and Columbia
M240L: Contracts through FN Herstal and Belgium
M2: Afghanistan, Iraq, Jordan, Pakistan, Uganda and Kenya
MK19: Iraq, Pakistan, Lebanon, Tunisia, Afghanistan, Saudi Arabia and Mexico

CONTRACTORS

M249: Fabrique National Manufacturing, LLC (Columbia, SC)
M240B: Fabrique National Manufacturing, LLC (Columbia, SC)
Colt Defense, LLC (West Hartford, CT)
M240L: Fabrique National Manufacturing, LLC (Columbia, SC)
M2 and M2A1: General Dynamics Ordnance and Tactical Systems (Williston, VT; Saco, ME)
Capco (Grand Junction, CO)
MK19: General Dynamics Armament and Technical Products (Saco, ME);
Alliant Techsystems (Mesa, AZ)

SPECIFICATIONS

	M249	M240	M2/M2A1	MK19
Length	30.75 inches -36.25 inches	44.5 inches	67.75 inches	43.1 inches
Weight	17.95 pounds	27.3 pounds (B), 21.8 pounds (L), 5.5 pounds (barrel)	86 pounds (barrel 26 pounds)	77.6 pounds
Caliber	5.56, maximum effective range 800 meters (area), 600 meters (point)	7.62, maximum effective range 800 meters (bipod), 1,800 meters (tripod)	12.7 mm (NATO), maximum effective range 1,829 meters; maximum range 6,764 meters	40 mm, maximum effective range 2,212 meters (area), 1,500 meters (point)
Rate of fire (rounds/minute)	700-850	550-650	450-600	325-375

Small Arms – Individual Weapons

PEO Soldier | Fort Belvoir, VA

WARFIGHTING FUNCTION

Mission Command

Movement and Maneuver

Intelligence

Fires

Sustainment

Maneuver Support and Protection

Engagement

ACQUISITION LIFECYCLE PHASE

Materiel Solution Analysis

Technology Maturation & Risk Reduction

Engineering & Manufacturing Development

Production & Deployment

Operations & Support

MILESTONE DECISION AUTHORITY

Defense Acquisition Executive

Army Acquisition Executive

Program Executive Officer

DESCRIPTION

The M4/M4A1 5.56 mm Carbine is designed for lightness, speed, mobility and firepower. The weapon incorporates more than 90 improvements since its inception. In post-combat surveys, 94 percent of Soldiers rate the M4 as an effective weapon system.

HQDA G-3/5/7 authorized the M4A1 as the standard carbine for the Army in 2010. In 2014, the Army decided to update its service rifle inventory from a mix of M16A2/A4 Rifles and M4 Carbines to an inventory of 5.56 mm M4A1 Carbines.

The M320 Grenade Launcher Module (GLM) is the replacement to all M203 series of grenade launchers on M16 Rifles and M4 Carbines. A modular system, it attaches under the barrel of the rifle or carbine, and can also convert to a stand-alone weapon. The M320 GLM has an integrated leaf sight and improved safety features. It also has a side-loading unrestricted breech to allow the system to fire longer 40 mm low-velocity projectiles (NATO standard and nonstandard).

The lightweight M26 12-Gauge Modular Accessory Shotgun System (MASS) attaches to the M4 Carbine and zeroes to the host weapon. It is also designed to operate as a stand-alone system, and comes with a recoil-absorbing, collapsible buttstock. The Picatinny rail mounted on top allows accessory equipment to be mounted on the shotgun.

The XM17 Modular Handgun System will replace the Army's M9 and M11 pistols. The Army is taking a noncaliber-specific approach in seeking the best-value solution through full and open competition among mature nondevelopmental designs in the procurement of a new handgun.

BENEFIT TO THE WARFIGHTER

The M4/M4A1 Carbine enables a Soldier operating in close quarters to engage targets at extended range with accurate, lethal fire. The M320 enables the Soldier to engage the enemy accurately in daylight or total darkness with a safer, more reliable grenade launcher. It reduces aiming error and increases first-round hit probability. The M26 MASS enables Soldiers to transition between lethal and less-than-lethal fires and adds the capability of a separate shotgun without carrying a second weapon. The XM17, the Army's next handgun, will be more capable than the M9 pistol in the areas of lethality, terminal effects, ergonomics, reliability, durability and maintainability.

PROGRAM STATUS

M4/M4A1:
- **2QFY14:** Army Decision to "Pure Fleet" the M4A1
- **2QFY15:** FN Manufacturing LLC deliveries commence for the Army
- **4QFY15:** Contract Awards to FN Manufacturing LLC and Colt Defense (292,000 systems)

M320:
- **3QFY14-3QFY15:** Heckler and Koch Defense Inc. production and deliveries (12,400 systems)

M26:
- **3QFY15:** Final M26 delivered

XM17:
- **4QFY15:** Solicitation released

PROJECTED ACTIVITIES

M4/M4A1:
- **FY16-FY17:** M4-to-M4A1 field conversions continue
- **2QFY17:** FN Manufacturing LLC and Colt Defense deliveries commence

M320:
- **3QFY16:** Grenadier Sighting System contract award

M26:
- **1QFY17:** New Leaf Sight incorporated to fire nonlethal extended-range rounds

XM17:
- **2QFY16:** Solicitation closes and bid sample testing commences
- **3Q-4QFY16:** Soldier participation (ergonomics and warfighter acceptance)

M4A1

M320

M26

FOREIGN MILITARY SALES
M4/M4A1: Iraq, Afghanistan, Slovakia, Grenada and Romania

CONTRACTORS
M4 Carbine: Colt Defense LLC. (West Hartford, CT)
M320 Grenade Launcher Module: Heckler and Koch Defense Inc. (Ashburn, VA)
M26 Modular Accessory Shotgun System: Vertu Corp. (Warrenton, VA)

SPECIFICATIONS

	M4/M4A1 5.56 mm Carbine	M320	M26	XM17 (Army Requirements)
Length	30.57 inches (retracted); 33.82 inches (extended)	11.2 inches (stand-alone)	16.5 inches (stand-alone); 25 inches (stand-alone)	Less than 8.7 inches; 7.5 inches for the compact
Weight	7.46 pounds (M4); 7.74 pounds (M4A1)	6.48 pounds (stand-alone, empty); 3.42 pounds (mounted, empty)	5.5 pounds (stand-alone, empty); 3.5 pounds (mounted, empty)	Less than 36 ounces; 34.5 ounces for the compact
Caliber	5.56 mm	40 mm	12-gauge	To be decided
Range	500 meters point target	550-650	25 meters	0-50 meters

Small Arms – Precision Weapons

PEO Soldier | Fort Belvoir, VA

DESCRIPTION

The M107 Semi-Automatic Long-Range Sniper Rifle fires .50 Caliber ammunition and is capable of delivering precise, rapid fire on targets out to 2,000 meters, greatly exceeding the terminal effect capability of other sniper rifles in use by U.S. forces. Its primary mission is to engage and defeat materiel targets at extended ranges.

The M2010 Enhanced Sniper Rifle is a bolt-action, magazine-fed weapon system that utilizes .300 WinMag ammunition. The rifle is built around a rechambered M24 Sniper Weapon System receiver. The M2010 is equipped with a fully adjustable, right-folding chassis system featuring accessory cable routing channels and Military-Standard 1913 Picatinny rails that mount a Leupold 6-20 x 50 mm variable power Day Optic Scope with advanced scalable H-58 ranging and targeting reticle. The M2010 is also equipped with a sound suppressor and adjustable bipod. The shooter interface can be tailored to accommodate a wide range of shooter preferences and its folding stock provides Soldiers flexibility in transporting the weapon during operations.

The M110 7.62 mm Semi-Automatic Sniper System (SASS) is an anti-personnel and light materiel weapon that fires 7.62 mm ammunition out to a maximum effective range of 800 meters. The M110's Leupold Mark IV 3.5–10x scope provides both a wide field of view at low magnification for close-in engagements and a narrow field of view for precision long shots at high magnification. The SASS leverages a rapid fire and rapid reload design, variable-power day optic sight, and 10- or 20-round detachable magazines.

BENEFIT TO THE WARFIGHTER

The M107 completes missions that cannot be accomplished with current sniper rifles. The ability to engage both personnel and light skinned vehicles at range provides Soldiers a tremendous tactical advantage. It is especially valuable during military operations in urban terrain where greater firepower and standoff ranges provide counter-sniper capability while enhancing sniper survivability. The M2010 exceeds the rate of

fire and lethality of the M24, the previous medium-caliber sniper rifle with a 50 percent increase in range. It bridges the capability gap between the M110 and the M107, allowing precision engagements in daylight and limited visibility, using a clip-on sniper night sight, out to 1,200 meters. The M110 SASS provides the capability for rapid and focused engagements on several targets with multiple follow-on shots. It is the first Army weapon system that integrates a quick attach and detach suppressor to reduce the weapon's firing signature. The M110 provides the warfighter with increased lethality, situational awareness from an enhanced scope, and survivability from the flash and sound suppressor.

PROGRAM STATUS

M107:

- **Current:** Fielded to Explosive Ordnance Disposal teams; 2,681 total systems in the field

M2010:

- **4QFY13:** Full Material Release
- **Current:** Completed fielding; 2,083 total systems in the field

M110:

- **Current:** Completed fielding; 2,621 total systems in the field

PROJECTED ACTIVITIES

M107:

- System in sustainment
- Residual maintenance work order/upgrade remaining

M2010:

- System in sustainment
- **2QFY16:** Contract award for Compact Semi-Automatic Sniper System (CSASS)
- **4QFY17:** Begin fielding CSASS

M110:

- System in sustainment

M107

M2010

M110

FOREIGN MILITARY SALES

M107: Thailand, Columbia, Kenya, Yemen, Hungary, Slovakia, Romania, Peru, Philippines and Chad

M110: Hungary, Senegal, Romania, Slovakia, Chad, Cameroon, Kenya, Latvia, Tunisia, Peru, Mexico, Iraq and Czech Republic

M2010: None

CONTRACTORS

M107: Barrett Firearms Manufacturing (Murfreesboro, TN)

XM2010: Remington Arms Co. Inc. (Illion, NY)

M110: Knight's Armament Co (Titusville, FL)

SPECIFICATIONS

	M107	M2010	M110
Length	57 inches	52.2 inches	46.5 inches
Weight	30.9 pounds	18.7 pounds	17.3 pounds (with suppressor)
Caliber	.50 BMG (12.7 x 99 mm NATO)	.30	.308 Win (7.62 x 51 mm NATO)
Range	2,000 meters (materiel) 1,000 meters (personnel)	1,200 meters	800 meters

Small Caliber Ammunition

PEO Ammunition | Picatinny Arsenal, NJ

WARFIGHTING FUNCTION

Mission Command

Movement and Maneuver

Intelligence

Fires

Sustainment

Maneuver Support and Protection

Engagement

ACQUISITION LIFECYCLE PHASE

Materiel Solution Analysis

Technology Maturation & Risk Reduction

Engineering & Manufacturing Development

Production & Deployment

Operations & Support

MILESTONE DECISION AUTHORITY

Defense Acquisition Executive

Army Acquisition Executive

Program Executive Officer

DESCRIPTION

Small Caliber Ammunition is .50 Caliber and below. Conventional Small Caliber Ammunition in production and deployment consists of 5.56 mm, 7.62 mm, 9 mm, 10- and 12-gauge, .22 Caliber, .30 Caliber, .38 Caliber, .45 Caliber, .300 WinMag and .50 Caliber. The 5.56 mm cartridge is used in the M16 Rifle, M4 Carbine and M249 Squad Automatic Weapon. The 7.62 mm cartridge is used in the M240 Machine Gun, as well as the M24, M110 and M14 Enhanced Battle Rifle Sniper Rifles. The 9 mm cartridge is fired in the M9 Pistol. The M2010 Sniper Rifle uses the .300 WinMag cartridge. The M2 Machine Gun and the M107 Sniper Rifle use .50 Caliber cartridges. The remaining Small Caliber Ammunition is used in a variety of pistols, rifles and shotguns.

Small Caliber Ammunition in research and development consists of Lightweight Case to lighten the Soldier's load, Advanced Armor Piercing Capabilities, Reduced Range Training Ammunition and One Way Luminescent Trace Ammunition.

Three categories of Small Caliber Ammunition are currently in use. War Reserve Ammunition is ammunition with overmatch capability that supports individual and crew-served weapons during combat operations. Training Standard Ammunition is dual-purpose, and can be used to support both training and operational requirements. Training Unique Ammunition is designed specifically for use in training and is not for combat use, i.e., blank, dummy-inert, Close Combat Man-Marking Kit and short-range training ammunition.

BENEFIT TO THE WARFIGHTER

Standard ammunition provides the warfighter with the necessary lethality needed to defeat the enemy.

SPECIFICATIONS

Various specifications used are dependent on weapon platform, caliber and target set and effect.

PROGRAM STATUS

- **4QFY14:**
  - › M80A1/M62A1 Low-Rate Production Initiated
  - › 7.62 mm M80A1 Enhanced Performance Round (EPR)/M62A1 Fielding Approval
- **Current:** 7.62 mm XM1158 Advanced Armor Piercing, Pre-Engineering & Manufacturing Development (EMD) Materiel Development Decision (MDD) Approval

PROJECTED ACTIVITIES

- **2QFY16:** Second Source 5-year Indefinite Delivery Indefinite Quantity Contract Award
- **1QFY17:**
  - › 7.62 mm One Way Luminescent, Pre-EMD MDD
  - › 7.62 mm XM1158 Advanced Armor Piercing, Milestone B

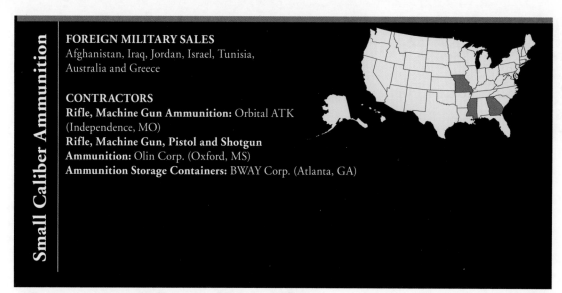

FOREIGN MILITARY SALES
Afghanistan, Iraq, Jordan, Israel, Tunisia, Australia and Greece

CONTRACTORS
Rifle, Machine Gun Ammunition: Orbital ATK (Independence, MO)
Rifle, Machine Gun, Pistol and Shotgun Ammunition: Olin Corp. (Oxford, MS)
Ammunition Storage Containers: BWAY Corp. (Atlanta, GA)

Small Caliber Ammunition Family

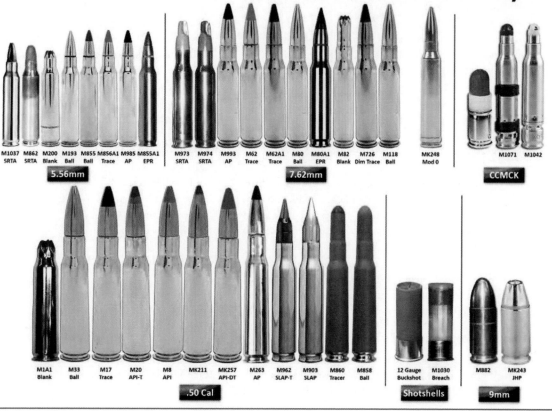

5.56mm

| M1037 SRTA | M862 SRTA | M200 Blank | M193 Ball | M855 Ball | M856A1 Trace | M985 AP | M855A1 EPR |

7.62mm

| M973 SRTA | M974 SRTA | M993 AP | M62 Trace | M62A1 Trace | M80 Ball | M80A1 EPR | M82 Blank | M726 Dim Trace | M118 Ball |

| MK248 Mod 0 |

CCMCK

| M1071 | M1042 |

.50 Cal

| M1A1 Blank | M33 Ball | M17 Trace | M20 API-T | M8 API | MK211 | MK257 API-DT | M263 AP | M962 SLAP-T | M903 SLAP | M860 Tracer | M858 Ball |

Shotshells

| 12 Gauge Buckshot | M1030 Breach |

9mm

| M882 | MK243 JHP |

Soldier Protection System (SPS)

PEO Soldier | Fort Belvoir, VA

WARFIGHTING FUNCTION

Mission Command

Movement and Maneuver

Intelligence

Fires

Sustainment

Maneuver Support and Protection

Engagement

ACQUISITION LIFECYCLE PHASE

Materiel Solution Analysis

Technology Maturation & Risk Reduction

Engineering & Manufacturing Development

Production & Deployment

Operations & Support

MILESTONE DECISION AUTHORITY

Defense Acquisition Executive

Army Acquisition Executive

Program Executive Officer

DESCRIPTION

The Soldier Protection System (SPS) is the Army's next generation Personal Protective Equipment (PPE) system. SPS is a modular, scalable, tailorable system designed to defeat current threats at a reduced weight in comparison to the Army's existing PPE. The SPS is based on the parallel development of five subsystems.

The Vital Torso Protection (VTP) includes lighter-weight Enhanced Small Arm Protective Inserts/Enhanced Side Ballistic Inserts (ESAPI/ESBI) as well as the X Threat Small Arms Protective Inserts (XSAPI)/X Threat Side Ballistic Inserts (XSBI) for deployers.

The Torso and Extremity Protection (TEP) is further comprised of multiple components to include the Modular Scalable Vest (MSV), the Ballistic Combat Shirt (BCS), the Blast Pelvic Protector (BPP) and the Load Distribution System (LDS).

The Integrated Head Protection System (IHPS) will include a 5 percent-lighter-weight helmet system comprised of helmet/maxillofacial and passive hearing protection with increased blunt impact performance.

The Transition Combat Eye Protection (TCEP) will include ballistic protective eyewear capable of transitioning from light to dark and dark to light in less than one second, providing a 10 percent increase in fragmentation. This capability aids Soldiers in a combat environment to move rapidly in varying light conditions.

The Integrated Soldier Sensor System (ISSS) will include a multifaceted sensor system capable of measuring heart rate, temperature and hydration levels, and will include a data retrieval system.

BENEFIT TO THE WARFIGHTER

SPS increases the warfighter's lethality, mobility and modularity by optimizing Soldier protection while effectively reducing weight with the latest technologies and managing all lifecycle aspects of personal protective equipment. SPS replaces the capability of multiple current systems to provide the Soldier with an overall 10 percent weight reduction. SPS provides the Soldier with multiple levels of ballistic protection tailorable to a broad range of missions. This modular, scalable approach increases Soldier survivability and mobility and contributes to increased force protection.

SPECIFICATIONS

- VTP achieves 8-14 percent weight reduction over the current plates
  › ESAPI and XSAPI sizes: XS, S, M, L, XL and Small Long
  › ESBI and XSBI sizes: 7x8 inches, 6x8 inches and 6x6 inches
  › Weight: ESAPI, 5 pounds; ESBI, 2.03 pounds; XSAPI, 5.5 pounds; XSBI, 2.39 pounds
- TEP achieves 26 percent weight reduction over current soft armor vest/plate carrier
  › Number of sizes: MSV, 15; BCS, 6; BPP, 4; LDS, 5
  › Weight (medium size): MSV, 6.19 pounds; BCS, 2.89 pounds; BPP, 1.68 pounds; LDS, 2.3 pounds

PROGRAM STATUS

- **3QFY15:**
  › VTP Milestone (MS) C, entering Production
  › TEP MS C, entering Production
  › Live Fire Testing
  › Initial Operational Test and Evaluation

PROJECTED ACTIVITIES

- **4QFY16:**
  › Full-Rate Production Decision for VTP and TEP
  › Full and Open Competition Award for VTP and TEP
- **1QFY17:**
  › IHPS MS C, entering Production
  › TCEP MS C, entering Production
- **2QFY17:** ISSS MS C, entering Production

Enhanced Small Arms Protective Insert (ESAPI)

X Threat Small Arms Protective Insert (XSAPI)

Enhanced Side Ballistic Insert (ESBI)

X Threat Side Ballistic Insert (XSBI)

VTP

  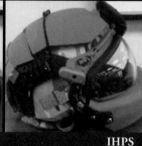

IHPS

VTP includes Modular Scalable Vest, Ballistic Combat Shirt, Blast Pelvic Protector and Load Distribution System

Tier 2: Low Visibility
+ Concealable Carrier
+ Soft armor ballistic inserts
+ SAPIs

Concealable
Concealable Carrier
Soft armor ballistic inserts

Tier 3: Tactical
+ Tactical Carrier
+ Shoulder Pads
+ Soft armor ballistic inserts
+ SAPIs
+ ESBIs

Tier 4: Full Spectrum
+ Tactical Carrier
+ Shoulder Pads
+ Soft armor ballistic inserts
+ SAPIs
+ ESBIs
+ Ballistic Combat Shirt
+ Blast Pelvic Protector
+ Load Distribution System

TEP

TCEP

FOREIGN MILITARY SALES
None

CONTRACTORS
Engineering & Manufacturing Development Contractors:
IHPS: Ceradyne, Inc. (Costa Mesa, CA), Gentex Corp. (Carbondale, PA), Revision Military Ltd. (Essex Junction, VT)
TCEP: AlphaMicron (Kent, OH)
ISSS: BAE Systems (Phoenix, AZ), Georgia Tech Research Institute (Atlanta, GA)
Low-Rate Initial Production Contractors:
VTP: BAE Systems (Phoenix, AZ), Ceradyne, Inc. (Costa Mesa, CA)
TEP:
- MSV: Bethel Industries (Jersey City, NJ), Hawk Protection (Pembroke Pines, FL), KDH Defense Systems (Eden, NC)
- BCS: Carter Enterprises, LLC (Brooklyn, NY), Point Blank Enterprises, Inc. (Pompano Beach, FL), Short Bark Industries (SBI) (Vonore, TN)
- BPP: Bethel Industries (Jersey City, NJ), Hawk Protection (Pembroke Pines, FL), KDH Defense Systems (Eden, NC)
- LDS: Carter Enterprises, LLC (Brooklyn, NY), Revision Military Ltd. (Essex Junction, VT)

Spider – Command Destruct Networked Command Munition Dispensing Set Increment 1A

PEO Ammunition | Picatinny Arsenal, NJ

WARFIGHTING FUNCTION

Mission Command

Movement and Maneuver

Intelligence

Fires

Sustainment

Maneuver Support and Protection

Engagement

ACQUISITION LIFECYCLE PHASE

Materiel Solution Analysis

Technology Maturation & Risk Reduction

Engineering & Manufacturing Development

Production & Deployment

Operations & Support

MILESTONE DECISION AUTHORITY

Defense Acquisition Executive

Army Acquisition Executive

Program Executive Officer

DESCRIPTION

M7 Spider Increment 1 is a hand-emplaced, remotely controlled, Man-in-the-Loop, anti-personnel munition system that is currently being fielded. M7E1 Spider Increment 1A is being developed as a follow-on incremental development to the baseline Spider Program. Spider Increment 1A is not a replacement for the Spider Increment 1 system. Spider Increment 1A will develop and provide an enhanced control station that will utilize the common Increment 1 munitions and accessories. Spider Increment 1A will retain all current features of Spider Increment 1, with the addition of the following:

- New control station, which will include an enhanced mapping capability
- Control station will be capable of seamlessly communicating the munition field status and location to the Mission Command, provided an unclassified network is available
- Ability to employ legacy government off-the-shelf munitions
- Will be compliant with U.S. National Landmine Policy, as is Spider Increment 1

Spider Increment 1A is a Special Interest Program with Office of the Secretary of Defense oversight (operational testing only). The Under Secretary of Defense for Acquisition, Technology and Logistics memo, dated January 10, 2011, directed the Army to "fully fund, develop, and field an alternative(s) for persistent anti-vehicle landmines as part of the Spider program." Although Spider Increment 1A is an incremental modification to the baseline M7 Spider Increment 1 program, from a funding perspective Spider Increment 1A was considered a new start because the M7 Spider Increment 1 Research, Development, Test, & Evaluation funding line had closed. Spider Increment 1A is being developed as an evolutionary acquisition in an incremental approach. It entered the acquisition lifecycle at Milestone B.

BENEFIT TO THE WARFIGHTER

Spider Increment 1A will provide the warfighter with an improved networked munition control station, and the ability to employ and control fielded Army common Anti-Personnel (AP) and Anti-Vehicle (AV) lethal and nonlethal munitions and effects.

SPECIFICATIONS

- Latest computer controller technology and operating system with map background and open system software architecture to support integration of future munitions
- Ability to employ fielded Army blasting-cap-initiated AP and AV munitions and effects
- Capable of seamless interoperability with Mission Command
- Self-destruct and self-deactivate capabilities
- Command reset and recycle self-destruct
- Transfer of control
- Interface to Mission Command and Joint Battle Command – Platform via removable media
- Command destruction
- On-off-on (safe passage/maintenance)
- Multiple effects (lethal, nonlethal, demo)
- Intrusion detection
- Anti-tamper and self-protection
- Reuse

PROGRAM STATUS

- **1QFY16:** Functional Qualification Test

PROJECTED ACTIVITIES

- **2QFY16:** System Verification Test
- **2QFY16-3QFY16:** Conduct Risk Management Framework Testing
- **3QFY16:**
  › Obtain Interim Authority To Test
  › Network Integration Evaluation 16.2
- **4QFY16:** Obtain Authority To Operate

Spider

FOREIGN MILITARY SALES
None

CONTRACTORS
SI1A: Northrop Grumman Corp. (Redondo Beach, CA)
SI1: Joint Venture between Textron Defense Systems (Wilmington, MA) and Orbital ATK (Plymouth, MN)

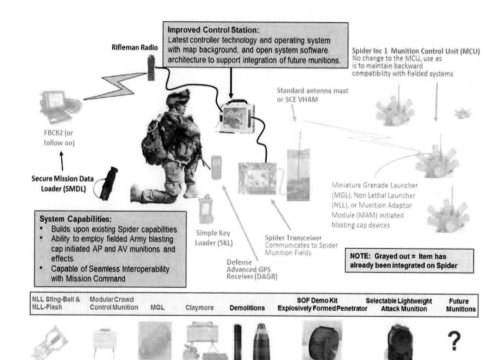

Rifleman Radio

Improved Control Station:
Latest controller technology and operating system with map background, and open system software architecture to support integration of future munitions.

Spider Inc 1 Munition Control Unit (MCU)
No change to the MCU, use as is to maintain backward compatibility with fielded systems

Standard antenna mast or SCE VHAM

FBCB2 (or follow on)

Secure Mission Data Loader (SMDL)

Miniature Grenade Launcher (MGL), Non Lethal Launcher (NLL), or Munition Adaptor Module (MAM) initiated blasting cap devices

System Capabilities:
* Builds upon existing Spider capabilities
* Ability to employ fielded Army blasting cap initiated AP and AV munitions and effects
* Capable of Seamless Interoperability with Mission Command

Simple Key Loader (SKL)

Spider Transceiver
Communicates to Spider Munition Fields

Defense Advanced GPS Receiver (DAGR)

NOTE: Grayed out = Item has already been integrated on Spider

NLL Sting-Ball & NLL-Flash	Modular Crowd Control Munition	MGL	Claymore	Demolitions	SOF Demo Kit Explosively Formed Penetrator	Selectable Lightweight Attack Munition	Future Munitions

Synthetic Training Environment (STE)

PEO Simulation, Training, and Instrumentation | Orlando, FL

OTHER

WARFIGHTING FUNCTION

- Mission Command
- Movement and Maneuver
- Intelligence
- Fires
- Sustainment
- Maneuver Support and Protection
- Engagement

ACQUISITION LIFECYCLE PHASE

- Materiel Solution Analysis
- Technology Maturation & Risk Reduction
- Engineering & Manufacturing Development
- Production & Deployment
- Operations & Support

MILESTONE DECISION AUTHORITY

- Defense Acquisition Executive
- Army Acquisition Executive
- Program Executive Officer

DESCRIPTION

The Synthetic Training Environment (STE) is designed to provide a cognitive, collective, multi-echelon training and mission rehearsal capability for the operational, institutional and self-development training domains. It brings together the virtual, constructive and gaming training environments into a single STE for Army Active and Reserve Components as well as civilians. It will provide training services to ground, dismounted and aerial platforms and command post (CP) points of need (PoN).

The Synthetic Training Environment will interact with and augment live training, which is the primary training approach for the Army. This concept will allow the Army to provide a single STE that delivers a training service to the PoN. The capability will train all Warfighting Functions and the human dimension across all echelons with Joint and Unified Action Partners in the context of Unified Land Operations.

BENEFIT TO THE WARFIGHTER

Warfighters will benefit from a single STE built on One World Terrain concepts within a Common Operating Environment (COE).

SPECIFICATIONS

- Training and mission rehearsal capability
- Interfaces with operational networks and Network-Enabled Mission Command Initial Capability Document-defined platforms and CP
- Interfaces with live training instrumentation
- Native interoperability with the COE
- STE Virtual Military Equipment leverages commercial off-the-shelf (COTS) and government off-the-shelf (GOTS) hardware
  › Will provide immersive and semi-immersive training capability
- STE is a software solution and will not require production line for custom hardware
  › Will instead utilize integration line to integrate COTS and GOTS hardware

PROGRAM STATUS

- **Current:** Program is in the Pre-Materiel Development Decision (MDD) phase
  › Milestone Decision Authority and ACAT to be determined at MDD

PROJECTED ACTIVITIES

- **1QFY17:** Pre-MDD

T-9 Medium Dozer

PEO Combat Support and Combat Service Support | Detroit Arsenal, MI

WARFIGHTING FUNCTION

Mission Command

Movement and Maneuver

Intelligence

Fires

Sustainment

Maneuver Support and Protection

Engagement

ACQUISITION LIFECYCLE PHASE

Materiel Solution Analysis

Technology Maturation & Risk Reduction

Engineering & Manufacturing Development

Production & Deployment

Operations & Support

MILESTONE DECISION AUTHORITY

Defense Acquisition Executive

Army Acquisition Executive

Program Executive Officer

DESCRIPTION

The T-9/D7R dozer model is a medium drawbar, air-transportable by C-5 and C-17, diesel-engine-driven crawler tractor with a dozer blade and optional winch (Type I) or ripper (Type II). The medium dozer is a commercial vehicle with military modifications to include NATO start, arctic kit, rifle rack and armor C-Kit capability.

The vehicle provides cutting, moving and finish-grading capabilities to support various construction tasks such as building and maintaining roads, airfields and shelters.

BENEFIT TO THE WARFIGHTER

The T-9/D7R-II medium dozer is used to build and maintain air and ground lines of communication such as airfields and main supply routes, which enhances infrastructure and force protection for the warfighter.

SPECIFICATIONS

- Maximum speed: 6.6 mph forward, 8.4 mph reverse
- 105,820 pounds drawbar pull
- 3 forward and 3 reverse gears
- Dimensions:
  › With winch: 273 inches long, 139 inches high and 145 inches wide; Weight: 62,000 pounds without armor; 66,000 pounds with armor
  › With ripper: 289 inches long, 139 inches high and 145 inches wide; Weight: 65,000 pounds without armor; 69,000 pounds with armor

PROGRAM STATUS

- **Through FY15:**
  › Fielded 1,002 dozers
  › Trained 1,106 Soldiers from 166 units

PROJECTED ACTIVITIES

- **Through FY16:** Continue fielding and training
- **4QFY16:** Scheduled to complete fielding

T-9 Medium Dozer

FOREIGN MILITARY SALES
Uganda

CONTRACTORS
Caterpillar Inc. (Peoria, IL)
BAE Systems (Cincinnati, OH)

Tactical Electric Power (TEP)

PEO Combat Support and Combat Service Support | Detroit Arsenal, MI

ACAT II/III

WARFIGHTING FUNCTION

Mission Command

Movement and Maneuver

Intelligence

Fires

Sustainment

Maneuver Support and Protection

Engagement

ACQUISITION LIFECYCLE PHASE

Materiel Solution Analysis

Technology Maturation & Risk Reduction

Engineering & Manufacturing Development

Production & Deployment

Operations & Support

MILESTONE DECISION AUTHORITY

Defense Acquisition Executive

Army Acquisition Executive

Program Executive Officer

DESCRIPTION

Tactical Electric Power (TEP) provides a standardized family of tactical electric power sources to DoD in accordance with DoD Directive 4120.11, Standardization of Mobile Electric Power (MEP) Generating Sources.

The TEP program consists of a variety of generator set sizes. Small Generators: 2kW Military Tactical Generators (MTG), 3kW Tactical Quiet Generators (TQG), Small Tactical Electric Power (STEP); Medium Generators: 5, 10, 15, 30 and 60kW TQGs; Advanced Medium Mobile Power Sources (AMMPS), trailer-mounted Power Units and Power Plants; Large Generators: 100-200kW TQGs, Large Advanced Mobile Power Sources (LAMPS); 840kW Deployable Power Generation and Distribution System (DPGDS); Power Distribution: Power Distribution Illumination System Electrical (PDISE) and Management and Distribution Control (MDC) (microgrid intelligent power management and distribution).

The STEP, AMMPS and LAMPS are the third generation of mobile electric power generation systems, and will replace the TQG over time.

BENEFIT TO THE WARFIGHTER

The next generation of TEP will benefit the warfighter by offering increased system efficiency, reliability, mobility and maintainability. Units will see a significant reduction in fuel consumption, thereby reducing refueling operations, which decreases the overall risk to the warfighters.

SPECIFICATIONS

- Maximized fuel efficiency, diesel/JP8-based and eliminates gasoline on battlefield
- AMMPS offers a fleet-weighted average of 21 percent improved fuel efficiency over the medium TQGs

- Increased reliability (AMMPS, 750 hours mean time between failures), maintainability and transportability via skid or trailer mount
- Improved sustainability; operates at rated loads in all military environments
- Minimized weight and size while meeting all user requirements with military ruggedized commercial components
- Reduced infrared signature and noise (AMMPS, less than 70 decibels at 7 meters)
- Survivability in chemical, biological and nuclear environments
- Advanced Technology, including digital controls
- Standard DoD military tactical generator fleet that meets power generation and conditioning standards in accordance with Military Standard 1332B, Definitions of Tactical, Prime, Precise and Utility Terminologies for Classification of the DoD Mobile Electric Power Engine Generator Set Family
- Man-portability with 2kW MTG and 3kW TQG generators

PROGRAM STATUS

- **1QFY13-4QFY15:** Continued production and/or fielding of the following systems: 2kW MTG, 3kW TQG, 5-, 10-, 15- and 30kW AMMPS, 100kW TQG and PDISE

PROJECTED ACTIVITIES

- **3QFY16:** DPGDS Recapitalization contract award
- **4QFY16:**
  › AMMPS production rebuy contract award
  › STEP Milestone B, entering Engineering and Manufacturing Development (EMD)
- **2QFY17:** MDC Milestone B, entering EMD
- **3QFY17:** LAMPS Milestone C, entering production
- **FY16-17:** Continue production and fielding of 3kW TQG

FOREIGN MILITARY SALES
None

CONTRACTORS
3kW TQG: Fidelity Technologies
Corp. (Reading, PA)
AMMPS 5–60kW: Cummins Power
Generation (Minneapolis, MN)
LAMPS: L3 Westwood (Tulsa, OK)
DPGDS: DRS Fermont (Bridgeport, CT)
PDISE: Fidelity Technologies Corporation (Reading, PA)

Tank Ammunition

PEO Ammunition | Picatinny Arsenal, NJ

WARFIGHTING FUNCTION

Mission Command

Movement and Maneuver

Intelligence

Fires

Sustainment

Maneuver Support and Protection

Engagement

ACQUISITION LIFECYCLE PHASE

Materiel Solution Analysis

Technology Maturation & Risk Reduction

Engineering & Manufacturing Development

Production & Deployment

Operations & Support

MILESTONE DECISION AUTHORITY

Defense Acquisition Executive

Army Acquisition Executive

Program Executive Officer

DESCRIPTION

The current 120 mm family of tactical tank ammunition consists of fourth-generation kinetic energy, multipurpose and canister ammunition.

Kinetic Energy (KE) ammunition lethality is optimized by firing a maximum-weight subcaliber projectile at the greatest velocity possible, defeating advanced-threat armor. The M829A3 kinetic energy cartridge provides armor-defeat capability. The M829A4, the next generation KE cartridge, is currently in production.

Multipurpose ammunition uses a high-explosive warhead to provide blast, armor penetration and fragmentation effects. The Advanced Multi-Purpose (AMP) cartridge, is a 120 mm high-explosive multi-purpose munition. When fired from a platform equipped with the Ammunition Data Link already being incorporated into the Abrams tank, the cartridge can be programmed for one of three modes, including Point Detonate, Point Detonate Delay, or Airburst. AMP will consolidate the capabilities of currently fielded high-explosive munitions including the M830A1 and the M908 as well as the M1028, which is a shotgun-shell-like canister cartridge that provides the Abrams tank with effective, short-range, rapid, lethal fire against massed assaulting Infantry.

The 120 mm family has dedicated training cartridges in production: the M865, with its reduced range, simulates KE tactical trajectory to 2,500 meters; and the M1002, which simulates the M830A1 size, weight and nose switch. To support the Stryker force, the 105 mm Mobile Gun System uses M1040 canister cartridges. The M1040 canister cartridge provides rapid, lethal fire against massed assaulting Infantry at close range. The new 105 mm M724A1E1 is a reduced-range training cartridge intended to provide the Soldier the training capability to maximize the effectiveness of the tactical 105 mm M900 KE cartridge, which provides armor-defeat capability. The M724A1E1 is a ballistic match for the M900. The cartridge will be used in the Stryker Mobile Gun System (MGS). The 105 mm M467A1 training cartridge is a ballistic match to the M393A3 tactical round. The MGS employs the M68A1/A2 105 mm

rifled gun tube with a Muzzle Reference System and an autoloader for storage and handling of its 105 mm ammunition.

BENEFIT TO THE WARFIGHTER

Standard ammunition provides the warfighter with the necessary lethality needed to defeat the enemy.

SPECIFICATIONS

Various specifications used depend on weapon platform, caliber, target set and effect.

PROGRAM STATUS

- **Current:** M829A3, M830, M830A1, M1002, M908, M1028, M1040, M393A3, M467A1 are fielded
- **FY13:**
  › M1002 in production
  › M865, M831A1 in recapitalization
  › M724A1E1 Milestone (MS) C
- **FY15:**
  › AMP MS-B and competitive Phase 1 Engineering & Manufacturing Development (EMD) contract awards
  › M829A4 Type Classified – Standard (TC-STD)

PROJECTED ACTIVITIES

- **FY16:**
  › M724A1E1 TC-STD, Full Materiel Release (FMR), and Full-Rate Production Decision Review (FRPDR)
  › 829A4 FMR and FRPDR
- **FY17:** AMP down-select to single contractor for EMD Phase 2

FOREIGN MILITARY SALES
M831A1, M865, M1028, M830A1, M908, and
KEW-A1 (Tungsten Penetrator): Iraq
KEW-A1 (Tungsten Penetrator): Kuwait

CONTRACTORS
**M1002, M865, M724A1E1, AMP EMD Phase
1, and M829A4:** Orbital ATK (Plymouth, MN)
**M1002, M865, AMP EMD Phase 1, and
KEW-A1 (Tungsten Penetrator):** General Dynamics Ordnance and Tactical
Systems (St. Petersburg, FL)
M1040: L-3 Communications (Lancaster, PA)

Large Caliber Ammunition Family

AMP — Devel.

M829A4 M724A1E1 KEWA1 M1002 M865 IM HE-T — Production

M1028 M829A3 M830A1 M831A1 M908 M829A1 M829A2 M830 M1040 M393A3 M467A1 M900 M274A1 M456A2 M490A1 — Sustainment

105mm
FMS Only

Test Equipment Modernization (TEMOD)

PEO Combat Support and Combat Service Support | Detroit Arsenal, MI

DESCRIPTION

The Test Equipment Modernization (TEMOD) program replaces obsolete General Purpose Electronic Test Equipment with new state-of-the-art equipment. This new equipment reduces the proliferation of test equipment, modernizes the Army's current existing inventory and strongly supports other weapon systems. Acquisitions are commercial items that have significant impact on readiness, power projection, safety and training operations of the Army, Army Reserve, and National Guard. The TEMOD program has procured 38 products that replace more than 334 models.

BENEFIT TO THE WARFIGHTER

TEMOD improves the readiness of Army weapon systems; minimizes test, measurement and diagnostic equipment proliferation and obsolescence; and reduces operations and support costs.

SPECIFICATIONS

Equipment includes:

- **High Frequency Signal Generator (SG-1366/U):** This is a signal source to test electronic receivers and transmitters of all types throughout the Army and provide standards to compare signals
- **Radar Test Set Identification Friend or Foe (IFF) Upgrade Kit and Radar Test Set with Mode S enhanced and Mode 5 cryptography (TS-4530A/UPM):** Personnel use this equipment to perform pre-flight checks on aviation and missile transponders and interrogators to alleviate potential fratricide concerns
- **Multimeter (AN/GSM-437):** The multimeter enables quick, reliable troubleshooting that positively affects operational availability
- **Radio Test Set (AN/PRM-36):** This set diagnoses the condition of various radios in the field
- **Ammeter (ME-572/U):** The ammeter measures and displays alternating and direct current without interrupting the measured circuit
- **Telecommunication System Test Set (TS-4544/U):** This set measures and displays information related to digital transmissions

- **Future TEMOD projects:** Upcoming TEMOD equipment includes two oscilloscopes, the OS-305/U, a bench-top instrument, and the OS-307/U a portable, hand-held instrument; the Radio Frequency Power Test Set, the TS-4548/P, for general purpose digital measurement of radio frequency power; and an Optical Time Domain Reflectometer, the TS-4558/U which will include an optical power meter for testing of fiber-optic cables

PROGRAM STATUS

- **2QFY14:** Multimeter Full-Rate Production (FRP)
- **3QFY14:** Oscilloscope (bench-top) issue Letter Request For Bid Samples (LRFBS); Oscilloscope (portable) issue LRFBS; Radio Frequency Power Test Set issue LRFBS
- **4QFY14:** IFF Radar Test Set Mode S (Enhanced) Mode 5 Modification Work Order (MWO) Kits FRP; Radio Test Set FRP
- **1QFY15:** Telecommunication System Test Set issue LRFBS
- **2QFY15:** Oscilloscope (bench-top) Bid Sample Testing complete; Oscilloscope (portable) Bid Sample Testing complete; Optical Time Domain Reflectometer market research
- **4QFY15:** Telecommunication System Test Set Bid Sample Testing complete; Ammeter, preparing Milestone (MS) C package; Radio Frequency Power Test Set Bid Sample Testing complete

PROJECTED ACTIVITIES

- **2QFY16:** Ammeter MS C and Contract Award; Radio Frequency Power Test Set MS C and Contract Award
- **3QFY16:** Oscilloscope (bench-top) MS C and Contract Award; Oscilloscope (portable) MS C and Contract Award; Ammeter Low-Rate Initial Production (LRIP); Telecommunications System Test Set MS C; Optical Time Domain Reflectometer issue LRFBS
- **4QFY16:** Telecommunications System Test Set Contract Award; Oscilloscope (bench-top) LRIP; Oscilloscope (portable) LRIP; Radio Frequency Power Test Set LRIP
- **1QFY17:** Radio Test Set fielding complete; Multimeter contract end; Telecommunication System Test Set LRIP

FOREIGN MILITARY SALES
IFF Radar Test Set Mode S (Enhanced)
Mode 5: Azerbaijan, Greece, Hungary, Kuwait, Netherlands, Norway, Portugal, Saudi Arabia, Singapore and United Kingdom

CONTRACTORS
High Frequency Signal Generator: Keysight Technologies (Englewood, CO)
IFF Radar Test Set Mode S (Enhanced) Mode 5: Tel-Instrument Electronics Corp. (East Rutherford, NJ)
Multimeter: Fluke Corporation (Everett, WA)
Radio Test Set: DRS Technologies (St. Louis, MO)
Ammeter: TBD
Telecommunication System Test Set: TBD
Oscilloscope (bench-top): TBD
Oscilloscope (portable): TBD
Radio Frequency Power Test Set: TBD
Optical Time Domain Reflectometer: TBD

Signal Generator SG-1366/U

Multimeter AN/GSM-437

Radar Test Set TS-4530A/UPM

Radio Test Set AN/PRM-36

Ammeter ME-572/U

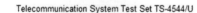

Telecommunication System Test Set TS-4544/U

Transportable Tactical Command Communications (T2C2)

PEO Command, Control and Communications – Tactical | Aberdeen Proving Ground, MD

WARFIGHTING FUNCTION

Mission Command

Movement and Maneuver

Intelligence

Fires

Sustainment

Maneuver Support and Protection

Engagement

ACQUISITION LIFECYCLE PHASE

Materiel Solution Analysis

Technology Maturation & Risk Reduction

Engineering & Manufacturing Development

Production & Deployment

Operations & Support

MILESTONE DECISION AUTHORITY

Defense Acquisition Executive

Army Acquisition Executive

Program Executive Officer

DESCRIPTION

Transportable Tactical Command Communications (T2C2) provides satellite capability to small detachments and teams operating in remote locations without network infrastructure. The man-portable T2C2 Lite version can be rapidly set up and provides satellite capability to small detachments and teams operating in these remote locations. The heavy version of T2C2 provides a high-bandwidth tactical network extension for small companies and small forward operating bases working beyond-line-of-sight from their higher headquarters.

Many systems with capabilities similar to T2C2 have been fielded over the years to address operational needs, however T2C2 product selection is not expected until 2QFY16. Reset and upgraded Secure Internet Protocol Router Network/Non-secure Internet Protocol Router Network (SIPRNet/NIPRNet) Access Points (SNAP) and even smaller suitcase-sized Global Rapid Response Information Packages, which reduce size, weight and power and increase bandwidth, are being used as bridging capabilities until the respective heavy and light versions of the T2C2 program are ready to begin fielding.

BENEFIT TO THE WARFIGHTER

T2C2 enables the warfighter to securely relay classified and time-sensitive information, increasing the situational awareness for the entire operation.

SPECIFICATIONS

T2C2 Lite (V1):
- Man-portable (carried by one Soldier)
- Sets up rapidly; can be on the air in less than 10 minutes
- Will support military Ka and X bands and commercial Ku band capability for integration into WIN-T tactical network

T2C2 Heavy (V2):
- Will leverage capabilities based on SNAP terminal solution
- Will support company-sized elements and small forward operating bases
- V2 will support military Ka and X bands and commercial Ku band for integration into WIN-T tactical network

PROGRAM STATUS
- **1QFY16:** Milestone C Decision

PROJECTED ACTIVITIES
- **2QFY16:** Product Selection
- **FY16-FY17:** Initial Fielding

Unified Command Suite (UCS)

JPEO for Chemical and Biological Defense | Aberdeen Proving Ground, MD

WARFIGHTING FUNCTION

Mission Command

Movement and Maneuver

Intelligence

Fires

Sustainment

Maneuver Support and Protection

Engagement

ACQUISITION LIFECYCLE PHASE

Materiel Solution Analysis

Technology Maturation & Risk Reduction

Engineering & Manufacturing Development

Production & Deployment

Operations & Support

MILESTONE DECISION AUTHORITY

Defense Acquisition Executive

Army Acquisition Executive

Program Executive Officer

DESCRIPTION

The Unified Command Suite (UCS) vehicle is a self-contained, stand-alone, C-130-air-mobile communications platform that provides both voice and data communications capabilities to civil support team (CST) commanders.

The UCS consists of a combination of commercial and existing government off-the-shelf communications equipment (both secure and nonsecure data) to provide the full range of communications necessary to support the CST mission. It is the primary means of reachback communications for the Analytical Laboratory System and acts as a command-and-control hub to deliver a common operational picture for planning and fulfilling an incident response.

BENEFIT TO THE WARFIGHTER

UCS gives the warfighter communications interoperability with federal, state, local and military emergency response elements at an incident scene. It also provides reachback capability, which allows incident commanders the ability to assess an incident scene, advise responders and facilitate access to DoD information.

SPECIFICATIONS

- Digital voice and data over satellite network
- Secure Internet Protocol Router Network (SIPRNET) and Non-Secure (NIPRNET)
- Radio remote and intercom with cross-banding
- Over-the-horizon communication interoperable interface with state emergency management and other military units

PROGRAM STATUS

- **Current:**
  - › Modernization of communication-on-the-move system, radio cross-banding system and secondary reachback system
  - › Platform integration and modernization

PROJECTED ACTIVITIES

- **Current:** Production and deployment

UCS

FOREIGN MILITARY SALES
None

CONTRACTORS
UCS Vehicle: Wolf Coach, Inc., an L-3
Communications Co. (Auburn, MA)
UCS Communications System Integrator: Naval
Air Warfare Center Aircraft Division (Patuxent
River, MD)

Unit Water Pod System (Camel II)

PEO Combat Support and Combat Service Support | Detroit Arsenal, MI

WARFIGHTING FUNCTION

Mission Command

Movement and Maneuver

Intelligence

Fires

Sustainment

Maneuver Support and Protection

Engagement

ACQUISITION LIFECYCLE PHASE

Materiel Solution Analysis

Technology Maturation & Risk Reduction

Engineering & Manufacturing Development

Production & Deployment

Operations & Support

MILESTONE DECISION AUTHORITY

Defense Acquisition Executive

Army Acquisition Executive

Program Executive Officer

DESCRIPTION

The Unit Water Pod System (Camel II) is the Army's primary water distribution system. Camel II replaces the M107, M149 and M1112 series water trailers. It consists of an 800- to 900-gallon-capacity baffled water tank with integrated freeze protection and all hoses and fittings necessary to dispense water by gravity flow.

The system provides a one-day supply of potable water for drinking and other purposes. If the unit has another source of drinking water, such as bottled water, then the Camel II can provide two days of potable water for other purposes. The system also contains six positions for filling canteens and five-gallon water cans.

BENEFIT TO THE WARFIGHTER

The Camel II receives, stores and dispenses potable water to warfighter units at all echelons throughout the battlefield.

SPECIFICATIONS

- Mounts on an M1095 trailer, allowing for better on- and off-road transportability by utilizing the family of medium tactical vehicle trucks
- Provides one-day supply of potable water
- Provides two-day supply for purposes other than drinking
- Operational from minus 25 degrees to more than 120 degrees Fahrenheit

PROGRAM STATUS

- **2QFY15:** Full Materiel Release

PROJECTED ACTIVITIES

- **3QFY16:** Contract award of remaining 161 systems

Camel II

FOREIGN MILITARY SALES
None

CONTRACTORS
Choctaw Manufacturing Defense Contractors
(McCalester, OK)

ARMY SCIENCE
AND TECHNOLOGY

Army Science and Technology

The Army Science and Technology (S&T) mission is to identify, develop and demonstrate technology options that inform and enable effective and affordable capabilities for the Soldier. The Army S&T program balances investments between "revolutionary" and "evolutionary" research to improve the performance of existing warfighting systems and provide new capabilities. The Army S&T program is guided by and aligned to higher level Army, DoD and National strategies and policies. The program is informed by current and emerging threats. In addition, the Army identified enduring capability challenges necessary to conduct future operations to frame Army modernization and prevent, shape and win conflicts. The enduring capability challenges align to the U.S. Army Training and Doctrine Command's (TRADOC) Army Warfighting Challenges and are subsequently matched to TRADOC Capability Needs Analysis gaps, which provide a focus for Army S&T investment. The Army is committed to ensuring that its Soldiers remain the most capable in the world. Consistent with this commitment is the Army's S&T vision to provide Soldiers with the technology to win.

The Army S&T Enterprise is comprised of the Office of the Deputy Assistant Secretary of the Army (Research and Technology (ODASA(R&T)) and the five S&T executing commands/agencies. They are responsible for technical leadership, scientific advancement and support for the acquisition process. On behalf of the Assistant Secretary of the Army (Acquisition, Logistics and Technology), the ODASA(R&T) is responsible for civilian oversight and governance of the Army S&T Enterprise relating to budget and policy matters. The five S&T executing commands and agencies are:

- The U.S. Army Materiel Command's (AMC) Research, Development and Engineering Command (RDECOM)
- The U.S. Army Corps of Engineers' Engineer Research and Development Center (ERDC)
- The U.S. Army Medical Command's Medical Research and Materiel Command (MRMC)

- The U.S. Army Space and Missile Defense Command/Army Forces Strategic Command's Space and Missile Defense Command Technical Center (SMDC-TC)
- HQDA G-1's U.S. Army Research Institute (ARI) for Behavioral and Social Sciences

In 2015, the Army S&T Enterprise included civilian manpower totaling about 17,000, with approximately 11,000 scientists and engineers in 16 laboratories and engineering centers. These include seven AMC/RDECOM organizations (six Research, Development and Engineering Centers (RDECs) and the U.S. Army Research Laboratory), six MRMC laboratories, ARI, SMDC-TC and ERDC at seven laboratories.

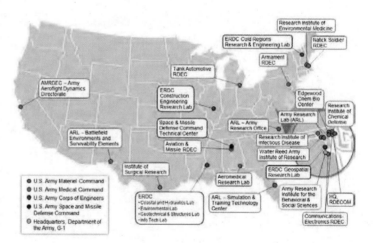

Army S&T Commands, Laboratories and RDECs in the United States

The Army S&T program is executed through a variety of funding strategies, mechanisms and partnerships. The majority (64 percent) of the Army's basic research Budget Activity (BA) 1 is conducted externally through grants to universities and contracts with industry.

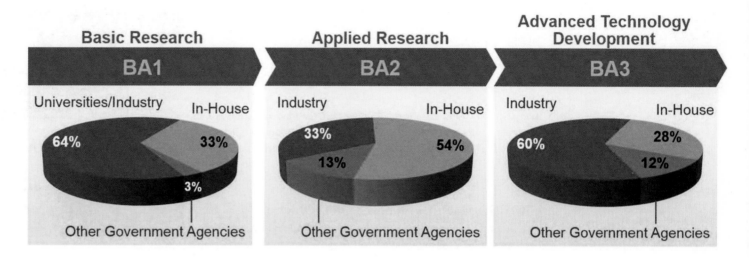

Basic Research — BA1
- Universities/Industry: 64%
- In-House: 33%
- Other Government Agencies: 3%

Applied Research — BA2
- Industry: 33%
- In-House: 54%
- Other Government Agencies: 13%

Advanced Technology Development — BA3
- Industry: 60%
- In-House: 28%
- Other Government Agencies: 12%

Broad Overview of Army S&T Investments (FY15)

Army scientists working at Army S&T laboratories and centers conduct the remaining basic research. Army scientists and engineers conduct approximately half (54 percent) of the Army's applied research (BA2), with the remaining contracted to industry and other organizations and government agencies. A majority (60 percent) of the advanced technology development (BA3) program is contracted to industry, with the remaining portion performed within Army and other government laboratories and centers. The figure above shows the split of in-house versus external work for Fiscal Year (FY) 2015, by budget activity.

Army S&T is responsible for some advanced component development and rapid prototyping (BA4) and operational system development efforts, including Manufacturing Technology (ManTech) (BA7). BA4 and BA7 resources support technology maturation and technology manufacturing efforts across S&T portfolios and help enable the transition of new and affordable capabilities to Army acquisition programs and ultimately to the field. The Army S&T Enterprise also executes Research and Development funding allocated to Small Business Innovation Research programs for the Army and DoD.

For coordination and oversight across the Army S&T Enterprise, the ODASA(R&T) organizes the S&T budget and programs into eight S&T Portfolios. Each portfolio is overseen by a portfolio director within the ODASA(R&T) who coordinates the Planning,

Programming, Budgeting and Execution process inputs and other oversight actions specific to that portfolio. The Army S&T Portfolios address challenges across six Army wide capability areas: Ground Maneuver, Soldier/Squad, Air, Command, Control, Communications and Intelligence (C3I), Lethality and Medical portfolios. There are also two S&T enabling portfolios: Innovation Enablers and Basic Research.

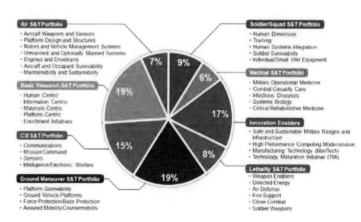

Army S&T Enterprise Program Funding Percentage Breakdown by Portfolio

Army S&T investment portfolios support Army modernization goals to develop and field affordable equipment in a rapidly changing technological and economic environment. The S&T Enterprise addresses this need by fostering technology invention, innovation, demonstration and maturation for the current and future fight.

GROUND MANEUVER S&T PORTFOLIO

The Ground Maneuver S&T Portfolio supports BA2 and BA3 research, development and demonstration of technologies to ensure Army freedom of maneuver. The Ground Maneuver S&T Portfolio focuses on technologies to provide survivability for combat and tactical vehicles and bases, power and mobility for ground vehicles, technology to support debarkation and embarkation of U.S. Forces and countermobility/counter improvised explosive device technologies to ensure freedom of maneuver. The Ground Maneuver S&T Portfolio's vision is to maintain U.S. overmatch in military vehicles for offensive and defensive capabilities. This portfolio also manages ground maneuver related projects from the BA4 Technology Maturation Initiative (TMI) and BA7 ManTech S&T programs.

The Ground Maneuver S&T investment strategy has subportfolios, including survivability for ground vehicles, survivability for protective structures, ground vehicle platforms, assured mobility/countermobility and ground vehicle robotics. Industry is a key partner to ensure the success of this portfolio by developing technologies to enable future and modernized ground vehicles for the Army. Industry participates in a range of S&T efforts that help shape that future, from vehicle concepts to developing standards, such as Vehicular Integration for Command, Control, Computers, Communications, Intelligence, Surveillance and Reconnaissance/Electronic Warfare (C4ISR/EW) Interoperability and Active Protection Systems (APS). Two of the Ground Maneuver Portfolio's major strategic efforts were initiated in FY15.

The **Combat Vehicle Prototyping (CVP)** Program matures technologies to address technical and integration challenges facing the ground combat fleet in the areas of mobility, survivability, lethality and vehicle architecture. The CVP focuses on maturation and demonstration of technologies such as engines, transmissions, integrated starter generators, ballistic protection, blast mitigation, advanced material technologies, lethality subsystems and advanced fire controls. The goal is to deliver a portfolio of mature technologies and subsystems by FY19. This effort informs the requirements for future fighting vehicles, identifies insertion opportunities for the legacy ground platform fleet and drives down future Program of Record (PoR) and Engineering Change Proposal risk.

The **Modular Active Protection System (MAPS)** Program is developing technologies to increase vehicle survivability and protection against current and emerging advanced threats. MAPS is focused on developing and demonstrating active protection, using a modular framework (A-Kit) that will facilitate commonality across the Army's ground vehicle fleets but with sensor and countermeasure sets (B-Kit) tailored to each vehicle's assigned threats. The modular approach will help alleviate integration issues and costs across the military vehicle fleets and be upgradable as new APS components and threats emerge. The effort's overall goal is to demonstrate component capability and validate architecture design to ease integration and facilitate fielding of

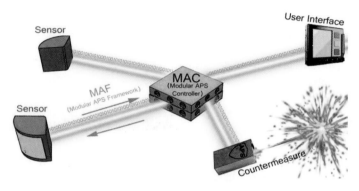

APS on Army platforms across the ground vehicle fleet. This effort will demonstrate a MAPS compliant soft-kill capability in FY17 and a hard-kill capability in FY19.

SOLDIER/SQUAD S&T PORTFOLIO

The Soldier/Squad S&T Portfolio supports BA2 and BA3 research, development and demonstration of technologies in lightweight, energy efficient, human centric systems and equipment, training technologies, training methods and personnel measures, all of which enable, protect and sustain dismounted Soldiers and Squads. Using both systems engineering and human science research, this portfolio influences many aspects of Doctrine, Organization, Training, Materiel, Leadership, Personnel, Facilities and Policy to satisfy capabilities gaps. The technologies protect, sustain and enable Soldiers operating within Squads who execute a variety of missions while deployed and at home stations. Geopolitical drivers include drawdown of deployed Soldiers abroad, requiring increased training at home station, reduction in the total force requiring greater innovative manpower efficiencies and growing complexity in the mission. These drivers require optimization of human capital and enabling technologies. Small, niche companies make up the research industrial base supporting this portfolio, and the Army S&T community accomplishes much of the technology integration.

The Soldier/Squad S&T Portfolio investment strategy is comprised of subportfolios, including personnel, tactical training, Soldier systems integration, situational awareness, survivability and sustainment.

One important initiative, the development of a **Soldier Systems Engineering Architecture**, is underway. This initiative is designed to make major inroads into our efforts to lighten the Soldier's load. This architecture, developed in concert with our acquisition and requirements community, is an analytical decision-based model where changes in Soldier system inputs (loads, technology/equipment, physiological and cognitive state, stress levels, training, etc.) may be assessed to predict changes in Soldier performance in operationally relevant environments. By using a systems engineering approach, the model will result in a full system-level analysis capable of predicting impacts of both materiel and nonmateriel solutions on fully equipped Soldiers performing operational missions or tasks.

The **Force Protection Soldier & Small Unit (FPS&SU) Program** seeks to make significant improvements in Soldier and Small Unit Protection. The spectrum of threats encountered by Soldiers in small units is varied and complex with current equipment, clothing and other protective measures providing adequate protection but introducing significant mobility challenges. The FPS&SU program, created to address these mobility shortfalls, has been organized into four thrust areas: human performance, ballistics and blast protection, integrated protection (protective clothing and concealment tools) and squad protection. Technologies within these four thrust areas provide an integrated solution, improving protection technologies and methods while reducing the cognitive and physical burden on the Soldier.

AIR S&T PORTFOLIO

The Air S&T Portfolio supports BA2 and BA3 research, development and demonstration of technologies for aviation systems to provide game-changing survivability, lethality, range, payloads and speed for the Army and DoD. The Air Portfolio's goals include longer persistence, improved payloads, increased speed, combat overmatch and battlefield dominance with overall lower cost of ownership.

The Air S&T investment strategy is divided into seven subportfolios: platform design and structures, engine and drives technology, aircraft and occupant survivability, maintainability and sustainability, rotors and vehicle management, aircraft weapon and sensors, and unmanned and optionally manned systems. Over 50 percent of the funding for the Air portfolio is dedicated to two major strategic efforts.

The **Joint Multi-Role Technology Demonstrator (JMR TD)** S&T program is aligned with the Joint/DoD Future Vertical Lift (FVL) effort. The JMR TD S&T effort is exploring rotor systems, drives, propulsion systems, structures, platform configurations, mission systems architectures and other associated technologies to support the FVL strategy.

In early FY15, two JMR TD competitors were selected to complete their flight demonstrator designs with the goal of executing flight tests starting in FY17. These flight tests will demonstrate critical technologies that best inform the requirements for FVL.

Because operations in Degraded Visual Environments (DVE) are the leading contributor to rotorcraft accidents and reduced operational effectiveness, the Air S&T Portfolio has the **Degraded Visual Environment Mitigation (DVE-M)** program. The DVE-M Program seeks to combine multispectral sensor systems (sensors that cover a wide spectrum from Ultra-Violet to InfraRed to Radio Frequencies (RF)), modernized flight control laws (algorithms that manage handling qualities of the aircraft), advanced cueing to enable pilotage in all DVEs and weather conditions and 360-degree situational awareness to aid pilot decision making. Flight trials to demonstrate the technology are scheduled for FY16 and FY17. Knowledge developed during the DVE-M program is intended to inform leadership on improvements to platform survivability and specific implementation decisions.

COMMAND, CONTROL, COMMUNICATIONS AND INTELLIGENCE S&T PORTFOLIO

The C3I S&T Portfolio provides oversight of BA2 and BA3 research, development and demonstration efforts that provide information and analysis for commanders' decisions and responsive capabilities for the future in congested electro-magnetic environments. These capabilities are supported by sustained efforts in sensors, communications, defensive and offensive cyber, EW, intelligence, mission command and information fusion in dynamic, congested and austere (disconnected, intermittent and limited) environments.

Areas of emphasis in the C3I portfolio include efforts in RF, hardware and software convergence, Positioning, Navigation and Timing (PNT), and technology red teaming and vulnerability analysis. The Army continues to investigate and improve electronic warfare to perform characterization and analysis of devices to develop detection

In FY17, S&T will integrate software into the Army Brigade network providing holistic cyber situational awareness...

and characterization techniques, tactics and technologies to mitigate the effects of contested environments (such as jamming) on Army C4ISR systems.

Army S&T is developing **Assured PNT (A-PNT)** technologies to provide dismounted and mounted Soldiers the capability to attain trusted PNT information while operating in conditions that impede or deny access to the Global Positioning System (GPS). These technologies include GPS antennas for mounted platforms and dismounted Soldiers, and pseudolite transceivers as an alternative source of GPS-like signals. In FY17, Army S&T will transition A-PNT solutions for mounted and dismounted applications to the Army's A-PNT PoR. Mounted and dismounted efforts are structured to provide a hub capability that delivers a position and timing signal to all vehicle or Soldier systems that require PNT.

The **RF Hardware/Software Convergence** effort is integrating multiple RF functions, such as communications, electronic warfare, PNT and signals intelligence into a common chassis with architecture standards and a common backplane. RF functions are built into cards that fit into

the chassis. This reduces size, weight and power requirements, enables interoperability and enables easy upgrades based on technology refresh or threat for specific mission applications.

The **Cyber S&T** efforts are aligned to operational gaps identified in the cyber capability based assessment, TRADOC emerging doctrine and requirements and the Army Cyber Materiel Development Strategy. Near-term defensive efforts focus on protection technologies that enhance resiliency, trust and agility of tactical networks and information as well as addressing top-tier threat actors. Near-term offensive efforts focus on technologies that provide robust and scalable architectures and cyber geolocation. In FY17, S&T will integrate software into the Army Brigade network providing holistic cyber situational awareness for assurance teams to assess the cyber battle space, detect/defend against known cyber weapons and enable network adaptation.

LETHALITY S&T PORTFOLIO

The Lethality S&T Portfolio supports BA2 and BA3 research, development and demonstration of offensive and defensive overmatch technologies for Army weapons. Ongoing efforts are focused on affordability, increasing range and precision, and improving the breadth of effects available to the Army. The Lethality S&T Portfolio is divided into air and missile defense, fire support, close combat, Soldier weapons, directed energy and weapon enablers subportfolios. Key enabling technology areas include: energetic materials, warheads and scalable effects, guidance and controls, rocket and gun propulsion, fuses and seekers. For directed energy, enabling technologies for both high-energy laser and high-power microwave technologies are being investigated.

Achieving tactical overmatch includes providing the Army with the capability for long-range fires and air and missile defense technologies to enable Army operations, especially in an Anti-Access/Area-Denial (A2/AD) environment, providing greater force protection and reducing life-cycle costs. Current programs are enhancing Army capabilities.

The **High Energy Laser (HEL) Tactical Vehicle Demonstrator** will demonstrate a mobile HEL integrated onto a Family of Medium Tactical Vehicle to defeat rocket, artillery and mortar, unmanned aerial vehicles, and intelligence, surveillance and reconnaissance threats. This effort supports the Indirect Fire Protection Capability PoR with the plan to transition a 100 kW laser system with precision targeting and tracking in degraded atmospheric conditions by FY22.

The **Long-Range Fires for Artillery and Rockets** program will enhance the Army's posture for A2/AD environments. The Lethality S&T Portfolio is developing long-range fires for both rockets and artillery technologies. For rockets, S&T is focusing on dual-pulse solid rocket motor propulsion to provide longer range rockets, maintaining precision in GPS-denied environments and providing both area and point lethal effects from a single warhead. For artillery, Army S&T is focused on the

whole system, looking to provide incremental improvements in the near term by reducing barrel weight and increasing its length, along with other weapon system improvements. In the longer term, Army S&T is looking at novel propellants, lightweight barrel materials and ammunition improvements to achieve a leap-ahead, long-range capability.

The Lethality Portfolio is also investing on technologies to increase the overmatch of **Soldier Weapons**. The key S&T technology areas are focused on reducing weapon weight while improving accuracy, lethality, capability and effective ranges to stay ahead of future threats and defeat targets in defilade.

To support these capabilities, the Army is conducting research on new energetic materials, called **Disruptive Energetics**, and is working toward both propulsive and explosive applications. These materials have significantly higher energetic yield than current materials and will increase the effectiveness and reduce the size of Army systems. This effort's goal is to increase the energy density of energetic materials by a factor of 3 to 10, which could revolutionize weapon systems.

MEDICAL S&T PORTFOLIO

The Medical S&T Portfolio supports BA2 and BA3 research, development and demonstration technologies regarding the wellness and fitness of our Soldiers from accession through training, deployment, treatment of injuries and return to duty or civilian life. Ongoing efforts address multiple threats to our Soldiers' health and readiness. The Medical S&T Portfolio's mission is to develop capabilities that ensure forces sustain optimal health, are protected from disease and injury, and receive optimal care in the event of injury or illness.

The Medical S&T Portfolio investment strategy covers subportfolios that include clinical and rehabilitative medicine, combat casualty care, military infectious disease, military operational medicine and systems biology. The Medical S&T Portfolio is focused on materiel and knowledge-based medical solutions including the delivery of improved combat casualty care, enhanced survivability, reduced impact due to injury and optimized downrange medical footprint. The portfolio also is seeking ways to enhance recovery, rehabilitation and reintegration of our Wounded Warriors in terms of duty, performance and quality of life.

The portfolio is also developing capability options to improve diagnosis, prevention and treatment of diseases with major impact on mission effectiveness and will enhance physiological performance in a variety of mission settings through solutions focused on maintaining, restoring and improving warfighter health and readiness, injury prevention and reduction, environmental health and protection, and psychological health and resilience. The Medical S&T Portfolio is preserving combat effectiveness and survivability through medical countermeasures to chemical and biological threats and clinical diagnostic capabilities.

Industry partners are an integral part of medical capability development and fielding. Army medical S&T labs collaborate with university and industrial partners to develop diagnostic tools and medical countermeasures (vaccines, therapeutics), in addition to capitalizing on the industrial base for use of diagnostic equipment supporting both the continental U.S. and deployed medical functions.

For example, **Psychological Health and Resilience and Traumatic Brain Injury** (TBI) research efforts support laboratory validation studies and field demonstrations of biomedical products designed to counteract myriad environmental and physiological stressors and materiel hazards Soldiers encounter in training and operational environments. The resulting biomedical capabilities are focused on protecting, sustaining and enhancing Soldiers' cognitive, physiological, physical and social performance. Key efforts are providing capability solutions in the form of technologies and tools that enhance warfighter survivability, assessment and prediction of injuries, assessments for postconcussive syndrome, and enhancing performance during continuous operations. Physiological health and environmental protection, injury prevention and reduction and psychological health and resilience are the three main thrust areas.

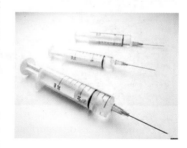

The Army's **Infectious Diseases (Drugs and Vaccines)** efforts will mature and demonstrate medical countermeasures, such as drugs and vaccines, and diagnostic tools for wound infections and militarily important naturally occurring infectious diseases yielding capabilities approved by the Food and Drug Administration. Research priorities are identified by worldwide medical surveillance and military threat analysis. These S&T efforts also support testing of personal protective measures such as repellents and insecticides regulated by the Environmental Protection Agency. The portfolio also develops and evaluates vaccine candidates to prevent diseases that impact warfighter readiness, such as the three major

The S&T portfolio is an essential enabler to critical requirements for sustainable training and operations.

causes of diarrhea (E. coli, Campylobacter and Shigella), Hemorrhagic Fever with Renal Syndrome and other hantavirus diseases, like those transmitted by contact with rodents and naturally found throughout Asia and Europe.

Our **Combat Casualty Care** efforts mature, demonstrate and validate promising medical technologies and methods, including control of severe bleeding, treatment for TBI, revival and stabilization of trauma patients, acute treatment of extremity (arms and legs) and facial injuries, treatment of severe burn wounds, treatment of single and multiple organ failures due to trauma and predictive indicators and decision aids for life support systems, including:

- Preclinical studies on contributions of the immune system and blood products to the body's ability to properly clot blood following trauma.
- Advanced patient monitoring technologies that rapidly and accurately detect early-onset of blood loss, continuously estimate blood loss volume and predict patient's risk for cardiovascular collapse.

- New methods to control life-threatening bleeding from areas of the body where tourniquets may not be used effectively, such as within the chest and abdomen, and from injuries to the armpit or groin.
- Improved blood platelet, an important factor required for blood clotting, storage technologies suitable for far-forward use.

Efforts in **Clinical Rehabilitative Medicine** support validation studies on safety and effectiveness of drugs, biologics (medical products derived from living organisms), medical devices and medical procedures intended to minimize long-term effects from battlefield injuries. Clinical Rehabilitative Medicine focuses on the execution of advanced technology development and clinical studies for treatment of ocular and visual system traumatic injury, and conducts regenerative medicine clinical studies enabling restoration of function and appearance by regenerating skin, muscle, nerve, vascular, bone and soft tissue (including genitals and abdomen) in battle-injured casualties. Areas of interest for regenerative medicine include healing without scarring, repair of compartment syndrome (muscle and nerve damage following reduced blood flow caused by swelling), replacement skin and facial reconstruction.

INNOVATION ENABLERS S&T PORTFOLIO

The Innovation Enablers S&T Portfolio includes activities that indirectly support PoRs and enable the Army to be successful. Within this portfolio we conduct research to minimize chemical and material environmental impacts, ensure the long-term viability of sustainable training infrastructure and contingency bases, and provide High Performance Computing Centers that conduct highly complex research and system design. This portfolio is an essential enabler to critical requirements for sustainable training and operations.

The S&T Innovation Enablers investment strategy includes the following subportfolios: ManTech; TMI; Environmental Quality Technology; and the High Performance Computing and Modernization Program.

The **Army ManTech Program** provides affordable and timely manufacturing solutions that address the Army's highest priority needs. It accomplishes this through technology developments and demonstrations that value the most effective, efficient and adaptable advanced manufacturing processes, procedures and standards. The program encourages strong internal and external partnerships across the manufacturing technologies community.

In a time of decreased modernization funds, it is incumbent upon the S&T Enterprise to drive down the technical risks associated with developing new capabilities. The **Technology Maturation Initiative** drives down technical risk, informs future requirements and provides affordable capabilities for the Army of the future. The Army TMI is a strategic partnership between the S&T Enterprise and acquisition community established to enable the transition of priority technologies at reduced cost and risk. This is done by partnering with acquisition program offices to further mature, prototype and validate emerging technologies beyond technology readiness levels typical of S&T products.

A current priority under TMI is the set of efforts focused on driving down cost and technical risk for technologies that provide dismounted and mounted Soldiers with trusted PNT information, while operating in conditions that impede or deny access to the GPS. The S&T Enterprise is addressing risk in four thrust areas. The first is pseudolites (pseudo-satellites) that augment or replace military GPS signals by developing a terrestrial/aerial based GPS-like signal, enabling signal acquisition/tracking, navigation and timing in degraded or denied environments. The second is a PNT hub for vehicular applications that develops a robust system to support all PNT needs on the platform and maintains PNT capability during operations in GPS-denied environments. Third, the S&T Enterprises are developing a PNT hub for dismounted Soldiers systems that has low size, weight and power and can provide assured PNT signals for all Soldier equipment. Finally, anti-jam antennas that enable GPS signal acquisition and tracking in degraded or denied environments are being investigated.

These PNT efforts leverage traditional S&T and TMI investments and have a direct tie into the A-PNT PoR. By further developing these technologies to a relatively high-maturity level, we are driving down the PoR's technical risk, accelerating capability and ensuring that our troops can operate in a contested environment.

The **High Performance Computing Modernization Program** provides supercomputing resources to DoD scientists and engineers to conduct advanced research and design by demonstrating and maturing the most advanced, leading-edge computational architectures and exploiting these systems with complementary specialized expertise. The program is maturing the Defense Research and Engineering Network, a leading-edge digital network that securely delivers computational capabilities to the distributed DoD Research, Development, Test and Evaluation (RDT&E) community. The program leverages specialized expertise from DoD, other Federal departments, industry and academia to demonstrate leading-edge software application codes. These synergistic activities collectively demonstrate horizontal technologies that are exploited throughout the DoD RDT&E community to ensure DoD maintains the most advanced research ecosystem in the areas of computationally intensive modelling and design.

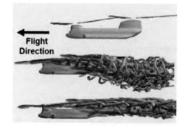

The **Engineered Resilient Systems Program** applies high-performance modeling and simulation tools from concept generation through tradespace analysis to virtual prototyping and testing to increase affordability, adaptability and effectiveness of acquisition processes.

The **Environmental Quality Technology** focus area investigates and evaluates enabling tools and methods that support the sustainment of Army training and testing activities. A specific focus is maintaining regulatory compliance while limiting future Army liability in operations and training. Environmental effects of new materials (such as nano-materials) developed by the Army are investigated to mitigate threats to the environment. The goal of the Environmental Quality and Technology focus area is to develop the understanding required to limit environmental impacts of Army operations and training.

BASIC RESEARCH S&T PORTFOLIO

The Basic Research (BA1) S&T Portfolio is the Army's primary driver to enabling leap-ahead technologies that will enhance Soldier capability and increase Soldier protection. It is focused on discovering and understanding of fundamental science through Army-led investigations and by assessing break-through innovations to improve overall scientific knowledge. It is the critical hedge for acquiring new knowledge in areas that hold great promise in advancing new and technically challenging Army capabilities and concepts. Basic research investment generates new knowledge for the Army to address diverse, rapidly evolving threats, while simultaneously attracting the country's most talented and gifted scientists and engineers to the future workforce.

The basic research strategy includes investing in Army labs and university-based research. For example, the Army uses University Affiliated Research Centers, Collaborative Research Alliances, Multi-Disciplinary University Research Initiatives and the Single Investigator Program, all of which enable the Army to take advantage of innovation and research opportunities through academic and industry partnerships. Collaboration among industry, academia and the Army is a key element of this strategy, as each member brings a distinctly different approach to research. Academia is known for cutting-edge innovation. Industry partners leverage existing research results for transition and deal with technology bottlenecks, and Army researchers keep the program focused on solving complex Army technical problems. Major strategic efforts for basic research and their associated collaborative alliances are below.

By using **Multiscale Modeling of Materials**, fundamental materials science research will reduce the time from materials-based discovery to capability delivery by half and the cost to a fraction of what it is today. The new paradigm is to manipulate matter at any scale, at the atomic level if necessary, to create the required properties for a range of material classes (structural, electronic, energetic, etc.) The result will be a materials-by-design capability for ballistic protection, energetic and electronic materials built using a multiscale approach, heavily leveraging computational materials science.

Research into **Intelligent Systems** will discover, develop and enable robotic devices and systems with highly sophisticated sense, response and processing systems approaching that of biological systems. We are developing truly intelligent systems with a high degree of autonomous capability. This research endeavors to develop autonomous systems that can act appropriately in uncertain environments and team with Soldiers. This includes autonomous navigation and exploration in static and dynamic urban and complex environments, logical understanding of actions taken by other autonomous agents or humans, and creative, adaptable intelligent architectures that expand capabilities.

Research into **Human Sciences and Cybernetics** science and modeling of human-machine behavior can provide critical insights enabling next-generation Soldier-system interactions. Basic research seeks to understand  control and communication in complex human systems to capture social processes, structure and change in extrasensory patterns of physical energy in the environment and real-time cortical brain dynamics.

The objective is to provide new principles, algorithms and technical approaches that drive innovation for future Soldier-systems interaction and enable better control of technology or weapons systems and reduce Soldiers' cognitive workloads.

Army research into **Quantum Effects and Quantum Information Sciences** focuses on generating advances in quantum science. Quantum science is the study of the behavior of matter and its interactions with energy on the scale of atoms and subatomic particles. This research will enable revolutionary approaches to information processing, secure communications and cryptography, jam-proof position and navigation, and ultraprecise sensing and imaging.

CONCLUSION

As the Army S&T program continues to identify and harvest technologies suitable for transition to our force, we aim to remain ever vigilant of potential and emerging threats. We are implementing a strategic approach to modernization that includes an awareness of existing and potential gaps, and we continue to work towards understanding emerging threats, knowledge of state-of-the-art commercial, academic and government research, and understanding competing needs for limited resources. Army S&T will sharpen research efforts to focus upon these core capabilities it needs to sustain while identifying promising or disruptive technologies. Ultimately, our focus remains on Soldiers. Army S&T consistently seeks new avenues to increase Soldiers' capabilities and ensure their technological superiority today, tomorrow and decades from now. The Army S&T mission is never complete. We will continue working to ensure that our Soldiers are always equipped with the technology to win.

Appendices

Army Combat Organizations

Army organizations are inherently built around people and the tasks they must perform. Major combat organizations are composed of smaller forces, as shown here.

SQUAD
- Leader is a sergeant
- Smallest unit in Army organization
- Size varies depending on type: Infantry (9 Soldiers), Armor (4 Soldiers), Engineer (10 Soldiers)
- Three or four squads make up a platoon

PLATOON
- Leader is a lieutenant
- Size varies: Infantry (40 Soldiers), Armor (4 tanks, 16 Soldiers)
- Three or four platoons make up a company

COMPANY
- Leader is a captain
- Usually up to 220 Soldiers
- Artillery unit of this size is called a battery
- Armored Cavalry or Air Cavalry unit is called a troop
- Basic tactical element of the maneuver battalion or cavalry squadron
- Normally 5 companies make up a battalion

BATTALION
- Leader is a lieutenant colonel
- Tactically and administratively self-sufficient
- Armored Cavalry and Air Cavalry equivalents are called squadrons
- Two or more combat battalions make up a brigade

BRIGADE
- Leader is a colonel
- May be employed on independent or semi-independent operations
- Combat, Combat Support or Service Support elements may be attached to perform specific missions
- Normally 3 combat brigades are in a division

DIVISION
- Leader is a major general
- Fully structured division has own brigade-size artillery, aviation, engineer, combat support and service elements
- Two or more divisions make up a corps commanded by a lieutenant general

To better confront current and future threats, the Army transformed its force structure into Brigade Combat Teams (BCT). The goal is to provide more flexible and self-contained forces with the capability of rapid deployment and the ability to engage in the full spectrum of warfare without sacrificing lethality and staying power on the battlefield. These BCT are organized as Infantry (IBCT), Heavy (HBCT) and Stryker (SBCT).

Glossary of Terms

ACQUISITION CATEGORIES (ACAT)

ACAT I

ACAT I programs are Major Defense Acquisition Programs (MDAP) that are estimated to achieve the statutorily defined MDAP cost threshold or are designated MDAP by the Army Acquisition Executive (AAE) or the Defense Acquisition Executive (DAE).

Dollar value: estimated by the Under Secretary of Defense for Acquisition, Technology and Logistics (USD(AT&L)) to require an eventual total expenditure for research, development, test and evaluation (RDT&E) of more than $480 million in Fiscal Year (FY) 2014 constant dollars or, for Procurement, of more than $2.790 billion in FY 2014. ACAT I programs have two subcategories:

1. **ACAT ID,** for which the Milestone Decision Authority (MDA) is the USD(AT&L) acting as the DAE. The "D" refers to the Defense Acquisition Board, which advises the DAE at major decision points.
2. **ACAT IC,** for which the MDA is the DoD Component Head or, if delegated, the DoD Component Acquisition Executive (CAE). The "C" refers to Component; for the Army, the MDA is the AAE. The DAE designates programs ACAT ID or ACAT IC.

ACAT IA programs are Major Automated Information System (MAIS) acquisition programs, or programs designated by the USD(AT&L) to be ACAT IA.

Dollar value: estimated to exceed $40 million in FY 2014 constant dollars for all expenditures, for all increments, regardless of the appropriation or fund source, directly related to the Automated Information System (AIS) definition, design, development and deployment, and incurred in any single fiscal year; or $165 million in FY 2014 constant dollars for all expenditures, for all increments, regardless of the appropriation or fund source, directly related to the AIS definition, design, development and deployment, and incurred from the beginning of the Materiel Solution Analysis Phase through deployment at all sites; or $520 million in FY 2014 constant dollars for all expenditures, for all increments, regardless

of the appropriation or fund source, directly related to the AIS definition, design, development, deployment, operations and maintenance, and incurred from the beginning of the Materiel Solution Analysis Phase through sustainment for the estimated useful life of the system.

ACAT IA programs have two subcategories:
1. **ACAT IAM**, for which the MDA is the DAE or as delegated. The "M" refers to the Major Automated Information System Review Council. (Change 4, 5000.2-R).
2. **ACAT IAC**, for which the MDA is the head of the DoD component or, if delegated, the CAE. The "C" refers to Component.

ACAT II programs are defined as those acquisition programs that do not meet the criteria for an ACAT I acquisition program or are programs designated ACAT II by the MDA. The dollar value is estimated to require total expenditure for RDT&E of more than $185 million in FY 2014 constant dollars, or for Procurement of more than $835 million in FY 2014 constant dollars.

ACAT III programs are defined as those acquisition programs that do not meet the criteria for an ACAT I, an ACAT IA or an ACAT II. The MDA is designated by the AAE and shall be at the lowest appropriate level, typically the Program Executive Officer. The estimated costs for ACAT III acquisition programs are below the thresholds for ACAT II acquisition programs. ACAT III also includes AIS acquisition programs that do not exceed the threshold of MAIS acquisition programs.

ACQUISITION PHASE

Each acquisition phase encompasses all the tasks and activities needed to bring a program to the next major milestone. Each acquisition lifecycle phase provides a logical means of progressively translating broadly stated mission needs into well-defined system-specific requirements and ultimately into operationally effective, suitable and survivable systems. The acquisition phases for the systems described in this handbook are defined below:

Materiel Solution Analysis Phase

The purpose of this phase is to conduct the analysis and other activities needed to choose the concept for the product that will be acquired, to begin translating validated capability gaps into system-specific requirements including the Key Performance Parameters and Key System Attributes, and to conduct planning to support a decision on the acquisition strategy for the product. Analysis of Alternatives (AoA), key trades among cost, schedule, performance, affordability analysis, risk analysis and planning for risk mitigation are key activities in this phase.

Technology Maturation & Risk Reduction (TMRR) Phase

The purpose of this phase is to reduce technology risk, determine and mature the appropriate set of technologies to be integrated into a full system, and demonstrate critical technology elements on prototypes. This phase is a continuous discovery and development process reflecting close collaboration between the Science and Technology (S&T) community, the user and the system developer. It is an iterative process designed to assess the viability of technologies while simultaneously refining requirements. Entrance into this phase depends on the completion of the AoA, a proposed materiel solution and full funding for planned TMRR activity.

Engineering & Manufacturing Development (EMD) Phase

The purpose of the EMD Phase is to develop a system or an increment of capability; complete full system integration; develop an affordable and executable manufacturing process; ensure operational supportability with particular attention to minimizing the logistics footprint; implement human systems integration; design for producibility; ensure affordability; protect critical program information by implementing appropriate techniques such as anti-tamper; and demonstrate system integration, interoperability, safety and utility. The Capability Development Document, Acquisition Strategy, Systems Engineering Plan and Test and Evaluation Master Plan shall guide this effort. Entrance into this phase depends on technology maturity (including software), approved requirements and full funding. Unless some other factor is overriding in its impact, the maturity of the technology shall determine the path to be followed.

Production & Deployment Phase

The purpose of the Production & Deployment Phase is to achieve an operational capability that satisfies mission needs. Operational test and evaluation shall determine the effectiveness and suitability of the system. The Milestone Decision Authority shall make the decision to commit DoD to production at Milestone C and shall document the decision in an Acquisition Decision Memorandum. Milestone C authorizes entry into Low-Rate Initial Production (LRIP) (for Major Defense Acquisition Programs (MDAP) and major systems), into production or procurement (for nonmajor systems that do not require LRIP), or into limited deployment in support of operational testing for Major Automated Information System programs or software-intensive systems with no production components. Entrance into this phase depends on the following criteria: acceptable performance in Developmental Test and Evaluation and Operational Assessment for Defense Operational Test and Evaluation oversight programs; mature software capability; no significant manufacturing risks; manufacturing processes under control when Milestone C is a Full-Rate Production (FRP) decision; an approved Initial Capability Document if Milestone C is program initiation; an approved Capability Production Document (CPD); a refined integrated architecture; acceptable interoperability; acceptable operational supportability; and demonstration that the system is affordable throughout the lifecycle, fully funded and properly phased for rapid acquisition. The CPD reflects the operational requirements, informed by EMD results, and details the performance expected of the production system. If Milestone C approves LRIP, a subsequent review and decision shall authorize FRP.

Operations & Support Phase

The purpose of the Operations & Support Phase is to execute a support program that meets materiel readiness and operational support performance requirements, and sustains the system in the most cost-effective manner over its total lifecycle. Planning for this phase shall begin prior to program initiation and shall be documented in the Life-Cycle Sustainment Plan (LCSP). The Operations and Support Phase has two major efforts: Life-Cycle Sustainment and Disposal. Entrance into the Operations and Support Phase depends on meeting the following criteria: an approved CPD, an approved LCSP and a successful FRP decision.

ACQUISITION PROGRAM

An acquisition program is a directed, funded effort designed to provide a new, improved or continuing weapon system or Automated Information System capability in response to a validated operational need. Acquisition programs are divided into different categories that are established to facilitate decentralized decision making, execution and compliance with statutory requirements. See Acquisition Category, above.

ADVANCED CONCEPT TECHNOLOGY DEMONSTRATIONS (ACTD)

ACTD are a means of demonstrating the use of emerging or mature technology to address critical military needs. ACTD themselves are not acquisition programs, although they are designed to provide a residual, usable capability upon completion. If the user determines that additional quantities are needed beyond the residual capability and that these quantities can be funded, the additional procurement shall constitute an acquisition program with an acquisition category generally commensurate with the dollar value and risk of the additional buy.

AUTOMATED INFORMATION SYSTEM (AIS)

An AIS is a combination of computer hardware and software, data, or telecommunications that performs functions such as collecting, processing, transmitting and displaying information. Excluded are computer resources, both hardware and software that are physically part of, dedicated to, or essential in real-time to the mission performance of weapon systems.

COMMERCIAL AND NON-DEVELOPMENTAL ITEMS

Market research and analysis shall be conducted to determine the availability and suitability of existing Commercial and Non-Developmental Items prior to the commencement of a development effort, during the development effort and prior to the preparation of any product description. For ACAT I and IA programs, while few commercial items meet requirements at a system level, numerous commercial components, processes and practices have application to DoD systems.

DEMILITARIZATION AND DISPOSAL

At the end of its useful life, a system must be demilitarized and disposed. During Demilitarization and Disposal, the program manager shall ensure materiel determined to require demilitarization is controlled and shall ensure disposal is carried out in a way that minimizes DoD's liability due to environmental, safety, security and health issues.

DEVELOPMENTAL TEST AND EVALUATION (DT&E)

DT&E shall identify potential operational and technological capabilities and limitations of the alternative concepts and design options being pursued; support the identification and description of design technical risks; and provide data and analysis in support of the decision to certify the system ready for operational test and evaluation.

FULL MATERIEL RELEASE

This process ensures all Army materiel is safe, operationally suitable and supportable before release of issue to users. The assigned Program Manager determines necessary activities to certify materiel release readiness. This decision should be accomplished prior to Full-Rate Production.

JOINT PROGRAM MANAGEMENT

Any acquisition system, subsystem, component or technology program that involves a strategy that includes funding by more than one DoD component during any phase of a system's lifecycle shall be defined as a Joint program. Joint programs shall be consolidated and co-located at the location of the lead component's program office, to the maximum extent practicable.

LIVE FIRE TEST AND EVALUATION (LFT&E)

LFT&E must be conducted on a covered system, major munition program, missile program, or a product improvement to a covered system, major munition program or missile program before it can proceed beyond Low-Rate Initial Production (LRIP). A covered system is any vehicle, weapon platform or conventional weapon system that includes features designed to provide some degree of protection to users in combat and that is an ACAT I or II program. Depending upon its intended use, a Commercial or Non-Developmental Item may be a covered system or a part of a covered system. Systems requiring LFT&E may not proceed beyond LRIP until realistic survivability or lethality testing is completed and the report required by statute is submitted to the prescribed Congressional committees.

LOW-RATE INITIAL PRODUCTION (LRIP)

The objective of this activity is to produce the minimum quantity necessary to provide production-configured or representative articles for operational tests; establish an initial production base for the system; and permit an orderly increase in the production rate for the system, sufficient to lead to Full-Rate Production upon successful completion of Operational Testing. The LRIP quantity may not exceed 10 percent of the total production quantity without an approved waiver by the Acquisition Executive and documented in the Acquisition Decision Memorandum.

MAJOR AUTOMATED INFORMATION SYSTEM (MAIS) ACQUISITION PROGRAM

A MAIS is an AIS acquisition program that is designated by the Under Secretary of Defense for Acquisition, Technology and Logistics as a MAIS, or estimated to require program costs in any single year in excess of $40 million in Fiscal Year (FY) 2014 constant dollars, total program costs in excess of $165 million in FY 2014 constant dollars, or total lifecycle costs in excess of $520 million in FY 2014 constant dollars. MAIS do not include highly sensitive, classified programs.

MAJOR DEFENSE ACQUISITION PROGRAM (MDAP)

An MDAP is an acquisition program that is not a highly sensitive, classified program as determined by the Secretary of Defense and that is designated by the Under Secretary of Defense for Acquisition, Technology and Logistics (USD(AT&L)) as an MDAP, or estimated by the USD(AT&L) to require an eventual total expenditure for research, development, test and evaluation of more than $480 million in Fiscal Year (FY) 2014 constant dollars or, for Procurement, of more than $2.790 billion in FY 2014 constant dollars.

MAJOR MILESTONE

A major milestone is the decision point that separates the phases of an acquisition program. MDAP milestones include, as examples, the decisions to authorize entry into the Engineering & Manufacturing Development Phase or Full-Rate Production. MAIS milestones may include, for example, the decision to begin Technology Maturation and Risk Reduction (TMRR).

- **Milestone A:** Entry into the TMRR Phase
- **Milestone B:** Entry into the Engineering & Manufacturing Development Phase
- **Milestone C:** Entry into the Production & Deployment Phase

MAJOR SYSTEMS

Dollar value: estimated by the DoD Component Head to require an eventual total expenditure for research, development, test and evaluation of more than $185 million in Fiscal Year (FY) 2014 constant dollars, or for Procurement, of more than $835 million in FY 2014 constant dollars. (Lowest category for major system designation is ACAT II).

MILESTONE

The point at which a recommendation is made and approval sought regarding starting or continuing an acquisition program, e.g., proceeding to the next phase.

MILESTONE DECISION AUTHORITY (MDA)

This is the individual designated in accordance with criteria established by the Under Secretary of Defense for Acquisition, Technology and Logistics for Automated Information System acquisition programs, to approve entry of an acquisition program into the next phase.

- **Defense Acquisition Executive (DAE):** The individual responsible for supervising the Defense Acquisition System. The DAE takes precedence on all acquisition matters after the Secretary of Defense and the Deputy Secretary of Defense.
- **Army Acquisition Executive (AAE):** The individual solely responsible for acquisition matters within the Department of the Army and the single decision authority for all Army acquisition matters. The AAE is responsible for approving requests to initiate new acquisition programs, and will do so only when they are supported by approved capability documents, requisite funding and program documentation.
- **Program Executive Officer:** A military or civilian assigned program responsibilities for the execution and management of ACAT II and III programs, or for any other program determined by the AAE to require dedicated executive management.

MODIFICATIONS

Any modification that is of sufficient cost and complexity that it could itself qualify as an ACAT I or ACAT IA program shall be considered for management purposes as a separate acquisition effort. Modifications that do not cross the ACAT I or IA threshold shall be considered part of the program being modified, unless the acquisition program is no longer in production. In that case, the modification shall be considered a separate acquisition effort.

OPERATIONAL TEST AND EVALUATION (OT&E)

OT&E shall be structured to determine the operational effectiveness and suitability of a system under realistic conditions, e.g., combat, and to determine that the operational performance requirements are satisfied. The following procedures are mandatory: Threat or threat representative forces, targets, and countermeasures, validated in coor-

dination with the Defense Intelligence Agency, shall be used; typical users shall operate and maintain the system or item under conditions simulating combat stress and peacetime conditions; the independent Operational Test Activity shall use production or production representative articles for the dedicated phase of OT&E that supports the Full-Rate Production decision, or for ACAT IA or other acquisition programs, the Deployment decision; and the use of modeling and simulation shall be considered during test planning.

OPERATIONS AND SUPPORT

The objectives of this activity are the execution of a support program that meets the threshold values of all support performance requirements and sustainment of them in the most lifecycle-cost-effective manner. A Follow-on Operational Test and Evaluation program that assesses performance and quality, compatibility, and interoperability, and identifies deficiencies shall be conducted, as appropriate. This activity shall also include the execution of operational support plans, to include the transition from contractor to organic support, if appropriate.

WARFIGHTING FUNCTIONS

A Warfighting Function is a group of tasks and systems (people, organizations, information and processes) united by a common purpose that commanders use to accomplish missions. The Army's Warfighting Functions are fundamentally linked to the Joint functions.

Mission Command

The Mission Command Warfighting Function develops and integrates those activities enabling a commander to balance the art of command and the science of control. This fundamental philosophy of command places people, rather than technology or systems, at the center. Under this philosophy, commanders drive the operations process through their activities of understand, visualize, describe, direct, lead and assess. They develop teams, both within their own organizations and with Joint, interagency and multinational partners. Commanders inform and influence audiences, inside and outside their organizations. The commander leads the staff's tasks under the science of control.

The four primary staff tasks are conduct the operations process (plan, prepare, execute and assess); conduct knowledge management and information management; conduct, inform and influence activities; and conduct cyber electromagnetic activities.

Movement and Maneuver
The Movement and Maneuver Warfighting Function is the related tasks and systems that move and employ forces to achieve a position of relative advantage over the enemy and other threats. Direct fire and close combat are inherent in maneuver. This function includes tasks associated with force projection related to gaining a positional advantage over the enemy.

Intelligence
The Intelligence Warfighting Function is the related tasks and systems that facilitate understanding the enemy, terrain and civil considerations. It includes the synchronization of collection requirements with the execution of tactical tasks such as reconnaissance, surveillance and related intelligence operations. This Warfighting Function includes specific intelligence and communication structures at each echelon.

Fires
The Fires Warfighting Function is the related tasks and systems that provide collective and coordinated use of Army indirect fires, air and missile defense, and Joint fires through the targeting process.

Sustainment
The Sustainment Warfighting Function is the related tasks and systems that provide support and services to ensure freedom of action, extended operational reach and prolonged endurance. The endurance of Army forces is primarily a function of their sustainment. Sustainment determines the depth and duration of Army operations. It is essential to retaining and exploiting the initiative.

Maneuver Support and Protection
The Maneuver Support and Protection Warfighting Function is the related tasks and systems that preserve the force so the commander can apply maximum combat power to accomplish the mission. Preserving the force includes protecting personnel (friendly combatants and noncombatants) and physical assets of the United States, host-nation and multinational military and civilian partners.

Engagement
The Engagement Warfighting Function is the related tasks and systems that influence the behaviors of a people, security forces and governments.

ADDITIONAL RESOURCES

For additional information on acquisition terms, or terms not defined, please refer to DoD Directives, available on the Internet at http://www.dtic.mil/whs/directives/corres/dir.html; DoD Instruction 5000.02, Operation of the Defense Acquisition System, available on the Internet at http://www.dtic.mil/whs/directives/corres/pdf/500002p.pdf; or the Defense Acquisition Guidebook, available on the Internet at https://dag.dau.mil/Pages/Default.aspx.

Systems by Contractors

AAI Corporation
- RQ-7Bv2 Shadow Tactical Unmanned Aircraft System (TUAS)

AASKI Technology
- Defense Enterprise Wideband SATCOM System (DEWSS)
- Global Command and Control System – Army (GCCS-A)
- Tactical Mission Command (TMC)

Acambis plc
- Medical Countermeasure Systems – Joint Vaccine Acquisition Program (JVAP) and Bioscavenger

Accenture Federal Services
- General Fund Enterprise Business Systems (GFEBS)

Action Manufacturing Company
- 2.75 Inch Rocket Systems (Hydra-70)
- Artillery Ammunition

Adams Communication & Engineering Technology, Inc.
- Airborne Reconnaissance Low (ARL)
- Enhanced Medium Altitude Reconnaissance and Surveillance System (EMARSS)
- Fixed Wing

AeroVironment, Inc.
- RQ-11B Raven Small Unmanned Aircraft System (SUAS)

Airborne Systems North America
- Joint Precision Airdrop System (JPADS)

Airbus Defense and Space, Inc.
- Lakota UH-72A Light Utility Helicopter (LUH)

Airbus Helicopters, Inc.
- Lakota UH-72A Light Utility Helicopter (LUH)

Allison Transmission
- Family of Medium Tactical Vehicles (FMTV)

AlphaMicron, Inc.
- Soldier Protection System (SPS)

AM General LLC
- High Mobility Multipurpose Wheeled Vehicle (HMMWV)
- Improved Ribbon Bridge (IRB)

American Defense Systems, Inc. (ADSI)
- High Mobility Engineer Excavator (HMEE) I and III

American Ordnance LLC
- Artillery Ammunition

American Science & Engineering, Inc.
- Non-Intrusive Inspection Systems (NIIS)

AMT
- Mortar Systems

AMTEC Corporation
- Medium Caliber Ammunition (MCA)

Anniston Army Depot
- Assault Breacher Vehicle (ABV)

Mine Protection Vehicle Family (MPFV), Mine Clearing Vehicle (MCV), Explosive Hazard Pre-Detonation (EHP)

Applied Companies
- Aviation Combined Arms Tactical Trainer (AVCATT)

ArgonST (A Boeing Company)
- Guardrail Common Sensor (GR/CS)

Armtec
- Artillery Ammunition

Army Aviation and Missile Research Development and Engineering Center (AMRDEC) Prototype Integration Facility (PIF), Redstone Defense Systems
- Black Hawk UH/HH-60

AT&T
- Installation Information Infrastructure Modernization Program (I3MP)

Avon Protection Systems, Inc.
- Joint Service General Purpose Mask (JSGPM) M-50/M-51

Systems by Contractors

Avox Systems
- Joint Service Aircrew Mask – Rotary Wing (JSAM RW) (MPU-5)

AVT Simulation
- Aviation Combined Arms Tactical Trainer (AVCATT)
- Close Combat Tactical Trainer (CCTT)

BAE Systems
- 2.75 Inch Rocket Systems (Hydra-70)
- Airborne Reconnaissance Low (ARL)
- Armored Multi-Purpose Vehicle (AMPV)
- Common Missile Warning System (CMWS), Laser Detection System (LDS), Radar Warning Receiver (RWR), Advanced Threat Infrared Countermeasures (ATIRCM) and Common Infrared Countermeasure (CIRCM) programs
- Enhanced Night Vision Goggle (ENVG)
- Family of Weapon Sights – Individual (FWS-I)
- High Mobility Engineer Excavator (HMEE) I and III

- Joint Effects Targeting System (JETS) Target Location Designation System (TLDS)
- Lightweight 155 mm Howitzer System (LW155)
- M109 Family of Vehicles (FOV) (Paladin/FAASV, PIM SPH/CAT)
- Mine Protection Vehicle Family (MPFV), Mine Clearing Vehicle (MCV), Explosive Hazard Pre-Detonation (EHP)
- Soldier Protection System (SPS)
- T-9 Medium Dozer

BAE Systems, Inc.
- Bradley Fighting Vehicle Systems (BFVS)
- M88A2 Improved Recovery Vehicle HERCULES (Heavy Equipment Recovery Combat Utility Lift and Evacuation System)

Barrett Firearms Manufacturing
- Small Arms – Precision Weapons

Battelle Memorial Institute
- Chemical Biological Medical Systems – Therapeutics
- Next Generation Chemical Detector (NGCD)

Bechtel National, Inc.
- Assembled Chemical Weapons Alternatives (ACWA)

Bechtel Parsons Blue Grass
- Assembled Chemical Weapons Alternatives (ACWA)

Berg Companies, Inc.
- Force Provider (FP)

Bethel Industries
- Soldier Protection System (SPS)

BioFire Defense, LLC
- Medical Countermeasure Systems (MCS) – Diagnostics

Birdon Corporation
- Improved Ribbon Bridge (IRB)

Bluegrass Army Depot
- Artillery Ammunition

Boeing
- AH-64D/E Apache
- CH-47F Chinook
- Enhanced Medium Altitude Reconnaissance and Surveillance System (EMARSS)
- Integrated Family of Test Equipment (IFTE)

Boeing Defense, Space and Security
- Fixed Wing

Booz Allen Hamilton
- Army Key Management System (AKMS)
- Common Hardware Systems (CHS)
- Distributed Common Ground System – Army (DCGS-A) Increment 1
- Integrated Personnel and Pay System – Army (IPPS-A)

Bruker Detection Corporation
- Next Generation Chemical Detector (NGCD)

Buffalo Turbine
- Mine Protection Vehicle Family (MPFV), Mine Clearing Vehicle (MCV), Explosive Hazard Pre-Detonation (EHP)

BWAY Corporation
- Small Caliber Ammunition

CACI International, Inc.
- Army Key Management System (AKMS)
- Enhanced Medium Altitude Reconnaissance and Surveillance System (EMARSS)
- Fixed Wing
- Integrated Personnel and Pay System – Army (IPPS-A)
- Nuclear Biological Chemical Reconnaissance Vehicle (NBCRV) – Stryker Sensor Suites

Cangene Corporation
- Medical Countermeasure Systems – Joint Vaccine Acquisition Program (JVAP) and Bioscavenger

Capco, Inc.
- Small Arms – Crew Served Weapons

Carleton Technologies, Inc.
- Air Warrior (AW)

Carnegie Robotics LLC
- Autonomous Mine Detection System (AMDS)

Carter Enterprises, LLC
- Soldier Protection System (SPS)

Case New Holland
- High Mobility Engineer Excavator (HMEE) I and III

Casteel Manufacturing, Inc.
- Line Haul Tractor

Caterpillar, Inc.
- 120M Motor Grader
- 621G Scraper
- Family of Medium Tactical Vehicles (FMTV)
- T-9 Medium Dozer

Ceradyne, Inc.
- Soldier Protection System (SPS)

CGI Federal
- Common Missile Warning System (CMWS), Laser Detection System (LDS), Radar Warning Receiver (RWR), Advanced Threat Infrared Countermeasures (ATIRCM) and Common Infrared Countermeasure (CIRCM) programs

Charleston Marine Containers, Inc.
- Force Provider (FP)

ChemImage Corporation
- Next Generation Chemical Detector (NGCD)

Chemring Detection Systems
- Joint Biological Tactical Detection System (JBTDS)
- Next Generation Chemical Detector (NGCD)

Chemring Ordnance
- Artillery Ammunition

Choctaw Manufacturing Defense Contractors
- Unit Water Pod System (Camel II)

Cole Engineering Services, Inc.
- Aviation Combined Arms Tactical Trainer (AVCATT)
- One Semi-Automated Force (OneSAF)

Colt Defense LLC
- Small Arms – Crew Served Weapons
- Small Arms – Individual Weapons

Communications & Ear Protection, Inc.
- Air Warrior (AW)

Computer Sciences Corporation
- Common Missile Warning System (CMWS), Laser Detection System (LDS), Radar Warning Receiver (RWR), Advanced Threat Infrared Countermeasures (ATIRCM) and Common Infrared Countermeasure (CIRCM) programs
- Global Command and Control System – Army (GCCS-A)
- Medical Simulation Training Center (MSTC)
- Tactical Mission Command (TMC)

Systems by Contractors

CONCO
- 2.75 Inch Rocket Systems (Hydra-70)

Connected Logistics, Inc.
- General Fund Enterprise Business Systems (GFEBS)

Crane Army Ammunition Activity
- Artillery Ammunition

Critical Solutions International, Inc.
- Mine Protection Vehicle Family (MPFV), Mine Clearing Vehicle (MCV), Explosive Hazard Pre-Detonation (EHP)

Cubic Global Defense
- Engagement Skills Trainer (EST)
- Home Station Instrumentation Training System (HITS)
- Instrumentable – Multiple Integrated Laser Engagement System (I-MILES)

Cummins Power Generation
- Tactical Electric Power (TEP)

CymSTAR LLC
- Aviation Combined Arms Tactical Trainer (AVCATT)

Daimler Trucks North America LLC/Freightliner
- Line Haul Tractor

David H. Pollock Consultants
- Common Missile Warning System (CMWS), Laser Detection System (LDS), Radar Warning Receiver (RWR), Advanced Threat Infrared Countermeasures (ATIRCM) and Common Infrared Countermeasure (CIRCM) programs

Day & Zimmerman Lone Star LLC
- Artillery Ammunition

Dell
- Distributed Common Ground System – Army (DCGS-A) Increment 1

Detroit Diesel
- Line Haul Tractor

DOK-ING d.o.o.
- M160 Robotic Mine Flail

Draper Laboratory, Inc.
- Joint Precision Airdrop System (JPADS)

DRS Environmental Systems, Inc.
- Improved Environmental Control Units (IECU)

DRS Fermont
- Tactical Electric Power (TEP)

DRS Sustainment Systems, Inc.
- Modular Fuel System (MFS)

DRS Technologies, Inc.
- Assault Breacher Vehicle (ABV)
- Combat Service Support Communications (CSS Comms)
- Enhanced Night Vision Goggle (ENVG)
- Family of Weapon Sights – Individual (FWS-I)
- Heavy Equipment Transporter System (HETS)
- Joint Battle Command – Platform (JBC-P)
- Joint Effects Targeting System (JETS) Target Location Designation System (TLDS)

- Joint Service Transportable Decontaminating System Small Scale (JSTDS-SS) M26
- Test Equipment Modernization (TEMOD)

Dynetics, Inc.
- Calibration Sets Equipment (CALSETS)

DynPort Vaccine Company LLC
- Medical Countermeasure Systems – Joint Vaccine Acquisition Program (JVAP) and Bioscavenger

Elbit Systems of America
- Mortar Systems

Emergent BioSolutions (BioPort)
- Medical Countermeasure Systems – Joint Vaccine Acquisition Program (JVAP) and Bioscavenger

Engineering Solutions and Products
- Warfighter Information Network – Tactical (WIN-T) Increment 1

Entwistle
- Load Handling System Compatible Water Tank Rack (Hippo)

Esri
- Distributed Common Ground System – Army (DCGS-A) Increment 1

Fabrique National Manufacturing, LLC
- Small Arms – Crew Served Weapons

Fidelity Technologies Corporation
- Tactical Electric Power (TEP)

FLIR Systems, Inc.
- Chemical, Biological, Radiological, Nuclear Dismounted Reconnaissance Sets, Kits, and Outfits (CBRN DR SKO)
- Next Generation Chemical Detector (NGCD)

Fluke Corporation
- Calibration Sets Equipment (CALSETS)
- Test Equipment Modernization (TEMOD)

Future Skies
- Tactical Mission Command (TMC)

Garrett Container Systems, Inc.
- Family of Military Working Dogs Equipment and Kennel

General Atomics Aeronautical Systems, Inc.
- MQ-1C Gray Eagle Unmanned Aircraft System (UAS)

General Dynamics
- 2.75 Inch Rocket Systems (Hydra-70)
- Advanced Field Artillery Tactical Data System (AFATDS)
- Common Hardware Systems (CHS)
- Distributed Common Ground System – Army (DCGS-A) Increment 1
- Global Command and Control System – Army (GCCS-A)
- Installation Information Infrastructure Modernization Program (I3MP)
- Tactical Mission Command (TMC)
- Warfighter Information Network – Tactical (WIN-T) Increment 2

- Warfighter Information Network – Tactical (WIN-T) Increment 3

General Dynamics Armament and Technical Products
- Small Arms – Crew Served Weapons

General Dynamics C4 Systems, Inc.
- Warfighter Information Network – Tactical (WIN-T) Increment 1

General Dynamics Communication Systems
- Cryptographic Systems

General Dynamics European Land Systems
- Improved Ribbon Bridge

General Dynamics Information Technology
- Joint Effects Model (JEM)

General Dynamics Land Systems
- Abrams Tank Upgrade
- Mine Protection Vehicle Family (MPFV), Mine Clearing Vehicle (MCV), Explosive Hazard Pre-Detonation (EHP)

- Nuclear Biological Chemical Reconnaissance Vehicle (NBCRV) – Stryker Sensor Suites
- Stryker Family of Vehicles

General Dynamics Land Systems – Canada
- Mine Protection Vehicle Family (MPFV), Mine Clearing Vehicle (MCV), Explosive Hazard Pre-Detonation (EHP)

General Dynamics Mission Systems
- Intelligence Electronic Warfare Tactical Proficiency Trainer (IEWTPT)
- Prophet

General Dynamics Ordnance and Tactical Systems
- 2.75 Inch Rocket Systems (Hydra-70)
- Artillery Ammunition
- Medium Caliber Ammunition (MCA)
- Tank Ammunition

General Dynamics Ordnance and Tactical Systems— Scranton Operations
- Artillery Ammunition

Systems by Contractors

General Dynamics SATCOM Technologies
- Warfighter Information Network – Tactical (WIN-T) Increment 1

General Electric
- Black Hawk UH/HH-60

Gentex Corporation
- Air Warrior (AW)
- Soldier Protection System (SPS)

Georgia Tech Applied Research Corporation
- Common Missile Warning System (CMWS), Laser Detection System (LDS), Radar Warning Receiver (RWR), Advanced Threat Infrared Countermeasures (ATIRCM) and Common Infrared Countermeasure (CIRCM) programs

Georgia Tech Research Institute
- Soldier Protection System (SPS)

Gibson & Barnes
- Air Warrior (AW)

Goodrich Corporation
- CH-47F Chinook

GPS Source, Inc.
- NAVSTAR Global Positioning System (GPS)

Griffon Aerospace
- Air Defense Artillery (ADA) Targets

Gulfsteam
- Fixed Wing

Harris Corporation
- Cryptographic Systems
- Defense Enterprise Wideband SATCOM System (DEWSS)
- Enhanced Night Vision Goggle (ENVG)
- Handheld, Manpack and Small Form Fit (HMS)
- Mid-Tier Networking Vehicular Radio (MNVR)

Hawk Protection
- Soldier Protection System (SPS)

Hawker Beechcraft Corporation
- Enhanced Medium Altitude Reconnaissance and Surveillance System (EMARSS)

- Fixed Wing

Heckler & Koch Defense, Inc.
- Small Arms – Individual Weapons

Highland Engineering, Inc.
- Family of Military Working Dogs Equipment and Kennel

Holston Army Ammunition Plant
- Artillery Ammunition

Honeywell
- CH-47F Chinook

HP
- Distributed Common Ground System – Army (DCGS-A) Increment 1

Hunter Manufacturing Company
- Force Provider (FP)

Hydrema
- Mine Protection Vehicle Family (MPFV), Mine Clearing Vehicle (MCV), Explosive Hazard Pre-Detonation (EHP)

IBM
- Distributed Common Ground System – Army (DCGS-A) Increment 1

INMARSAT
- Combat Service Support Communications (CSS Comms)

Intelligent Decisions
- Close Combat Tactical Trainer (CCTT)

Intrepid
- Army Integrated Air and Missile Defense (AIAMD)

Intuitive Research and Technology Corporation
- Common Missile Warning System (CMWS), Laser Detection System (LDS), Radar Warning Receiver (RWR), Advanced Threat Infrared Countermeasures (ATIRCM) and Common Infrared Countermeasure (CIRCM) programs

IRTC
- AN/MPQ-64 Sentinel

Isometrics, Inc.
- Modular Fuel System (MFS)

JANUS
- Warfighter Information Network – Tactical (WIN-T) Increment 1

Javelin Joint Venture LLC – Raytheon and Lockheed Martin
- Javelin

JCB, Inc.
- High Mobility Engineer Excavator (HMEE) I and III

Johns Hopkins University Applied Physics Laboratory
- Defense Enterprise Wideband SATCOM System (DEWSS)

Kalmar RT Center LLC
- Light Capability Rough Terrain Forklift (LCRTF)

KDH Defense Systems, Inc.
- Soldier Protection System (SPS)

Keysight Technologies, Inc.
- Calibration Sets Equipment (CALSETS)
- Test Equipment Modernization (TEMOD)

Kforce Government Solutions, Inc.
- Medical Simulation Training Center (MSTC)

King Aerospace, Inc.
- Airborne Reconnaissance Low (ARL)
- Fixed Wing

Kipper Tool Company
- Family of Engineer Combat & Construction Sets (ECACS)

Knight's Armament Company
- Small Arms – Precision Weapons

Kongsberg Defense & Aerospace
- Common Remotely Operated Weapon Station (CROWS)

L-3 Communications
- Bradley Fighting Vehicle Systems (BFVS)
- Combat Service Support Communications (CSS Comms)
- Cryptographic Systems
- Distributed Common Ground System – Army (DCGS-A) Increment 1

- Guardrail Common Sensor (GR/CS)
- Tank Ammunition

L-3 Communications – East
- Force Protection Systems

L-3 Communications Mission Integration
- Enhanced Medium Altitude Reconnaissance and Surveillance System (EMARSS)

L-3 Communications Systems – West
- Enhanced Medium Altitude Reconnaissance and Surveillance System (EMARSS)

L-3 Fuzing & Ordnance Systems
- Mortar Systems

L-3 MID
- Fixed Wing

L-3 Vertex
- Fixed Wing

L-3 Warrior Systems
- Enhanced Night Vision Goggle (ENVG)

L-3 Westwood
- Tactical Electric Power (TEP)

Laerdal
- Medical Simulation Training Center (MSTC)

Leidos, Inc.
- Airborne Reconnaissance Low (ARL)
- Distributed Common Ground System – Army (DCGS-A) Increment 1
- Fixed Wing
- One Semi-Automated Force (OneSAF)

Letterkenny Army Depot
- Force Provider (FP)

Lex Products Corporation
- Force Provider (FP)

Litton Advanced Systems
- Airborne Reconnaissance Low (ARL)

LMI Consulting
- General Fund Enterprise Business Systems (GFEBS)

Lockheed Martin

- AH-64D/E Apache
- AN/TPQ-53 Counterfire Target Acquisition Radar
- Airborne Reconnaissance Low (ARL)
- Distributed Common Ground System – Army (DCGS-A) Increment 1
- Guardrail Common Sensor (GR/CS)
- Guided Multiple Launch Rocket System (GMLRS) DPICM/Unitary/Alternative Warhead
- HELLFIRE Family of Missiles
- Joint Air-to-Ground Missile (JAGM)
- Multiple Launch Rocket System (MLRS) M270A1
- PATRIOT Advanced Capability-3 (PAC-3)
- Warfighter Information Network – Tactical (WIN-T) Increment 3

Lockheed Martin Missiles and Fire Control

- Guided Multiple Launch Rocket System (GMLRS) DPICM/Unitary/Alternative Warhead

Lockheed Martin Mission Systems and Training

- Close Combat Tactical Trainer (CCTT)
- Joint Land Component Constructive Training Capability (JLCCTC)

LogiCore Corporation

- Common Missile Warning System (CMWS), Laser Detection System (LDS), Radar Warning Receiver (RWR), Advanced Threat Infrared Countermeasures (ATIRCM) and Common Infrared Countermeasure (CIRCM) programs

Longbow LLC

- AH-64D/E Apache

M-7 Aerospace

- Fixed Wing

Mainstream Engineering Corporation

- Improved Environmental Control Units (IECU)

Mandus Group

- Mobile Maintenance Equipment Systems (MMES)

MaTech

- Mortar Systems

ManTech, Inc.

- Distributed Common Ground System – Army (DCGS-A) Increment 1

Marsh Industrial

- Force Provider (FP)

McAlester Army Ammunition Plant

- Artillery Ammunition

MediVector, Inc.

- Chemical Biological Medical Systems – Therapeutics

Meggitt Training Systems

- Engagement Skills Trainer (EST)

Meritor, Inc.

- Family of Medium Tactical Vehicles (FMTV)
- Line Haul Tractor

Mil-Mar Century, Inc.

- Load Handling System Compatible Water Tank Rack (Hippo)

MITRE Corporation

- Distributed Common Ground System – Army (DCGS-A) Increment 1
- General Fund Enterprise Business Systems (GFEBS)

Naval Air Warfare Center Aircraft Division

- Unified Command Suite (UCS)

Navistar Defense

- Mine Resistant Ambush Protected Vehicles (MRAP), Army

NetApp

- Distributed Common Ground System – Army (DCGS-A) Increment 1

NITEK

- Husky Mounted Detection System (HMDS)

Nomadics, Inc.

- Next Generation Chemical Detector (NGCD)

Northrop Grumman
- AH-64D/E Apache
- Air and Missile Defense Planning and Control System (AMDPCS)
- Army Integrated Air and Missile Defense (AIAMD)
- Biometric Enabling Capability (BEC)
- Common Missile Warning System (CMWS), Laser Detection System (LDS), Radar Warning Receiver (RWR), Advanced Threat Infrared Countermeasures (ATIRCM) and Common Infrared Countermeasure (CIRCM) programs
- Defense Enterprise Wideband SATCOM System (DEWSS)
- Global Combat Support System – Army (GCSS-Army)
- Guardrail Common Sensor (GR/CS)
- Integrated Family of Test Equipment (IFTE)
- Rocket, Artillery, Mortar (RAM) Warn
- Spider – Command Destruct Networked Command Munition Dispensing Set Increment 1A

Northrop Grumman Electronic Systems
- Joint Tactical Ground Station (JTAGS)

Northrop Grumman Information Technology
- Joint Warning and Reporting Network (JWARN)

Northrop Grumman Laser Systems
- Lightweight Laser Designator Rangefinder (LLDR) AN/PED-1 & AN/PED1A

Northrop Grumman Mission Systems
- Joint Effects Model (JEM)

Northrop Grumman Technical Services
- Fixed Wing

Nova Technologies
- Call For Fire Trainer (CFFT) Immersive System
- Call For Fire Trainer Increment 3 (CFFT 3)

Olin Corporation
- Small Caliber Ammunition

Optimal Technologies International
- Medical Simulation Training Center (MSTC)

Orbital ATK
- Artillery Ammunition
- Counter Defilade Target Engagement (CDTE) – XM25
- Medium Caliber Ammunition (MCA)
- Precision Guidance Kit (PGK)
- Small Arms – Crew Served Weapons
- Small Caliber Ammunition
- Spider – Command Destruct Networked Command Munition Dispensing Set Increment 1A
- Tank Ammunition

Oshkosh Corporation
- Common Bridge Transporter
- Family of Medium Tactical Vehicles (FMTV)
- Heavy Expanded Mobility Tactical Truck (HEMTT)/HEMTT Extended Service Program (ESP)
- Heavy Equipment Transporter System (HETS)
- Improved Ribbon Bridge (IRB)
- Joint Light Tactical Vehicle (JLTV)
- Mine Resistant Ambush Protected Vehicles (MRAP), Army
- Palletized Load System (PLS) and PLS Extended Service Program (ESP)

Parsons Government Services, Inc.
- Assembled Chemical Weapons Alternatives (ACWA)

Penta Research, Inc.
- Common Missile Warning System (CMWS), Laser Detection System (LDS), Radar Warning Receiver (RWR), Advanced Threat Infrared Countermeasures (ATIRCM) and Common Infrared Countermeasure (CIRCM) programs

Pine Bluff Arsenal
- Artillery Ammunition
- Chemical, Biological, Radiological, Nuclear Dismounted Reconnaissance Sets, Kits, and Outfits (CBRN DR SKO)
- Mortar Systems

PM Ground Soldier
- Mortar Systems

POCAL Industries, Inc.
- Mortar Systems

Point Blank Enterprises, Inc.
- Soldier Protection System (SPS)

Potomac Fusion, Inc.
- Distributed Common Ground System – Army (DCGS-A) Increment 1

PULAU Corporation
- Medical Simulation Training Center (MSTC)

Radiation Safety & Control Services
- Joint Personal Dosimeter (JPD)

Rapiscan Systems
- Non-Intrusive Inspection Systems (NIIS)

Raytheon
- Advanced Field Artillery Tactical Data System (AFATDS)
- Army Integrated Air and Missile Defense (AIAMD)

- Distributed Common Ground System – Army (DCGS-A) Increment 1
- Excalibur Precision 155 mm Projectiles
- Improved Target Acquisition System (ITAS)
- Joint Air-to-Ground Missile (JAGM)
- PATRIOT Advanced Capability-3 (PAC-3)
- Secure Mobile Anti-Jam Reliable Tactical Terminal (SMART-T)

Raytheon Missile Systems
- Counter-Rocket, Artillery, Mortar (C-RAM) Intercept Land-Based Phalanx Weapon System (LPWS)
- Tube-Launched, Optically Tracked, Wireless-Guided (TOW) Missiles

Raytheon Technical Services
- Air Warrior (AW)

Red Hat
- Distributed Common Ground System – Army (DCGS-A) Increment 1

Red River Army Depot
- High Mobility Multipurpose Wheeled Vehicle (HMMWV)

Remington Arms Company, Inc.
- Small Arms – Precision Weapons

Revision Military Ltd.
- Soldier Protection System (SPS)

Rini Technologies, Inc.
- Air Warrior (AW)

Rock Island Arsenal
- Line of Communications Bridge (LOCB)

Rock Island Arsenal – Joint Manufacturing & Technology Center
- High Mobility Multipurpose Wheeled Vehicle (HMMWV)
- Mobile Maintenance Equipment Systems (MMES)

Rockwell Collins, Inc.
- CH-47F Chinook
- Close Combat Tactical Trainer (CCTT)

- Common Missile Warning System (CMWS), Laser Detection System (LDS), Radar Warning Receiver (RWR), Advanced Threat Infrared Countermeasures (ATIRCM) and Common Infrared Countermeasure (CIRCM) programs
- Enhanced Medium Altitude Reconnaissance and Surveillance System (EMARSS)
- NAVSTAR Global Positioning System (GPS)

Saab Training USA, LLC
- Instrumentable – Multiple Integrated Laser Engagement System (I-MILES)

SafeNet
- Cryptographic Systems

Sarepta Therapeutics
- Chemical Biological Medical Systems – Therapeutics

Science and Engineering Services, Inc.
- Air Warrior (AW)

Science Applications International Corporation (SAIC)
- Non-Intrusive Inspection Systems (NIIS)

Scientific Resource Corporation
- Army Watercraft Systems (AWS)

Short Bark Industries, Inc.
- Soldier Protection System (SPS)

Siemens
- Installation Information Infrastructure Modernization Program (I3MP)

Sierra Nevada Corporation
- Airborne Reconnaissance Low (ARL)
- Army Key Management System (AKMS)
- Enhanced Medium Altitude Reconnaissance and Surveillance System (EMARSS)
- Fixed Wing

Sigmatech, Inc.
- Joint Tactical Ground Station (JTAGS)

Signature Science, LLC
- Next Generation Chemical Detector (NGCD)

Sikorsky
- Black Hawk UH/HH-60

Simetri, Inc.
- Medical Simulation Training Center (MSTC)

SKEDCO, Inc.
- Medical Simulation Training Center (MSTC)

Smiths Detection, Inc.
- Chemical Biological Protective Shelter (CBPS) – M8E1
- Joint Chemical Agent Detector (JCAD) M4A1
- Next Generation Chemical Detector (NGCD)

Software Engineering Directorate, AMRDEC
- Joint Battle Command – Platform (JBC-P)

Southwest Research Institute
- Chemical Biological Medical Systems – Therapeutics

SRCTec, LLC
- AN/TPQ-50 Lightweight Counter Mortar Radar (LCMR)

STERIS Corporation
- Joint Service Equipment Wipe (JSEW)

Switlik Parachute Company, Inc.
- Air Warrior (AW)

Tekmira Pharmaceutical Corporation
- Chemical Biological Medical Systems – Therapeutics

Tel-Instrument Electronics Corporation
- Test Equipment Modernization (TEMOD)

Telephonics Corporation
- Air Warrior (AW)

Textron Defense Systems
- Spider – Command Destruct Networked Command Munition Dispensing Set Increment 1A

Textron/Overwatch Systems
- Distributed Common Ground System – Army (DCGS-A) Increment 1

Thales Defense & Security, Inc.
- Handheld, Manpack and Small Form Fit (HMS)

Thales Raytheon Systems
- AN/MPQ-64 Sentinel

Tobyhanna Army Depot
- Mobile Maintenance Equipment Systems (MMES)

Tri-Tech USA, Inc.
- Force Provider (FP)

Tucson Embedded Systems
- Distributed Common Ground System – Army (DCGS-A) Increment 1

URS Corporation
- Assault Breacher Vehicle (ABV)

URS Federal Services, Inc.
- Force Protection Systems

Systems by Contractors

Vertigo, Inc.
- Force Provider (FP)

Vertu Corporation
- Small Arms – Individual Weapons

ViaSat Inc.
- Cryptographic Systems
- Joint Battle Command – Platform (JBC-P)

ViaTech System, Inc.
- Distributed Common Ground System – Army (DCGS-A) Increment 1

Vision Ability Execution, Inc.
- Installation Information Infrastructure Modernization Program (I3MP)

Vision Technology Miltope Corporation
- Integrated Family of Test Equipment (IFTE)
- Mortar Systems

VMware, Inc.
- Distributed Common Ground System – Army (DCGS-A) Increment 1

Wavelink
- Common Missile Warning System (CMWS), Laser Detection System (LDS), Radar Warning Receiver (RWR), Advanced Threat Infrared Countermeasures (ATIRCM) and Common Infrared Countermeasure (CIRCM) programs

Watervliet Arsenal
- Mortar Systems

WESCAM
- Airborne Reconnaissance Low (ARL)

Wolf Coach, Inc., an L-3 Communications Company
- Unified Command Suite (UCS)

Wyle's CAS Group
- Common Missile Warning System (CMWS), Laser Detection System (LDS), Radar Warning Receiver (RWR), Advanced Threat Infrared Countermeasures (ATIRCM) and Common Infrared Countermeasure (CIRCM) programs

XMCO, Inc.
- Assault Breacher Vehicle (ABV)
- High Mobility Engineer Excavator (HMEE) I and III

Contractors by State ——————————

Alabama

- Anniston Army Depot
- Army Aviation and Missile Research Development and Engineering Center (AMRDEC) Prototype Integration Facility (PIF), Redstone Defense Systems (RDF)
- CGI Federal
- Communications & Ear Protection (CEP), Inc.
- Computer Sciences Corporation
- Dynetics, Inc.
- General Dynamics Mission Systems
- General Dynamics Ordnance and Tactical Systems
- Griffon Aerospace
- Intrepid
- Intuitive Research and Technology Corporation
- Javelin Joint Venture LLC – Raytheon and Lockheed Martin
- LogiCore
- Northrop Grumman
- Penta Research, Inc.
- Sigmatech, Inc.
- Science and Engineering Services, Inc.
- Software Engineering Directorate (SEC), AMRDEC
- Vision Technology Miltope Corporation
- Wavelink
- Wyle's CAS Group

Arizona

- BAE Systems
- Boeing
- General Dynamics
- General Dynamics Mission Systems
- Honeywell
- Javelin Joint Venture LLC – Raytheon and Lockheed Martin
- L-3 Communications
- Lockheed Martin
- Orbital ATK
- Raytheon
- Raytheon Missile Systems
- Tucson Embedded Systems

Arkansas

- AMTEC Corporation
- Lockheed Martin
- Pine Bluff Arsenal

California

- AeroVironment, Inc.
- Applied Companies
- ArgonST (A Boeing Company)
- ARMTEC
- BAE Systems
- Ceradyne, Inc.

- Cubic Global Defense
- DRS Technologies, Inc.
- Esri
- General Atomics Aeronautical
- General Dynamics Information Technology
- Gentex Corporation
- Gibson & Barnes
- HP
- Javelin Joint Venture LLC – Raytheon and Lockheed Martin
- Keysight Technologies, Inc.
- NetApp
- Northrop Grumman
- Northrop Grumman Mission Systems
- Parsons Government Services, Inc.
- Rapiscan Systems
- Science Applications International Corporation (SAIC)
- Thales Raytheon Systems
- Vertigo, Inc.
- ViaSat, Inc.
- VMware

Colorado

- Birdon Corporation
- Capco
- GPS Source, Inc.
- Keysight Technologies
- Lockheed Martin

- Northrop Grumman Electronic Systems

Connecticut

- Colt Defense, LLC
- DRS Fermont
- Goodrich
- Lex Products Corporation
- Sikorsky

Florida

- AVT Simulation
- Chemring Ordnance
- Cole Engineering Services, Inc.
- Computer Sciences Corporation
- DRS Technologies, Inc.
- General Dynamics
- General Dynamics Ordnance and Tactical Systems
- Harris Corporation
- Hawk Protection
- Javelin Joint Venture LLC – Raytheon and Lockheed Martin
- Knight's Armament Company
- Leidos, Inc.
- Lockheed Martin
- Lockheed Martin Mission Systems and Training
- Longbow LLC
- Mainstream Engineering Corporation
- Northrop Grumman Information Technology

- Northrop Grumman
  Laser Systems
- Nova Technologies
- Optimal Technologies
  International
- Point Blank Enterprises, Inc.
- PULAU Corporation
- Raytheon
- Rini Technologies
- Saab Training USA, LLC
- Simetri, Inc.
- Thales Raytheon Systems

Georgia
- BWAY Corporation
- General Dynamics
  SATCOM Technologies
- Georgia Tech Applied
  Research Corporation
- Georgia Tech
  Research Institute
- Gulfstream
- JCB, Inc.
- Kipper Tool Company
- Meggitt Training Systems
- Scientific Resource
  Corporation

Illinois
- Caterpillar, Inc.
- General Dynamics Ordnance
  and Tactical Systems
- Mandus Group
- Navistar Defense
- Northrop Grumman

- Rock Island Arsenal
- Rock Island Arsenal –
  Joint Manufacturing &
  Technology Center

Indiana
- Allison Transmission
- AM General
- Crane Army
  Ammunition Activity
- Raytheon
- Raytheon Technical Services

Iowa
- American Ordnance
- Rockwell Collins

Kansas
- Hawker Beechcraft
  Corporation

Kentucky
- Bechtel Parsons Blue Grass
- Bluegrass Army Depot
- CONCO
- DRS Environmental
  Systems, Inc.
- DRS Technologies, Inc.

Maine
- General Dynamics Armament
  and Technical Products

Maryland
- AAI Corporation

- Adams Communication and
  Engineering Technology, Inc.
- Booz Allen Hamilton
- CACI International, Inc.
- Computer Sciences
  Corporation
- DynPort Vaccine
- Engineering Solutions
  and Products
- FLIR Systems, Inc.
- Future Skies
- Garrett Container
  Systems, Inc.
- JANUS
- Johns Hopkins University
  Applied Physics Laboratory
- Litton Advanced Systems
- Lockheed Martin
- MaTech
- Naval Air Warfare Center
  Aircraft Division
- Northrop Grumman
- URS Federal Services, Inc.
- SafeNet
- Sierra Nevada Corporation
- Smiths Detection, Inc.
- Thales Defense &
  Security, Inc.

Massachusetts
- Acambis plc
- American Science &
  Engineering, Inc.
- Bruker Detection Corporation
- Draper Laboratory, Inc.

- General Dynamics
- General Dynamics C4
  Systems, Inc.
- General Dynamics
  Communication Systems
- General Electric
- MediVector, Inc.
- Raytheon
- Sarepta Therapeutics
- Textron Defense Systems
- Wolf Coach, Inc., an L-3
  Communications Company

Michigan
- AM General
- Avon Protection Systems
- Detroit Diesel
- Emergent BioSolutions
- General Dynamics
  Land Systems
- Highland Engineering, Inc.
- L-3 Communications
- March Industrial
- Meritor, Inc.
- XMCO, Inc.

Minnesota
- Cummins Power Generation
- Orbital ATK

Mississippi
- BAE Systems
- L-3 Vertex
- Olin Corporation
- Thales Raytheon Systems

Missouri
- Boeing
- Boeing Defense, Space and Security
- DRS Sustainment Systems, Inc.
- DRS Technologies, Inc.
- Orbital ATK

Nevada
- Sierra Nevada Corporation

New Hampshire
- BAE Systems
- L-3 Warrior Systems
- Radiation Safety & Control Services

New Jersey
- AASKI Technology, Inc.
- Airborne Systems North America
- AMT
- Bethel Industries
- Booz Allen Hamilton
- David H. Pollock Consultants
- L-3 Communications
- L-3 Communications – East
- MITRE
- Switlik Parachute Company
- Tel-Instrument Electronics Corporation
- ViaTech Systems, Inc.

New Mexico
- Lockheed Martin Missiles and Fire Control
- URS Corporation
- Raytheon

New York
- ADSI
- Avox Systems
- Buffalo Turbine
- Carleton Technologies, Inc.
- Carter Enterprises, LLC
- General Dynamics Information Technology
- Harris Corporation
- IBM
- L-3 Communications
- Laerdal
- Lockheed Martin
- Remington Arms Company, Inc.
- SRCTec, LLC
- Telephonics Corporation
- Watervliet Arsenal

North Carolina
- Chemring Detection Systems
- Daimler Trucks North America LLC/Freightliner
- Isometrics, Inc.
- KDH Defense Systems
- Red Hat

Ohio
- AlphaMicron

New Mexico
- BAE Systems
- Battelle Memorial Institute
- Hunter Manufacturing Company
- L-3 Fuzing and Ordnance Systems
- Mil-Mar Century, Inc.
- STERIS Corporation

Oklahoma
- Choctaw Manufacturing Defense Contractors
- CymSTAR LLC
- FLIR
- L-3 Westwood
- McAlester Army Ammunition Plant
- Nomadics, Inc.

Oregon
- Daimler Trucks North America LLC/Freightliner
- Skedco, Inc.

Pennsylvania
- Action Manufacturing
- BAE Systems
- BAE Systems, Inc.
- Boeing
- ChemImage
- Carnegie Robotics LLC
- Fidelity Technologies Corporation
- General Dynamics Ordnance and Tactical Systems

Pennsylvania (cont.)
- General Dynamics Ordnance and Tactical Systems – Scranton Operations
- Gentex Corporation
- Kongsberg Defense & Aerospace
- L-3 Communications
- Letterkenny Army Depot
- POCAL Industries, Inc.
- Tobyhanna Army Depot

Rhode Island
- General Dynamics Information Technology

South Carolina
- Caterpillar, Inc.
- Charleston Marine Containers, Inc.
- Critical Solutions International, Inc.
- Fabrique National Manufacturing, LLC

Tennessee
- Barrett Firearms Manufacturing
- Holston Army Ammunition Plant
- Short Bark Industries

Texas
- Airbus Helicopter, Inc.
- AT&T
- Casteel Manufacturing

Contractors by State

- Day & Zimmerman – Lone Star
- Dell
- DRS Technologies, Inc.
- Elbit Systems of America
- Javelin Joint Venture LLC – Raytheon and Lockheed Martin
- Kalmar RT Center LLC
- King Aerospace, Inc.
- L-3 Communications Mission Integration
- L-3 MID
- Lockheed Martin
- M-7 Aerospace
- Northrop Grumman Technical Services
- Oshkosh Corporation
- Potomac Fusion
- Raytheon
- Red River Army Depot
- Signature Science, LLC
- Southwest Research Institute
- Textron/Overwatch Systems
- Thales Raytheon Systems

Utah
- BioFire Defense, LLC
- L-3 Communications
- L-3 Communication Systems – West

Vermont
- General Dynamics
- General Dynamics Ordnance and Tactical Systems
- Revision Military Ltd.
- Tri-Tech USA, Inc.

Virginia
- Accenture Federal Services
- Adams Communication & Engineering Technology
- Airbus Defense and Space, Inc.
- BAE Systems
- Bechtel National, Inc.
- Booz Allen Hamilton
- CACI International, Inc.
- Connected Logistics, Inc.
- DRS Technologies, Inc.
- Entwistle
- General Dynamics
- Harris Corporation
- Heckler and Koch Defense, Inc.
- INMARSAT
- Intelligent Decision
- Kforce Government Solutions, Inc.
- Leidos, Inc.
- LMI Consulting
- ManTech
- MITRE
- NITEK
- Northrop Grumman
- PM Ground Soldier

- Technology and Supply Management LLC
- Vertu Corporation
- Vision Ability Execution

Washington
- Berg Companies, Inc.
- Fluke Corporation

West Virginia
- Northrop Grumman
- Orbital ATK

Wisconsin
- AMTEC Corporation
- Case New Holland
- Oshkosh Corporation

Washington, D.C.
- Booz Allen Hamilton
- Siemens

INTERNATIONAL CONTRACTORS

Canada
- Cangene, Corporation
- General Dynamics Land Systems – Canada
- General Dynamics Ordnance and Tactical Systems
- WESCAM
- Tekmira Pharmaceutical Corporation

Croatia
- DOK-ING d.o.o.

Denmark
- Hydrema

Germany
- General Dynamics European Land Systems – Germany

United Kingdom
- BAE Systems
- Raytheon

Points of Contact

120M Motor Grader
PEO Combat Support and
Combat Service Support
Product Manager Combat
Engineer/Material Handling
Equipment
SFAE-CSS-FP-C
6501 E. 11 Mile Road
Mail Stop 401
Detroit Arsenal, MI 48397-5000

**2.75 Inch Rocket Systems
(Hydra-70)**
PEO Missiles and Space
JAMS Project Office
SFAE-MSLS-JAMS
5250 Martin Road
Redstone Arsenal, AL
35898-8000

621G Scraper
PEO Combat Support and
Combat Service Support
Product Manager Combat
Engineer/Material Handling
Equipment
SFAE-CSS-FP-C
6501 E. 11 Mile Road
Mail Stop 401
Detroit Arsenal, MI 48397-5000

Abrams Tank Upgrade
PEO Ground Combat Systems
Main Battle Tank Systems
SFAE-GCS-MA
6501 E. 11 Mile Road
Detroit Arsenal, MI 48397-5000

**Advanced Field Artillery
Tactical Data System
(AFATDS)**
PEO Command, Control and
Communications – Tactical
Product Director Fire Support
Command and Control
SFAE-C3T-MC-FSC2
6007 Combat Drive
5th Floor
Aberdeen Proving Ground,
MD 21005

AH-64D/E Apache
PEO Aviation
PM Apache
SFAE-AV
5307 Sparkman Circle
Redstone Arsenal, AL 35898

**Air and Missile Defense
Planning and Control System
(AMDPCS)**
PEO Missiles and Space
Counter-Rocket, Artillery,
Mortar (C-RAM) Program
Directorate
SFAE-MSLS-CRAM
5250 Martin Road
Redstone Arsenal, AL
35898-5000

**Air Defense Artillery
(ADA) Targets**
PEO Simulation, Training, and
Instrumentation
Project Manager Instrumentation,
Targets and Threat Simulators
SFAE-STRI-ITTS
12350 Research Parkway
Orlando, FL 32826

Air Soldier System (Air SS)
PEO Soldier
Product Manager Air Warrior
SFAE-SDR-AW
6726 Odyssey Drive NW.
Redstone Arsenal, AL 35806

Air Warrior (AW)
PEO Soldier
Product Manager Air Warrior
SFAE-SDR-AW
6726 Odyssey Drive NW.
Redstone Arsenal, AL 35806

**Airborne and Maritime/Fixed
Station (AMF)**
PEO Command, Control and
Communications – Tactical
Project Manager Tactical Radios
SFAE-CCC-TR
6007 Combat Drive
Aberdeen Proving Ground,
MD 21005

**Airborne Reconnaissance
Low (ARL)**
PEO Aviation
Fixed Wing Project Office
SFAE-AV-FW
650 Discovery Drive
Redstone Arsenal, AL 35805

AN/MPQ-64 Sentinel
PEO Missiles and Space
Cruise Missile Defense Systems
Project
SFAE-MSL-CMA
5250 Martin Road
Redstone Arsenal, AL 35898

AN/TPQ-50 Lightweight Counter Mortar Radar (LCMR)
PEO Missiles and Space
Product Manager Radars
SFAE-MSL-CRR
6001 Combat Drive
Aberdeen Proving Ground, MD 21005

AN/TPQ-53 Counterfire Target Acquisition Radar
PEO Missiles and Space
Product Manager Radars
SFAE-MSL-CRR
6006 Combat Drive
Aberdeen Proving Ground, MD 21005

Armored Multi-Purpose Vehicle (AMPV)
PEO Ground Combat System
Program Manager Armored
Multi-Purpose Vehicle
SFAE-GCS-A
6501 E. 11 Mile Road
Mail Stop 463
Detroit Arsenal, MI 48397-5000

Army Integrated Air and Missile Defense (AIAMD)
PEO Missiles and Space
Integrated Air and Missile
Defense Project Office
SFAE-MSL-IA
5250 Martin Road
Redstone Arsenal, AL 35898-8000

Army Key Management System (AKMS)
PEO Command, Control and
Communications – Tactical
Project Director Network
Enablers
6007 Combat Drive
5th Floor
Aberdeen Proving Ground, MD 21005

Army Watercraft Systems (AWS)
PEO Combat Support and
Combat Service Support
SFAE-CSS-TS-AWS
6501 E. 11 Mile Road
Detroit Arsenal, MI 48397-5000

Artillery Ammunition
PEO Ammunition
PM Combat Ammunition
Systems
SFAE-AMO-CAS
Picatinny Arsenal, NJ 07806

Assault Breacher Vehicle (ABV)
PEO Combat Support and
Combat Service Support
PM Bridging Systems
SFAE-CSS-FP-H
6501 E. 11 Mile Road
Detroit Arsenal, MI 43897-5000

Assembled Chemical Weapons Alternatives (ACWA)
PEO Assembled Chemical
Weapons Alternatives
SFAE-ACW-Z
5183 Blackhawk Road
Aberdeen Proving Ground, MD 21010-5424

Autonomous Mine Detection System (AMDS)
PEO Ammunition
Project Manager Close Combat
Systems
SFAE-AMO-CCS
Building 1
Picatinny Arsenal, NJ 07806

Aviation Combined Arms Tactical Trainer (AVCATT)
PEO for Simulation, Training,
and Instrumentation
Project Manager Integrated
Training Environment
SFAE-STRI-PMITE
12350 Research Parkway
Orlando, FL 32826-3276

Battlefield Kitchen (BK)
PEO Combat Support and
Combat Service Support
Product Manager Force
Sustainment Systems
SFAE-CSS-E2-F
General Green Avenue
Natick, MA 01760-5057

Biometric Enabling Capability (BEC)
PEO Enterprise Information
Systems
PM DoD Biometrics
SFAE-PS-BI
200 Stovall Street
Suite 10N07
Alexandria, VA 22332

Black Hawk/UH/HH-60
PEO Aviation
Utility Helicopters Project Office
SFAE-AV-UH
5308 Patton Road
Redstone Arsenal, AL 35898-5000

Bradley Fighting Vehicle Systems (BFVS)
PEO Ground Combat Systems
Product Manager Bradley
Fighting Vehicle Systems
SFAE-GCS-FV
6501 E. 11 Mile Road
Building 229
Mail Stop 531
Detroit Arsenal, MI 48397-5000

Calibration Sets Equipment (CALSETS)
PEO Combat Support and
Combat Service Support
Product Director Test,
Measurement, and Diagnostic
Equipment
SFAE-CSS-JC-TM
3651 Army TACMS Drive
Redstone Arsenal, AL 35898

Call For Fire Trainer (CFFT) Immersive System
PEO for Simulation, Training,
and Instrumentation
Project Manager Instrumentation,
Targets and Threat Simulation
SFAE-STRI-ITTS
12350 Research Parkway
Orlando, FL 32826

Call For Fire Trainer Increment 3 (CFFT 3)
PEO for Simulation, Training,
and Instrumentation
Project Manager Instrumentation,
Targets and Threat Simulation
SFAE-STRI-ITTS
12350 Research Parkway
Orlando, FL 32826

CH-47F Chinook
PEO Aviation
SFAE-AV-CH-ICH
Building 5678
Redstone Arsenal, AL 35898

Chemical Biological Medical Systems – Therapeutics
JPEO for Chemical and
Biological Defense
Joint Project Manager Medical
Countermeasure Systems
1564 Freedman Drive
Fort Detrick, MD 21702

Chemical Biological Protective Shelter (CBPS) – M8E1
JPEO for Chemical and
Biological Defense
Joint Project Manager Protection
50 Tech Parkway
Suite 301
Stafford, VA 22556

Chemical, Biological, Radiological, Nuclear Dismounted Reconnaissance Sets, Kits, and Outfits (CBRN DR SKO)
JPEO for Chemical and
Biological Defense
Joint Project Manager NBC
Contamination Avoidance
SFAE-CBD-NBC-R
5183 Blackhawk Road
Building 2800
Aberdeen Proving Ground, MD
21010-5425

Close Combat Tactical Trainer (CCTT)
PEO for Simulation, Training,
and Instrumentation
Project Manager Integrated
Training Environment
SFAE-STRI-PMITE
12350 Research Parkway
Orlando, FL 32826-3276

Combat Service Support Communications (CSS Comms)
PEO Enterprise
Information Systems
PM Defense Communications
and Army Transmission Systems
SFAE-PS-TS
9350 Hall Road
Building 1445
Fort Belvoir, VA 22060

Common Bridge Transporter
PEO Combat Support and
Combat Service Support
PdM Bridging
SFAE-CSS-FP-H
6501 E. 11 Mile Road
Detroit Arsenal, MI 48397-5000

Common Hardware Systems (CHS)
PEO Command, Control and
Communications – Tactical
Product Director Common
Hardware Systems (PD-CHS)
SFAE-C3T-NE
6007 Combat Drive
Aberdeen Proving Ground, MD
21005

Common Missile Warning System (CMWS), Laser Detection System (LDS), Radar Warning Receiver (RWR), Advanced Threat Infrared Countermeasures (ATIRCM), and Common Infrared Countermeasure (CIRM) programs
PEO Intelligence Electronic
Warfare & Sensors
PM Aircraft Survivability
Equipment
SFAE-IEW-ASE
6726 Odyssey Drive
Redstone Arsenal, AL 35806

Common Remotely Operated Weapon Station (CROWS)
PEO Soldier
Project Manager Soldier Weapons
SFAE-SDR-SW
Building 151
Picatinny Arsenal, NJ 07806

Common Robotic System – Individual (CRS(I))
PEO Combat Support and
Combat Service Support
Unmanned Ground Vehicles
SFAE-CSS-FP
6501 E. 11 Mile Road
Detroit Arsenal, MI 48397

Counter Defilade Target Engagement (CDTE) – XM25
PEO Soldier
PM Soldier Weapons
SFAE-SDR-SW
Building 151
Picatinny Arsenal, NJ 07806

Counter-Rocket, Artillery, Mortar (C-RAM) / Intercept Land-Based Phalanx Weapon System (LPWS)
PEO Missiles and Space
C-RAM Intercept LPWS Product Office
SFAE-MSL-CR
5250 Martin Road
Redstone Arsenal, AL 35898-5000

Cryptographic Systems
PEO Command, Control and
Communications - Tactical
PD COMSEC
Cryptographic Systems
SFAE-CCC-CMC
6007 Combat Drive
F5-140-44
Aberdeen Proving Ground, MD 21005

Defense Enterprise Wideband SATCOM System (DEWSS)
PEO Enterprise
Information Systems
PM Defense Communications
and Army Transmission Systems
SFAE-PS-TS
9350 Hall Road
Building 1445
Fort Belvoir, VA 22060

Distributed Common Ground System – Army (DCGS-A) Increment 1
PEO Intelligence, Electronic
Warfare and Sensors
PM Distributed Common
Ground System–Army
(DCGS-A)
SFAE-IEW-DCG
6006 Combat Drive
Aberdeen Proving Ground, MD 21005-0001

Distributed Common Ground System – Army (DCGS-A) Increment 2
PEO Intelligence, Electronic
Warfare & Sensors
PM Distributed Common
Ground System – Army
(DCGS-A)
6006 Combat Drive
Room B2-133
Aberdeen Proving Ground, MD 21005

Early Entry Fluid Distribution System (E2FDS)
PEO Combat Support and
Combat Service Support
Petroleum and Water Systems
SFAE-CSS-FP
6501 E. 11 Mile Road
Mail Stop 111
Warren, MI48397

Engagement Skills Trainer (EST)
PEO for Simulation, Training,
and Instrumentation
Project Manager Instrumentation,
Targets and Threat Simulators
SFAE-STRI-ITTS
12350 Research Parkway
Orlando, FL 32826

Enhanced Medium Altitude Reconnaissance and Surveillance System (EMARSS)
PEO Aviation
Fixed Wing Project Office
SFAE-AV-FW
650 Discovery Drive
Redstone Arsenal, AL 35805

Enhanced Night Vision Goggle (ENVG)
PEO Soldier
PM Soldier Sensors and Lasers
SFAE-SDR-SSL
10125 Gratiot Road
Building 218
Fort Belvoir, VA 22060

Excalibur Precision 155 mm Projectiles
PEO Ammunition
PM Excalibur
SFAE-AMO-CAS-EX
Buffington Road
Building 172
Picatinny Arsenal, NJ 07806-5000

Expeditionary Water Packing System (EWPS)
PEO Combat Support and Combat Service Support
Petroleum and Water Systems
SFAE-CSS-FP
6501 E. 11 Mile Road
Mail Stop 111
Detroit Arsenal, MI 48397

Family of Engineer Combat and Construction Sets (ECACS)
PEO Combat Support and Combat Service Support
Product Manager Sets, Kits, Outfits, and Tools
SFAE-CSS-JC-SK
6501 E. 11 Mile Road
Mail Stop 640
Detroit Arsenal, MI 48397-5000

Family of Medium Tactical Vehicles (FMTV)
PEO Combat Support and Combat Service Support
Product Manager Medium Tactical Vehicles
SFAE-CSS
6501 E. 11 Mile Road
Detroit Arsenal, MI 43897-5000

Family of Military Working Dogs Equipment and Kennel
PEO Ammunition
Project Manager Close Combat Systems
SFAE-AMO-CCS
Building 1
Picatinny Arsenal, NJ 07806

Family of Weapon Sights – Crew Served (FWS-CS)
PEO Soldier
PM Soldier Sensors and Lasers
SFAE-SDR-SSL
10125 Gratiot Road
Building 318
Fort Belvoir, VA 22060

Family of Weapon Sights – Individual (FWS-I)
PEO Soldier
PM Soldier Sensors and Lasers
SFAE-SDR-SSL
10125 Gratiot Road
Building 318
Fort Belvoir, VA 22060

Family of Weapon Sights – Sniper (FWS-S)
PEO Soldier
PM Soldier Sensors and Lasers
SFAE-SDR-SSL
10125 Gratiot Road
Building 318
Fort Belvoir, VA 22060

Fixed Wing
PEO Aviation
Fixed Wing Project Office
SFAE-AV-FW
650 Discovery Drive
Redstone Arsenal, AL 35805

Force Protection Systems
JPEO for Chemical and Biological Defense
Joint Project Manager Guardian
SFAE-CBD-GN-F
E. 2800 Bush River Road
Aberdeen Proving Ground, MD 21010-5424

Force Provider (FP)
PEO Combat Support and Combat Service Support
PM Force Sustainment Systems
SFAE-CSS-FP-F
Kansas Street
Natick, MA 01760-5057

General Fund Enterprise Business Systems (GFEBS)
PEO Enterprise Information Systems
PM General Fund Enterprise Business System
SFAE-PS-GF
9350 Hall Road
Building 1445
Fort Belvoir, VA 22060

Points of Contact

Global Combat Support System – Army (GCSS-Army)
PEO Enterprise Information Systems
PM Global Combat Support Systems – Army
SFAE-PS-AE-GCS
9350 Hall Road
Building 1445
Fort Belvoir, VA 22060

Global Command and Control System – Army (GCCS-A)
PEO Command, Control and Communications – Tactical
Product Manager Strategic Mission Command
SFAE-C3T-MC-SMC
6007 Combat Drive
5th Floor
Aberdeen Proving Ground, MD 21005

Guardrail Common Sensor (GR/CS)
PEO Aviation
Fixed Wing Project Office
SFAE-AVN-FW
650 Discovery Drive
Redstone Arsenal, AL 35806

Guided Multiple Launch Rocket System (GMLRS) DPICM/Unitary/ Alternative Warhead
PEO Missiles and Space
Precision Fires Rocket and Missile Systems
SFAE-MSLS-PF
5250 Martin Road
Redstone Arsenal, AL 35898

Handheld, Manpack and Small Form Fit (HMS)
PEO Command, Control and Communications - Tactical
Program Manager
Tactical Radios
SFAE-CCC-TR
6007 Combat Drive
Aberdeen Proving Ground, MD 21005

Heavy Equipment Transporter System (HETS)
PEO Combat Support and Combat Service Support
PdM Heavy Tactical Vehicles
SFAE-CSS-TS-H
6501 E. 11 Mile Road
Mail Stop 429
Detroit Arsenal, MI 48397-5000

Heavy Expanded Mobility Tactical Truck (HEMTT)/ HEMTT Extended Service Program (ESP)
PEO Combat Support and Combat Service Support
PM Heavy Tactical Vehicles
SFAE-CSS-TS-H
6501 E. 11 Mile Road
Mail Stop 429
Detroit Arsenal, MI 48397-5000

HELLFIRE Family of Missiles
PEO Missiles and Space
JAMS Project Office
SFAE-MSLS-JAMS
5250 Martin Road
Redstone Arsenal, AL 35898

High Mobility Engineer Excavator (HMEE) I and III
PEO Combat Support and Combat Service Support
Product Manager Combat Engineer/Material Handling Equipment
SFAE-CSS-FP-C
6501 E. 11 Mile Road
Mail Stop 401
Detroit Arsenal, MI 48397-5000

High Mobility Multipurpose Wheeled Vehicle (HMMWV)
PEO Combat Support and Combat Service Support
Product Director Light Tactical Vehicles
SFAE-CSS-TS-LT
6501 E. 11 Mile Road
Mail Stop 245
Detroit Arsenal, MI 43897-5000

Home Station Instrumentation Training System (HITS)
PEO for Simulation, Training, and Instrumentation
Project Manager Training Devices
SFAE-STRI-TRADE
12350 Research Parkway
Orlando, FL 32826

Husky Mounted Detection System (HMDS)
PEO Intelligence, Electronic Warfare and Sensors
Project Manager Close Combat Systems
SFAE-AMO-CCS
183 Buffington Road
Picatinny Arsenal, NJ 07806

Improved Environmental Control Units (IECU)
PEO Combat Support and Combat Service Support
Project Manager Expeditionary & Sustainment System
SFAE-CSS-E2
5850 Delafield Road
Building 324
Fort Belvoir, VA 22060-5809

Improved Ribbon Bridge (IRB)
PEO Combat Support and Combat Service Support
PM Bridging Systems
SFAE-CSS-FP-H
6501 E. 11 Mile Road
Mail Stop 401
Detroit Arsenal, MI 43897-5000

Improved Target Acquisition System (ITAS)
PEO Missiles and Space
PM Close Combat Weapon Systems Project Office
SFAE-MSL-CWS-J
111 Hankins Drive
Redstone Arsenal, AL 35898

Indirect Fire Protection Capability Increment 2 – Intercept Block 1
PEO Missiles and Space
Cruise Missile Defense Systems Project Office
SFAE-MSL-CMM
5250 Martin Road
Redstone Arsenal, AL 35898

Installation Information Infrastructure Modernization Program (I3MP)
PEO Enterprise Information Systems
PM Installation Information Infrastructure Modernization Program
SFAE-PS-I3-MP
9350 Hall Road
Building 1445
Fort Belvoir, VA 22060

Instrumentable – Multiple Integrated Laser Engagement System (I-MILES)
PEO for Simulation, Training, and Instrumentation
Project Manager Training Devices
SFAE-STRI-PMTRADE
12350 Research Parkway
Orlando, FL 32826

Integrated Family of Test Equipment (IFTE)
PEO Combat Support and Combat Service Support
Product Director Test, Measurement, and Diagnostic Equipment
SFAE-CSS-JC-TM
3651 Army TACMS Drive
Redstone Arsenal, AL 35898

Integrated Personnel and Pay System – Army (IPPS-A)
PEO Enterprise Information Systems
PD Integrated Personnel and Pay System – Army
SFAE-PS-IP
9350 Hall Road
Building 1445
Fort Belvoir, VA 22060

Intelligence Electronic Warfare Tactical Proficiency Trainer (IEWTPT)
PEO for Simulation, Training, and Instrumentation
Project Manager Instrumentation, Targets and Threat Simulators
SFAE-STRI-ITTS
12350 Research Parkway
Orlando, FL 32826

Javelin
PEO Missiles and Space
PM Close Combat Weapon Systems Project Office
SFAE-MSL-CWS-J
111 Hankins Drive
Redstone Arsenal, AL 35898

Joint Air-to-Ground Missile (JAGM)
PEO Missiles and Space
Joint Air to Ground Missile Product Office
SFAE-MSL-JAMS-M
5250 Martin Road
Redstone Arsenal, AL 35898

Joint Assault Bridge
PEO Combat Support and Combat Service Support
PdM Bridging
SFAE-CSS-FP-H
6501 E. 11 Mile Road
Warren, MN 43897-5000

Joint Battle Command – Platform (JBC-P)
PEO Command, Control and Communications – Tactical
PM Mission Command
SFAE-CCC-MC
6007 Combat Drive
4th Floor
Aberdeen Proving Ground, MD 21005-1846

Points of Contact

Joint Biological Tactical Detection System (JBTDS)
JPEO for Chemical and Biological Defense
SFAE-CBD-BD-PD-FoS
5183 Blackhawk Road
Building E3549
Aberdeen Proving Ground, MD 21010-5424

Joint Chemical Agent Detector (JCAD) M4A1
JPEO for Chemical and Biological Defense
Joint Project Manager NBC Contamination Avoidance
SFAE-CBD-NBC
5183 Blackhawk Road
Building 2800
Aberdeen Proving Ground, MD 21010-5424

Joint Effects Model (JEM)
JPEO for Chemical and Biological Defense
Joint Project Manager Information System
4301 Pacific Highway
Building 0T3 Room 52142
San Diego, CA 92110

Joint Effects Targeting System (JETS) Target Location Designation System (TLDS)
PEO Soldier
Project Manager Soldier Sensors and Lasers
SFAE-SDR-SSL
10125 Gratiot Road
Building 318
Fort Belvoir, VA 22060

Joint Land Component Constructive Training Capability (JLCCTC)
PEO for Simulation, Training, and Instrumentation
Project Manager Integrated Training Environment
STRI-SFAE-ITE
12350 Research Parkway
Orlando, FL 32826

Joint Light Tactical Vehicle (JLTV)
PEO Common Support and Combat Service Support
JPEO Joint Light Tactical Vehicle (JLTV)
SFAE-CSS-JL
43087 Lake Street, NE
Building 301 Mail Stop 640
Harrison Twp, MI 48045-4941

Joint Personal Dosimeter (JPD)
JPEO for Chemical and Biological Defense
Joint Project Manager for Radiological and Nuclear Defense
SFAE-CBD-RND
5101 Hoadley Road
Aberdeen Proving Ground, MD 21010

Joint Precision Airdrop System (JPADS)
PEO Combat Support and Combat Service Support
PM Force Sustainment Systems
SFAE-CSS-FP-F
Kansas Street
Natick, MA 01760-5057

Joint Service Aircrew Mask – Rotary Wing (JSAM RW) (MPU-5)
JPEO for Chemical and Biological Defense
Joint Project Manager Protection
50 Tech Parkway
Suite 301
Stafford, VA 22556

Joint Service Equipment Wipe (JSEW)
JPEO for Chemical and Biological Defense
Joint Project Manager Protection
50 Tech Parkway
Suite 301
Stafford, VA 22556

Joint Service General Purpose Mask (JSGPM) M-50/M-51
JPEO for Chemical and Biological Defense
Joint Project Manager Protection
50 Tech Parkway
Suite 301
Stafford, VA 22556

Joint Service Transportable Decontaminating System Small Scale (JSTDS-SS) M26
JPEO for Chemical and Biological Defense
Joint Project Manager Protection
50 Tech Parkway
Suite 301
Stafford, VA 22556

Joint Tactical Ground Station (JTAGS)
PEO Missiles and Space
Missile Defense and Space
Systems Project Office
SFAE-MSL-MD
5250 Martin Road
Redstone Arsenal, AL
35898-8000

Joint Warning and Reporting Network (JWARN)
JPEO for Chemical and
Biological Defense
Joint Project Manager
Information System
4301 Pacific Highway
Building 0T3 Room 52142
San Diego, CA 92110

Lakota UH-72A Light Utility Helicopter (LUH)
PEO Aviation
Utility Helicopters Project Office
PEO AVN-UH-LUH
Lakota/UH-72A
5308 Patton Road
Redstone Arsenal, AL
35898-5000

Light Capability Rough Terrain Forklift (LCRTF)
PEO Combat Support and
Combat Service Support
Product Manager Combat
Engineer/Material
Handling Equipment
SFAE-CSS-FP-C
6501 E. 11 Mile Road
Mail Stop 401
Detroit Arsenal, MI 48397-5000

Lightweight 155 mm Howitzer System (LW155)
PEO Ammunition
JPMO Towed Artillery Systems
SFAE-AMO-TAS
Building 151
Picatinny Arsenal, NJ 07806

Lightweight Laser Designator Rangefinder (LLDR) AN/PED-1 and AN/PED-1A
PEO Soldier
PM Soldier Sensors and Lasers
10125 Gratiot Road
Building 318
Fort Belvoir, VA 22060

Line Haul Tractor
PEO Combat Support and
Combat Service Support
PM Heavy Tactical Vehicles
SFAE-CSS-TV-H
6501 E. 11 Mile Road
Mail Stop 429
Detroit Arsenal, MI 48397-5000

Line of Communications Bridge (LOCB)
PEO Combat Support and
Combat Service Support
PdM Bridging
SFAE-CSS-FP-H
6501 E. 11 Mile Road
Detroit Arsenal, MI 43897-5000

Load Handling System Compatible Water Tank Rack (Hippo)
PEO Combat Support and
Combat Service Support
PM Petroleum and Water Systems
SFAE-CSS-FP-P
6501 E. 11 Mile Road
Mail Stop 111
Detroit Arsenal, MI 43897

Long Range Precision Fires (LRPF)
PEO Missiles and Space
Precision Fires Rocket and
Missile Systems
SFAE-MSLS-PF
5250 Martin Road
Redstone Arsenal, AL 35898

M109 Family of Vehicles (FOV) (Paladin/FAASV, PIM SPH/CAT)
PEO Ground Combat Systems
SFAE-GCS-F
6501 E. 11 Mile Road
Mail Stop 531
Detroit Arsenal, MI 48397

M160 Robotic Mine Flail
PEO Combat Support and
Combat Service Support
Appliqué and Large Unmanned
Ground Systems
SFAE-CSS-FP
6501 E. 11 Mile Road
Detroit Arsenal, MI 48397

M88A2 Improved Recovery Vehicle HERCULES (Heavy Equipment Recovery Combat Utility Lift and Evacuation System)
PEO Ground Combat Systems
PM Combat Recovery Systems
SFAE-GCS-MR
650 E. 11 Mile Road
Detroit Arsenal, MI 48397-5000

Man Transportable Robot System (MTRS) Increment 2
PEO Combat Support and
Combat Service Support
Unmanned Ground Vehicles
SFAE-CSS-FP
6501 E. 11 Mile Road
Detroit Arsenal, MI 48397

Medical Communications for Combat Casualty Care (MC4)
PEO Enterprise Information
Systems
PM Medical Communications for
Combat Casualty Care (MC4)
SFAE-PS-MC
9350 Hall Road
Building 1445
Fort Belvoir, VA 22060

Medical Countermeasure Systems (MCS) – Diagnostics
JPEO for Chemical and
Biological Defense
JPM Chemical Biological
Medical Systems
1564 Freedman Drive
Fort Detrick, MD 21702

Medical Countermeasure Systems (MCS) – Joint Vaccine Acquisition Program (JVAP) and Bioscavenger
JPEO for Chemical and
Biological Defense
Joint Project Manager Chemical
Biological Medical Systems
1564 Freedman Drive
Fort Detrick, MD 21702

Medical Simulation Training Center (MSTC)
PEO for Simulation, Training,
and Instrumentation
Project Manager Training
Devices (TRADE)
SFAE-STRI-TRADE
12350 Research Parkway
Orlando, FL 32826-3276

Medium Caliber Ammunition (MCA)
PEO Ammunition
PM Maneuver Ammunition
Systems
SFAE-AMO-MAS
Building 351
Picatinny Arsenal, NJ 07806

Mid-Tier Networking Vehicular Radio (MNVR)
PEO Command, Control and
Communications – Tactical
Project Manager Tactical Radios
SFAE-CCC-TR
6007 Combat Drive
Aberdeen Proving Ground,
MD 21005

Mine Protection Vehicle Family (MPVF), Mine Clearing Vehicle (MCV), Explosive Hazard Pre-Detonation (EHP)
PEO Combat Support and
Combat Service Support
Product Manager Assured
Mobility Systems
SFAE-CSS-MRA
6501 E. 11 Mile Road
Detroit Arsenal, MI 43897-5000

Mine Resistant Ambush Protected Vehicles (MRAP), Army
PEO Command Support and
Combat Service Support
Army Project Office MRAP
SFAE-CSS-MR
6501 E. 11 Mile Road
Detroit Arsenal, MI 48397

Mobile Maintenance Equipment Systems (MMES)
PEO Combat Support and
Combat Service Support
PdM Sets, Kits, Outfits and Tools
SFAE-CSS
6501 E. 11 Mile Road
Detroit Arsenal, MI 48397

Modular Fuel System (MFS)
PEO Combat Support and
Combat Service Support
PM Petroleum and Water Systems
SFAE-CSS-FP
6501 E. 11 Mile Road
Mail Stop 111
Detroit Arsenal, MI 48397

Mortar Systems
PEO Ammunition
PM Combat Ammunition
Systems
SFAE-AMO-CAS-MS
B162S
Picatinny Arsenal, NJ 07806

MQ-1C Gray Eagle Unmanned Aircraft System (UAS)
PEO Aviation
Project Manager Unmanned Aircraft Systems
SFAE-AV-UAS
5300 Martin Road
Redstone Arsenal, AL
35898-5000

Multiple Launch Rocket System (MLRS) M270A1
PEO Missiles and Space
Project Office Precision Fires Rocket and Missile Systems
SFAE-MSL-PF-FAL
Building 112
Redstone Arsenal, AL 35898

NAVSTAR Global Positioning System (GPS)
PEO Intelligence, Electronic and Sensors
Program Manager Navigation and Timing
SAAL-SSI-PNT
6006 Combat Drive
B2101
Aberdeen Proving Ground, MD 21005

Nett Warrior (NW)
PEO Soldier
Project Manager Soldier Warrior
SFAE-SDR-SWAR
10125 Kingman Road
Building 317
Fort Belvoir, VA 22060

Next Generation Chemical Detector (NGCD)
JPEO for Chemical and Biological Defense
Joint Project Manager for Nuclear, Biological and Chemical Contamination
SFAE-CBD-NBC-R
5183 Blackhawk Road
Aberdeen Proving Ground, MD 21010

Non-Intrusive Inspection Systems (NIIS)
JPEO for Chemical and Biological Defense
Joint Project Manager Guardian
SFAE-CBD-GN
E. 2800 Bush River Road
Aberdeen Proving Ground, MD 21010-5424

Nuclear Biological Chemical Reconnaissance Vehicle (NBCRV) – Stryker Sensor Suites
JPEO for Chemical and Biological Defense
Joint Project Manager NBC Contamination Avoidance
SFAE-CBD-NBC-R
5183 Blackhawk Road
Building 2800
Aberdeen Proving Ground, MD 21010-5425

One Semi-Automated Force (OneSAF)
PEO for Simulation, Training, and Instrumentation
Project Manager Integrated Training Environment
SFAE-STRI-ITE
12350 Research Parkway
Orlando, FL 32826

Palletized Load System (PLS) and PLS Extended Service Program (ESP)
PEO Combat Support and Combat Service Support
PM Heavy Tactical Vehicles
SFAE-CSS-TS-H
6501 E. 11 Mile Road
Mail Stop 429
Detroit Arsenal, MI 48397-5000

PATRIOT Advanced Capability – 3 (PAC-3)
PEO Missiles and Space
Project Manager Lower Tier Project Office
SFAE-MSLS-LT
5250 Martin Road
Redstone Arsenal, AL 35898-8000

Precision Guidance Kit (PGK)
PEO Ammunition
PM Combat Ammunition Systems
SFAE-AMO-CAS
Picatinny Arsenal, NJ 07806

Prophet
PEO Intelligence, Electronic Warfare and Sensors
PM PROPHET
SFAE-IEW EWP
Building 5100
Aberdeen Proving Ground, MD 21005

Points of Contact

Radiological Detection System (RDS)
JPEO for Chemical and Biological Defense
Joint Project Manager for Radiological Nuclear Detection
SFAE-CBD-RND
5101 Hoadley Road
Aberdeen Proving Ground, MD 21010

Rocket, Artillery, Mortar (RAM) Warn
PEO Missiles and Space
Counter-Rocket, Artillery, and Mortar (C-RAM) Program Directorate
SFAE-MSL-CR
5250 Martin Road
Redstone Arsenal, AL 35898

Route Clearance Interrogation System (RCIS) Type 1
PEO Combat Support and Combat Service Support
Appliqué and Large Unmanned Ground Systems
SFAE-CSS-FP
6501 E. 11 Mile Road
Detroit Arsenal, MI 48397-5000

RQ-7Bv2 Shadow Tactical Unmanned Aircraft System (TUAS)
PEO Aviation
Project Manager Unmanned Aircraft Systems
SFAE-AV-UAS
5300 Martin Road
Redstone Arsenal, AL 35898-5000

RQ-11B Raven Small Unmanned Aircraft System (SUAS)
PEO Aviation
Project Manager Unmanned Aircraft Systems (UAS)
SFAE-AV-UAS
5300 Martin Road
Redstone Arsenal, AL 35898-5000

Secure Mobile Anti-Jam Reliable Tactical Terminal (SMART-T)
PEO Command, Control and Communications – Tactical
PM WIN-T
SFAE-CCC-WTS
6010 Frankford Street
Aberdeen Proving Ground, MD 21005

Small Arms – Crew Served Weapons
PEO Soldier
PM Soldier Weapons
SFAE-SDR-SW
Building 151
Picatinny Arsenal, NJ 07806

Small Arms – Individual Weapons
PEO Soldier
PM Soldier Weapons
SFAE-SDR-SW
Building 151
Picatinny Arsenal, NJ 07806

Small Arms – Precision Weapons
PEO Soldier
Project Manager Soldier Weapons
SFAE-SDR-SW
Building 151
Picatinny Arsenal, NJ 07806

Small Caliber Ammunition
PEO Ammunition
PM Maneuver Ammunition Systems
SFAE-AMO-MAS
Building 351
Picatinny Arsenal, NJ 07806

Soldier Protection System (SPS)
PEO Soldier
Product Manager Soldier Protection and Individual Equipment
SFAE-SDR-SPE
10170 Beach Road
Building 325
Fort Belvoir, VA 22060

Spider – Command Destruct Networked Command Munition Dispensing Set Increment 1A
PEO Ammunition
PM Close Combat Systems
SFAE-AMO-CCS
183 Buffington Road
Picatinny Arsenal, NJ 07806-5000

Stryker Family of Vehicles
PEO Ground Combat Systems
Project Manager Stryker Brigade Combat Team
SFAE-GCS-BCT MS 325
6501 E. 11 Mile Road
Detroit Arsenal, MI 48397

Synthetic Training Environment (STE)
PEO for Simulation, Training, and Instrumentation
Project Manager Integrated Training Environment
SFAE-STRI-ITE
12350 Research Parkway
Orlando, FL 32826

T-9 Medium Dozer
PEO Combat Support and Combat Service Support
Product Manager Combat Engineer/Material Handling Equipment
SFAE-CSS-FP-C
6501 E. 11 Mile Road
Mail Stop 401
Detroit Arsenal, MI 48397-5000

Tactical Electric Power (TEP)
PEO Combat Support and Combat Service Support
Project Manager Expeditionary Energy and Sustainment System
SFAE-CSS-E2
5850 Delafield Road
Building 324
Fort Belvoir, VA 22060-5809

Tactical Mission Command (TMC)
PEO Command, Control and Communications – Tactical
SFAE-C3T-MC-TMC
6007 Combat Drive
Floor 5
Aberdeen Proving Ground, MD 21005

Tank Ammunition
PEO Ammunition
SFAE-AMO-MAS
Building 351
Picatinny Arsenal, NJ 07806

Test Equipment Modernization (TEMOD)
PEO Combat Support and Combat Service Support
Product Director Test, Measurement, and Diagnostic Equipment
SFAE-CSS-JC-TM
3651 Army TACMS Drive
Redstone Arsenal, AL 35898

Transportable Tactical Command Communications (T2C2)
PEO Command, Control and Communications – Tactical
Project Manager Warfighter Information Network – Tactical
SFAE-CCC-WT

6010 Frankford Street
Aberdeen Proving Ground, MD 21005

Tube-Launched, Optically Tracked, Wireless-Guided (TOW) Missiles
PEO Missiles and Space
PM Close Combat Weapon Systems Project Office
SFAE-MSL-CWS-T
111 Hankins Drive
Redstone Arsenal, AL 35898

Unified Command Suite (UCS)
JPEO for Chemical and Biological Defense
Joint Project Manager Guardian
SFAE-CBD-GN
5183 Blackhawk Road
Building E4465
Aberdeen Proving Ground, MD 21010

Unit Water Pod System (Camel II)
PEO Combat Support and Combat Service Support
PM Petroleum and Water Systems
SFAE-CSS-FP
6501 E. 11 Mile Road
Mail Stop 111
Detroit Arsenal, MI 43897

Warfighter Information Network – Tactical (WIN-T) Increment 1
PEO Command, Control and Communications – Tactical
PM WIN-T
SFAE-CCC-WT
6010 Frankford Street
Aberdeen Proving Ground, MD 21005

Warfighter Information Network – Tactical (WIN-T) Increment 2
PEO Command, Control and Communications – Tactical
PM WIN-T
SFAE-CCC-WT
6010 Frankford Street
Aberdeen Proving Ground, MD 21005

Warfighter Information Network – Tactical (WIN-T) Increment 3
PEO Command, Control and Communications – Tactical
PM WIN-T
SFAE-CCC-WT
6010 Frankford Street
Aberdeen Proving Ground, MD 21005

Assistant Secretary of the Army for Acquisition, Logistics and Technology (ASA(ALT))

MISSION STATEMENT:

Provide our Soldiers a decisive advantage in any mission by maintaining quality acquisition professionals to develop, acquire, field and sustain the world's best equipment and services through efficient leveraging of technologies and capabilities to meet current and future Army needs.

VISION STATEMENT:

Best equipped Army that maintains the technological advantage and capabilities against any threat in any environment.

PREPARED BY:

Assistant Secretary of the Army for
Acquisition, Logistics and Technology (ASA(ALT))
103 Army Pentagon, Room 2E251
Washington, DC 20310-0103